우루과이라운드

서비스 협상 1

우루과이라운드

서비스 협상 1

한국학술정보

| 머리말

우루과이라운드는 국제적 교역 질서를 수립하려는 다각적 무역 교섭으로서, 각국의 보호무역 추세를 보다 완화하고 다자무역체제를 강화하기 위해 출범되었다. 1986년 9월 개시가 선언되었으며, 15개 분야의 교섭을 1990년 말까지 진행하기로 했다. 그러나 각 분야의 중간 교섭이 이루어진 1989년 이후에도 농산물, 지적소유권, 서비스무역, 섬유, 긴급수입제한 등 많은 분야에서 대립하며 1992년이 돼서야 타결에 이를 수 있었다. 한국은 특히 농산물 분야에서 기존 수입 제한 품목 대부분을 개방해야 했기에 큰 경쟁력 하락을 겪었고, 관세와 기술 장벽 완화, 보조금 및 수입 규제 정책의 변화로 제조업 수출입에도 많은 변화가 있었다.

본 총서는 우루과이라운드 협상이 막바지에 다다랐던 1991~1992년 사이 외교부에서 작성한 관련 자료를 담고 있다. 관련 협상의 치열했던 후반기 동향과 관계부처회의, 무역협상위원회 회의, 실무대책회의, 규범 및 제도, 투자회의, 특히나 가장 많은 논란이 있었던 농산물과 서비스 분야 협상 등의 자료를 포함해 총 28권으로 구성되었다. 전체 분량은 약 1만 3천여 쪽에 이른다.

2024년 3월

한국학술정보(주)

| 일러두기

· 본 총서에 실린 자료는 2022년 4월과 2023년 4월에 각각 공개한 외교문서 4,827권, 76만여 쪽 가운데 일부를 발췌한 것이다.

· 각 권의 제목과 순서는 공개된 원본을 최대한 반영하였으나, 주제에 따라 일부는 적절히 변경하였다.

· 원본 자료는 A4 판형에 맞게 축소하거나 원본 비율을 유지한 채 A4 페이지 안에 삽입하였다. 또한 현재 시점에선 공개되지 않아 '공란'이란 표기만 있는 페이지 역시 그대로 실었다.

· 외교부가 공개한 문서 각 권의 첫 페이지에는 '정리 보존 문서 목록'이란 이름으로 기록물 종류, 일자, 명칭, 간단한 내용 등의 정보가 수록되어 있으며, 이를 기준으로 0001번부터 번호가 매겨져 있다. 이는 삭제하지 않고 총서에 그대로 수록하였다.

· 보고서 내용에 관한 더 자세한 정보가 필요하다면, 외교부가 온라인상에 제공하는 『대한민국 외교사료요약집』 1991년과 1992년 자료를 참조할 수 있다.

| 차례

정 리 보 존 문 서 목 록

기록물종류	일반공문서철	등록번호	2019080102	등록일자	2019-08-14
분류번호	764.51	국가코드		보존기간	영구
명 칭	UR(우루과이라운드) / GNS(서비스협상그룹) 회의, 1991. 전5권				
생 산 과	통상기구과	생산년도	1991~1991	담당그룹	
권 차 명	V.1 1-3월				
내용목차					

0001

오

경 제 기 획 원

통조삼 10502-15　　503-9149　　1991. 1. 9.

수신 외무부장관

제목 주제네바 대표부 경협관보의 귀국기간 연장 협조요청

1. 통조삼 10502-834 ('90.12.22)와 관련입니다.

2. 주제네바 대표부의 경협관보가 현재 일시 귀국하여 UR/서비스협상과 관련한 아국의 최초의 양허계획표(Initial Offer List)를 작성하는 작업에 참여하고 있는바, 막대한 작업량으로 인해 다음과 같이 귀국기간을 연장하여 협상대책 수립에 만전을 기하고자 하오니 조치해 주시기 바랍니다.

다 음

	당 초	변 경
귀국기간	'91.1.1-'91.1.9 (8박 9일)	'91.1.1-'91.1.12 (11박 12일)

끝.

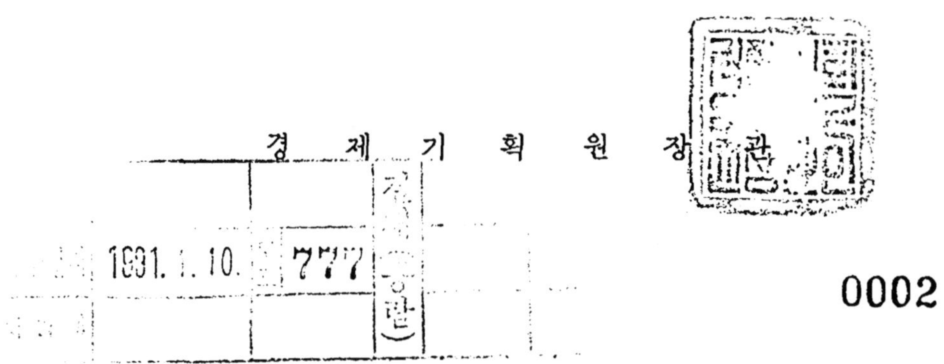

경 제 기 획 원 장 관

0002

분류번호	보존기간

발 신 전 보

번 호 : WGV-0039 910109 1810 CG 종별 :

수 신 : 주 제네바 대사대리 ~~대사. 총영사~~

발 신 : 장 관 (통기)

제 목 : 주재관 귀국기간 연장

귀관 한철수 경협관보의 귀국기간을 Offer list 작성에 따르는 작업량이 과다로 91.1.12 까지 연장 하니 양지 바람. 끝.

(통상국장 김 삼훈)

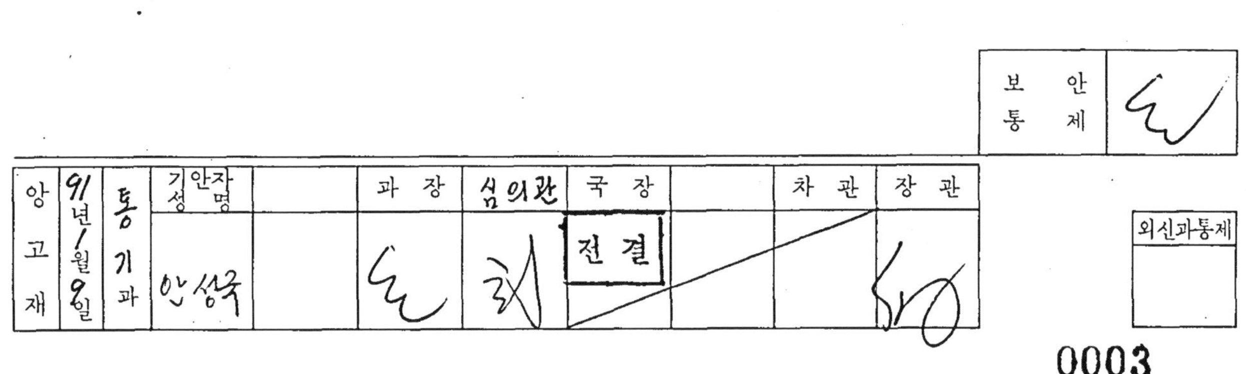

앙 고 재	91년 1월 9일	통기과	기안자 성명		과 장	심의관	국 장		차 관	장 관
			안성국		(서명)	(서명)	전결			(서명)

보안 통제 (서명)

외신과통제

0003

關係長官 會議資料

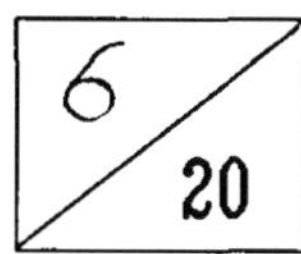

UR/서비스協商關聯

最初의 讓許計劃表 提出對策

'91. 1. 7

經 濟 企 劃 院

0004

目 次

0005

1. 主要國家의 讓許計劃表 提出 動向

- 美國, EC, 스위스, 日本, 濠洲, 뉴질랜드, 스웨덴, 카나다, 홍콩등 9個國이 브랏셀 閣僚會議時까지 條件付로 最初의 讓許計劃表를 제출하였음.

  o 대부분의 國家가 現在의 서비스交易에 대한 國內規制水準을 凍結(Standstill)하고 一部業種의 自由化計劃을 포함하는 水準의 讓許計劃表를 提出

  o 스웨덴등 一部國家는 선언적인 讓許計劃表를 提出하였으나 美國, EC등은 비교적 充實한 讓許計劃表를 提出

- 이와같이 美國, EC등 主要協商國家가 충실한 讓許計劃表를 提出한 것은 기타 國家에도 이에 상응한 讓許計劃表의 提出을 촉구하는 것을 의미함.

- 브랏셀 閣僚會議時 我國을 포함한 未提出 國家들도 조속한 時日內에 讓許計劃表를 提出할 의사를 表明한 바 있음.

2. 我國의 讓許計劃表 提出의 意義

- 我國도 當初 브랏셀 閣僚會議時까지 條件付로 讓許計劃表의 提出을 추진하였으나 방대한 作業量으로 인해 提出치 못함으로써 브랏셀 閣僚會議에서 我國의 協商力을 強化할 기회를 喪失하였음.

- 그러나 我國이 브랏셀 閣僚會議以後 처음으로 開催된 貿易協商委員會에 讓許計劃表를 제출할 경우 交錯狀態에 빠진 서비스協商의 진전에 기여한 것으로 評價받을 수 있음.

- 또한 金融, 通信分野등에서의 雙務的 通商壓力을 완화하기 위해서도 最初의 讓許計劃表를 조속히 제출하는 것이 효과적임.

0006

3. 我國의 讓許計劃(案)의 內容

가. 讓許計劃表 作成의 基本指針

- 서비스協商에서 論議된 業種을 최대한 포괄하여 我國의 協商力을 強化

- 自由化水準은 現存規制의 凍結을 原則으로 하되 一部自由化가 確定된 事項을 추가하는 水準으로 讓許

- 金融, 通信, 流通분야 등은 향후 韓.美間 雙務協商에서 論議될 內容을 감안하여 적정한 開放水準을 設定

나. 讓許計劃表의 內容

(1) Covernote

- 서비스協商의 核心爭點인 包括業種範圍 및 最惠國待遇(MFN) 問題에 대해서 Universal Coverage와 無條件的 MFN原則을 천명

- 外資導入法 및 外國換管理法에 의한 外國企業의 國內進出에 대한 一般的인 制限事項을 규정

- 外國人土地法에 의한 外國企業의 土地에 대한 制限事項 및 出入國管理法에 의한 規制事項을 명시

- 서비스一般協定 및 分野別 附屬書, 各國의 讓許計劃內容에 따라 修正, 補完, 撤回할 수 있는 권리를 유보

0007

(2) 市場開放約束

<包括業種>

o 金融, 通信, 運送, 流通, 건설, 事業서비스등 서비스협상에서 논의되던 主要한 業種을 대부분 포함

<除外業種>

o 教育 및 保健서비스 全體, 流通分野中 貿易業, 事業서비스중 法務서비스등

<自由化水準>

o 대부분 現存開放 및 規制水準을 凍結하는 정도에서 제시

o 美國등 主要國의 關心事項에 대해서는 추가적인 自由化計劃을 포함

o 특히 通信分野에 있어서는 美國側의 要求事項을 전향적으로 反映

다. 豫想되는 問題点

(1) 讓許計劃表에 除外된 業種의 開放問題

- 讓許計劃表에 除外된 것이 최종적으로 開放對象에서의 除外를 의미하는 것은 아니므로 教育 및 保健서비스등 대해서 美國, EC등 主要先進國이 開放要求를 할 可能性이 있음.

0008

(2) 讓許計劃表에 포함된 業種에 대한 追加 自由化問題

- 金融, 流通등 讓許計劃表에 포함시킨 業種에 대해서도 包括範圍의 擴大 및 보다 높은 水準의 自由化 要求 可能性이 있음.

  o 특히 金融分野는 現存 規制水準을 凍結하는 線에서 自由化 計劃을 提示하였으나, 先進國의 主要關心 業種이므로 向後 金融分野의 附屬書에 대한 協商動向을 감안하여 伸縮的인 對處 必要

4. 協商推進對策

가. 最初의 讓許計劃表의 提出 및 補完

- '91.1.15일 開催되는 무역협상위원회 이전에 提出

- 正式으로 각국에 배포하기에 앞서 GATT事務局과 非公式的인 協議를 進行

  o GATT事務局의 客觀的인 諮問內容을 가능한 範圍內에서 讓許計劃表에 反映

나. 讓許協商에의 徹底한 對應

- 美國, EC등 先進國으로부터 開放要求가 있을 것으로 예상되는 분야에 대하여 協商代案 및 協商論理를 개발하는 동시에 相對國에 대한 要求事項(Request List)을 徹底히 準備하여 我國의 利害關係를 反映할 수 있도록 努力

0003

- 必須專門人力 및 숙련노동인력의 國境間移動에 대한 具體的인 方案을 講究하여 建設등 勞動集約的인 서비스의 海外進出이 可能하도록 함.

- 各部處에 構成되어 있는 18개 分野別 對策班에 通商協商에 대한 經驗과 知識을 갖고있는 專門家를 참여시키는등 아국의 讓許協商팀을 補強

다. 國內 補完對策의 推進

- 지금까지 把握된 國內規制現況을 바탕으로 各部處는 民間의 자유로운 競爭을 저해하는 不必要한 規制 制度를 整備

- 長期的인 次元에서 各部處는 서비스협상을 契機로 所管業種에 대한 國際競爭力의 強化, 國際化戰略 등을 포함한 產業構造調整 방안을 綜合的으로 推進

0010

(별첨).

分野別 市場開放 約束에 대한 評價

<視聽覺서비스>

o 영화, 음반 및 비디오, 定期刊行物등만 포함되어있고 放送 및 書籍分野는 除外되었으며 다른 國家와 비교하면 中間 程度의 自由化 水準임.

<事業서비스>

o 會計, 稅務, 廣告, 엔지니어링서비스등 10개 業種을 포함하여 다른國家와 비교하여 볼때 대체적으로 동일한 水準임.

o 技術用役育成法에 의해 많은 규제가 있는 엔지니어링서비스등 一部業種을 除外하고는 다른 國家의 自由化 水準과 유사한 水準이며 특히 廣告등 非認可서비스업종은 비교적 높은 수준의 自由化 計劃을 提示함.

<通 信>

o 電話,電信등을 제외한 대부분의 電氣通信서비스를 포함하고 있어 美國,EC등 先進國과 동일한 水準의 包括範圍를 提示함.

o 自由化 水準과 關聯하여 外國人投資 지분을 制限하고 있으나 向後 自由化 計劃을 구체적으로 제시하여 韓.美通信 協商에도 前向的인 對應이 可能함.

0011

<建　設>

o 土木施工, 建設엔지니어링, 建築士등을 포함하고 있어 包括範圍는 美國, EC등 先進國과 同一한 水準임.

o 외국인투자지분제한, 建築士 資格制限등 比較的 많은 內容의 制限事項을 담고 있으나 향후 自由化計劃을 구체적으로 提示하여 美國의 要求事項을 적절히 반영하고 있음.

<流　通>

o 都賣業과 小賣業을 포함시키되 貿易業은 除外하여 美國, EC, 日本등 主要先進國의 包括範圍보다 낮은 수준임.

o 現在狀態의 開放 및 規制水準을 동결하는 내용을 담고 있어 自由化 水準도 상대적으로 높지 않음.

<金　融>

o 國內金融市場을 개방할 主要分野를 기존의 我國立場인 Positive System에 따라 提示하였으나 全般的으로 볼때 包括範圍가 좁은편임.

o 自由化 水準과 관련하여 현재의 開放 및 規制 水準을 凍結하는 線에서 提示하였으나 향후 金融分野 附屬書에 대한 協商動向등을 감안하여 伸縮的으로 대처할 필요성이 있음.

0012

<運 送>

o 航空補助서비스, 海運서비스, 貨物트럭킹서비스등 대부분의 運送서비스를 포함하여 美國, 日本등 運送分野를 包括하지 않은 一部國家에 비해 적극적인 立場

o 自由化水準과 관련하여 我國은 국적선이용제도, 外國人投資制限事項등을 규정하여 EC, 뉴질랜드등에 비해서 대체로 보수적인 立場을 견지

<觀 光>

o 觀光호텔業, 觀光宿泊業, 旅行斡旋業등 주요관광서비스를 包含하여 여타 先進國의 包括範圍와 유사한 수준임.

o 讓許業種에 대해서 外國企業에 대한 특별한 制限事項이 없어 先進國과 마찬가지로 비교적 높은 水準의 自由化 計劃을 提示

0013

관리 번호	91-55

	분류번호	보존기간

발 신 전 보

번　　호 : WGV-0068　　910112 1435 AO 종별 :

수　　신 : 주 제네바　　　대사. ~~총영~~사

발　　신 : 장　관　(통기)

제　　목 : UR/ 서비스 협상관련 양허 계획표 제출

연 : WGV - 0022

아국의 표제 양허 계획표를 귀관 한철수 경협관보가 지참하여 1.12 (토) 귀지 도착 예정이니 동 양허 계획표를 연호에 따라 91.1.14 (월) 한 갓트 사무국에 제출 바람.　　끝.

(통상국장 김 삼훈)

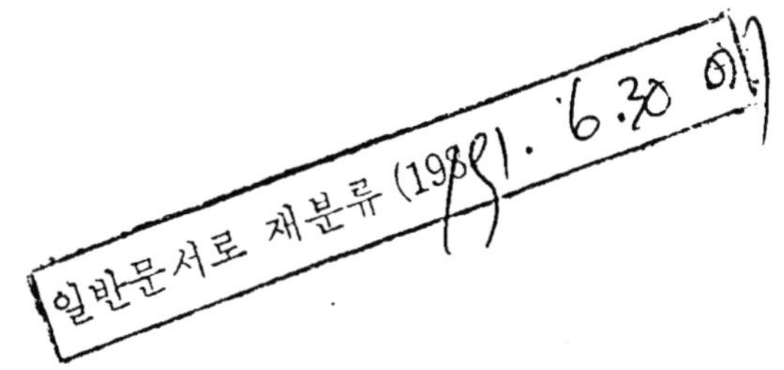

앙 고 재	91년 1월 12일	통기과	기안자		과 장	심의관	국 장		차 관	장 관
			김봉주				전결			

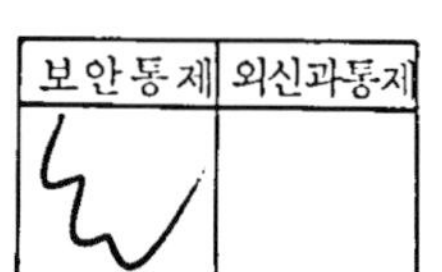

보안통제	외신과통제

0014

관리 번호 91-61

원 본

외 무 부

종 별 : 지 급

번 호 : USW-0170 일 시 : 91 0114 1845

수 신 : 장관(통기,통일)

발 신 : 주 미 대사

제 목 : HILLS USTR 대표 면담

대 WUS-0081,0103,0104,0105

1. 본직은 금 1.14(월) HILLS USTR 대표를 면담, 대호 UR 에 관한 아국 입장을 설명하고 UR 협상 성공과 한미간 통상 마찰 해소를 위하여 한국측이 진지한노력을 한 결과임을 강조하였음.

2.HILLS 대표는 한국측의 조정된 UR 입장을 환영하는 바이나, 한국측의 좀더 과감한 결단을 내려 HELLSTROM 의장안을 협상 기초로 수락하는 자세를 보이기를 희망한다고함.

3. 동 대표는 UR 농산물 분야 협상에서는 아직 아무런 새로운 진전이 없으나, 서비스 분야에서는 협상이 계속되고 있고 한국측의 전향적인 입장 제시(INITIAL OFFER)를 환영한다고 함. 서비스 분야 관련, 한국측과 1.29 제네바에서 한.미 양자간 협상을 갖기를 원한다고 하면서 아측 수락 여부를 문의하여옴(본건은 이봉서 상공장관에게 전화로 기 요청하였다 함)

4. 본직이 대호 담배, 쇠고기, 운송 분야에서의 아측 입장을 통보해준데 대해 HILLS 대표는 사의를 표한후 작년봄 이후 한미 통상관계가 많이 악화되었고 그 시점이 미국 경제가 나빠지는 시점과 일치되어 미 의회, 업계 등 보호주의 성향이 있는측에게 좋은 구실을 제공해준것을 감안, 이를 개선하기 위하여 더욱 많은 노력이 필요할것이라고 언급함.

(대사 박동진-장관)

91.6.30 까지

일반문서로 재분류 (1991 . 6 . 30)

통상국	장관	차관	1차보	2차보	통상국	청와대	상공부

PAGE 1

91.01.15 11:33

외신 2과 통제관 BW

0015

관리번호	91-70

외 무 부

종 별 : 지 급

번 호 : USW-0193 일 시 : 91 0115 1747

수 신 : 장관(통일,통기,체신부) 사본:주제네바대사(본부중계필)

발 신 : 주 미 대사

제 목 : 한.미 통신 협의

당관 이종순 통협관은 금 1.15 표제 관련 NANCY ADAMS USTR 부대표보와 면담한바, 하기 보고함(서용현 서기관 동석)

1. 한. 미 양자 협의의 시기및 장소 문제

0 ADAMS 부대표보는 종합 통상법상의 시한(2.23)전에 미측이 취해야할 국내절차(행정부내 의견 조정, 대의회 보고등)를 감안, 1.27 시작주 또는 늦어도 2 월 첫주초까지는 양자 협의가 개최되어야함을 강조함.

0 이 통협관은 양국은 양국 통신 업계간 회의가 1.31 워싱턴에서 개최키로 예정되어 있는바 정부간 협의가 실질적인 것이 되기 위하여는 업계 협의의 결과를 기초로 함이 적절한 것이라는점을 지적함.

0 이에 대해 동 부대표보는 정부간 협의를 업계 협의후에 개최할 필요성에 대해 동의하면서 개인 의견임을 전제, 업계 협의와의 연계상 2.1 또는 2.2 워싱턴에서 정부간 협의를 개최하는 방안을 제시함.

0 이 통협관은 이에 대해 UR 과의 연계 문제, ~~한국 정부 관계관들이 UR 과의 연계 문제,~~ 한국정부 관계관들이 UR 서비스 협상과 관련하여 동 시기에 제네바에 파견될 가능성등을 고려할때 아측이 1 차적으로 희망하는 회의 장소는 제네바라고 함.

0 이에 대해 동 부대표보는 전반적 UR 서비스 문제는 당연히 제네바에서 취급되어야할것이나, 서비스 양자 협상은 그중 일부인 통신 분야를 따로 분리하여 양자/ 다자 문제간 연계하에 워싱턴에서 협상할수도 있을것이라고 하면서, 이와관련, 미측이 한국측에 제시한 UR 서비스 양자 협상 개최 일자(1.29 또는 30)를 한국측이 수락치 않고 있어 UR 서비스 양자 협상 일자가 유직 유동적임을 지적함. 동 부대표보는 양측이 모두 내부 협의를 거친후에 회의 개최 장소, 일시 문제를 추후 타결 짓자고 하였는바, 동건 관련 본부 입장 조속 회시 바람(미측도 제네바 개최에

통상국	장관	차관	1차보	2차보	통상국	안기부	체신부

91.01.16 08:45

외신 2과 통제관 BW

원칙적으로 이의가 없으나, 워싱턴 개최시 실무 기술 인력의 조언 확보및 업계 접촉의 용이성등을 감안, 워싱턴 개최를 고려하는것으로 보임)

2. 한. 미 협의시 미측 관심 사항

0 ADAMS 부대표보는 지난 90.7 자신이 방한시 거론했던(동 자료를 근거로 하여 90.2 한. 미 통신 ROU 상 괄호로 표시된 미결 사항들을 해소하기 위한) 각종의 새로운 조치및 이행 상황들에 관하여 한국측이 구체적 영문자료를 금번 회의시 제시할수 있기를 희망함.

0 금번 협의시 주요 협의 의제로는 기기 표준 제정 절차에 있어 투명성 확보를 위한 조치, 정부 조달의 GATT 가입 이행문제, 서비스 시장의 추가 개방및 이와 관련한 INTRACORPORATE NETWORK 의 개방문제등에 관하여 폭넓게 협의할수 있기를 희망함.

(참사관 최영진-국장)

91.6.30 까지

경 제 기 획 원

통조삼 10502-

503-9149

1991. 1. 14.

수신 외무부장관

제목 UR/서비스협상관련 아국의 최초의 양허계획표 제출

1. 통조삼 10502-8451 ('90.12.28)와 관련입니다.

2. UR/서비스협상의 진전에 기여하고 아국의 협상력을 강화하기 위하여 '91.1.15일 제네바에서 개최되는 무역협상위원회에 별첨과 같이 최초의 양허계획표를 제출코자 하니 조치해 주시기 바랍니다.

첨부: 1. 한국의 최초의 양허계획표(국문) 2부.

2. Conditional Offer by Korea of Initial Commitment on Trade in Services 2부. 끝.

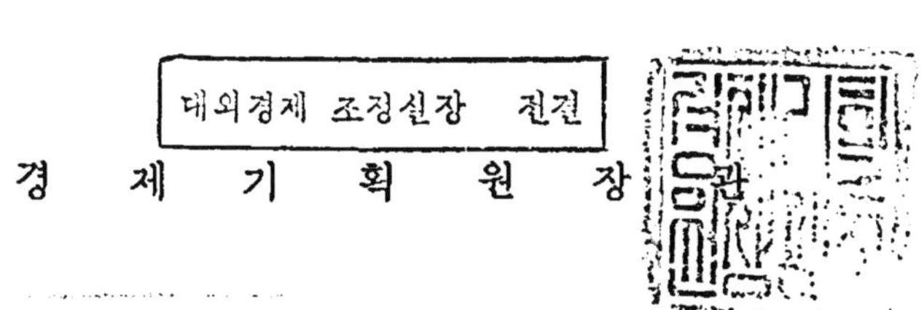

대외경제 조정실장 전결

경 제 기 획 원 장

0018

UR/서비스協商
關聯資料

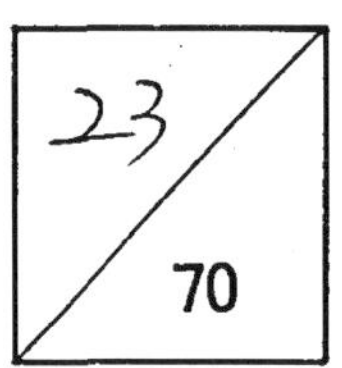

韓國의 最初의 讓許計劃表

1991. 1. 11

對外協力委員會

0013

目　　次

I. 前 文

1. 一般事項

- 韓國은 世界서비스交易의 擴大 및 서비스協商의 進展에 寄與하기 위해 그동안 서비스協商에서 대체로 合意에 接近된 基本骨格에 따라 制限된 時間內에 최대한 충실한 內容의 讓許計劃表를 作成하였음

- 서비스業種의 大分類體系는 가급적 GATT 事務局서비스分類表 (MTN/GNS/W/50)를 참조하였으나 細部分類方法은 國內制度에 따른 分類方法을 주로 使用하였음

- 韓國은 向後 서비스協商의 進展狀況 및 各國의 讓許內容에 따라 讓許計劃表를 修正·補完·철회할 수 있는 權利를 留保하며 技術的인 修正을 할 수 있는 權利도 留保함

- 韓國은 1990.11.1 現在의 各種法令을 基準으로 하여 offer List를 作成하였음

- 韓國政府는 offer List에 열거되지 않은 1991.1.1 現在의 강제적인 法令上의 制限事項도 준수해야 할 의무가 있음

2. 모든 서비스에 適用되는 制限事項

가. 商業的 駐在

- 外國會社의 合作投資會社, 子會社, 支社(支店, 出張所, 事務所) 設立을 위해서는 外資導入法 또는 外國換管理法에 의한 節次를 거쳐야 함

  外國人投資制度는 Negative System이나 Negative List에 열거된 業種에 대해서도 일정한 基準을 充足할 경우 投資가 허용됨

  國內支社設置에 대해서는 外國人投資制度가 一般的으로 준용되나 一部 一致되지 않은 業種에 대해서는 別添 offer List에 個別的으로 表示되어 있음

- 外國人이 國內會社의 구주를 取得하여 國內會社를 合併 또는 買收하는 것은 外國換管理法 또는 外資導入法에 의해 關係當局의 許可를 받은 경우에 한해 許容됨

- 外國人投資認可制度는 1993年까지 段階的으로 申告制로 轉換될 計劃임

  ○ 단, 國內市場에서의 獨占的 또는 市場支配的 관행을 초래하는 投資등은 制限을 가할 수 있음

0022

나. 土地取得 및 利用

- 外國人과 外國人으로 의제되는 外國投資家가 出資한 國內法人의 土地取得은 外國人土地法에 따라 關係當局의 許可를 받아야함. 그러나 外國會社의 國內支社(支店, 出張所, 事務所)의 경우는 不動產取得이 許容되지 않으며 賃借 및 전세권만 認定됨.

다. 外 換

- 國內居住者가 外換管理規定에 規定된 일부 外貨支給用役契約을 체결하기 위해서는 關係當局으로 부터 許可를 받아야 함.

라. 人力移動

- 國內에 商業的駐在를 한 外國企業이 서비스를 供給하는데 필수적인 人力은 入國이 許容되나 就業關聯 비자취득등 出入國管理法上의 節次를 필하여야 함.

- 人力移動範圍에 관해서는 追加的인 檢討를 하고 있으며 向後 讓許協商 과정에서 分野別로 구체적인 人力移動約束을 할 용의가 있음

Ⅱ. 分野別 市場開放約束

* (1) 國境間提供
(2) 海外消費
(3) 商業的駐在

1. 視聽覺 서비스

分　野	供給樣式	市場接近에 대한 制限·條件	內國民待遇에 대한 條件·制約
映畵輸入·配給	(1)	Unbound	條件 또는 制約없음
	(2)	制限 또는 條件없음	條件 또는 制約없음
	(3)	外國人投資認可指針上의 制限業種에 대한 投資許容基準에 따름	條件 또는 制約없음
音盤 및 비디오輸入	(1)	Unbound	條件 또는 制約없음
	(2)	制限 또는 條件없음	條件 또는 制約없음
	(3)	外國人 및 外國法人에 대한 登錄 制限撤廢('92.1)	條件 또는 制約없음

註: 外國映畵輸入 및 音盤, 비디오輸入에 대한 主務長官 추천 또는 許可와 輸入映畵의 프린트벌수에 대한 制限이 있으나 商品貿易과 視聽覺서비스貿易과의 關係가 明確하지 않으므로 기재하지 않았음.

ㅇ 프린트벌수에 대한 制限은 '94年까지 段階的으로 撤廢 豫定 ('91 : 14벌, '92 : 15벌, '93 : 16벌)

0024

2. 事業서비스

分 野	供給樣式	市場接近에 대한 制限·條件	內國民待遇에 대한 條件·制約
廣 告	(1)	外國廣告物을 國內에 輸入·使用하는 경우 主務長官의 輸入 推薦 必要(映畫法 第 10 條, 音盤에 관한 法律 第 8 條)	條件 또는 制約없음
	(2)	制限 또는 條件없음	條件 또는 制約없음
	(3)	合作投資許容(99 %까지) 支社 및 子會社 設置許容 ('91.1) ○ 放送廣告代行의 경우 韓國放送廣告公社法 및 同法施行令과 韓國放送廣告公社의 放送廣告代行規定 遵守 ○ 新聞廣告代行의 경우 韓國新聞協會 廣告協議會의 新聞廣告代行規則 遵守	條件 또는 制約없음

分 野	供給樣式	市場接近에 대한 制限・條件	內國民待遇에 대한 條件・制約
엔지니어링* 서비스	(1)	Unbound	條件 또는 制約없음
	(2)	制限 또는 條件없음	條件 또는 制約없음
	(3)	登錄要件으로 技術士等 專門 技術人力 雇傭義務 賦課 (技術用役育成法 第3條)	條件 또는 制約없음
컴퓨터關聯 서비스	(1)	制限 또는 條件없음	條件 또는 制約없음
	(2)	制限 또는 條件없음	條件 또는 制約없음
	(3)	制限 또는 條件없음	條件 또는 制約없음
소프트웨어 開發業	(1)	制限 또는 條件없음	條件 또는 制約없음
	(2)	制限 또는 條件없음	條件 또는 制約없음
	(3)	制限 또는 條件없음	條件 또는 制約없음
經營管理 컨설팅	(1)	制限 또는 條件없음	條件 또는 制約없음
	(2)	制限 또는 條件없음	條件 또는 制約없음
	(3)	制限 또는 條件없음	條件 또는 制約없음
엔지니어링 디자인	(1)	Unbound	條件 또는 制約없음
	(2)	制限 또는 條件없음	條件 또는 制約없음
	(3)	登錄要件으로 技術士等 專門 技術人力 雇傭義務 賦課 (技術用役育成法 第3條)	條件 또는 制約없음

註 : * 엔지니어링자문, 產業 및 建設엔지니어링 包含

0026

分 野	供給樣式	市場接近에 대한 制限·條件	內國民待遇에 대한 條件·制約
事業管理 (Project Manage- ment)	(1)	Unbound	條件 또는 制約없음
	(2)	制限 또는 條件없음	條件 또는 制約없음
	(3)	登錄要件으로 技術士等 專門 技術人力 雇傭義務 賦課 (技術用役育成法 第3條)	條件 또는 制約없음
翻 譯	(1)	制限 또는 條件없음	條件 또는 制約없음
	(2)	制限 또는 條件없음	條件 또는 制約없음
	(3)	制限 또는 條件없음	條件 또는 制約없음
公認會計	(1)	國內에서 會計士 業務를 수행하려면 韓國公認會計士 資格 取得 必要(公認會計士法 第2條, 第4條, 第5條) ○ 韓國의 會計士 資格을 認定하는 國家에서 會計士 資格을 取得한 外國公認會計士는 韓國政府의 資格認可를 받은 후 本國企業이 50%以上 出資한 合作企業이나	條件 또는 制約없음

分　野	供給樣式	市場接近에 대한 制限·條件	內國民待遇에 대한 條件·制約
		本國企業이 이해관계를 가진 企業體에 대한 會計監査業務를 遂行할 수 있음	
	(2)	Standstill	Standstill
	(3)	Unbound	Unbound
稅務서비스	(1)	國內에서 稅務業務를 遂行하려면 韓國稅務士 資格 取得 必要 ○ 韓國의 稅務士 資格을 認定하는 國家에서 稅務士 資格을 取得한 外國稅務士는 國內稅法 전형을 거치고, ○ 外國公認會計士나 辯護士는 國內公認會計士나 辯護士의 資格을 取得하고 그 本來資格 取得國이 韓國公認會計士나	條件 또는 制約없음

0028

分　野	供給樣式	市場接近에 대한 制限・條件	內國民待遇에 대한 條件・制約
		辯護士에게 稅務士資格을 自動 認定하는 경우에 기장대리업무, 稅務調整業務, 租稅相談 諮問만 가능함.	
	(2)	Standstill	Standstill
	(3)	Unbound 但, 韓國稅務士資格을 認定받고 登錄을 필하면 個人事務所 開設은 可能	Unbound

0029

3. 通 信

分 野	供給樣式	市場接近에 대한 制限·條件	內國民待遇에 대한 條件·制約
On-line 情報檢索(DB), 단순資料處理(RCS) 서비스 ①	(1)	制限 또는 條件없음	條件 또는 制約없음
	(2)	該當事項없음	該當事項없음
	(3)	國內서비스만 許容 ○ 國際서비스 '91.7 부터 일정기준에 의한 登錄要件을 賦課하여 許容 (公衆電氣通信事業法 第73條의 2)	條件 또는 制約없음
情報通信役務提供業 ②	(1)	制限 또는 條件없음	條件 또는 制約없음
	(2)	該當事項없음	該當事項없음
	(3)	外資 50%以下 合作投資企業의 國內서비스만 許容하며 一定基準에 의한 登錄要件 賦課(外資導入法 第9條 및 公衆電氣通信事業法 第73條의 2) ○ 國際서비스 許容('91.7) ○ 外資制限廢止('94.1)	條件또는 制約없음
데이타 單純 傳送서비스 ③	(1)	制限 또는 條件없음	條件 또는 制約없음
	(2)	該當事項없음	該當事項없음

0030

分　　野	供給樣式	市場接近에 대한 制限・條件	內國民待遇에 대한 條件・制約
	(3)	ㅇ '91.7부터 外資 50%以下의 合作投資企業으로서 ②의 서비스를 提供하는 情報通信役務 提供業者에게 國內 서비스만 許容하며 一定 基準에 의한 登錄要件賦課 (外資導入法 第9條 및 公衆電氣通信事業法 第73條의2)	條件 또는 制約없음

註：① DB, RCS : 公衆通信事業者의 通信回線을 利用하여 他人의 通信을 媒介하지 아니하는 情報通信役務를 提供하는 事業

② 情報通信 役務提供業：公衆通信事業者의 通信回線을 利用하여 非實時間으로 利用者가 提供하는 情報를 蓄積하여 傳送하거나 處理하여 전송하는 情報通信役務를 提供하는 事業(코드 및 프로토콜 變換서비스 包含)

③ 데이타 單純傳送서비스：公衆通信事業者의 通信回線을 利用하여 利用者가 提供하는 情報를 內容變更없이 實時間으로 傳送하거나 交換하는 서비스(음성서비스, 텔렉스 및 FAX 서비스는 除外됨)

4. 建 設

分 野	供給様式	市場接近에 대한 制限・條件	內國民待遇에 대한 條件・制約
一般建設(土木,建築,土建)	(1)	Unbound	條件 또는 制約없음
	(2)	制限 또는 條件없음	條件 또는 制約없음
	(3)	國內建設業免許 取得이 必要하며 合作投資만 許容(外資導入法 第7條, 建設業法 第7條) ○ 100% 投資許容('94.1) ○ 支社의 活動許容('96.1)	Unbound
專門建設(特殊,專門,電氣,電氣通信,消防設備)	(1)	Unbound	條件 또는 制約없음
	(2)	制限 또는 條件없음	條件 또는 制約없음
	(3)	國內建設業免許 取得이 必要하며 合作投資만 許容(外資導入法 第7條) ○ 100% 投資許容('96.1) ○ 支社의 活動許容('98.1)	Unbound
建築士業	(1)	建築士業 登錄 必要(建築士法 第23條) ○ 國內法人建築事務所와의 共同契約 可能('96.1)	條件 또는 制約없음

0032

分 野	供給樣式	市場接近에 대한 制限・條件	內國民待遇에 대한 條件・制約
	(2)	制限 또는 條件없음	條件 또는 制約없음
	(3)	韓國建築士 資格取得 및 登錄 必要(建築士法 第7條 및 第23條)	條件 또는 制約없음

5. 流 通

分 野	供給様式	市場接近에 대한 制限・條件	內國民待遇에 대한 條件・制約
都 賣①	(1)	制限 또는 條件없음	條件 또는 制約없음
	(2)	制限 또는 條件없음	條件 또는 制約없음
	(3)	制限 또는 條件없음②	條件 또는 制約없음
小 賣③	(1)	制限 또는 條件없음	條件 또는 制約없음
	(2)	制限 또는 條件없음	條件 또는 制約없음
	(3)	賣場面積 700㎡미만의 單一店舖를 運營하는 경우에 한해 許容 (外資導入法 第7條)	條件 또는 制約없음

註 : ① 穀物, 고기, 果實 및 菜蔬, 알콜성음료, 肥料, 農藥, 書籍 및 新聞都賣, 連鎖化事業, 一般貿易, 貿易仲介 除外

② 水產物, 醫藥品, 비료, 農藥, 시계, 보석, 人蔘등을 販賣하거나 農・水產物 都賣市場을 開設하고자 하는 경우 個別法上의 許可取得 必要

③ 담배, 골동품 및 예술품, 穀物, 고기, 菜蔬, 과실소매, 달리 分類되지 않은 飮食料品 및 담배소매업, 醫藥品, 化粧品, 書籍小賣, 注油所運營, 가스충전, 煉炭, 石油, 가스소매 除外

0034

6. 金 融

分 野	供給樣式	市場接近에 대한 制限·條件	內國民待遇에 대한 條件·制約
〈銀行 및 其他 銀行附隨業〉			
銀 行	(1)	Standstill	Standstill
	(2)	Standstill	Standstill
	(3)	事務所, 一定基準에 의한 支店만 許容(銀行法 第9條)	受信, 與信, 換業務 許容 ○ 資本金(또는 營業基金)增額時 金通委認可 ○ 一定條件下의 ATM設置 許容
其他 銀行附隨業	(1)	Standstill	Standstill
	(2)	Standstill	Standstill
	(3)	銀行支店의 形態로 國內進出한 경우만 許容(銀行法 第9條)	다음과 같은 附隨業務를 許容 ○ 商業어음, 貿易어음, 一般賣出業務

分 野	供給樣式	市場接近에 대한 制限·條件	內國民待遇에 대한 條件·制約
			○ 相互賦金業務 ○ 支給保證業務
信 託	(1)	Standstill	Standstill
	(2)	Standstill	Standstill
	(3)	銀行支店의 形態로 國內進出한 경우만 許容(銀行法 第9條)	信託業法에 의한 信託業 許容
〈證 券〉	(1)	Standstill	Standstill
	(2)	Standstill	Standstill 委託賣買, 自己賣買, 有價證券 引受業務 許容
	(3)	一定基準에 따라서 事務所, 支店, 合作法人(40%이상~50%미만)만 許容 ○ 旣存證券社의 持分參與는 外國證券社當 10%미만 總 50%미만만 許容	○ 資本金 또는 營業 ○ 基金 下限設定 證券去來所 會員加入은 去來所會員 總會에서 決定

0036

分　野	供給樣式	市場接近에 대한 制限・條件	內國民待遇에 대한 條件・制約
〈保　險〉			
原保險	(1)	輸出海上積荷保險에 限하여 許容 ○ 輸入海上積荷保險 許容 ('95.1)	Standstill
	(2)	外國居住時 締結한 保險契約을 保險期間이 경과되기 전에 國內에서 그 契約을 契約期間 동안 지속시키는 경우와 輸出積荷保險에 限하여 許容 ○ 輸入海上積荷保險 許容 ('95.1)	Standstill
	(3)	모든 保險社는 일정기준에 의해 許可를 取得하여야 하며 특히 損害保險業의 경우는 아래 형태의 進出만을 許容함 (保險業法 第5條) ○ 支店 ○ 既存社에 대한 20% 未滿의 持分 參與	Standstill

分 野	供給樣式	市場接近에 대한 制限・條件	內國民待遇에 대한 條件・制約
再保險 및 再再保險	(1)	國內社 우선출재의무를 除外하고는 制限없음(保險業法 第18條)	Standstill
	(2)	國內社 우선출재의무를 除外하고는 制限없음(保險業法 第18條)	Standstill
	(3)	모든 保險社는 일정기준에 의해 許可를 取得하여야 하며 특히 損害保險業의 경우는 아래 형태의 進出만을 許容함(保險業法 第5條) ○ 支店 ○ 旣存社에 대한 20% 未滿의 持分 參與	Standstill
保險과 關聯한 附隨業務(諮問, 保險計理, 損害査正, 危險管理)	(1)	一定基準에 의해 財務部長官이 認定하는 者로서 保險監督院에 登錄된 者에 限해 許容	Standstill
	(2)	Standstill	Standstill

0038

分　　野	供給樣式	市場接近에 대한 制限・條件	內國民待遇에 대한 條件・制約
	(3)	一定基準에 의해 財務部長官의 許可를 取得한 경우에 限해 許容	Standstill

註：金融서비스 Initial offer 作成時 考慮事項

① 金融分野의 自由化 推進方式은 Framework상의 自由化 推進方式에 따라서 作成되었음.

② 內國民待遇는 傳統的인 槪念의 內國民待遇로 限定하였으므로 市場 慣行에 의한 差別은 內國民待遇의 對象이 아님.

③ 政府의 影響力이 미치지 못하는 純粹한 民間自律規制團體는 서비스協定의 規制對象이 아닌 것으로 간주하였음.

④ 金融機關進出時 相互主義 適用國家에 대해서는 相互主義原則이 適用됨.

⑤ 預金者, 投資者, 保險加入者 등을 保護하기 위한 規制 및 金融制度의 安定性과 健全性을 유지하기 위한 Prudential Regulation이 適用됨.

7. 運 送

가. 航 空

分 野	供給樣式	市場接近에 대한 制限·條件	內國民待遇에 대한 條件·制約
地上操業	(1)	制限 또는 條件없음	條件 또는 制約없음
서비스	(2)	制限 또는 條件없음	條件 또는 制約없음
	(3)	外國人 投資持分 50%未滿의 合作投資 許容('97.1)	條件 또는 制約없음
航空서비스	(1)	制限 또는 條件없음	條件 또는 制約없음
販賣 및	(2)	制限 또는 條件없음	條件 또는 制約없음
마케팅	(3)	外國人 投資持分 50%未滿의 合作投資許容('97.1)	條件 또는 制約없음
컴퓨터豫約	(1)	制限 또는 條件없음('94.1)	條件 또는 制約없음
시스템	(2)	制限 또는 條件없음	條件 또는 制約없음
(CRS)	(3)	制限 또는 條件없음('94.1)	條件 또는 制約없음
航空機修繕	(1)	制限 또는 條件없음	條件 또는 制約없음
및 維持	(2)	制限 또는 條件없음	條件 또는 制約없음
	(3)	外國人 投資持分 50%未滿의 合作投資 許容('97.1)	條件 또는 制約없음

0040

나. 海 運

分 野	供給樣式	市場接近에 대한 制限·條件	內國民待遇에 대한 條件·制約
外航旅客運送	(1)	制限 또는 條件없음. 다만 정기선(liner)의 경우 政府의 認可必要(海運業法 第4條)	條件 또는 制約없음
	(2)	制限 또는 條件없음	條件 또는 制約없음
	(3)	代表者가 內國人인 外國人 投資持分 50% 未滿의 合作投資 許容(船舶法 第2條)	條件 또는 制約없음
外航貨物運送	(1)	國籍船優先利用制度撤廢('95.1)	條件 또는 制約없음
	(2)	制限 또는 條件없음	條件 또는 制約없음
	(3)	免許를 取得해야 하며 代表者가 內國人인 定期船 및 特殊貨物에 대한 合作投資 및 支社設置 許容(海運業法 第26條의 2 및 第27條)	條件 또는 制約없음
海上運送부대사업(주선, 대리점업) 중개, 선박관리, 선박대여)	(1)	Unbound	Unbound
	(2)	制限 또는 條件없음	條件 또는 制約없음
	(3)	代表者가 內國人인 外國人 投資持分 50% 未滿의 合作投資許容(海運業法 第35條의 2) o 外國船社가 海運代理店 合作投資時 營業範圍는 自社貨物에 限定	該當事項없음

다. 陸 運

分 野	供給樣式	市場接近에 대한 制限·條件	內國民待遇에 대한 條件·制約
貨物트럭킹	(1)	制限 또는 條件없음	條件 또는 制約없음
	(2)	制限 또는 條件없음	條件 또는 制約없음
	(3)	Unbound o 一般區域貨物自動車 運送事業限定 免許許容('97.1)	條件 또는 制約없음
倉 庫 業	(1)	制限 또는 條件없음	條件 또는 制約없음
	(2)	制限 또는 條件없음	條件 또는 制約없음
	(3)	許可取得必要(創庫業法 第3條)	條件 또는 制約없음

0042

8. 觀 光

分 野	供給樣式	市場接近에 대한 制限·條件	內國民待遇에 대한 條件·制約
觀光호텔業, 유스호스텔, 가족호텔업, 한국전통 호텔업	(1)	制限 또는 條件없음	條件 또는 制約없음
	(2)	制限 또는 條件없음	條件 또는 制約없음
	(3)	一定基準에 의한 登錄要件 賦課(觀光振興法 第4條)	條件 또는 制約없음
外國人專用 觀光記念品 販賣業	(1)	制限 또는 條件없음	條件 또는 制約없음
	(2)	制限 또는 條件없음	條件 또는 制約없음
	(3)	一定基準에 의한 登錄要件 賦課(觀光振興法 第4條)	條件 또는 制約없음
其他 觀光 關聯事業 (國際會議 用役業)	(1)	制限 또는 條件없음	條件 또는 制約없음
	(2)	制限 또는 條件없음	條件 또는 制約없음
	(3)	一定基準에 의한 登錄要件 賦課(觀光振興法 第4條)	條件 또는 制約없음
旅行斡旋業	(1)	制限 또는 條件없음	條件 또는 制約없음
	(2)	外貨旅行經費 소지한도 制限 (外國換管理法 第21條)	條件 또는 制約없음
	(3)	一定基準에 의한 登錄要件 賦課(觀光振興法 第4條)	條件 또는 制約없음

Conditional Offer by the Republic of Korea of Initial Commitments on Trade in Services

1991. 1

The Republic of Korea

Conditional Offer by the Republic of Korea of Initial Commitments on Trade in Services

I. General Comments

Korea respectfully presents its conditional offer of initial commitments on trade in services as indicated in the attached list. The Korean government places great importance on bringing to fruition successful services negotiations which will provide a strong foundation for the expansion of world trade in services. Despite lack of sufficient time and guidance, Korea has made best efforts to prepare the most comprehensive offer possible.

In most cases, major classifications of the service sectors follow the reference list set out in the document MTN.GNS/W/50, whereas sub-sector classifications are mainly based upon domestic regulations and institutions in Korea.

This offer is conditional. Korea reserves the right to modify, add, or withdraw this offer at any time prior to the closure of the negotiations on services, depending on the degree to which other parties' offers are equivalent and mutually acceptable, and the final text of the framework agreement and its sectoral annexes. Korea further reserves the right to make technical changes to its offer.

This offer has been prepared based upon the regulatory regime in force on November 1, 1990. Some additional clarifications and/or amendments to this offer may be necessary if, due primarily to time constraints or oversight, some restrictions are omitted in error.

0045

Ⅱ. Limitations, Conditions and Qualifications Applicable to All Service Sectors

1. Commercial Presence

The establishment of a joint-venture company, subsidiary, or branch office of a foreign corporate entity (liaison or representative office or branch) is subject to the procedural requirements in accordance with the Foreign Capital Inducement Act or the Foreign Exchange Control Act, as the case may be. Since 1984 Korea has adopted a negative system in allowing foreign direct investment, under which foreign direct investment is generally allowed except for in the sectors specifically listed in the Negative List. Foreign direct investment in those sectors on the Negative List may also be allowed if they meet certain additional requirements. As indicated in the attached list, some sectors may have different limitations and/or conditions for the establishment of a branch office from those of a joint-venture company or subsidiary.

Mergers and acquisitions of domestic firms by foreigners through the acquisition of issued and outstanding stocks are subject to the approval of concerned Authorities in accordance with the Foreign Exchange Control Act or the Foreign Capital Inducement Act.

The Korean government is in the process of further liberalizing its foreign direct investment policy by converting the current approval system to a notification system by 1993. However, restrictions may be imposed on foreign direct investments which are likely to lead to monopolistic or predatory practices in the domestic market.

0046

2. Acquisition and Usage of Land

The acquisition of land by foreigners or domestic companies which are deemed foreigners because of foreign equity ownership is subject to the approval of concerned Authority in accordance with the Alien Land Acquisition Law. However, in the case of a branch office of a foreign corporate entity (liaison or representative office or branch), the acquisition of the ownership interest in land is prohibited, although such office is permitted to hold lease right in land.

3. Foreign Exchange Control

In accordance with the Foreign Exchange Control Act, contracts for certain services by domestic residents requiring payment of foreign exchange require approval from the relevant Authorities.

4. Movement of Personnel

Entrance of foreign personnel who are essential to the supply of services in Korea may be allowed subject to procedural requirements such as acquiring a work-visa in accordance with the Immigration Control Law. Korea is in the process of further examining the scope of movement of personnel. In future negotiations, Korea has a willingness to make a more specific commitment regarding the movement of personnel in each sector.

0047

Ⅲ. Sectoral Commitment

- Mode of Delivery (1): Cross-border Supply
- Mode of Delivery (2): Consumption Abroad
- Mode of Delivery (3): Commercial Presence

1. Audio-Visual Services

Sub-sector	Mode of Delivery	Limitations and Conditions on Market Access	Conditions and Qualifications on National Treatment
Import & Distribution of Motion Picture	(1)	Unbound	No conditions or qualifications
	(2)	No limitations or conditions	No conditions or qualifications
	(3)	Foreign investment is subject to the Criteria for Permitting Foreign Investment in Restricted Industries in the Guidelines for Foreign Investment.	No conditions or qualifications
Import of Sound Recording & Video Tape Recording	(1)	Unbound	No conditions or qualifications
	(2)	No limitations or conditions	No conditions or qualifications
	(3)	Restriction on the registration of foreigner and foreign legal entity. The restriction will be removed from Jan. 1992 (subject to the approval of the National Assembly).	No conditions or qualifications

Note: The requirement for concerned ministry's recommendation or permission for the import of foreign motion picture, video tape recording and sound recording has not been indicated since the distinction between finished product trade and audio-visual service trade is still unclear. The limitation on the number of foreign motion picture prints is scheduled to be gradually liberalized by 1994. ('91: 14 prints, '92: 15 prints, '93: 16 prints)

0048

2. Business Services

Sub-sector	Mode of Delivery	Limitations and Conditions on Market Access	Conditions and Qualifications on National Treatment
Advertising	(1)	Import and use of foreign made advertising materials require a letter of recommendation from the minister concerned (Art. 10 Motion Picture Act, Art. 8 Disk Law)	No conditions or qualifications
	(2)	No limitations or conditions	No conditions or qualifications
	(3)	Joint ventures permitted with up to 99% share holding by foreign agencies Establishment of branch offices or sub-sidiaries permitted from Jan. 1991 . The Law on the Korea Broadcasting Advertising Corporation(KOBACO) should be observed by agencies applying for accreditation from KOBACO. . The Rules of the Newspaper Advertising Council of the Korea Newspaper Publishers Association should be observed by agencies applying for accreditation to the Council.	No conditions or qualifications
Engineering Service *	(1)	Unbound	No conditions or qualifications
	(2)	No limitations or conditions	No conditions or qualifications
	(3)	Registration required (Art. 3 Engineering Services Promotion Law)	No conditions or qualifications

Note: * includes advisory and consultative engineering, industrial and construction engineering.

0043

Sub-sector	Mode of Delivery	Limitations and Conditions on Market Access	Conditions and Qualifications on National Treatment
Computer-related Services	(1)	No limitations or conditions	No conditions or qualifications
	(2)	No limitations or conditions	No conditions or qualifications
	(3)	No limitations or conditions	No conditions or qualifications
Software Development	(1)	No limitations or conditions	No conditions or qualifications
	(2)	No limitations or conditions	No conditions or qualifications
	(3)	No limitations or conditions	No conditions or qualifications
Management & Administrative Consulting	(1)	No limitations or conditions	No conditions or qualifications
	(2)	No limitations or conditions	No conditions or qualifications
	(3)	No limitations or conditions	No conditions or qualifications
Engineering Design	(1)	Unbound	No conditions or qualifications
	(2)	No limitations or conditions	No conditions or qualifications
	(3)	Registration required (Art. 3 Engineering Services Promotion Law)	No conditions or qualifications
Project Management	(1)	Unbound	No conditions or qualifications
	(2)	No limitations or conditions	No conditions or qualifications

0050

Sub-sector	Mode of Delivery	Limitations and Conditions on Market Access	Conditions and Qualifications on National Treatment
	(3)	Registration required (Art. 3 Engineering Services Promotion Law)	No conditions or qualifications
Translation Services	(1)	No limitations or conditions	No conditions or qualifications
	(2)	No limitations or conditions	No conditions or qualifications
	(3)	No limitations or conditions	No conditions or qualifications
Certified Public Accountant (CPA) Services	(1)	To practice as a CPA in Korea, Korean CPA qualification is required (Art. 2,4,5 Certified Public Accountant Act) . A foreign CPA who has obtained his license in a country where Korean CPA licenses are regarded as being valid, following the attainment of an appropriate license from the Korean government, is allowed to provide auditing services to joint venture companies that are more than 50% owned by corporations or citizens of his own country and to other local companies in which corporations or citizens of his own country have interests.	No conditions or qualifications
	(2)	Standstill	Standstill
	(3)	Unbound	Unbound

0051

Sub-sector	Mode of Delivery	Limitations and Conditions on Market Access	Conditions and Qualifications on National Treatment
Certified Tax Accountant (CTA) Services	(1)	Practice of Tax Accountancy is permitted subject to obtaining a Korean CTA license. Foreign CTAs, CPAs and Lawyers may practice bookkeeping and tax consulting in the following cases: . CTAs licensed by a foreign country which recognizes Korean licenses as being valid shall acquire Korean CTA qualification by passing domestic tex exams. . CPAs and Lawyers licensed by a foreign country which recognizes CTA privileges of CPAs and Lawyers shall retain such privileges upon acquiring Korean CPA or Lawyer qualification respectively.	No conditions or qualifications
	(2)	Standstill	Standstill
	(3)	Unbound except for the establishment of an individual office.	Unbound

0052

3. Telecommunications

Sub-sector	Mode of Delivery	Limitations and Conditions on Market Access	Conditions and Qualifications on National Treatment
On-line Database and Remote Computing Services ①	(1)	No limitations or conditions	No conditions or qualifications
	(2)	Not applicable	Not applicable
	(3)	Domestic services only . International services allowed from July 1991, subject to registration (Art. 73-2 Public Telecommunications Business Law)	No conditions or qualifications
Computer Communication Services ②	(1)	No limitations or conditions	No conditions or qualifications
	(2)	Not applicable	Not applicable
	(3)	Domestic services only allowed to companies with less than 50% foreign equity, subject to registration (Art. 9 Foreign Capital Inducement Act, Art. 73-2 Public Telecommunications Business Law) . International services allowed from July 1991. . Elimination of foreign equity restrictions from Jan. 1994.	No conditions or qualifications
Data Transmission Services ③	(1)	No limitations or conditions	No conditions or qualifications
	(2)	Not applicable	Not applicable

0053

Sub-sector	Mode of Delivery	Limitations and Conditions on Market Access	Conditions and Qualifications on National Treatment
	(3)	Prohibited . Domestic and international services allowed to companies which are providing Computer Communication Services above and with less than 50% foreign equity from July 1991, subject to registration (Art. 9 Foreign Capital Inducement Act, Art. 73-2 of Public Telecommunications Business Law)	Prohibited No conditions or qualifications

Note: ① telecommunications services which are carried over common carriers' networks and which do not mediate third party communications.

② telecommunications services which are carried over common carriers' networks and which store and forward, or process and forward customer's information on a non-real time base other than those ① above (code and protocol conversion services included).

③ telecommunications services which are carried over common carriers' networks and which transmit and/or exchange customer's information without change in the form or content on a real-time base (voice telephony, telex, facsimile services excluded).

0054

4. Construction

Sub-sector	Mode of Delivery	Limitations and Conditions on Market Access	Conditions and Qualifications on National Treatment
General Construction (civil works, building)	(1)	Unbound	No conditions or qualifications
	(2)	No limitations or conditions	No conditions or qualifications
	(3)	License required (Art. 6 Construction Business Act), joint venture permited . Foreign equity restrictions will be eliminated from Jan. 1994 . Branch will be allowed from Jan. 1996	Unbound
Special Construction (special construction, specialist construction, electrical works, communication works, anti-fire equipment installation)	(1)	Unbound	No conditions or qualifications
	(2)	No limitations or conditions	No conditions or qualifications
	(3)	Liscence required (Art. 6 Construction Business Act, Art. 5 Electrical Construction Business Act, Art. 5 Communication Construction Business Act, Art. 42-2 Anti-fire Act), joint venture permited . Foreign equity restrictions will be eliminated from Jan. 1996 . Branch will be allowed from Jan. 1998	Unbound
Architectural Services	(1)	Registration required (Art. 23 Architect Act) . Joint contracts with domestic architectural firms will be allowed from Jan. 1996	No conditions or qualifications
	(2)	No limitations or conditions	No conditions or qualifications
	(3)	Domestic license required to register (Art. 7, 23 Architect Act)	No conditions or qualifications

0055

5. Distribution ①

Sub-sector	Mode of Delivery	Limitations and Conditions on Market Access	Conditions and Qualifications on National Treatment
Wholesale ②	(1)	No limitations or conditions	No conditions or qualifications
	(2)	No limitations or conditions	No conditions or qualifications
	(3)	No limitations or conditions	No conditions or qualifications
Retail ③	(1)	No limitations or conditions	No conditions or qualifications
	(2)	No limitations or conditions	No conditions or qualifications
	(3)	A business establishing a single shop, the floor area of which is below 700m², is allowed	No conditions or qualifications

Note: ① Businesses selling Fisheries, Drugs, Fertilizers, Pesticides, Watches, Jewellery, Ginseng etc and establishing a shop, the floor area of which is not less than 700m² and Agricultural and Fishery wholesale market are subject to approval under individual law.

② Excluding Wholesale of Grain, Meats, Fruits, Vegetables, Alcoholic Beverages, Fertilizers, Pesticides, Books & Newspapers, Brokers-Chain Market, General Foreign Trade, Foreign Trade Brokers.

③ Excluding Retail of Tobacco, Antiques & Art, Grain, Meats, Fruits, Vegetables, Food Beverages & Tobacco n.e.c., Drugs, Comestics, Books, Oil Service Stations, Gas Services Stations, Coal Briquettes, Fuel Oil, Bottled Gas.

0056

6. Financial Services

Sub-sector	Mode of Delivery	Limitations and Conditions on Market Access	Conditions and Qualifications on National Treatment
<Banking>			
Banking	(1)	Standstill	Standstill
	(2)	Standstill	Standstill
	(3)	Representative offices, and branches upon the fullfilment of guidelines only.	Only the acceptance of deposits, loans, and exchange business are allowed. . Capital (or operating funds) increases allowed subject to the Monetary Board's approval . Establishments of ATMs allowed subject to existing criteria
Services Auxiliary to Banking	(1)	Standstill	Standstill
	(2)	Standstill	Standstill
	(3)	Bank branches only	Only the following auxiliary services are allowed: . Sales of commercial bills and trade bills . Mutual installment deposits . Guarantees
Trust Business	(1)	Standstill	Standstill
	(2)	Standstill	Standstill
	(3)	Bank branches are subject to guideline.	Trust business as stipulated by the Trust Business Law.

0057

Sub-sector	Mode of Delivery	Limitations and Conditions on Market Access	Conditions and Qualifications on National Treatment
<Securities Business>	(1)	Standstill	Standstill
	(2)	Standstill	Standstill
	(3)	Approvals for representative offices, branches and joint ventures are subject to specified requirements: . Foreign partners must have equity participation in joint ventures of at least 40 percent up to, but not including 50 percent. . Currently, foreign equity participation in existing securities firms is possible with less than 50 percent (less than 10 percent for each).	Only brokerage, dealing and underwriting are allowed. . A minimum is required for paid-in capitals or operating funds. . Membership to the Stock Exchange will be decided by the existing members.
<Insurance>			
Direct Insurance	(1)	Marine Cargo only (Marine Cargo on import goods: permitted from Jan. 1995)	Standstill
	(2)	Marine Cargo (Marine Cargo on imported goods: permitted from Jan. 1995) and any remaining active policies which were issued during foreign residence, until their expiration.	Standstill

Sub-sector	Mode of Delivery	Limitations and Conditions on Market Access	Conditions and Qualifications on National Treatment
	(3)	Required to obtain licenses under certain guidelines. For the non-life insurance business in particular, only the following modes of entry are permitted: branch or equity participation of less than 20% in existing non-life insurance companies.	Standstill
Reinsurance & Retrocession	(1)	No restrictions other than the obligation of priority reinsurance cessions to domestic insurers.	Standstill
	(2)	The same as above	Standstill
	(3)	The same as commercial presence for Direct Insurance.	Standstill
Insurance Auxiliary Services (consulting, actuarial, claim handling, risk management)	(1)	Required to register with the Insurance Supervisory Board under the guidelines set by the Ministry of Finance.	Standstill
	(2)	Standstill	Standstill
	(3)	Required to obtain licenses from the Ministry of Finance under certain guidelines.	Standstill

0059

Note: In preparing this list of offers on financial services, Korea takes into account the following matters:

(1) Application
In consideration of the unique characteristics of Korea's financial system, Korea has chosen the form of binding consistent with the Services Framework, namely the positive approach.
With regard to national treatment, the traditional definition of national treatment should be applied, as in such instances, market practices are considered outside the scope of the Services Framework.

(2) Self-regulatory body
When a self-regulatory body does not exercise its authority through statutory powers, the party is unable to ensure the application of national treatment to financial service providers of other parties.

(3) Reciprocity
Authorization for the establishment of banks or other financial institutions is subject to reciprocity requirements only for those countries which impose reciprocity requirements.

(4) Prudential measures
Certain requirements exist due to prudential reasons and to ensure the integrity and stability of the financial system.

7. Transportation

A. Air Transportation

Sub-sector	Mode of Delivery	Limitations and Conditions on Market Access	Conditions and Qualifications on National Treatment
Ground Handling Services	(1)	No limitations or conditions	No conditions or qualifications
	(2)	No limitations or conditions	No conditions or qualifications
	(3)	Permission for Joint Ventures with less than 50% foreign equity from Jan. 1997	No conditions or qualifications
Selling and Marketing of Air Transport Services	(1)	No limitations or conditions	No conditions or qualifications
	(2)	No limitations or conditions	No conditions or qualifications
	(3)	Permission for Joint Ventures with less than 50% foreign equity from Jan. 1997	No conditions or qualifications
Computer Reservation Systems	(1)	No limitations or conditions	No conditions or qualifications
	(2)	No applicable	Not applicable
	(3)	Domestic services only allowed to companies with less than 50% foreign equity, subject to registration (Art. 9 Foreign Capital Inducement Act, Art. 73-2 Public Telecommunications Business Law) . international services subject to further consideration.	No conditions or qualifications
Aircraft Repair and Maintenance	(1)	No limitations or conditions	No conditions or qualifications
	(2)	No limitations or conditions	No conditions or qualifications
	(3)	Permission for Joint Ventures with less than 50% foreign equity from Jan. 1997	No conditions or qualifications

0061

B. Maritime Transportation

Sub-sector	Mode of Delivery	Limitations and Conditions on Market Access	Conditions and Qualifications on National Treatment
International Deep-sea Passenger Shipping	(1)	No limitations except for approval of liner service	No conditions or qualifications
	(2)	No limitations or conditions	No conditions or qualifications
	(3)	An applicant for a joint venture shall obtain approval from the Administrator of the KMPA (Art. 4, MTBA) . The foreign equity shall be less than 50%. . The juridical representative of the joint venture shall be a national.	No conditions or qualifications
International Deep-sea Cargo Shipping	(1)	A person who intends to transport the marine cargoes as prescribed in the Presidential Decree shall utilize Korean flag vessels (Art. 16-1, MTIFA) . Cargo preference system will be phased out by Jan. 1995.	No conditions or qualifications
	(2)	No limitations or conditions	No conditions or qualifications
	(3)	A foreign maritime cargo transporter shall obtain permission from the Administrator of the KMPA to establish a branch office (Art. 26-2, MTIFA).	No conditions or qualifications

0062

Sub-sector	Mode of Delivery	Limitations and Conditions on Market Access	Conditions and Qualifications on National Treatment
		A license to a foreign investor for a joint venture on specific liners and specific cargoes is required. (Art. 27-2, MTBA) . The juridical representative of the joint venture shall be a national.	
Auxiliary Services (freight forwarding, ship brokering, ship management, ship leasing, shipping agency)	(1)	Unbound	Unbound
	(2)	No limitations or conditions	No conditions or qualifications
	(3)	. Joint ventures are permitted with the condition that foreign equity shall be less than 50%. . The juridical representative of the joint venture shall be a national. . Joint ventures of the shipping agency invested by foreign shipping company shall be an agent only for his own cargoes and vessels.	No conditions or qualifications

Note: KMPA : Korea Maritime and Port Administration
MTBA : Maritime Transportation Business Act
MTIFA: Maritime Transportation Industry Fostering Act

0063

C. Road Transportation

Sub-sector	Mode of Delivery	Limitations and Conditions on Market Access	Conditions and Qualifications on National Treatment
Freight Transport by Road	(1)	No limitations or conditions	No conditions or qualifications
	(2)	No limitations or conditions	No conditions or qualifications
	(3)	Licenses for general local freight transport will be permitted from Jan. 1997	No conditions or qualifications
Storage and Warehousing	(1)	No limitations or conditions	No conditions or qualifications
	(2)	No limitations or conditions	No conditions or qualifications
	(3)	No limitations except for a license under Storage and Warehousing Law	No conditions or qualifications

0064

8. Tourism

Sub-sector	Mode of Delivery	Limitations and Conditions on Market Access	Conditions and Qualifications on National Treatment
Tourist Hotels, Youth-Hostels, Family Hotels, Korean Traditional Hotels	(1)	No limitations or conditions	No conditions or qualifications
	(2)	No limitations or conditions	No conditions or qualifications
	(3)	Registration reguired (Art. 4 Tourism Promotion Law)	No conditions or qualifications
Foreigner's Tourist Souvenir Shops	(1)	No limitations or conditions	No conditions or qualifications
	(2)	No limitations or conditions	No conditions or qualifications
	(3)	Registration reguired (Art. 4 Tourism Promotion Law)	No conditions or qualifications
Professional Convention Organizers	(1)	No limitations or conditions	No conditions or qualifications
	(2)	No limitations or conditions	No conditions or qualifications
	(3)	Registration required (Art. 4 Tourism Promotion Law)	No conditions or qualifications
Travel Agencies	(1)	No limitations or conditions	No conditions or qualifications
	(2)	Limitations on travel expenses (Art. 21 Foreign Exchange Control Law)	No conditions or qualifications
	(3)	Registration required (Art. 4 Tourism Promotion Law)	No conditions or qualifications

0065

분류기호 문서번호	통기20644-1159	기 안 용 지 (전화 :)	시 행 상 특별취급	
보존기간	영구·준영구. 10. 5. 3. 1.	장 관		
수 신 처 보존기간				
시행일자	1991. 1.16.			

보조기관			협조기관		문 서 통 제
	국 장	전결			
	심의관				
	과 장				발 송 인
기안책임자		김 봉 주			

경 유 수 신 참 조	경제기획원장관	발신명의		
제 목	UR/서비스 분야 한·미간 양자 협상			

1. 91.1.14(월) 주미 아국대사의 Hills USTR 대표와의 면담시 동 대표는 UR/서비스 분야 협상과 관련하여 91.1.29(화) 제네바에서 한·미간 양자협상을 갖기를 원한다고 하면서 아측의 수락 여부를 문의하여 왔다고 합니다.

2. 이와 관련하여 상기 미국 제의의 수락 여부를 1.16(수)한 전언통신으로 통보하여 주시기 바랍니다. 끝.

0066

1505-25(2-1) 일(1)갑
85. 9. 9. 승인

190mm×268mm 인쇄용지 2급 60g/m²
가 40-41 1986. 2. 13.

수신 : 통상조정3과 구종호

발신 : 통상기구과 현학승

통화시간 : 91. 1. 16(수) 11:44

0067

91- 1-17 ; 16:28 ; ;# 1

經濟企劃院 對外經濟調整室

427-760
京畿道 果川市 中央洞 1番地
政府 第2廳舍
Tel (02) 503-9130
Fax (02) 503-9138

Facsimile 送 信 表 紙

日字 : 1991. 1. 16.

受信 : 외무부 통상기구과 (김봉주 서기관)

參照 :

發信 : E.P.B. 통상조정3과

題目 :

發送枚數 : 3 (表紙包含)

※ 내용중 명확하지 않은 부분이 있거나 누락된 부분이 있을 경우에는 연락하여 주시기 바랍니다.

0068

분류기호 문서번호	통조삼 10502-	기 안 용 지 (전화: 503-9149)	시 행 상 특별취급	
보존기간	영구·준영구. 10. 5. 3. 1.	장 관		
수 신 처 보존기간				
시행일자	'91.1.			
보조기관 실 장	전 결	협조기관		문 서 통 제
국 장				
과 장				
기안책임자	김 용 준			발 송 인
경 유 수 신 참 조	외무부장관	발신명의		
제 목	UR/서비스분야 한.미간 양자협상			

1. 외기 20644-1159('91.1.16)와 관련임.

2. UR/서비스분야의 한.미간 양자협의 개최와 관련하여 당원의 대외경제조정실장은 S. Kristoff USTR 부대표와 1.15(화) 면담시 다음과 같은 협의원칙을 합의하였음.

- UR Service 협상의 기본 frame에 의하면 91.3까지 각국의 initial offer 제출후 91.4. 이후 개별협상은 하도록 일정이 되어 있음에 유의함.
- 한.미간의 협의는 UR/서비스협상의 테두리내에서 아국을 포함한 여러국가가 참여하는 쌍무협의의 일환으로 추진되어야 함.
- 아국은 Offer List에 포함된 업종에 대한 실질협상을 진행하는데 상당한 준비가 필요한 점을 감안 본 한.미간의 협의는 아국의

1505-25(2-1) 일(1)갑
85. 9. 9. 승인 "내가 아낀 종이 한장 늘어나는 나라살림"

190mm×268mm 인쇄용지 2급 60g/m²
1 10-11 1990. 9. 15.

0069

Offer List에 대한 설명과 상호관심사항에 대한 의견청취에 중점을

두어 진행토록 함.

3. 상기 합의내용은 아국의 상공부장관과 미국의 L.Williams USTR부대표 및

M.Farren 상무성차관과의 당일 회동시 재차 확인되었으며, S.Kristoff USTR 부대표는

이러한 합의내용을 귀국후 C.Hills USTR대표에게 보고키로 하였음.

4. 상기 합의된 원칙의 테두리내에서 아국은 '91.1.29 제네바에서

UR/서비스분야에 관한 한.미간 양자협의를 개최할 방침임을 미측에 통보하여 주기

바랍니다. 끝.

0070

1505-25(2-2) 일 1)을
85. 9. 9. 승인 "내가아낀 종이 한장 늘어나는 나라살림"

190mm×268mm 인쇄용지 2급 60g/m²
가 40-41 1990. 3. 15

전 언 통 신 문

통조3 10502-3

수신 외무부장관

발신 경제기획원장관

제목 UR/서비스 분야 한·미간 양자협상

1. 통기 20644-1159 (91.1.16)와 관련임

2. UR/서비스 분야의 한·미간 양자협의 개최와 관련하여 당원의 대외경제 조정실장은 S. Kristoff USTR 부대표와 1.15(화) 만찬시 다음과 같은 협의 원칙을 합의 하였음.

   - UR/서비스 협상의 기본 Frame 의하면 91.3월까지 각국이 initial offer 제출 후 91.4 이후 개별 협상을 갖도록 일정이 되어 있음에 유의함.
   - 한·미간 협의는 UR/서비스 협상의 테두리 내에서 아국을 포함한 여러 국가가 참여하는 쌍무협의의 일환으로 추진되어야 함.
   - 아국은 Offer List 에 포함된 업종에 대한 실질협상을 진행하는데 상당한 준비가 필요한 점을 감안, 본 한·미간의 협의는아국의 Offer List 에 대한 설명과 상호 관심사항에 대한 의견청취에 중점을 두어 진행토록 함.

3. 상기 합의내용은 아국의 상공부장관과 미국의 L. Williams USTR 부대표 및 M. Farren 상무성 차관과의 동일 회동시 재차 확인되었으며 S. Kristoff USTR 부대표는 이러한 합의 내용을 귀국후 C. Hills USTR 대표에게 보고키로 하였음.

4. 상기 합의된 원칙의 테두리 내에서 아국은 91.1.29. 제네바에서 UR/서비스 분야에 관한 한·미간 양자협의에 응할 방침임을 미측에 통보하여 주시기 바랍니다.   끝.

공람	통상기구과	91년 1월 17일	담 당	과 장	심의관	국 장	차관보	차 관	장 관
			김봉주	(서명)					

봉화시간 : 1.17 13:30

송 화 자 : 강 병 제

수 화 자 : 김 봉 주

0071

관리 번호	91-81

	분류번호	보존기간

발 신 전 보

번 호 : WUS-0190 910117 1840 DP 종별 :

수 신 : 주 미 대사. ~~총영사~~ (사본 : 주제네바, 카나다대사) WGV -0090 WCN -0066

발 신 : 장 관 (통기)

제 목 : UR/서비스 분야 한·미간 양자협상

대 : USW - 0170, 0193

일반문서로 재분류 (1991. 6. 30.)

1. 표제 협상과 관련, 1.15(화) 경기원 대조실장과 Kristoff USTR 부대표간 면담을 통하여 아래와 같은 협의 원칙에 합의 하였음.
   - ㅇ UR/서비스 협상의 기본 Frame 의하면 91.3월까지 각국의 initial offer 제출 후 91.4 이후 개별 협상을 갖도록 일정이 되어 있음에 유의함.
   - ㅇ 한·미간 협의는 UR/서비스 협상의 테두리 내에서 아국을 포함한 여러 국가가 참여하는 쌍무협의의 일환으로 추진되어야 함.
   - ㅇ 아국은 Offer List 에 포함된 업종에 대한 실질협상을 진행하는데 상당한 준비가 필요한 점을 감안, 본 한·미간의 협의는아국의 Offer List 에 대한 설명과 상호 관심사항에 대한 의견청취에 중점을 두어 진행토록 함.

2. 상기 합의내용은 아국의 상공부장관과 미국의 L. Williams USTR 부대표 및 M. Farren 상무성 차관과의 동일 회동시 재차 확인되었으며 S. Kristoff USTR 부대표는 이러한 합의 내용을 귀국후 C. Hills USTR 대표에게 보고키로 하였음.

3. 상기 합의된 원칙의 테두리 내에서 아국은 91.1.29(화) 제네바에서 UR/서비스 분야에 관한 한·미간 양자협의에 응할 방침임을 미측에 통보하기 바람. 끝.

(통상국장 김 삼훈)

앙 고 재	91년 1월 17일	통기과	기안자	김낙주	과 장	(서명)	국 장	전결	차 관	장 관 (서명)

보안통제	외신과통제
(서명)	

0072

서비스 分野 最初 讓許 計劃書 提出의 背景 및 內容

o 政府는 지난 1.14. 우리나라의 서비스 讓許 計劃書를 GATT에 提出하였음.

o 政府가 提出한 讓許 計劃書는 金融, 通信, 運送, 流通, 建設, 觀光, 事業서비스, 시청각 서비스등 서비스 協商에서 論議되었던 主要業種을 대부분 포함하고 있으나, 敎育, 保健 서비스, 流通서비스중 貿易業, 事業서비스중 法務서비스는 除外하였음.

o 讓許計劃書에 포함된 業種에 대한 自由化 水準도 通信, 建設등 一部分野에서 主要 國家의 關心事項을 고려한 一部 追加自由化 內容을 담고 있는 외에는 대부분 현재 시행되고 있는 規制 및 開放水準을 凍結하는 內容임.

o 이러한 讓許計劃書 提出은 90.10.그린룸會議에서 合意된 바에 따른 措置로서, 우리나라 외에도 美國, EC, 日本, 스위스, 濠州, 뉴질랜드, 카나다, 홍콩, 스웨덴등 9개국이 이미 提出하였음.

0073

o 서비스 交易規模가 89년도 基準 205억불, 世界 18위로서 商品分野에서 뿐만 아니라 서비스 分野에 있어서도 對外依存度가 매우 높은 우리나라로서는 全體 UR 協商時 조기 妥結에 기여하고 向後 서비스 協商에서의 우리나라 協商力을 强化시키고자 하는 目的과 金融, 通信서비스 分野등에서의 雙務的 開放 要求를 多者的 次元으로 對處하는 것이 바람직하다는 判斷下에 同 讓許計劃書를 提出하였음.

0074

(참고자료)

아국 最初의 讓許 計劃書 內容

① 讓許計劃 提示에 있어서 我國의 基本立場

- ㅇ 서비스 協商에서 대체로 合意가 이루어진 基本構造 및 그간 주장해온 立場을 土臺로하여 作成
- ㅇ 現行 國內法에 의해 一般的으로 適用되는 外國人의 國內營業活動에 관한 制限事項은 基本的으로 維持

  (例 : 外資導入法, 外國換管理法, 外國人土地法, 出入國管理法등)
- ㅇ 서비스 一般協定 및 分野別 附屬書, 各國의 讓許計劃 內容이 具體化될 경우 우리 立場의 補完, 調整이 可能

② 分野別 市場開放 約束

(對象業種)

- ㅇ 金融, 通信, 運送, 流通, 建設, 觀光, 事業서비스, 視聽覺 서비스등 서비스 協商에서 論議된 주요한 業種을 大部分 包含
- ㅇ 敎育 및 保健서비스 全體, 流通分野中 貿易業, 事業서비스중 法務서비스 등은 除外

(自由化 水準)

- ㅇ 대부분 現存開放 및 規制水準을 凍結하는 정도에서 提示
- ㅇ 通信分野를 비롯한 美國등 主要國의 關心事項에 대해서는 追加的인 自由化 計劃을 包含

0075

③ 追加的인 自由化 計劃

o 視聽覺 서비스

- 音盤 및 비디오 輸入 關聯, 外國人 및 外國法人에 대한 登錄制限 撤廢 (92.1)

o 通信

- 情報檢索, 單純 資料 處理 및 情報通信 役務 提供 國際 서비스 許容 (91.7.)
- 情報 通信 役務 제공업 外資制限 撤廢(94.1.)
- 데이타 單純 傳送 서비스 國內 서비스 許容 (91.7.)

o 建設

- 一般建設 100% 投資許容(94.1.) 및 支社의 活動許容(96.1.)
- 專門建設 100% 投資許容(96.1.) 및 支社의 活動許容(98.1.)
- 國內法人 建築事務所와의 共同契約 可能 (96.1.)

o 保險

- 輸入海上 積荷 保險 許容 (95.1.)

o 航空

- 地上操業, 航空 서비스 販賣 및 마켓팅, 航空機 수선 및 유지분야 外國人 投資持分 50% 未滿의 合作投資 許容 (97.1.)
- 컴퓨터 豫約 서비스의 國境間 提供 및 商業的 주재 許容(94.1.)

o 海運

- 國籍船 優先 利用 制度 撤廢 (95.1.)

o 陸運

- 一般 區域 貨物自動車 運送 事業 限定 免許許容(97.1.)

0076

경 제 기 획 원

통조삼 10502- 45　　　　503-9149　　　　1991. 1. 19.

수신 수신처장관 (외무부 통상기구과)

제목 UR/서비스협상관련 양허협상대책 회의개최　　　기 FAX송부

1. '91.1.9 개최된 제9차 대외협력위원회의 결정에 따라 GATT에 제출한 아국의 최초의 양허계획표를 별첨과 같이 송부하니 업무에 참고하기 바랍니다.

2. 아울러 동 양허계획표의 제출을 계기로 아국은 본격적인 양허협상 대책의 추진이 필요한바 이와 관련한 대책회의를 다음과 같이 개최코자 하니 필히 참석해 주기 바랍니다.

다　　음

가. 일　　시: '91.1.22(화)　15:00-17:00

나. 장　　소: 경제기획원 대회의실 (1동 727호)

다. 의　　제: UR/서비스협상관련 양허협상대책

- 양허협상팀 구성문제

- 양허협상 자료준비문제

라. 참석범위: (별첨 참조)

첨부: 1. 한국의 최초의 양허계획표 1부.

2. 참석범위 1부.　끝.

경 제 기 획 원 장관

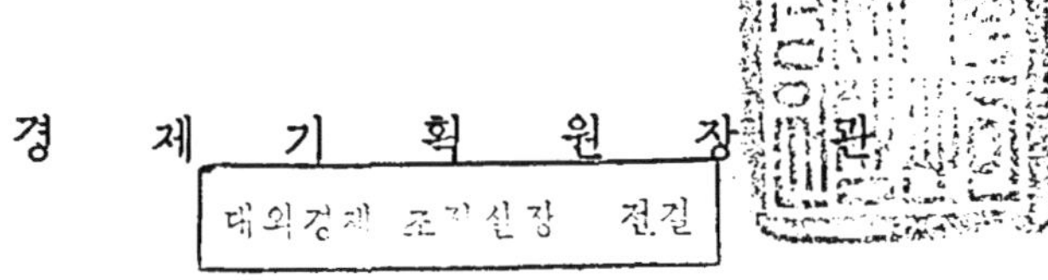

대외경제 조정실장 전결

수신처 : 외무부장관, 재무부장관, 법무부장관, 문교부장관, 문화부장관, 상공부장관, 교통부장관, 건설부장관, 보사부장관, 노동부장관, 체신부장관, 과기처장관, 공보처장관, 환경처장관, 해운항만청장, 특허청장, 대한무역진흥공사장, 대외경제정책연구원장, 한국개발연구원장, 산업연구원장.

0077

1991. 1. 2073

참 석 범 위

소속기관	참 석 자
경제기획원	대외경제조정실장 (회의주재) 제2협력관 정책조정국장 공정거래 총괄정책국장
외 무 부	통 상 국 장
재 무 부	국제금융국장
법 무 부	섭외법무심의관
문 교 부	사회국제교육국장
상 공 부	국제협력관
건 설 부	건설경제국장
보 사 부	기획관리실장
노 동 부	직업안정국장
교 통 부	수송정책국장
체 신 부	통신정책국장
문 화 부	예술진흥국장
과학기술처	기술협력관
공 보 처	광고진흥국장
환 경 처	기획관리실장
해운항만청	해 운 국 장
특 허 청	기획관리관
대한무역진흥공사	무역정보본부장
대외경제정책연구원	박태호 연구위원
한국개발연구원	유정호 연구위원
산업연구원	이영세 연구위원

0078

UR/서비스協商
關聯資料

最初의 讓許計劃表提出의 意義 및 內容

1991. 1

經濟企劃院
對外經濟調整室

0079

目　　次

1. 最初의 讓許計劃表 提出의 意義

- UR서비스協商에서 各國의 서비스市場開放은 讓許計劃表를 바탕으로 한 讓許協商(Concession Negotiation)을 통해서 確定하기로 合意

  o 서비스協商이 成功的으로 마무리지어질 경우 ① 서비스一般協定, ② 分野別 附屬書, ③ 各國의 讓許計劃表가 同時에 發效될 豫定이며 UR協商 終了 以後에 各國의 自由化水準을 擴大하기 위한 讓許協商이 주기적으로 이루어질 展望

- 이와같은 讓許協商의 重要性을 勘案하여 GATT 事務局은 讓許計劃表의 提出을 促進시키기 위해 2段階 節次를 마련

  o 서비스協商에 積極的으로 參與하겠다는 政治的 意志를 表現하는 性格의 最初의 讓許計劃表(Initial Offer List)를 브랏셀 閣僚會議 以前에 提出

  o 브랏셀 閣僚會議 以前에 최초의 讓許計劃表를 提出하지 못한 國家는 '91. 3月까지 讓許計劃表를 提出토록 하여 '91. 4부터 讓許協商을 進行

— 美國, EC, 스위스, 日本, 濠洲, 뉴질랜드, 스웨덴, 카나다, 홍콩등 9個國은 브랏셀 閣僚會議 以前에 最初의 讓許計劃表를 提出

  ○ 大部分의 國家가 서비스交易에 대한 現在의 國內規制制度를 凍結 (Standstill)하는 水準의 讓許計劃表를 提出

  ○ 한편 스웨덴등 一部國家는 宣言的인 讓許計劃表를 提出하였으나 美國, EC등은 비교적 충실한 內容의 讓許計劃表를 提出

— 이와같이 美國, EC등 主要協商國家가 충실한 內容의 讓許計劃表를 提出한 것은 다른 國家에도 이에 相應한 讓許計劃表의 提出을 促求하는 것으로 判斷됨.

— 브랏셀 閣僚會議 議長은 最初의 讓許計劃表를 提出한 國家가 世界 서비스貿易에서 차지하는 比重이 80%에 달한다고 指摘하고 各國 代表를 非公式的으로 面談하여 早速히 自國의 讓許計劃表를 提出할 것을 要請

  ○ 이에따라 我國을 비롯한 未提出 國家들은 議長面談 過程에서 早速히 提出할 意思를 表明

— 我國도 當初 브랏셀 閣僚會議時까지 讓許計劃表를 提出코자 推進 하였으나 방대한 作業量으로 인해 未提出

— 그러나 我國이 제네바 貿易協商委員會에 對備하여 讓許計劃表를 提出할 경우 교착상태에 빠진 서비스協商의 進展에 寄與하고 我國의 協商力을 强化할 수 있을 것으로 判斷

  ○ 아울러 金融, 通信分野등에서의 雙務的 通商壓力을 緩和하는데에도 바람직할 것으로 보임.

0082

2. 我國의 讓許計劃表의 內容

가. 讓許計劃表 作成의 基本指針

- 서비스協商에서 論議된 業種을 최대한 包括하여 我國의 協商力을 强化

- 自由化水準은 現存 規制의 凍結을 原則으로 하되 一部自由化가 確定된 事項을 추가하는 水準으로 讓許

- 金融, 通信, 流通分野 등은 向後 韓·美間 雙務協商에서 論議될 內容을 勘案하여 適正한 開放水準을 設定

나. 讓許計劃表의 內容

(1) 前 文

- 서비스協商의 進展에 寄與하기 위해 最大한 充實한 內容의 讓許計劃表를 作成했음을 言及

- 外資導入法 및 外國換管理法에 의한 外國企業의 國內進出에 대한 一般的인 制限事項을 規定

- 外國人土地法에 의한 外國企業의 土地에 대한 制限事項 및 出入國管理法에 의한 規制事項을 明示

— 國境間人力移動의 範圍에 대해서는 追加的인 檢討를 하고 있으며 向後 讓許協商過程에서 分野別로 具體的인 自由化 約束을 할 用意가 있음을 言及

— 서비스一般協定 및 分野別 附屬書, 各國의 讓許計劃內容에 따라 修正, 補完, 撤回할 수 있는 權利를 留保

(2) 市場開放約束

〈包括業種〉

○ 視聽覺서비스, 事業서비스, 通信, 建設, 流通, 金融, 運送, 觀光등 서비스協商에서 論議되던 主要한 業種을 大部分 包含

* 敎育 및 保健서비스 全體, 流通分野中 貿易業, 事業서비스중 法務서비스등은 除外

〈自由化水準〉

○ 大部分 現存開放 및 規制水準을 凍結하는 정도에서 提示

○ 美國등 主要國의 關心事項에 대해서는 追加的인 自由化 計劃을 包含

○ 특히 通信分野에 있어서는 美國側의 要求事項을 전향적으로 反映

0084

3. 向後協商 推進對策

가. 讓許協商에의 徹底한 對應

- 最初의 讓許計劃表에서 除外되었다 하더라도 最終的으로 開放 對象에서 除外되는 것은 아니므로 教育 및 保健서비스 등에 대해서 美國, EC등 主要先進國이 開放要求를 할 可能性이 있음.

- 또한, 金融, 流通등 讓許計劃表에 包含시킨 業種에 대해서도 包括範圍의 擴大 및 보다 높은 水準의 自由化를 要求할 可能性이 큼.

- 따라서 主要協商 對象國家로부터 開放要求가 있을 것으로 豫想되는 分野에 대하여 協商代案을 開發하는 同時에 相對國에 대한 要求事項(Request List)을 철저히 準備

- 아울러 各部處에 構成되어 있는 18個 分野別 對策班에 協商專門家를 參與시키는등 讓許協商팀을 補强

- 必須專門人力 및 숙련노동인력의 國境間移動에 대한 具體的인 方案을 講究하여 建設등 勞動集約的인 서비스의 海外進出이 可能하도록 함.

나. 國內補完對策의 推進

- 지금까지 把握된 國內 規制現況을 바탕으로 各部處는 民間의 自由로운 競爭을 沮害하는 規制制度를 整備

- 長期的인 次元에서 各部處는 서비스協商을 契機로 所管業種에 대한 國際競爭力의 强化方案 등을 包含한 產業構造調整方案을 綜合的으로 推進

0086

(別添 1)

다른國家의 讓許內容과의 比較

가. 全般的인 評價

- 包括範圍는 全般的으로 볼때 既提出한 9個 先進國과 유사한 水準이며 특히, 運送分野(陸運, 海運, 航空)를 包含하여 美國, 日本등 運送分野를 包含하지 않은 一部國家에 비해 積極的인 편임.

- 自由化 水準은 대부분 現存規制 및 開放水準을 凍結하는 線에서 그쳤기 때문에 保守的인 편이나 通信, 建設, 廣告, 會計, 經營 컨설팅에 대한 主要國家의 關心事項은 追加自由化 計劃의 提示 등으로 적절히 反映하고 있는 것으로 評價됨.

  o 다만, 金融, 流通등 一部業種의 自由化 水準은 先進國에 비해 相對的으로 낮은 편으로써 讓許協商에 대한 徹底한 對備가 必要하다고 思料됨.

나. 分野別 評價

〈視聽覺서비스〉

o 映畫, 音盤 및 비디오 등만 包含되어있고 放送 및 書籍分野는 除外되었으며 다른 國家와 比較하면 中間程度의 自由化 水準임.

〈事業서비스〉

ㅇ 會計, 稅務, 廣告, 엔지니어링서비스등 10個 業種을 包含하여 다른國家와 比較하여 볼때 대체적으로 同一한 水準임.

ㅇ 技術用役育成法에 의해 많은 規制가 있는 엔지니어링서비스 등 一部業種을 除外하고는 다른 國家의 自由化 水準과 類似한 水準의 自由化 計劃을 提示함.

〈通 信〉

ㅇ 電話, 電信등을 除外한 대부분의 電氣通信서비스를 包含하고 있어 美國, EC등 先進國과 同一한 水準의 包括範圍를 提示함.

ㅇ 自由化 水準과 關聯하여 外國人投資 持分을 制限하고 있으나 向後 自由化 計劃을 具體的으로 提示하여 韓·美通信 協商에도 前向的인 對應이 可能함.

〈建 設〉

ㅇ 土木施工, 建設엔지니어링, 建築士등을 包含하고 있어 包括範圍는 美國, EC등 先進國과 同一한 水準임.

ㅇ 外國人投資持分制限, 建築士 資格制限등 比較的 많은 內容의 制限事項을 담고 있으나 向後 自由化計劃을 具體的으로 提示하여 美國의 要求事項을 적절히 反映하고 있음.

〈流 通〉

ㅇ 都賣業과 小賣業을 包含시키되 貿易業은 除外하여 美國, EC, 日本등 主要先進國의 包括範圍보다 낮은 水準임.

ㅇ 現在狀態의 開放 및 規制水準을 凍結하는 內容을 담고 있어 自由化 水準도 相對的으로 높지 않음.

0088

〈金 融〉

○ 國內金融市場을 開放할 主要分野를 旣存의 我國立場인 Positive System에 따라 提示하였으나 全般的으로 볼때 包括範圍가 좁은 편임.

○ 自由化 水準과 關聯하여 現在의 開放 및 規制 水準을 凍結하는 線에서 提示하였으나 向後 金融分野 附屬書에 대한 協商動向등을 勘案하여 伸縮的으로 對處할 必要性이 있음.

〈運 送〉

○ 航空補助서비스, 海運서비스, 貨物트럭킹서비스등 대부분의 運送서비스를 包含하여 美國, 日本등 運送分野를 包括하지 않은 一部國家에 비해 積極的인 立場

○ 自由化水準과 關聯하여 我國은 國籍船利用制度, 外國人投資制限事項등을 規定하여 EC, 뉴질랜드등에 비하여 대체로 보수적인 立場을 堅持

〈觀 光〉

○ 觀光호텔業, 觀光宿泊業, 旅行斡旋業등 主要觀光서비스를 包含하여 餘他 先進國의 包括範圍와 類似한 水準임.

○ 讓許業種에 대하여 外國企業에 대한 特別한 制限事項이 없어 先進國과 마찬가지로 比較的 높은 水準의 自由化計劃을 提示

(別添 2)

主要國家의 要求事項 反映與否

가. 主要國家의 開放要求 事項

— 現在까지 UR서비스協商을 통하여 我國에게 開放要求事項 (Request List)을 提示한 國家는 美國 뿐임.

○ 美國은 지난 '90.6 我國을 包含한 28個國에 대하여 開放要求事項(Request List)을 提示

— 美國의 Request List에 包含되어 있는 業種은 會計, 廣告등 8個 業種이며 대부분 韓·美 雙務間 協商에서 提起되었던 事項을 言及

○ 包括業種 : 會計서비스, 廣告, 視聽覺서비스(Audio/Visual Works), 建設(엔지니어링 包含), 프렌차이징, 保險仲介業, 經營컨설팅, 通信

○ 要求水準 : 同 8個業種에 存在하고 있는 市場接近의 制限措置, 外國人에 대한 差別待遇, 政府補助金의 支給등 서비스 交易의 障壁을 緩和 및 撤廢

— 同 開放 要求事項은 서비스協商의 進展을 促進하기 위해서 美國이 서둘러서 作成한 것으로서 最終的인 內容은 아니며 追加的인 開放 要求事項이 있을 것으로 豫測됨.

0090

나. 我國의 讓許計劃表에의 反映與否

- 包括範圍와 關聯하여 美國이 提示한 8個業種中 會計, 廣告, 視聽覺서비스, 建設, 經營컨설팅, 通信등 6個分野를 我國의 讓許計劃表에 包含시킴.

  o 프렌차이징은 外國人投資制限業種으로써 다른 流通分野의 外國人投資制限業種과 함께 提示함.

  o 保險仲介業(獨立代理店 包含)은 國內保險會社에 대해서도 아직 施行되고 있지 않는 새로운 制度로서 除外시킴.

- 讓許計劃表에 包含시킨 6個業種에 대하여 대부분 現存制度를 凍結하는 線에서 提示하였으나 通信, 建設등에 관한 要求事項중 일부는 向後 自由化 計劃을 提示

  o 附加價値 通信서비스市場에 대하여 '91.7부터 一定한 登錄要件을 갖출 경우 外國人投資比率 50%未滿의 合作投資를 許容

  o 一般建設業등에 대하여 外國企業의 單獨投資를 '94.1부터 許容

    · 但, 國內建設免許取得 必要

0091

(別添 3)

既提出한 9個國家의 最初 讓許計劃表 槪要

가. 美 國

— 提出時期 : '90.11.13

— 性 格 : UR/서비스協商完了 以前에 언제든지 서비스協定의 Framework 와 附屬書의 最終案, 他國의 Offer 水準에 따라 修正이 可能하며, National Schedule 樣式에 記入해 넣는 技術的인 方法의 變更도 可能하다는 條件附 Offer List 임.

— 包括業種 : 自國에게 脆弱한 海運·航空, 基本通信등의 業種은 除外하고 거의 大部分의 業種을 包含하고 알파벧 順序로 羅列.

○ 會計, 建築서비스, 放送, 컴퓨터서비스, 建設, 엔지니어링서비스, 裝備賃貸, 프랜차이징, 病院 및 保健서비스, 法務서비스, 經營컨설팅, 鑛山 및 油田서비스, 映畵 및 비디오프로그래밍, 出版, 音聲錄音, 附加價値 通信서비스, 觀光, 陸運(트럭킹, 버스, 鐵道), 保險, 銀行 및 其他 金融서비스

— 特 徵 : 市場接近이 許容된 모든 業種(放送 및 金融業은 除外)에 있어서 經營者(manager), 任員(executive), 專門家(specialist)의 一時的 入國(3年~5年)을 許容

0092

나. 스위스

- 提出時期 : 서비스協定의 Framework, 分野別 附屬書의 最終內容 및 相對國의 Offer 水準에 따라 언제든지 修正 및 增減할 수 있는 條件附 提案
- 包括業種 : GATT 事務局이 作成한 分類體系 (MTN/GNS/50)에 따라 金融 및 運送分野등 거의 모든 서비스業種을 列擧
  - ○ 視聽覺서비스, 裝備의 賃貸 및 維持・補修, 會計, 經營 및 管理 서비스, 廣告, 엔지니어링, 컴퓨터關聯서비스, 旅行斡旋業, 빌딩淸掃, 鋪裝, 飜譯, 印刷, 通信, 建設, 流通, 保險, 銀行, 證券, 호텔 및 레스토랑, 航空, 陸運, 海運
- 特 徵
  - ○ 1986年 現在의 羈束的인 立法事項 (Mandatory legislation)과 재량적인 規制措置 (Discretionary measures)를 明示하였으나 혹시 Offer List의 作成過程에서 政府의 權限으로 措置할 수 없는 기속적인 立法事項이 누락됨으로써 自由化되는 잘못을 防止하기 위하여 Subject to Mandatory legislation이라는 表現을 挿入
  - ○ 市場接近과 關聯해서는 서비스 供給의 네가지 形態中 國境間 移動 (Cross-border trade), 消費者의 移動, 商業的駐在 (Commercial presence)에 對해서는 거의 아무런 制限이 없으며 勞動力의 移動 (Movement of personnel)에 對해서만은 例外없이 모든 業種에 걸쳐 아무런 自由化 約束을 하지 않고 있음.
  - ○ 內國民待遇와 關聯해서 個別業種 次元에서는 外國人에 대한 特別한 差別待遇는 거의 없으나 모든 業種에 걸쳐 理事會의 任員의 過半數 以上이 스위스 市民일 것을 要求하고 있음.

다. EC

— 提出時期 : '90.12.4

— 性 格 : 서비스協定의 Framework와 分野別 附屬書에 대한 協商結果에 따라 修正·撤回할 수 있는 條件附 提案

〈서비스協商結果를 評價하는 主要 考慮事項〉

- ㅇ 效果的인 MFN原則의 適用
- ㅇ Universal Coverage
- ㅇ 모든 規制當局에 對한 適用
- ㅇ 協商力을 强化시키는 措置를 취하지 않겠다는 凍結約束

— 包括業種 : GATT 事務局이 作成한 參考目錄 (MTN.GNS/W/50)에 열거된 거의 모든 業種을 包含

ㅇ 設備賃貸서비스, 不動産서비스, 設置 및 組立서비스, 設備의 維持 및 補修서비스, 專門職業서비스 (法務, 會計, 建築, 醫師, 齒科醫師, 獸醫師, 廣告, 엔지니어링, 旅行斡旋業등), 빌딩淸掃서비스, 印刷業, 通信, 視聽覺서비스, 뉴스 및 新聞, 代理店, 建設, 流通 (都賣, 小賣, 貿易業), 敎育, 保健서비스, 호텔 및 레스토랑, 個人서비스 (집안淸掃, 育兒), 레져서비스, 銀行, 保險, 航空, 海運, 陸運등

— 特 徵

ㅇ 모든 業種에 걸쳐 現存 規制水準의 凍結 (Standstill) 約束을 함.

ㅇ 勞動力의 移動에 대해서는 附屬書의 制定이 必要하고 EC도 向後 어느정도의 自由化 約束을 할 것이나 一律的으로 모든 業種에 대해 追加的인 考慮對象 (subject to further consideration)이라고 規定

0094

라. 日 本

- 提出時期 : '90.11.29
- 性 格 : 서비스協定의 Framework와 分野別 附屬書의 最終內容에 따라 언제든지 修正 및 增減할 수 있는 條件附 提案
- 包括業種 : 金融, 運送등 重要한 서비스業種이 除外되어 있으며 일정한 分類體系없이 알파벧順으로 個別業種들을 열거
  - ○ 廣告, 農業·林業·漁業서비스, 建築서비스, 會計, 엔지니어링, 建設, 稅關代行業, 流通, 敎育, 호텔 및 레스토랑, 保健서비스, 情報서비스, 賃貸, 法務서비스, 圖書館서비스, 映畵産業 및 映畵館, 個人看護 서비스(personal care services), 寫眞, 出版, R & D서비스, 레져 및 文化서비스, 소프트웨어서비스, 土地測量, 通信, 飜譯, 旅行斡旋業, 獸醫業, 쓰레기處分業
- 特 徵
  - ○ 外國人은 不動産에 關한 權利의 取得 및 行使에 共通的인 制限이 있다고 하는 것을 强調
  - ○ 서비스協定에 一致하지 않는 制限事項등만 열거하고 일부 無差別的인 要求事項(例 : 專門資格要員등)에 對해서는 明示하지 않음.
  - ○ 勞動力의 移動에 對해서는 一律的으로 아무런 自由化 約束을 하지 않음(Unbound)
  - ○ 1986年 以來 自由化한 內容에 對해서는 別途로 區分하여 Credit을 받고자함.

마. 濠 洲

— 提出時期: '90.12.4

— 性 格: 서비스協定의 最終形態, 特히 包括的인 包括範圍 (comprehensive sectoral coverage) 및 强力한 MFN規定에 대한 滿足할 만한 協商結果에 따라 修正 및 撤回할 수 있는 條件附 提案

— 對象業種: 特別한 分類體系없이 個別業種을 열거했으며 金融, 通信, 建設, 海運, 流通등 主要한 서비스들이 除外되어 있음. 다만 金融서비스의 경우는 同 分野의 註釋書가 制定되는 대로 最初의 自由化 約束을 위한 協商에 參與할 準備가 되어있다는 內容 言及

○ 廣告, 컨설팅, 飜譯, 마케팅, 有害物規制서비스(Pest control services), 臨時 雇傭서비스, 輿論調査, 뉴스代行, 레크레이션 서비스, 航空補助서비스, 會議서비스, 호텔 및 飮食配達서비스 (catering), 旅行案內

— 特 徵

○ 市場接近의 形態中 商業的駐在에 對해서는 모든 業種에 대하여 反復해서 自國의 外國人投資 政策指針에 따른 制限以外에는 制限事項이 없다고 規定하고 있으며, 또한 自國의 List에 包含된 어떤 內容도 關聯法과 政策에 따라 外國人投資를 規制하는 自國의 權利에 影響을 주지 않는다는 點을 明示

○ 國境間의 勞動力移動은 自國의 移民規制制度와 節次(immigrational requlations and procedures)에 從屬된다는 點을 反復해서 言及하고 있음.

○ Offer List에 包含된 各 業種에 대한 정의 및 包括範圍를 規定

0096

바. 뉴질랜드

- 提出時期 : '90.12.5
- 性 格 : 서비스協定의 最終形態, 特히 MFN, 內國民待遇, 市場接近 및 資格의 認定 (recognition of qualification)에 關한 規定의 最終形態와 Offer List를 提出한 國家의 숫자 및 同 Offer List의 自由化 程度에 따라 언제든지 修正 및 增減할 수 있는 條件附 提案
- 包括業種 : GATT事務局의 參考目錄 (MTN.GNS/W/50)의 分類體系에 따라 거의 모든 業種을 包含.
  - ㅇ 視聽覺서비스, 事業서비스 (裝備賃貸, 不動産서비스등), 專門職業 서비스 (法務서비스, 會計 및 稅務서비스등), 엔지니어링, 旅行 斡旋業, 建物의 淸掃, 飜譯, 通信, 建設, 流通, 敎育서비스, 金融 서비스, 호텔 및 레스토랑, 陸運, 海運, 航空
- 特 徵 : Offer List에 包含된 모든 業種에 適用되는 一般的인 提案事項을 다음과 같이 明示
  - ㅇ 25%以上의 持分率取得등 일정한 種類의 外國人投資는 海外投資 委員會 (Overseas Investment Commission)의 承認 必要
  - ㅇ 外國企業에 대해서는 國內企業 보다 差別的으로 높은 稅率을 適用
  - ㅇ 法務서비스, 會計, 建設 및 엔지니어링 (컨설팅包含), 農業서비스, 醫療 및 看護서비스, 不動産서비스, 海運, 陸運 및 航空서비스, 保險 및 金融서비스에는 專門的인 資格要件등이 있으나 Offer List 상에는 言及하지 않음.
  - ㅇ 移民政策, 勞使關係, 競爭促進, 消費者保護 등을 위한 法과 制度는 계속 適用될 것이나 이러한 事項을 Offer List에 列擧하지는 않음.

사. 홍 콩

- 提出時期 : '90.12.4

- 性　　格 : 서비스協定의 最終形態, 특히 MFN規定의 만족스런 解決에 따라 언제든지 修正 및 增減할 수 있는 條件附 提案

- 包括業種 : GATT事務局의 參考目錄(MTN.GNS/W/50)의 分類體系에 따라 自國의 關心分野를 열거하고 있으나 建設, 航空등 많은 分野가 除外되어 있음.

  ○ 事業서비스(裝備賃貸, 빌딩淸掃, 飜譯등), 專門職業서비스(컨설팅, 廣告, 市場調査, 소프트웨어開發, 旅行斡旋業등), 커뮤니케이션서비스(配達, 通信, 映畵配給, 圖書館서비스), 都賣, 호텔 및 레스토랑, 海運貨物處理, 倉庫, 保險, 銀行 및 其他 金融서비스

  ○ 海運分野에 대한 協商結果에 따라 國際運送(ocean freight) 및 선박전세 서비스를 包含시킬 準備가 되었있다고 明示

- 特　徵

  ○ Offer List에 包含시킨 모든 業種에 대하여 一律的으로 國境間移動(Cross border-trade)과 勞動力의 移動(Movement of personnel)은 아무런 自由化約束을 하지 않음(Unbound)

  ○ 반면에 消費者의 移動 및 商業的駐在, 內國民待遇에 대하여는 아무런 制限事項을 規定하고 있지 않음.

0098

아. 카나다

- 提出時期 : '90.12.4

- 性　格 : 餘他國家의 서비스市場 開放程度, 서비스 一般協定 (Framework) 및 그 附屬書, 특히 電氣通信 및 金融서비스分野의 協商結果에 따라 修正・撤回할 수 있다는 條件附 提案

- 包括業種 : 海運, 航空, 流通, 保健서비스등 많은 業種이 除外되어 있으며 GATT事務局이 作成한 參考目錄(MTN.GNS/W/50)의 分類體系와는 상이한 方式으로 作成

  ○ 鑛業關聯서비스, 建設, 金融, 商業서비스, (裝備賃貸, 專門職業서비스, 訓練서비스, 市場調査서비스등), 컴퓨터關聯서비스, 電氣通信서비스, 觀光서비스등

- 特　徵

  ○ National schedule 樣式없이 서비스業種의 名稱만 열거하고 있으며 열거된 業種에 대하여 國境間移動(cross-border movement) 및 商業的駐在의 현존 規制水準의 동결을 宣言

  ○ 서비스販賣者(service seller), 重役(executives), 管理者 (managers), 專門家(specialists)는 모든 서비스業種의 供給을 위하여 必要한 경우 別途의 就業許可 節次없이 일시적인 國境間 移動을 許容

    • 上記 4個形態의 勞動力에 대하여 槪念을 定義

자. 스웨덴

— 提出時期 : '90.12.5

— 性　　格 : 서비스協定에 包含될 原則, 다른國家로부터의 Offer 內容 및 最初의 自由化 約束을 위한 協商方法(modality)에 따라 修正할 수 있는 條件附 提案

— 特 徵

○ 다른 國家의 Offer List와는 달리 National Schedule의 樣式에 따른 別途의 List가 없음.

○ 모든業種(all services sectors)에 대하여 現在의 市場接近水準과 現在의 內國民待優 水準을 凍結시킨다고 宣言하고 向後 追加的인 自由化約束을 위한 協商에 參與할 準備가 되어 있음을 明示

○ 스웨덴의 서비스協商에 대한 다음과 같은 基本立場을 다시한번 强調

① 强力한 內容의 MFN原則을 바탕으로 한 法的條約(legal treaty)의 마련

② 同 條約은 서비스交易의 擴大를 위한 토대가 되어야 하며 모든 서비스業種을 包括해야 함.

③ 各國의 自由化約束은 서비스協定의 意味있는 執行 및 各國의 規制措置의 豫測可能性, 交易環境의 安定性을 保障해야 함.

0100

UR/서비스協商
對策會議 資料

讓許協商對應方案

1991. 1

經 濟 企 劃 院
對外經濟調整室

0101

目　　次

0102

Ⅰ. 지금까지의 論議內容

- 최초의 自由化約束(Initial Commitment)을 확정하기 위한 讓許協商에 대해서는 서비스協定의 基本構造(Framework), 分野別 附屬書(Sectoral Annexes)등 規範制定 分野에 대한 協商不振으로 具體的인 論議를 하지 못한 실정임.

  o 讓許協商方式에 대해서 ① R/O(Request/Offer)방식 ② 公式適用(Formular)방식 ③ 全面 凍結措置(Across-the border freeze)등 세가지 방식이 提示되었으나 심층적인 討議를 進行하지 못함.

  o 美國은 '90.6月 28個國에 대한 Request List를 배포하고 讓許協商을 '90.9-11중에 진행할 것을 主張하였으나 協商相對國의 호응이 없어 실행되지 못함.

- 스위스는 '90.10月 서비스協商의 進展을 촉구하고 協商妥結에 대한 政治的 意志를 表明하기 위해 各國이 자발적으로 最初의 讓許計劃表(Initial Offer List)를 提出할 것을 提議

- UR/서비스協商그룹 議長은 '90.12월 主要國家들의 意見을 참고로 하여 讓許協商指針(Guideline for Initial Commitment)을 作成

  o 同指針에 따르면 각국은 '91.3월말까지 Offer List를 提出하고 구체적인 讓許協商은 '91.4-10중에 진행

- 美國은 '91.1月초 Fast-track 時限과 관련하여 我國을 포함한 10여국가에 대하여 '91.1月말경에 Initial Offer List에 대한 雙務間 協議를 進行할 것을 要請

  o 我國은 일정한 조건하에 同協議에 응할 것을 約束

Ⅱ. 向後展望

- UR協商이 전반적으로 不透明하며, MFN일탈문제등 서비스協商의 主要爭點에 대해서 協商參加國들이 계속해서 첨예하게 立場對立을 하고 있기 때문에 正確한 展望을 하기가 대단히 어려운 實情에 있음.

- 특히 Gulf 戰爭으로 말미암아 UR協商이 다소 연기되는 것이 不可避할 것으로 전망되지만 我國은 이를 讓許協商對應 作業과 國內補完對策 推進의 계기로 활용해야 될 것으로 보임.

- 이러한 관점에서 지금까지의 서비스協商 動向 및 對內協商對策 推進의 必要性에 비추어 概略的으로 다음과 같이 協商日程을 設定하고 協商方式 및 場所에 대한 展望을 해 볼수 있음.

〈讓許協商의 時期〉

- 브랏셀 閣僚會議에서는 Framework과 分野別 附屬書 및 最初의 自由化約束을 일괄적으로 終結짓기로 合意를 하였으며 이에 따르면 美國의 Fast-track 時限과 관련하여 協商主導國의 關心分野에 대한 讓許協商을 중심으로 하여 UR/서비스協商을 妥結

  o 일단 1月末에 Initial Offer List를 提出한 國家들이 相對國의 Offer List에 대한 疑問事項을 確認하고 自國의 Offer List를 설명하는 非公式協議를 進行

  o Framework과 分野別 附屬書의 制定을 위한 協商을 再開하는 問題는 他協商그룹의 進展狀況과 밀접히 관련을 맺고 있기 때문에 다소 지체될 可能性도 있음.

- 그러나 Gulf戰爭으로 말미암아 美國이 Fast-track 時限을 6個月정도 延長할 경우 당초 서비스協商그룹 議長이 提示한 讓許協商 指針에 따라 協商이 進行될 可能性이 있음.

  o 本格的인 讓許協商을 '91.4-10중에 진행
    . 每月 1回(총5~6회)씩 主要協商國間에 讓許協商을 진행하며 매 1回의 協商期間은 10여일 이상이 所要될 것으로 豫想

  o 개별적인 雙務協商 結果를 바탕으로 各國의 이익을 綜合的으로 評價하는 會議를 '91.11月 한달동안 진행하여 各國의 讓許計劃表를 확정

  o 일정수의 國家가 加入한 시점에서 서비스一般協定(GATS) 및 各國의 讓許計劃表가 발효됨 ('92年 初가 될 것으로 전망)

<讓許協商의 場所>

- 特別한 사정이 없는 한 雙務間協商은 해당국의 제네바대표부에서 상호 교대로 進行할 것임.

  o 金融등 一部 主要業種에 대해서는 별도의 場所에서 빈번한 非公式協議가 開催될 可能性이 많음.

<讓許協商의 方式>

- 정확한 예측은 어려우나 公式適用方式과 全面凍結措置 方式이 部分的으로 사용되고 주로 R/O方式이 사용될 可能性이 큼.

  o 公式適用方式은 서비스交易에 대한 各種 복잡한 規制制度를 일률적으로 완화 및 撤廢하는데 限界가 있음.

o 그러나 公式適用 方式이 컴퓨터관련서비스, 엔지니어링등 一部業種에 있어서 시도될 可能性을 排除할 수 없으며 특히 免許, 資格, 標準등에 대한 規制制度를 調和 및 統一시키기 위한 協商에 使用될 可能性도 있음.

o 또한 全面的인 凍結措置는 各國의 開放 및 規制水準이 상이한 상태에서 市場開放 水準의 현저한 不均衡을 초래하는 限界가 있음.

- 金融등 一部業種에 있어서 국내에 진출하는 外國企業의 숫자를 쿼터로 制限하는등 양적인 制限이 不可避하다고 인정되는 경우 동 쿼터를 公平하게 配分하는 問題는 어려운 難題가 될 것임.

o 資本金 規模 및 國際的인 信認度, 양국간의 去來規模등 객관적인 基準을 設定하여 배분하나 최종적으로는 추첨제나 競賣制등이 도입될 可能性도 전혀 排除할수 없음.

Ⅲ. 主要課題 推進對策

1. 讓許協商팀의 構成

가. 基本指針

- 經濟企劃院이 讓許協商에서도 綜合調整 機能을 遂行하고 分野別 協商班을 총괄함.

  o 國內弘報 問題 및 國會에서 承認을 받는 問題에 대해서도 綜合的인 對策推進

- 個別分野에 대해서는 主務部處가 현지 協商에 직접참여하며 所管業種에 대한 協商結果에 대해서 책임을 부담

  o 現地 協商에 直接參與하지 못하는 부처는 協商代案을 반드시 訓令으로 送付

나. 構成

- 協商總括調整機能은 經濟企劃院 對外經濟調整室 第2協力官이 담당하며 제네바 대표부의 經協官이 현지에서 協調하고 分野別 協商責任者는 各分野의 主務部處 課長으로 구성

- 讓許協商팀의 支援 및 有機的인 業務協助를 위한 國內對應 作業은 지금까지 各部處에 設置.運營되어 오던 18개 分野別 對策班이 계속해서 必要한 業務를 遂行

0107

다. 機能 및 活動

〈讓許協商팀〉

- 讓許協商팀에 편성된 協商責任者는 每會議때마다 一慣性있게 參席

- 各分野別 協商責任者는 各種 協商對策 資料를 준비하여 협상에 참석하며 首席代表등과 협의하여 所管分野에 대한 公式.非公式會議에서 아국의 입장을 발언
  - o 協商對象 業種의 範圍가 넓고 協商對象 國家가 많은 점에 비추어 綜合的인 機能을 遂行하는 首席代表와의 緊密한 협조가 必要

- 諮問官은 每會議時 協商責任者와 함께 現地協商에 參席
  - o 특히 各部處는 所屬研究機關등과 협조하여 同諮問官이 國內協商 對策會議 및 現地協商에 최우선적으로 참여할 수 있도록 協商諮問官으로 지정하며 필요한 行政的인 支援을 提供

〈國內對應 作業班〉

- 協商期間中 國內에서 讓許協商팀과 긴밀한 業務協調 및 連絡體制를 유지하며 讓許協商팀의 要請事項을 檢討.對處하고 內部的인 報告機能을 수행

- 相對國으로 부터 開放要求 事項이 있을경우 신속히 國內對應作業을 推進

- 法令改定作業, 國際競爭力 強化方案등 國內補完對策 등을 계속성있게 추진

2. 協商資料의 準備

① 我國의 讓許計劃表에 대한 解說資料

<資料의 種類>

- 前文(Covernote)에 나타난 공통적인 制限事項에 대한 細部 說明內容
- 讓許計劃表에 明示되어 있는 各業種의 具體的인 包括範圍 및 細部業種
- "Unbound 및 凍結(Standstill)"이라고 표시한 경우의 현존 規制制度 및 開放水準
- "免許 또는 登錄取得 必要" 라고 표시한 경우 同 免許 및 登錄의 要件, 基準과 根據法令
- 市場接近에 대한 制限事項을 포함시킨 부분에 대해서는 讓許協商過程에서 상대국을 설득할 수 있는 正當한 事由
- 追加的인 自由化 約束을 제시한 경우 특정한 時期를 설정한 논리

<推進對策>

- 各部處가 提出한 分野別 解說資料를 바탕으로 하여 경제기획원은 1.24까지 綜合的인 解說資料를 作成

② 我國의 讓許計劃表에서 제외시킨 업종에 대한 對策資料

<對象業種>

- 教育, 保健, 法務서비스, 貿易業, 不動産仲介業등

<推進對策>

- 讓許計劃表에 포함시킨 업종에 대한 解說資料와 동일한 內容을 準備하되 각부처는 2.10까지 分野別 對策資料를 작성하고 經濟企劃院은 2.20까지 綜合對策資料를 作成

③ 相對國에 대한 Request List

<對象國家>

- 기본적으로 美國, EC, 日本, 캐나다, 濠洲, 아세안등 6개국에 대한 Request List를 준비하고 各業種別로 추가적인 Request List를 準備

- 潛在的인 市場可能性이 큰 인도, 남미국가들에 대해서도 Request List 作成 可能性을 檢討

<對象分野>

- 國內企業이 잠재적인 비교우위가 있는 建設, 航空, 海運, 陸運등 勞動集約的인 서비스分野
(예시) 土木建設 시공분야에 대한 日本市場에의 進出

- 우수한 능력과 專門知識을 보유하고 있는 專門職種으로서 향후 海外進出 可能性이 있는 분야

(예시) 醫師, 會計士등 事業서비스 분야에 대한 先進國 市場에의 진출

* 先進國이 상호간에 關心을 갖고 있는 金融등의 分野에 대해서는 先進國間에 集中的인 R/O協商이 이루어지고 同 協商結果를 我國이 MFN原則에 의해 수혜를 받게될 可能性도 고려

<推進對策>

- UR協商을 海外市場 進出의 계기로 활용한다는 基本認識下에 主要交易相對國에 대한 Request List를 徹底히 準備

- 각부처는 '91.1-2月중에 民間業體 및 關聯研究機關 등과 공동으로 Request List 作成을 위한 海外現地調査 活動을 최대한 實施

  o 交易障壁이 되는 各種規制制度와 동 규제제도가 실제로 적용되고 있는 具體的인 事例를 생생하게 수집

- 2.28까지 各部處는 分野別 Request List를 작성하고 經濟企劃院은 3.10까지 綜合的인 Request List를 作成

④ 서비스交易에 대한 統計

<必要性>

- 讓許協商에서 利害得失에 대한 판단의 客觀的인 基準이 되므로써 相對國의 要求事項에 대한 對應資料 및 我國의 要求事項의 根據資料로 활용

<統計의 種類>

- 輸.出入規模등 서비스교역에 대한 國家別, 年度別統計

- 國內生産 및 雇傭에 대한 연도별 통계

- 國內에 活動하는 外國企業 (子會社, 合作投資, 支社)의 현황에 대한 國家別, 年度別 統計

- 外國에 진출한 國內企業의 現況에 대한 國家別,年度別統計

<推進對策>

- 各部處는 旣存 國內統計資料 및 外國의 統計資料 등을 활용하여 讓許協商에 活用할 수 있는 業種別 統計를 3.20까지 作成

  o 統計廳 및 韓國銀行은 各部處의 統計作成 業務에 필요한 關聯資料 및 情報를 提供하고 필요시 各分野別 統計를 綜合하는 機能을 遂行

0112

⑤ 勞動力移動 範圍

<必要性>

- 현재 勞動部 및 法務部는 分野別 勞動力移動 許容範圍에 대해서 具體的인 方向을 提示하고 있지 못함.

  o 특히 法務部는 出入國管理法과 관련하여 취업비자를 발급하는 과정에서 最終的인 裁量權을 留保하려는 立場堅持

- 各部處는 최소한 商業的 駐在와 관련한 필수 專門人力(Key-personnel)까지는 移動을 許容하는데 대체로 의견이 접근하고 있으며 建設部는 技術者(technician), 엔지니어(engineer)등 세부적인 勞動力移動 範圍를 설정한바 있음.

- 讓許協商過程에서 先.開途國으로 부터 구체적인 開放要求가 있을 것에 대비하여 조속히 分野別로 我國의 協商代案을 마련하는 것이 필요함.

<推進對策>

- 勞動力移動 分野의 作業班長을 맡고 있는 노동부가 법무부와 협조하여 2.10까지 勞動力移動에 대한 協商代案을 종합적으로 강구

  o 各分野에 필요한 勞動力의 移動範圍를 직종별로 검토
    (예시) 會計士, 엔지니어, 建築士, 經營컨설턴트

0113

o 모든 分野에 적용될 수 있는 人力의 移動範圍를 기능에 따라 分類하여 檢討

(예시) 事業目的上 訪問 (Business Visitors),
專門人力 (Professionals),
貿易業者 및 投資家 (Traders and Investors),
外國企業의 從事員 (Intra-Company Transferees)

- 各部處는 2.28까지 分野別 勞動力移動 許容範圍를 設定하고 勞動部 및 法務部는 3.10까지 綜合對策 資料를 作成

3. 國內補完 對策의 推進

<基本方向>

- 各部處는 讓許協商을 계기로 關聯法令 및 制度를 정비
  o 追加自由化 計劃을 제시한 분야는 약속한 내용에 따라 關聯法令 및 制度를 改善하여 차질없이 약속을 이행
  o 民間의 자유로운 競爭을 저해하는 各種規制制度는 자발적으로 整備하여 對外開放에 앞서 國內企業의 競爭體質을 強化

- 長期的인 次元에서 國際競爭力 強化方案 등을 포함한 産業構造調整 方案을 종합적으로 추진
  o 제조업의 國際競爭力 強化에 필수적인 서비스 産業은 적극적으로 지원
  o 比較優位가 있는 서비스산업은 輸出産業으로 유도하되 비생산적인 서비스産業에 대해서는 規制를 強化

0114

<推進對策>

- 經濟企劃院은 KIEP, KDI등과 協調하여 2.28까지 綜合的인 國內補完對策 推進計劃을 樹立

- 各部處는 分野別 補完對策을 마련하고 法令 및 制度改善 作業을 지속적으로 推進

- 經濟企劃院은 各部處의 補完對策을 바탕으로 하여 綜合的인 補完對策을 樹立

4. 業務推進 分擔表

구 분	추 진 과 제	담당부처
1. 讓許協商팀의 構成	- 分野別 協商責任者 및 國內對應擔當者의 지정	각부처
	- 諮問官 指定에 따른 行政的인 支援措置	각부처
	- 讓許協商팀에 대한 敎育實施 ○ 雙務間 協商의 經驗談 紹介 및 協商戰術의 敎育	경기원
	- 讓許協商에 參席 및 國內對應作業推進	경기원, 각부처
2. 讓許協商에 必要한 資料의 準備		
① 我國의 讓許計劃表에 대한 解說資料	- 分野別 解說資料 作成	각부처
	- 綜合的인 解說資料의 作成	경기원
② 我國의 讓許計劃表에서 除外시킨 業種에 대한 對策資料	- 分野別 對策資料의 作成	각부처
	- 綜合的인 對策資料의 作成	경기원

0116

(별첨 1)

UR/서비스협상관련 18개 분야별 대책반 현황

('91.1.22일 현재)

분 야	반 장	연구 책임자
<총괄반>		
- 서비스실무소위	경기원 대조실 제2협력관	대외경제정책연구원 박태호박사
<분과반>		
- 정보통신	체신부 통신정책국장	통신개발연구원 성극제박사
- 건 설	건설부 해외건설국장	국토개발연구원 김홍수박사
- 유 통	상공부 산업정책국장	대외경제정책연구원 이영세박사
- 금 융	재무부 국제금융국장	대외경제정책연구원 김태준박사
- 화물유통	교통부 수송정책국장	교통개발연구원 임호규박사
- 항 공	교통부 항공국장	해운산업연구원 이영혁박사
- 해 운	항만청 해운국장	해운산업연구원 김광태박사
- 관 광	교통부 관광국장	교통개발연구원 엄서호박사
- 보 건	보사부 기획관리실장	보건연구원 노인철박사
- 엔지니어링	과기처 기술협력관	한국기술용역협회 배정린전무
- 시청각서비스	문화부 예술진흥국장	서울신문사 이중한 논설위원
- 사업서비스		
o 노동력의 이동	노동부 고용관리과장	한국노동연구원 박영범박사
o 법무서비스	법무부 섭외법무검사	태평양법률사무소 이정훈변호사
o 교육서비스	문교부 교육협력과장	교육개발원 최운실이사
o 회계사	재무부 증권업무과장	공인회계사협회 김종기부회장
o 세무사	재무부 소득세제과장	세무사협회 김성한이사
o 광 고	공보처 광고정책과장	한국ABC협회 신인섭전무
o 부동산중개업	건설부 토지관리과장	부동산중개업협회 회장

* 주: UR대책 서비스실무소위원회 구성: 경기원(통상조정3과, 산업3과), 외무부, 상공부, 재무부, 건설부, 문공부, 교통부, 항만청, 체신부, 과기처등 10개부처 과장

길

경 제 기 획 원

통조삼 10502-61　　　　503-9149　　　　1991. 1. 24.

수신 수신처참조 (통상기구과)

제목 UR/서비스협상 대책회의 결과통보

'91.1.22(화)에 개최된 표제회의 결과를 별첨과 같이 통보하니 각부처(기관)는 향후 양허협상대책 및 국내보완대책의 추진에 만전을 기해 주기 바라며 분야별 협상책임자와 자문관을 지정하고 동 명단을 1.31(목)까지 송부해 주기 바랍니다.

첨부: UR/서비스협상 대책회의 결과 1부. 끝.

경 제 기 획 원 장관

수신처: 외무부장관, 재무부장관, 법무부장관, 교육부장관, 문화부장관, 농림수산부장관, 상공부장관, 교통부장관, 건설부장관, 보사부장관, 노동부장관, 동력자원부장관, 체신부장관, 체육청소년부장관, 과학기술처장관, 공보처장관, 환경처장관, 해운항만청장, 특허청장, 대한무역진흥공사장, 대외경제정책연구원장, 한국개발연구원장, 산업연구원장, 김&장법률사무소장.

1991. 　2566

0118

UR/서비스協商 對策會議 結果

('91.1.22, 15:00-16:20, 經濟企劃院 大會議室)

다음과 같이 서비스協商 對應方案을 確定하고 各部處(機關)別로 作業을 推進함.

1. 讓許協商팀의 構成

- 各部處는 分野別 讓許協商을 擔當할 協商責任者와 諮問官을 指定하여 1.31(木)까지 經濟企劃院에 通報

  o 특히 諮問官에 대하여 各部處는 所屬研究機關등과 協調하여 國內協商對策會議 및 現地協商에 최우선적으로 참여할수 있도록 行政的인 支援을 提供

2. 協商資料의 準備

- 各部處는 我國의 讓許計劃表에 대한 解說資料를 1.23(水)까지 經濟企劃院에 通報

- 各部處는 我國의 讓許計劃表에서 除外시킨 分野에 대한 對策資料를 2.20까지 經濟企劃院에 通報

- 各部處는 KOTRA등과 協調하여 相對國에 대한 Request List를 作成하여 2.28까지 經濟企劃院에 通報

  o 海外現地活動 등을 통하여 各種規制制度 및 事例등을 具體的으로 調査

0119

- 各部處는 기존 國內統計 및 外國의 統計資料 등을 바탕으로 讓許協商에 활용할 수 있는 分野別 統計를 作成하여 3.20까지 經濟企劃院에 通報

- 勞動力移動 問題와 관련하여 主要 關係部處가 조만간 別途의 會議를 開催하도록 하되 各部處는 分野別 勞動力移動 許容範圍를 설정하고 2.28까지 經濟企劃院에 通報

3. 國內補完 對策의 推進

- 各部處는 分野別 補完對策을 마련하고 法令 및 制度改善作業을 持續的으로 推進

  o 市場開放 約束을 한 事項은 차질없이 履行할수있도록 法令改定 作業을 計劃性 있게 推進

  o 서비스協商을 契機로 對內競爭 體制를 구축하고 國際競爭力을 強化할 수 있는 産業構造의 先進化 方案을 講究

0120

관리 번호	91-88

분류번호	보존기간

발 신 전 보

번 호 : WUS-0241 910121 1918 DA 종별 : 지급

수 신 : 주 미 대사 . 총영사 (사본 : 주제네바, 카나다 대사) WGV -0104 WCN -0074

발 신 : 장 관 (통 기)

제 목 : UR/서비스 분야 한, 미간 양자협상

일반문서로 재분류 (1991. 6. 30.)

연 : WUS-0190

아국은 미측의 제의를 수락, 1.29.(화) 제네바에서 서비스 협상에 관한 양자 협의를 갖기로 하고 동 방침을 미측에 통보토록 연호로 지시한 바, 최근 Gulf 전쟁발발등과 관련하여 제네바에서 예정된 주요국간 서비스 양자 협의가 예정대로 개최될 것인지의 여부를 파악 보고 바람. 끝.

(통상국장 김삼훈)

앙 고 재	91년 1월 21일	통기과	기안자	과 장	국 장	차 관	장 관
			김복수	(서명)	전결		(서명)

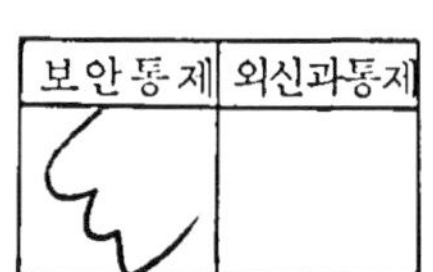

0121

관리 번호	91-90

원 본

외 무 부

종 별 :

번 호 : GVW-0125 일 시 : 91 0121 1800

수 신 : 장관(통기, 경기원)

발 신 : 주 제네바 대사대리

제 목 : UR/서비스 한.미 양자협상

대: WGV-0104

대호 관련, 당관이 파악한 사항을 하기 보고함.

1. 미국이 추진하고 있는 UR/ 서비스 양자협의는 당초 금주에 북구 및 캐나다와 미국간 양자협의가 예정되어 있었으나 GULF 전쟁으로 인하여 취소(미국 협상 대표들의 여행제한이 주요이유)되었으며 EC 와는 1.25(금)로 예정되어 있으나 상기 보안상의 이유로 개최 여부는 미정인 상태임.

2. 다음주에는 아국을 비롯하여 호주 및 홍콩(1.28), 뉴질랜드(1.30)등과 양자 협의가 예정되어 있으나 이역시 최종 개최여부 및 구체적 일정은 미정인 상태임.(금일 USTR 대표부가 휴일인 관계로 미측 입장 확인 불가)

이중 호주 및 뉴질랜드는 아국입장과 같은 맥락에서 본격적 협상이 아닌 1 차적 의견교환이라는 조건하에 미측 제의를 수락하였다고 하며 홍콩은 아직 미측 제의에 답변하지 않았으나 호주등과 같은 조건하에 수락할 가능성이 많은 것으로 판단되며, 일본은 FRAMEWORK 과 분야별 부속서에 대한 협상이 선행되어야 한다는 점을 들어 미측 제의에 대한 답변을 미루고 있는 상태라고 함.

3. 한편 EC 는 미국이 추진하고 있는 양자협상과는 별도로 OFFER 제출국간에 각국 OFFER 의 CLARIFICATION 과 FRAMEWORK 에 대한 협상을 위한 복수국간 협상을 추진하고 있는바 미국을 제외한 대부분의 나라가 지지 입장을 표명하고 있는 상태이며 다음주 중반에 개최될 가능성이 많은 것으로 판단됨.

아국에 대하여도 상기 협상에 참여요청이 있었는바 동 협상 참여여부에 대한 지침 회시 바람. 끝.

(대사대리 박영우-국장)

예고:91.6.30 까지

일반문서로 재분류(1991.6.30.)

통상국 2차보 경기원

PAGE 1 91.01.22 17:56

외신 2과 통제관 DO

0122

관리 번호	91-91

외 무 부

종 별 : 지 급

번 호 : USW-0357 일 시 : 91 0122 1811

수 신 : 장관(통일,통기,체신부)

발 신 : 주 미 대사

제 목 : UR 서비스 분야 한.미 양자 협상 및 한.미 통신협상

대:WUS-0241

연:USW-0193

당관 최영진 참사관과 이종순 통신협력관이 표제건과 관련, 1.22. N.ADAMS USTR 부대표보와 접촉한 결과를 하기 보고함.

1. UR/ 서비스 분야 한. 미 양자 협상은 걸프전쟁과 관계없이 1.29(화) 예정대로 개최될 것이라함.(미측 대표단 규모 및 명단은 추후 통보 예정)

2. 미측은 한. 미 통신협상을 동 UR/ 서비스 양자 협상(약 3 시간 정도 소요 예상)에 바로 속개하여 제네바에서 개최코자함.

3. 통신분야 협의는 우선 UR 다자간 통신 서비스의 관심분야를 논의하면서,정부조달, 통신기기 표준 제정에서의 투명성 보장등 양자간 현안문제도 동시에협의한다는것이 미측의 입장이라고 함.

4. 통신분야 협의 대표 구성은 NANCY ADAMS 가 수석대표가 되어 약 4 명정도로 구성할 예정이며 (구체명단 미확정), 가능한한 UR 서비스 협상에 참여하는 미측 대표를 활용할 방침이라함.

(대사 박동진-국장)

예고:91.6.30 까지

일반문서로 재분류 (1991. 6. 30.)

통상국	장관	차관	1차보	2차보	통상국	안기부	체신부

PAGE 1 91.01.23 08:30

외신 2과 통제관 BW

0123

미국의 한. 미 양자간 UR/서비스 협의 및 통신협의 제안 내용 요약

91.1.23.
통상기구과

1. 미측제안 내용

가. UR/서비스 협의

o 개최시기 및 장소 : 1.29(화), 제네바

o 미측희망 의제 : 양국이 시장접근 및 내국민대우에 대하여 공식 양허할 분야에 관한 토의

- 전면적 시장접근 및 내국민대우 허용 분야
- 부분적 허용분야 및 제한 조건등

※ 미측은 금번회의에서의 아측 거론 희망 의제를 가능한한 조속 통보 요망

o 미측 요청 사항

- 분야별 전문가 참여 희망(특히 통신 분야)
- 90.6월의 미측 request 에 대한 협의 희망
  . 특히 통신 system consultants의 자격 요건, 회계감사, 보험, 중개업, TV 광고, 시청각 분야 시장접근등

o 미측 request 분야

- 회계, 광고, 시청각, 건축, 건설, engineering, 법무서비스, 통신, 관광, 보험, 은행, 증권, 기타 금융서비스, 컴퓨터서비스, consulting, leasing, franchising

※ 아국이 Offer 한 분야 : 시청각, 사업서비스, 통신, 건설, 유통, 금융, 운송, 관광

※ 아국이 Offer 하지 않은 분야 : 법무서비스, leasing

- 노동력이동 분야에서 미국과 유사한 양허 희망

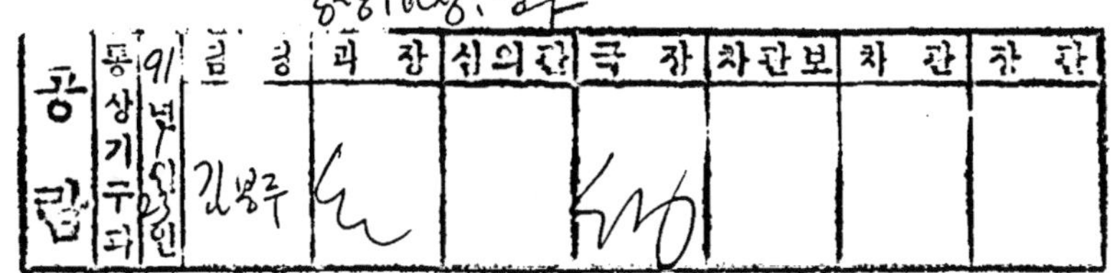

0124

나. 통신 협상

o 한.미 양자 협의 시한이 2.23인 점을 감안하여 미국의 통신분야 request 및 아국의 UR/서비스 분야의 최초 양허 계획서상의 Offer를 협의 희망

o 미측 토의 희망 분야
  - 표준과 정부조달
  - 기업간 통신 및 CUGS 문제등

o 양허 희망 분야
  - 모든 통신 증진 서비스의 시장접근 및 내국민대우 허용 및 외국인 전면투자 허용
  - 경쟁적으로 제공되는 서비스 범위에 대한 명확한 정의제공, 특히 시장 진입 절차
  - 외국회사의 사설 대여 회선 사용 및 기기와 software 선택 허용

o 미측 희망 사항
  - 양허 계획서상의 용어 설명
  - 개정된 공공 통신사업법 제공

다. 금융

o 미국이 외국 서비스업자에게 광범위한 시장접근, 내국민대우 및 동등한 경쟁기회를 허용하고 있는 만큼 미국도 미국의 금융 서비스 업자에게 비교가능하고 (comparable) 광범위한 시장접근, 내국민대우 및 동등경쟁 기회 제공 요청

라. 미국의 대표단

o Nancy Adams 외 7명

0125

2. 아측의 대응 (대책회의 개최)

o 91.1.22 15:00-17:00, 경기원 대회의실

o 참석자

- 주재 : 경기원 제2협력관
- 16개 관계부처 국장, KOTRA, 대외경제정책연구원등 연구기관 연구위원 3명

o 토의 내용

- 한. 미간 UR/서비스 협의
  . 91.1.29. 제네바에서 한. 미 양자협의 개최
  . 대표단은 별도 공문으로 관계 부처간 협의하여 임명
  . 동 협의를 위한 철저준비 필요
  . 노동력이동과 관련, 별도 회의를 개최하여 아국입장 정립
  . 아국이 각국에 제시할 request 작성 요망

- 한. 미간 통신 협의
  . 아국이 미국에 의한 PFC로 지정되었기 때문에 협의 필요
  . 제네바에서 개최를 희망하나 별도 회의를 개최하여 동건 토의 예정

- 여타 지금까지의 서비스 협상의 논의 내용, 향후 전망, 주요과제 추진 대책에 대하여 논의(상세 사항 별첨 자료 참조)

  ※ 주요과제 추진 대책

  ① 협상 팀구성
  - 협상 총괄 조정은 경기원 대조실 제2협력관이 담당
  - 제네바 경협관은 현지에서 협조
  - 분야별 협상 책임자는 각분야 주무부처 과장이 담당
  - 양허 협상 팀지원을 위한 국내대응 작업은 기존의 18개 분야별 대책반에서 수행

0126

② 협상자료 준비

- 아국의 양허 계획표에 대한 해설자료
- 아국의 양허 계획표에서 제외시킨 업종에 대한 대책자료
- 상대국에 대한 Request List 준비
- 서비스 교역에 대한 통계
- 노동력이동 범위 확정

③ 국내보완 대책 추진

- 경기원은 KIEP, KDI등과 협조 2.28까지 종합적인 국내 보완대책 추진 계획 수립

첨부 : 양허 협상 대응 방안 1부. 끝.

0127

JAN 22 '91 14:23 T

P.1

ECONOMIC SECTION, AMERICAN EMBASSY SEOUL, KOREA
82 SEJONG-RO, CHONGRO-KU
SEOUL 110-050, KOREA
FAX NO: 82-2-722-1429, TELEPHONE NO: 82-2-732-2601

UNCLASSIFIED

DATE: January 22, 1991

NUMBER OF PAGES INCLUDING COVER PAGE: 6

TO: Lee Sung Joo 이 성주 과장님
Multilateral Trade Affairs Division 통상기구과 외무부

FAX NO: 720-2686

FROM: James Gagnon
U.S. Embassy

SUBJECT: U.S. Proposal to Hold Bilateral Services and Telecommunications Consultations in Geneva, January 29, 1991

Attached is the text of a non-paper we received from the U.S. Trade Representative proposing that bilateral services and telecommunications consultations be held in Geneva, January 29, 1991. The non-paper outlines the services commitments we seek and the issues we would like to discuss.

0128

NON-PAPER FOR BILATERAL SERVICES AND TELECOMMUNICATIONS CONSULTATIONS

-- It is important that the services negotiations move ahead now. Too much remains unresolved; we cannot wait for a resolution of the agriculture issue before re-focussing attention on services. We urge that you agree to hold the first round of consultations on market access commitments on services in Geneva on January 29.

-- As you are aware, we also face another statutory deadline on February 23 in out bilateral Telecommunications Negotiations. The Telecommunications Negotiations overlap the Uruguay Round Services Market Access Negotiations, which also address other issues such as standards and government procurement. In the services negotiations, both the United States' Uruguay Round Services market access requests (and our offer) and Korea's services offer tabled January 15 address market access issues in telecommunications services.

SERVICES

-- We realize that a discussion of Uruguay Round market access and national treatment commitments may be complicated by the fact that the services framework agreement and annexes are not yet completed. However, we do not think this is a serious impediment to a useful bilateral negotiation of commitments for services in general and telecommunications in particular. The main focus of such a discussion should be on which sectors each country is prepared to make formal bindings for market access and national treatment, regardless of whether such bindings are linked to framework provisions. We recognize, of course, that substantial further work on the framework and annexes will also be necessary prior to the end of the Round. However, given the bilateral statutory deadline, it is essential that we make significant concrete progress on commitments in telecommunications services.

-- We suggest that both sides agree in advance that we will keep discussions of the framework and annexes during these bilateral market access talks to a minimum. Instead we will focus on whether each side is prepared to grant full market access and national treatment for each sector, and if not, specifically what sectors or sub-sectors will not receive full market access and national treatment, and what limitations and conditions on market access and national treatment for each mode of delivery are proposed.

-- Because your government has not submitted a request list, we are not sure what aspects of the U.S. offer your government may wish to raise with us. We suggest that you communicate to

0123

us as soon as possible before our scheduled bilateral what areas, if any, you would like to discuss, so that we may ensure that the appropriate experts are present and prepared to discuss your areas of interest in detail.

-- We suggest that both sides bring sectoral experts in areas requiring technical expertise, especially telecommunications.

-- The U.S. requests offers of commitments in at least the following service sectors: accounting, advertising, audio-visual, architecture, construction, engineering, legal services, telecommunications, tourism, insurance, banking, securities and other financial services, computer services, consulting, leasing, and franchising. We are currently reviewing the Korean offer in the context of these requests.

-- We hope that countries would include in their offers commitments similar to the U.S. offer on the movement of key or essential personnel.

-- The U.S. request list of June 1990 indicates the kinds of rollback we would like to achieve. We appreciate the detail that has been provided in the Korean offer. We hope the Korean government will be prepared to discuss further the requests on that list, including certification requirements for telecommunications system consultants, market access for audit corporations, market access in insurance/brokerage agency services, market access for television commercials, market access and national treatment in audio-visual services.

TELECOMMUNICATIONS

-- In addition, we have requested the following specific commitments in telecommunications services:

(A) We request that the Korean government extend market access and national treatment for the provision of all telecommunications enhanced services within Korea and across its border, allow full foreign investment in such services, and provide a transparent definition of the scope of such competitively-provided services, especially the procedure for market entry.

(B) We request that the Korean government guarantee foreign companies access to and use of private leased circuits at cost-oriented, flat-rate prices for all users, and permit companies to use the equipment and software of their choice, as long as such equipment does not harm the network.

0130

(C) We request that the Korean government allow foreign companies to participate in the decision-making process for setting telecommunications network standards.

(D) We request that the Korean government be prepared to describe its understanding of the following terms as they might appear in a national schedule of commitments: enhanced services, value-added services, computer-related services, software services, closed user groups, intracorporate communitations, and information services.

-- In addition, we would request that Korea be perpared to discuss the following issues:

(1) Intracorporate communications and closed-user groups (CUGS), which are restricted to data communications only and are not permitted to carry voice traffic. We would like to discuss the continuing requirement that international CUGS maintain a "closed" business relationship;

(2) The network attachment of multiplexers with a capacity of more than 2.048 MBPS with our ministerial approval. In addition, we would like to discuss the network attachment of packet switches in order to provide code and protocol processing as an independent service, distinct from EDI, message handling, or electronic mail services; and

(3) In addition, we ask that the Korean government provide us with copies of the amended public Telecom Business Law, enforcement decree, ministerial proclamation, and and relevant implementing regulations.

-- Also in telecommunications, we have outstanding issues on telecommunications standards and government procurement which must be duscussed.

FINANCIAL SERVICES

-- The U.S. has offered to other parties broad, deep commitments to market access and national treatment in financial services which would result in a guarantee of essentially a completely open U.S. market and equal competitive opportunities for foreign participants. In return the U.S. seeks comparable, broad commitments to market access, national traatment and equality of competitive opportunity for U.S. financial service providers. As we have stated in Geneva, the U.S. expects that these negotiations will result in a more level playing field in the financial services sector among countries. We are firmly convinced that commitments to open

0131

markets can only enhance the economic welfare of all countries.

-- The U.S. would hope that each country's initial offer on financial services would be available prior to the initiation of negotiations in order to facilitate a productive discussion. The U.S. expects a country's offer to reflect at least the current state of liberalization (a standstill) in countries that are already liberal and significant liberalization where extensive barriers exist.

0132

U.S. DELEGATION FOR BILATERAL SERVICES AND TELECOMMUNICATIONS CONSULTATIONS

NANCY ADAMS
Office of the U.S. Trade Representative

LAURA KNEALE ANDERSON
Office of the U.S. Trade Representative

BERNARD ASCHER
Office of the U.S. Trade Representative

JAY DOWLING
Department of Commerce

IVAN SHEFFRIN
Department of Commerce

JOHN COPES
Federal Communications Commission

RON DOBSON
Department of Labor

IAN DAVIS
Department of Commerce

0133

관리 번호	91-96

원 본

외 무 부

종 별 :

번 호 : GVW-0151 일 시 : 91 0124 1640

수 신 : 장관(통기,경기원)

발 신 : 주 제네바 대사대리

제 목 : UR/서비스 양자 협의

검 토 필(1991.6.30.)

일반문서로 재분류(1991.6.30.)

연: GVW-0125

대: WGV-0121

표제 양자 협의 추진 상황을 하기 보고함.

1. 미.북구간 및 미.스위스간 양자 협의가 1.23(수) 제네바 대표부 관계관간에 진행되엇으며, 1.25(금) 미.이씨간 양자 협의도 본부 대표는 참석하지 않고 제네바 대표부 관계관간에 양국 OFFER 의 CLARIFICATION 을 위한 협의로 진행될 계획임.

2. 다음주에 개최될 미국과의 양자 협의 입정은 1.28(월) 에 호주, 1.30(수)에는 뉴질랜드, 2.1(금)에 일본등이 예정되어 있으며, 홍콩은 양자 협의 자체는 수락하였으나 구체적 일정은 미정상태임. (미국은 1.28 을 제시하였으나 홍콩은 다음주 종반을 제시)

0 상기 국가들은 모두 실질협상이 아닌 각국 OFFER 의 CLARIFICATION 에 한한다는 조건하에 미국제의를 수락하였으며, 일본을 제외한 호주, 뉴질랜드, 홍콩은 본부 대표가 참석하지 않고 제네바 주재 관계관이 미국의 의문사항에 답변할 예정이라고 함.

0 특히 호주에 대하여 미국은 통신 분야의 실질 협상을 요청하였으나, 호주는 FRAMEWORK 과 분야별 부속서 특히 기본 통신에 MFN 문제가 선결되지 않은 상태에서는 실질 협상에 임할수 없다고 거부하였다고 함.

3. 이외에도 1.22 자 제네바 SUNS 지 보도와는 달리 다음주에 ASEAN (태국, 인니, 말련, 싱가폴)및 파키스탄 등 아세아 국가와 중남미 국가도 미국과의 양자 협의가 계획되어 있으며, 이와 관련 미국은 서비스 양허 협상팀을 5 개 지역(일본, 이씨, 기타 유럽국가 및 캐나다, 아세아 태평양지역, 중남미)으로 구분하여 운영하고 있다고 함.

통상국 2차보 경기원

PAGE 1 91.01.25 05:57

외신 2과 통제관 DO

0134

4. 한편, 이씨가 추진하고 있는 복수국간 협의는 1.31(목) 이씨 대표부에서 개최될 계획인바, 동 협의 역시 FRAMEWORK 등에 대한 협상은 하지 않고 각국 OFFER 에 대한 기술적인 CLARIFICATION 에 집중할 예정임. 끝

(대사대리 박영우-국장)

예고 91.6.30. 까지

관리 번호 91-98

외 무 부

종 별 : 지 급

번 호 : USW-0402 일 시 : 91 0124 1824

수 신 : 장관(통일,통기,경기원,체신부)

발 신 : 주 미 대사

제 목 : UR 및 한미 통신 협의

대: WUS-0288,0289

당관 최영진 참사관은 1.23(수) NANCY ADAMS USTR 부대표보와 접촉, 대호 내용을 통보하고 표제건에 관하여 협의한바, 동 결과 하기 보고함.

1. 한미 통신 협의

0 미측은 걸프 사태와 관련, 한미 통신 협의 장소에 관하여 금일 관계 부처간 긴급 회의를 개최한 결과, 당초 회의 장소로 제시한 제네바는 TRAVEL SECURITY상 문제가 있는것으로 결론 지었다함.

0 미측은 이와 관련, 회의 장소 수정을 제의하여 왔으며, 한국측이 서울 개최를 고집하지 않는다면 미측으로서는 하와이등 중간 지점에서 동 협의를 개최할것을 희망한다고 하면서 이에 관련 아측 입장을 긴급히 알려줄것을 요청해 왔음.

2.UR 관련 동향

0 ADAMS 부대표보에 의하면 대호 HELLSTROM 의장안 수정 협상을 위해 EC 대표단이 워싱턴을 방문, 오는 2.17-18간 미측과 회의를 개최할 예정이라함.

0 동 구체 내용 파악되는대로 추보 예정임.

(대사 박동진-국장)

91.6.30 까지

일반문서로 재분류 (1991. 6.30.)

통상국 통상국 체신부 경기원

PAGE 1

91.01.25 09:40

외신 2과 통제관 BT

0136

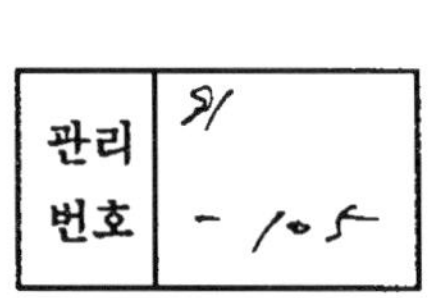

외 무 부

종 별 : 지 급

번 호 : USW-0412 일 시 : 91 0124 1859

수 신 : 장관(통일,체신부)

발 신 : 주 미 대사

제 목 : 한.미 통신 협상

1. 미 무역 대표부가 한. 미 통신 협상을 앞두고 미 상공회의소 등 업계 단체에 대하여 의존 조회시 나타난 미 무역 대표부의 한국 통신 분야에 대한 평가는 ROU 의 성실한 이행, 관세인하, GATT 정부 조달 가입신청등을 거론하며, 대체로 호의적이었다는 것이 업계의 의견이나

2. 한국측에서 관심을 두어야 할것은 1990.12 월까지 ROU 이행 사항에 대한공식적 통보 (USTR 이 주미 대사관에게 확인한다는것임)와 함께 동 조치에 대한주한 미 상공회의소의 반응에 유의해야 할것이라는 것임.

3. 또한 금번 한. 미 협상에서는 UR 에서 양국간에 이견이 있었든 INTRA-CORPORATE SERVICE 를 위시한 여러가지 현안에 대하여 이견들을 상당히 좁혀서 UR서비스 협상에 대응한다는것이 미측의 입장인만큼 상당 참고 바람.

(공사 손명현-국장)

91.6.30 까지

검 토 필(1991.6.30)

일반문서로 재분류(1991.12.31.)

통상국 통상국 체신부 경기원

(통상기구과)

PAGE 1 91.01.25 15:15

외신 2과 통제관 BT

0137

관리 번호	91-100

외 무 부

종 별 : 지 급

번 호 : USW-0430 일 시 : 91 0125 1745

수 신 : 장관(통일,통기,경기원,체신부)

발 신 : 주 미 대사

제 목 : 한미 통신 협상및 UR 서비스 양자 협의

대 WUS-0306

연 USW-0402

당관 최영진 참사관은 표제건과 관련, NANCY ADAMS USTR 부대표보와 면담 협의한바, 동 결과를 아래 보고함.

1. 미측은 아측의 한. 미 통신 협의 개최 장소 변경 수락에 사의를 표하고,개최 일자는 과거의 통신 협의시 시간에 쫓겨 충분한 토의가 어려웠던 적이 있었음을 감안, 2.4(월)-5(수)간 개최토록 제의해 옴.

2. 구체적 회의 장소는 미측이 물색, 내주초중 아측에 제안 하겠다함.

3.ADAMS 부대표보는 걸프 사태등 제반 사정상 한. 미간 UR 서비스 양자 협상을 연기 2.11-12 간 제네바에서 개최할것을 제안해 왔는바, 이에 대한 아측 입장 회시 바람.

(대사 박동진-국장)

91.6.30 까지

일반문서로 재분류 (1991. 6. 30.)

통상국	2차보	통상국	체신부	경기원

PAGE 1

91.01.26 10:08

외신 2과 통제관 FE

0138

원 본

외 무 부

종 별 :

번 호 : GVW-0167 일 시 : 91 0125 1700

수 신 : 장관(통기,경기원,재무부,상공부,건설부,교통부,체신부,문화부,공보처, 과기처)

발 신 : 주 제네바 대사대리

제 목 : UR/ 서비스 협상 비공식 협의

1.2/(금) 스웨덴 대표부에서 개최된 표제 협의내용을 하기 보고함.

(아국, 이씨, 스위스, 스웨덴, 노르웨이, 핀랜드, 캐나다, 호주, 오지리, 헝가리, 폴랜드, 유고, 멕시코, 우루과이, 알젠틴, 콜롬비아, 칠레, 모로코, 파키스탄,싱가폴 등 20개국 참석)

1. OFFER 제출 문제

- 싱가폴, 오지리, 멕시코 등이 내주 또는 그다음주에 OFFER 를 제출할 예정이라고 하였으며, 알제틴 및 우루과이는 1-2 주내에 OFFER 작성이 완료되나 UR 협상이공식적으로 재개되기 이전에는 제출하지 않을 방침이라고 하여 농산물과 연계 입장을 견지 하였음.

0 이외 헝가리, 폴랜드, 유고, 콜롬비아, 파키스탄등이 현재 OFFER 작성중에 있으나 구체적 제출시기는 밝힐수 없다고 하였음.

0 또한 스웨덴은 자국 OFFER 를 분야별로 구체화 하는 작업을 진행하고 있다고밝혔음.

2. 향후 협상 진행 절차

- 이씨, 캐나다, 호주, 스위스등은 FRAMEWORK 과분야별 부속서, 자유화 협상 세가지를 병행하는 접근 방법을 지지 하였으나, 오지리, 헝가리, 유고등은 FRAMEWORK과 분야별 부속서를 선결하는 순차적 접근 방식을 지지 하였음.

0 아국은 FRAMEWORK 과 분야별 부속서에 우선 순위가 두어져야 하며, 실질협상에 진입하기 전에 동 문제가 완료 되어야 하나 각국 OFFER 의 평가및 명료화가 어려운점을 고려할때 CLARIFICATION을 위한 협의는 개시할 필요가 있다고 언급하였음.

-기타 자유화 협상과 관련 각국 OFFER 에 제시된 서비스 분야간 비교 가능성 문제, 각국 OFFER 에 담긴 가치의 질적, 양적인 평가의 어려움, 운송분야를 제외하려는 미국

통상국 2차보 문화부 교통부 체신부 경기원 재무부
상공부 건설부 과기처 공보처

PAGE 1

91.01.26 04:18 DA
외신 1과 통제관

0139

업계의 입장고수 문제등이 향후 협상의 주요 문제점으로 지적되었음.

0 이와 관련 이씨가 추진하고 있는 기술적 CLARIFICATION 을 위한 복수국간 협의에 많은 나라가 지지 의사를 밝혔음.

3. 미국과의 양자협의

- 이씨를 비롯한 모든 나라가 실질적인 자유화 협상이 선행할수는 없다는 입장을견지 하였으며, 각국 OFFER 의 기술적 CLARIFICATION 과 관심사항을 알기 위한 협의에한 한다는 조건하에 미국의 양자 협의 제의를 수락하였다고 함.

- 금일 (1.25)로 예정되어 있던 미.이씨간 양자 협의는 취소되고 다음주로 미루어졌다고 하며, 대부분의 나라가 다음주에 미국 본부 대표 참석하에 양자 협의를가질것으로 알고 있었는바. 아국은 미국 본부대표가 다음주에도 제네바에 올수 없다는것을 오늘 아침 통보 받았다고 언급하였으며, 이와는 달리 호주는 역시 오늘아침 미국 대표들이 제네바에 올것이라고 본부로 부터 통보 받았다고함.

끝

(대사대리 박영우-국장)

PAGE 2

0140

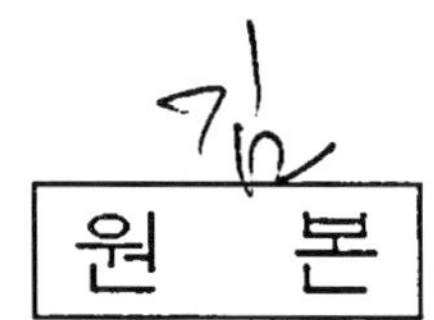

외 무 부

종 별 :

번 호 : GVW-0170 일 시 : 91 0125 1800

수 신 : 장관(통기,경기원)

발 신 : 주 제네바대사대리

제 목 : UR/ 서비스 한.미 양자협의

표제협의 관련 본직이 USTR STOLER 공사에게 확인한바 1.29(화) 개최 예정이던한.미 양자협의는 미측 본부대표가 불수없기 때문에 취소 되었다고 함.

(제네바주재 관계관간 의협의도 없음).

끝

(대사대리 박영우-국장)

통상국 경기원

PAGE 1

91.01.26 06:57 DA

외신 1과 통제관

0141

관리 번호	91-104

	분류번호	보존기간

발 신 전 보

번 호 : WGV-0142 910128 1530 DP 종별 :

수 신 : 주 제네바 대사. 총영사 (사본; 주미·EC 대사) WUS -0329 WEC -0057

발 신 : 장 관 (통 기)

제 목 : UR/서비스 복수국간 협의

대 : GVW-0125, 0151

대호, 1.31(목) 이씨대표부에서 개최 예정인 표제회의에 본부에서는 대표를 파견치 않을 예정인바, 귀관 관계관으로 참석토록 조치 바라며, 회의 결과 보고 바람. 끝.

(통상국장 김삼훈)

일반문서로 재분류 (1991. 6. 30.)

앙 고 재	91년 1월 28일	통기과	기안자 김봉주		과 장		국 장 전결		차 관	장 관

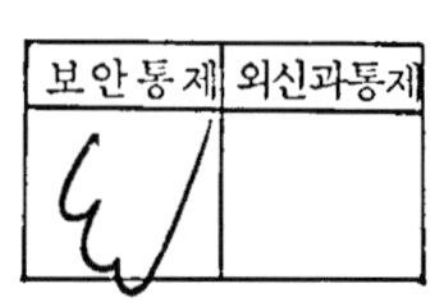

보안통제	외신과통제

0142

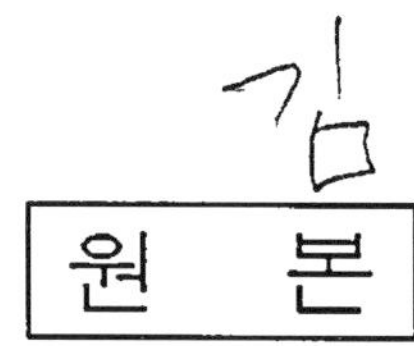

원 본

외 무 부

종 별 :

번 호 : GVW-0217 일 시 : 91 0201 1200

수 신 : 장 관 (통기,경기원,재무부,법무부,상공부,교육부,건설부

발 신 : 보사부,노동부,교통부,체신부,문화부,공보처,과기처,항만청)

제 목 : 주 제네바 대사대리

UR/ 서비스 비공식 협의(1)

1.31(목) EC 대표부에서 개최된 표제 협의내용을 하기 보고함.(이경협관, 한경협관보 참석)

1. 회의 진행 개요

- 아국 및 미국, 이씨, 일본, 스위스, 캐나다, 호주, 뉴질랜드, 스웨덴, 노르웨이, 핀랜드, 오지리, 헝가리, 폴랜드, 유고, 홍콩, 말련, 멕시코, 칠레, 우루과이, 인도, 이집트, 파키스탄등 23개국이 참석하였으며 본부대표가 참석한 나라는 미국, 이씨, 일본, 스위스등 4개국이었음.

- 회의 벽두 EC 대표는 본 협의가 상호교육 목적의 것이며 어떠한 공식협상 과정도 대체하는 것이 아닌 개인적인 비공식 협의라고 강조하였고 각국 OFFER 에서 공통적으로 제기되는 의문사항의 CLARIFICATION 에 한정하여 진행되었으며 많은 기술적문제가 제기되었으나 대부분 어떤 결론에 도달하지는 못하였으며 앞으로 계속하여 기술적 문제가 제기될 것으로 예상됨.

2. 일반 토의

- 동결(STANDSTILL): 어떤 MODE OF DELIVERY 에 단순히 STANDSTILL 이라고만 기재한 경우에는 양허협상을 하기가 어려우므로 실질적인 자유화수준이 어느정도인지 알수 있도록 구체적인 제한조치가 명시되어야 한다는데 의견이 합치되었음.

- 상호주의(RECIPROCIEY): 각국이 금융분야에 기재한 상호주의 조건과 관련, 어떤나라가 자국 양허표에 상호주의를 기재한다고 해서 MFN 의무로부터 벗어날수 있는 것은 아니라는데 의견이 일치하였으며 EC 는 자국의 엄격한 분야별상호주의를 요구하는 것은 아니며(협정 부적용문제는 별도) 최종 양허협상 결과가 대체적으로 균형을 이루어야 한다는 것을 의미한다고 함.

통상국	법무부	보사부	문화부	교통부	체신부	교육부	경기원	재무부
상공부	건설부	노동부	과기처	해항청	공보처			

PAGE 1 91.02.02 08:44 FC

외신 1과 통제관

0143

- 서비스 분류(NOMENCLATURE): 비록 아주 정확하지는 않더라도 공통의 분류체계를 발전시킬 필요가 있다는 의견 제시가 있었음.(이씨, 스위스)

- 양허표작성(SCHEDULING): 시장접근과 내국민대우를 구분하는 것이 아주 중요한문제는 아니나 한쪽을 BINDING 한 반면 다른 한쪽을 UNBOUND로 하였을 경우에는 두가지의 구분이 아주 중요하다는 점이 지적되었음(UNBOUND 된 쪽에 많은 제한조치를 도입함으로써 사실상 시장개방을 하지 않는 결과가 되기 때문)

0 일본은 자국 OFFER 에 'NO RESTRICTION'의 의미는 어떤 규제는 있더라도 차별적 규제가 없다는 것을 의미하며 거주요건이나 국적요건은 국내업자에게도 부과되는 조건이므로 기재하지 않았다고 한바, 미국, 인도, 뉴질랜드등은 단순히 차별여부만 가지고 판단해서는 않되며 내.외국인이 모두 시장진입이 불가능한 경우등 실제여건을알수 있도록 기재되어야 한다고 하였으며 또한 국적요건은 시장진입에 대한 제한이며 거주요건도 그 구체적 내용에 따라 시장접근에 대한 제한이 된다고 반박함.

- 양허협상 절차: 양자협상 결과의 다자화등 양허협상 절차가 규정되어야 한다는 인도의 주장에 대하여 미국, 일본은 관세분야에서 협상방법을 정하는데만 별 소득없이 수개월을 허비한 전례를 밟지 않도록 실용적 접근방법(공통된 절차없이 나라별로편의에 따라 양자협상을 추진하는 것을 의미)을 취하여야 한다고 한바 인도는 TNC/W/35 에 서도 양자협상 가이드라인을 정한 것처럼 OFFER 제출시한등 기본적인 절차는정하여야 한다는 의미라고 함.

- 지방정부의 의무부담: 호주가 모든 분야에 대하여, 미국이 금융분야에 대하여주정부의 의무부담을 회피한데 대하여 EC, 뉴질랜드등 많은 나라가 지방정부의 의무부담의 중요성을 강조하였음.

- 기타: 인력이동, CROSS BORDER TRADE 의 정의에 대하여 추가 작업이 필요하다는 점과 호주 OFFER 중 경우에 따라 외국인 부자정책, 법규에 의한 규제가 가능하다는부분은 사실상 아무런 BINDING도 하지 않게 되는 것을 의미하게 되므로 동제도(1천만 호주달러 이상 부자의 경우 FOREIGN INVESTMENT REVIEW BOARD 의 인가를 받아야 한다고 함)를 뉴질랜드 OFFER 와 같이 표시하여야할 것이라는 점에 대체로 견해가 일치하였음.

홍콩 OFFER 중 CROSS-BORDER TRADE 는 모두 UNBOUND 로 되어있는 이유에 대한 질의가 있었는바 홍콩은 각분야별로 동 MODE OF DELIVERY 의 구체적 의미가 정확하지않기 때문이라고 답변함.

PAGE 2

0144

(계속)

(대사대리 박영우-국장)

PAGE 3

0145

원 본

외 무 부

종 별 :

번 호 : GVW-0218 일 시 : 91 0201 1200

수 신 : 장관(통기,사본:수신처참조)

발 신 : 주제네바대사대리

제 목 : UR/서비스 비공식 협의(2)3.분야별 CLARIFICATION

가. 통신분야

- EC 측 통신 전문가로 부터 일본, 미국, 아국OFFER 에 대한 구체적 질문이 있었으나, 통신전문가 없이는 협의가 불가능하다는데 의견이 일치하여 토의를 중단하였음.

나. 사업 서비스 및 전문직업 서비스

- 전문직업 서비스에 있어 자격 취득 의무 기타 등록, 인가절차등의 기재 여부 문제가 제기된바,이씨는 등록, 인가등이 실제로 취득하기 어려우면SCHEDULE 에 기재되어야 할것이라고 한바 어떠한 등록기준.인가기준이 충족하기 어려운지, 쉬운지의구별이 어려울것이라는 문제점이 지적됨.

0 미국 및 스웨덴은 정보제공 차원에서 교육요건, 거주 요건, 등록의무등의 존재를 시장접근란에 기재하고 내국민 대우란에 동요건등에 차별이 있는지 기재할 것을제의한바 일본은 NATIONAL SCHEDULE 의 기본성격이 장벽을기재하는 것인지, 객관적인자격 요건등을 기재하는 것이 아니라고 반대하여 결론을 내리지못함.

- 아국은 엔지니어, 컨설턴트등 개별적인 서비스공급자(INDIVISUAL SELF SERVICE PROVIDER) 의 일시적이동(잠시 입국하여 서비스를 공급하고 귀국하는경우)이 CROSS-BOFDER TRADE 에 해당하는지,인력이동에 해당하는지 의문을 제기한바,스웨덴은 서비스 공급계약 및 댓가 지불에 따라달라질 것이며 서비스 공급댓가가 국경을 넘는경우에는 CROSS-BORDER TRADE 로 보아야 할것이라고한 반면, 일본 및 홍콩은 서비스 자체가 국경을넘은 것이 아니며, 국경을 넘은 사람에 의하여서비스가 공급된 것이므로 인력이동으로 보아야 한다고하였으며, 이씨 및 뉴질랜드는 양허 협상 결과에따라 최종적으로 SCHEDULE 이 어떻게작성되느냐에 따라 결정될 문제라고 하였음.

통상국	2차보	청와대	법무부	보사부	문화부	교통부	체신부	교육부
경기원	재무부	상공부	건설부	노동부	과기처	해항청	공보처	

PAGE 1

91.02.02 04:02 BX

외신 1과 통제관

0146

0 이와 관련 아국은 미국 OFFER 중 인력이동의양허 대상을 서비스 공급 기업에 1년이상 고용된인력에 한하고 있는바 이는 MODE OF DELIVERY 중인력이동을 상업적 주재에 따른 인력 이동에한하며, 개별 서비스 공급자의 이동은 CROSS-BORDERTRADE 로간주하는지 질의한바 미국은 우선 상업적주재에 관계된 인력중 특정범주의 인력을COMMITMENT 하는 것이라고 함.

다. 건설

- 시장접근과 내국민 대우중 한쪽은 COMMITMENT하면서 다른 한쪽은 UNBOUND 하는것이 무엇을의미하는가 하는 문제가 지적되었으며, CROSS BORDERTRADE 를 BOUND 하는 한편 인력이동을COMMITMENT 하지 않는다면 그러한 CROSS BORDERTRADE 의 BINDING 이 무슨의미가 있는지 하는문제가 제기되었음.

라. 운송

- 화물적재(FREIGHT FOWARDING) 서비스 분류문제(지상조업 서비스인지, 육운인지,사업서비스인지)와 항공기 수선, 유지서비스의분류(사업 서비스인지, 항공서비스인지)문제가제기됨.

마. 관광

- EC 는 여러가지 다른 서비스 분야의 복합체인관광이 별도 독립분야로 일부 국가의 OFFER 에나타난것이 놀랍다고 한바 이집트는 관광 버스운영, 여행자 수표, 여행자 보험등을 관광분야로볼것인지, 육운, 금융 서비스로 볼것인지 문제가있다고 하였으며, 미국은 관광에 오직 의미가있는 한가지는 해외 여행제한, 외화경비제한등 소비자 이동문제인바, 이를 표시하기위해 독립된 항목이 필요하다고 함.

바. 금융

- 일반 토의에서와 같이 상호주의, 주정부의의무부담 문제등이 지적된 외에 별다른 토의는없었으며, EC 는 아국 OFFER 중 '내국민대우의 전통적 정의'와 '시장관행'이 무엇을의미하는지 질의하였음.

4. 각국의 OFFER 제출 동향

- OFFER 를 수정제출 예정인국가: 일본은자국이 잘못 이해한 부분도 있고 기술적오류도있어 OFFER 를 전면 수정하여 제출할 예정이라고하였으며 이씨 역시 개정 2판(기재출 OFFER 중 'TO BE COMPLETED' 로 된 부분 보완)을 2-3주내에 낼 예정이라고함.

STANDSTILL 만을 제시한 카나다, 스웨덴,노르웨이, 핀랜드 등도 구체적 OFFER 를 제출할예정이라고 하였으며, 카나다는 2월중순 제출하겠다고 함.

- OFFER 작성중에 있으나 구체적 제출 시기를밝히지 않은 국가: 헝가리, 인도, 유고, 이집트, 말련, 폴란드, 칠레

- 멕시코는 다음주에 제출하겠다고 하였으며, 오지리는 금일 STANSTILL 약속 OFFER (FAX 편송부)를 제출하였으며, 2월말경 구체적인 OFFER를 내겠다고 함.

5. 향후 계획

- 이씨는 오늘과 같은 협의를 자국이 또다시주도하여 개최하기는 약간 거북하며, 전체적인 UR협상 진전상황에도 달려 있다고 하여 향후계획은 불투명한 상태임.

6. 관찰 및 건의

가. 아국 OFFER 에 대한 평가

- 비교적 자세하고 기술적으로 잘된 OFFER 라는반응이었음.

나. 향후 보안이 필요한 분야

- 금융서비스

0 STANDSTILL 로 표시된 부분의 시장접근, 내국민대우 제한, 조건의 구체적 명시

0 내국민 대우의 정의와 관련, '전통적인내국민 대우'의 개념을 명목상의 내국민대우로간주하고 이를 고수할 것인지, GATT 에서 사실상의내국민 대우로 해석되어 왔다면 이를 수용할것인지에 대한 분명하고 구체적인 입장 정립

0 MARKET PRACTICES 에 대한 구체적 정의- 건설

0 시장접근과 내국민 대우중 한쪽만 UNBOUND한 경우 두가지 개념의 구분 및 UNBOUND 한분야에 현재 있거나 향후 도입 가능성이 있는제한, 조건의 유형 정립

- 관광

0 호텔, 기념품점, 여행알선업등은 사업 서비스로재분류하고 미국, 스위스등의 OFFER 와 같이TOURISM 을 하나의 SUBSECTOR 로 하여 소비자이동에 있어서 회화 경비 제한만 표시하는 방안검토

첨부: 오지리의 OFFER 1 부 끝

(GVW(F)-48)

(대사대리 박영우-국장)

수신처: 사본배부처-경기원, 재무부, 법무부, 상공부, 교육부, 건설부, 보사부, 노동부, 교통부, 체신부, 문화부, 공보처, 과기처, 항만청)

PAGE 3

0148

GVW(CT)-0048 10201/200
// GVW-0218 첨부,

COMMUNICATION FROM AUSTRIA

Preliminary, conditional offer of Austria concerning initial commitments in trade in services

1. Creating a comprehensive regime for progressive liberalization of trade in services is for Austria an essential part of the Uruguay Round negotiations.

2. Austria has therefore been actively participating in the negotiating process and intends to continue to do so in order to further negotiations at all levels.

3. Austria considers the early submission of initial commitments necessary in order to revive the negotiating process; the subsequent negotiations should, however, attribute priority to the framework agreement and the sectorial annexes, on which the national liste will ultimately depend.

4. At this stage of negotiations Austria submits her initial offer of commitments. A more detailed offer is at present under preparation and will be submitted in due time.

5. Austria is prepared to bind in principle its existing market access and national treatment regimes with respect to measures affecting cross-border supply of specified services, movement of consumers and establishment of commercial presence by foreign service providers.

6. This offer pertains to measures at a national and sub-national level by governmental and non-governmental

48-2-1

0140

1991-02-01 20:52 KOREAN MISSION GENEVA 2 022 791 0525 P.12

regulatory bodies. New measures would on the whole not be more restrictive with regard to market access or national treatment than existing ones. The re-regulation of existing measures would follow the same principles.

7. This offer is conditional upon a satisfactory outcome of the current negotiations on trade in services. Austria therefore reserves the right to modify, supplement, reduce or withdraw this offer in view of the progress of negotiations on the framework agreement, the sectorial annexes, in particular the land-transport annex, the level of commitments assumed by other parties, as well as due to requirements resulting from ongoing regional integrations efforts.

8. This offer is presented as a basis for further discussions to secure comparability of initial commitments. Austria is prepared to enter into negotiations with other parties on additional market access and national treatment concessions in certain areas. A balanced outcome of negotiations would require corresponding commitments by other parties in areas of interest to Austria.

GNS協商終盤段階 課題와 對應

◇ 協 商 課 題 ◇

○ Framework에 관한 我國立場을 補完・發展하여 協商에 效率的으로 對處

○ 分野別 註釋書制定 작업에 積極的으로 參與

○ 讓許協商에 대한 準備作業 徹底

I. 一般協定內容에 대한 我國立場의 補完・發展

1. 立場點檢・補完의 必要性

— 我國은 當初부터 可能限 많은 開途國의 參與下에 모든 서비스分野를 對象으로 協定이 締結되도록 하기위해 基本構造 論議에 있어서 뿐 아니라 分野別 註釋書 制定, 讓許協商推進에 있어서도 開途國과 같은 立場을 취하여 왔음.

○ 公式・非公式會議를 통하여 점진적 自由化方式, 최초의 自由化約束, 市場接近 (MA), 內國民待遇 (NT)의 성격등에 관해 我國立場을 계속 견지하면서 美國, EC등에 대해 協商進展을 위해 신축성 賦與가 必要함을 强調

〈參考〉 **從來의 我國立場**

○ 協定適用對象 서비스：全體를 對象으로 하고 단순히 例示的 目的의 서비스目錄作成은 可能

○ 漸進的 自由化 推進方式：讓許한 分野 및 事項에 대하여만 서비스協定上의 義務를 負擔하는 Postive System을 主張

○ 市場接近 및 內國民 待遇：市場接近 및 內國民 待遇가 다같이 條件賦課 可能하도록 하고 協商에 의해 讓許되어야 함.

○ MFN / 無差別 主義：條件的 MFN이 될 경우 開途國 參與排除 우려, 다만, 特定 分野에서 일부 條件附 MFN수용을 檢討중

○ 최초의 自由化 約束：UR 期間內에는 協定만 制定하고 UR以後 주기적 協商으로 自由化 達成

- 그러나 7月 GNS 議長報告書論議를 계기로 協定妥結 및 開途國 參與의 可能性이 높아진 만큼 從來의 立場은 앞으로의 協商에서는 커다란 意味가 없게 되었음.

  ○ 議長報告書가 그동안 尖銳한 意見對立을 보여온 美·EC와 인도·멕시코 간의 집중적인 절충을 토대로 점진적 自由化方式에 관해 先·開途國間에 어느정도 Consensus 가 이루어져 採澤된만큼 我國으로서도 議長報告書에 제시된 方式을 수용하는데 큰 무리가 없음.

- 따라서 앞으로는 종래의 立場을 신축성있게 補完·發展시켜 先·開途國間 立場調整結果가 採澤되도록 하면서 남은 爭點들이 我國에게 유리한 方向으로 타결되도록 해야 함.

  ○ 協商日程으로 보아도 9-10月중 일부 남은 爭點을 解決하면서 Legal Drafting 作業이 進行되기 때문에 議長報告書에 대한 심층적인 檢討를 통해 보다 구체적인 立場을 發展시켜야만 協商에 積極的이고 實效性있게 參與할 수 있음.

2. 立場의 補完·調整 方案

◇ 基 本 方 向 ◇

○ 대다수 國家들에 의해 Consensus 가 형성된 Structure 에 대하여는 의장보고서 內容이 관철되도록 함.

○ 세부적인 쟁점이 남아 있는 分野에 대하여는 我國의 實利에 맞는 立場이 反映되도록 함.

○ 開發概念의 反映등에 대하여는 全體 Framework 協商 妥結에 지장이 없도록 均衡을 취함.

○ 全般的으로 Framework이 일관성(coherent)이 있으면서도 會員國間에 權利/義務의 均衡이 確保되도록 함.

— 定義(Definition)

○ 原則的으로 3 個의 基準을 배제하도록 하되 我國 立場의 적극 表明은 留保

— 協定 適用對象 서비스(Coverage)

○ 모든 서비스에 적용되도록 계속 주장

— 점진적 自由化 推進 方式

○ 議長報告書의 內容이 採擇되도록 하면서 남은 Negative System 要素의 縮小에 最大한 努力

— 最初의 自由化 約束 (Initial Commitment)

○ 開發程度에 따라 猶豫期間의 賦與를 保障

— 市場接近 및 內國民 대우 (Market access and National treatment)

○ 무조건적 義務로서 보다 條件을 賦課할 수 있도록 된만큼 議長報告書案을 受容

— 최혜국 대우 (MFN)

○ 非加入國에게만 提供된 惠澤도 모든 서비스協定加入國에 賦與되는 無條件的 MFN을 주장

— 開發概念 (Development Concept)

○ 現在 草案上에 상당부분 反映되었다고 일응 생각되나 앞으로 開途國의 구체적인 遇待方案에 대하여 先進國이 充分한 考慮를 하여 다수 開途國이 協定에 加入할 수 있도록 함

* 條文別 立場 檢討案 (別添)

3. Framework 作業에 대한 協商對策

— 書面檢討案의 마련 및 活用

○ 議長報告書 內容에 관한 條文別 我國立場과 事由를 理論的으로 정리하여 公式·非公式 會議에서 活用

○ 關聯國과의 協議를 통하여 書面 檢討案의 內容을 補完·發展시켜 必要時 書面提案도 檢討

Ⅱ. 分野別 註釋書 制定作業에의 活潑한 參與

- 그간의 分野別 會議를 통하여 我國은 先·開途國間의 立場을 調整하면서 적극 參與해왔음.
  - ○ 通信分野 附屬書案 提出(90.6)
  - ○ 建設分野 檢討案마련(90.8) 및 附屬書 作業 主導
  - ○ 其他分野에 있어서도 討議에 적극 參與
- 앞으로도 各 分野別 作業에 적극 參與함으로써 我國立場을 反映하는 한편 앞으로 있을 讓許協商에 必要한 註釋書의 解釋 및 適用에 있어 論理的 對應이 可能하도록 함.
  - ○ 金融分野와 關聯해서는 金融分野의 性格등을 고려, 我國의 必須的인 立場의 反映에 努力
  - ○ 建設分野 註釋書 또는 Foonote 制定 主導
  - ○ 勞動力 移動도 開途國 立場을 一部 反映한 細部檢討案 마련
- Framework 에 있어서의 立場調整을 勘案하여 註釋書作業에 있어서도 伸縮的인 立場을 취하면서 我國의 實益을 確保할 수 있는 方案마련에 努力함.
- 分野別 會議에는 同一한 關係部處 實務者가 계속 일관성있게 參席하여 蹉跌없이 協商 및 國內對應作業이 이루어지도록 함.

Ⅲ. 讓許協商에 대한 準備 철저

1. 讓許協商에 대한 我國立場의 發展

- 讓許交換時期는 協定制定 作業과 連繫하여 이루어져야 할 것을 主張
  - ○ 讓許交換協商이 조속히 進行되기 위해서는 서비스交易의 範圍 및 定義(Scope/Defininition)에 관한 合意를 促進해야 할 것임.
  - ○ 또한 Coverage 問題와 關聯하여 航空·海運分野를 포함해야 할 것임.
- 아울러 我國의 從前立場을 調整하여 UR 期間內 協商推進도 可能하다고 수용하면서 開途國에 대하여는 National Schedule 作成能力이 不足하므로 充分한 猶豫期間을 부여할 것을 主張
- 協商參加國間의 利益 및 義務와 權利의 均衡이라는 協商目標가 讓許協商을 통해 達成될 수 있도록 具體的 節次 및 方法에 관해 의견제시

2. 實質讓許協商 開始에 대비한 我國의 立場

- 금년내에 實質的인 讓許協商이 시작되는 경우 서비스協定에 따른 我國의 期待利益이 미미함을 주장하여 최소 範圍의 開放 및 長期間의 Time-Schedule 添附를 要求
- 先進國間의 協商이 먼저 이루어질 것을 주장하고 開途國에 대한 猶豫期間 賦與動向도 勘案하여 中間水準에서 讓許되도록 努力
  - ○ 雙務間 協商結果로 一部 開放이 可能한 分野에 대하여는 積極的인 기여도 檢討
  - ○ 協商順序 및 開放水準에 있어서 關係業界나 國民들의 批判的 시각을 고려하여 신중히 對處

3. 讓許協商 準備

- Request List 및 National Schedule를 作成하여 協商을 통해 留保 및 開放이 我國實情에 맞게 이루어지도록 準備
- 協商과 關聯된 國內政策 및 法令을 檢討하여 制度改善方案을 發展

관리 번호	91-121

	분류번호	보존기간

WUS-4711

발 신 전 보

번 호 : WGV-0182 910206 1145 AQ 종별 : 지급

수 신 : 주 미, 제네바 대사 . 총영사

발 신 : 장 관 (통 기)

제 목 : UR 서비스 한.미간 양자 협의

1. 미측은 작(2.5) 주한 미 대사관을 통하여 표제 협의를 제네바에서 2.11(월) 개최하되, 필요시 2.12(화) 오전까지 계속할 것을 제의하여 왔음.

2. 상기 미측 제의와 관련, 관계부처 관계관으로 구성된 본부대표단 파견에 참고코자 하니 아래 사항 파악 지급 보고바람.

가. 미측의 본부대표단 파견 여부 및 규모

나. 미측이 의도하는 표제 협의의 성격

다. 미국이 다른국가들과의 양자 협의 추진 실적 및 협의 성격

라. 아측 본부대표단 파견 필요성 및 규모에 대한 귀견. 끝.

(통상국장 김삼훈)

일반문서로 재분류 (1991. 6. 30)

앙 고 재	91년 2월 6일	통기과	기안자		과 장	신각란	국 장		차 관	장 관
			김성주		(서명)	(서명)	전결			(서명)

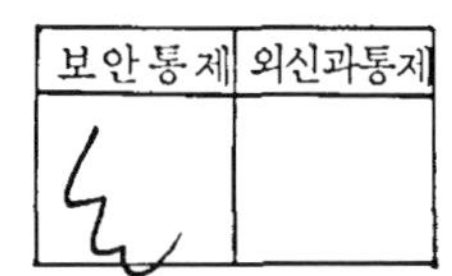

보안통제	외신과통제
(서명)	

0159

ECONOMIC SECTION, AMERICAN EMBASSY, SEOUL, KOREA
82 SEJONG-RO, CHONGRO-KU
SEOUL 110-050, KOREA
FAX NO: 82-2-722-1429, TELEPHONE NO: 82-2-732-4400

UNCLASSIFIED

DATE: February 6, 1991

NUMBER OF PAGES
INCLUDING COVER PAGE: 1

TO: KIM BONG SOO
MULTILATERAL TRADE AFFAIRS DIVISION, MOFA

FAX NO: 720-2686

FROM: James Gagnon
U. S. Embassy, Seoul

SUBJECT: Dates for Services Bilateral

Assistant USTR, Sandra Kristoff, has sent the Embassy a fax message proposing that the services bilaterals be held in Geneva on February 11. USTR, however, would like to hold open the morning of February 12 on an as needed basis.

0160

원 본

외 무 부

종 별 :

번 호 : GVW-0249 일 시 : 91 0206 1600

수 신 : 장 관(통기,경기원)

발 신 : 주 제네바 대사대리

제 목 : UR/ 서비스 한.미 양자협의

대호 관련사항을 하기 보고함.

1. 미국과 다른 국가와의 양자협의 실적 및 성격

가. 양자협의 실적

- 1.21 주: 북구, 스위스, 캐나다

- 1.28 주: EC, 호주, 일본, 홍콩

나. 협의성격

- 각 OFFER 에 대한 CLARIFICATION 및 관심사항 전달 (예: 호주의 경우 금융, 통신 분야 OFFER 제출 계획 문의 및 관심사항 전달)에 집중하였으며 1.28 주에 개최된 협의에는 미국, 일본측에서는 본부대표가 참석하였음

2. 아측 본부대표단 파견 필요성 및 규모에 대한의견

- 아국 OFFER 에 대한 질문사항에의 답변 및 미측관심사항의 파악, 아측 관심사항의 파악 및 전달등을 위하여 주요 분야별 관계관이 참석할 필요가 있는 것으로 판단됨.끝.

(대사대리 박영우-국장)

통상국 2차보 경기원

PAGE 1

91.02.07 09:05 WG

외신 1과 통제관 0161

김

관리번호	91-126

원 본

외 무 부

종 별 : 지 급

번 호 : USW-0656　　　　　일 시 : 91 0207 1810

수 신 : 장관(통기,통일,경기원,상공부)사본:주제네바대사-중계요

발 신 : 주 미 대사

제 목 : UR/서비스 양자 협의

대:WUS-0471

1. 대호 관련, 당관 손명현 공사가 금 2.7 KRISTOFF USTR 대표보와 접촉, 파악한바를 하기 보고함.

가. 미측 본부 파견 대표 (총 3 명):

USTR NANCY ADAMS 부대표보(수석 대표)

상무부 IAN DAVIS 한국담당

상무부 WILLIAM J. DOWLING 서비스 담당

나. 금번회의의 성격:

상호간의 정보교환을 위주로 하여 , UR 서비스 OFFER LIST 에 관한 질의 응답 형식으로 개최될것임.

다. 여타국과의 양자 협의 개최 여부

싱가폴, 뉴질랜드, 호주, EC, 스칸디나비아 국가등과 이미 상기 나항과 유사한 성격의 협의를 가진바 있다 함.

2. 미측에서 상기와같은 일련의 양자협의 개최를 추진하고 있는 배경에는 UR 협상 계속을 위한 FAST TRACK AUTHORITY 연장 신청과 관련하여 서비스 분야 협상에 진전이 있었다는 것을 의회에 과시하기 위한 목적도 있는것으로 관측됨.

3. 금번 회의가 실질 교섭보다는 FACT-FINDING 적 성격을 띄고 있으며, 금번 협의는 앞으로 계속될 서비스 양자 협상의 서막과같은 성격을 띠고 있음을 감안, 금번 아국 대표단은 제네바 주재 관계관들을 중심으로 하고 N.ADAMS 의 COUNTERPART 가 될 본부 수석대표와 서비스 문제 전반을 취급할수 있는 본부 실무급약간명을 보강하는 선에서 구성함이 적절한것으로 사료됨.(동 협의는 양자/ 다자의 성격을 공유하고 있는바, USTR, 상무부 등 미측 관계부처의 양자 문제 담당부서에서 동 협의를

통상국	장관	차관	1차보	2차보	통상국	청와대	총리실	안기부
경기원	상공부							

PAGE 1　　일반문서로 재분류 (1991. 6. 30.)　　91.02.08 10:44

외신 2과 통제관 FE

0162

주관하고 있는 만큼, 아측도 한, 미 양자간 통상문제 담당자도 동 협의에 참여케 함이 바람직할 것으로 사료됨.)

(대사 박동진-국장)

예고:91.6.30 까지

분류기호 문서번호	통기20644-	기 안 용 지 (전화 :)	시 행 상 특별취급	
보존기간	영구·준영구. 10. 5. 3. 1.	차 관	장 관	
수 신 처 보존기간		전결		
시행일자	1991. 2. 8.			

보조기관		협조기관		문 서 통 제
국 장			제2차관보	
심의관				
과 장				
기안책임자	김 봉 주			발 송 인

경 유 수 신 참 조	건 의	발신명의		
제 목	UR/서비스협상 한.미간 양자협의			

91.2.11-12간 스위스 제네바에서 개최되는 UR/서비스협상 한.미간 양자협의에 참가할 정부대표를 "정부대표 및 특별사절의 임명과 권한에 관한 법률"에 의거 아래와 같이 임명할 것을 건의하오니 재가하여 주시기 바랍니다.

- 아 래 -

1. 회 의 명 : UR/서비스협상 한.미간 양자협의

2. 회의기간 및 장소 : 91.2.11-12, 스위스 제네바

// 계 속 ......

0164

1505-25(2-1) 일(1)갑 190㎜×268㎜ 인쇄용지 2급 60g/㎡
85. 9. 9. 승인 "내가아낀 종이 한장 늘어나는 나라살림" 가 40-41 1990. 2. 10.

3. 정부대표

ㅇ 경제기획원 제2협력관 장승우

ㅇ 경제기획원 통상조정3과장 강병일

ㅇ 상 공 부 유통산업과장 박갑록

ㅇ 과 기 처 기술제도담당관 노흥길

ㅇ 경제기획원 통상조정3과 사무관 신호현

ㅇ 재 무 부 증권업무과 사무관 임동빈

ㅇ 문 화 부 영화진흥과 사무관 곽영진

ㅇ 교 통 부 국제협력과 사무관 황성연

4. 출장기간 : 91.2.9(토)-2.14(목) (5박6일)

5. 소요예산 : 소속부처 소관예산. 끝.

0165

경 제 기 획 원

통조삼 10502- 101   503-9149   1991. 2. 8.

수신 외무부장관

제목 UR/서비스협상 양자협의 참석

스위스 제네바에서 개최되는 미국과의 UR/서비스협상 양자협의(2.11-12)에 참석할 본부대표단의 일원을 다음과 같이 송부하니 조치해 주기 바랍니다.

다 음

가. 출 장 자

소 속	직 위	성 명
경제기획원 대외경제조정실 (Int'l Policy Coordination Office)	제 2 협 력 관 (Director General II)	장 승 우 (CHANG SEUNG WOO)
	통상조정 3과장 (Director, Multilateral Trade Division)	강 병 일 (KANG BYONG IL)
	통상조정3과 사무관 (Assistant Director)	신 호 현 (SHIN HO HYUN)

나. 출장기간: '91.2.9 - 2.14 (5박 6일)

다. 경비부담: 당원부담

첨부: 1. 출장일정 1부.

2. 협상대책자료 1부. 끝.

경 제 기 획 원 장

0166

출 장 일 정

'91. 2. 9(토)	12:40	서울 발 (KE 913)
	19:30	암스텔담 착
	21:35	암스텔담 발 (SR 795)
	22:45	제네바착
2. 11(월) ~ 2. 12(화)		미국과의 양자협의등 참석
2. 13(수)	11:00	제네바 발 (LH 1855)
	12:15	프랑크푸르트 착
	14:10	프랑크푸르트 발 (KE 904)
2. 14(목)	10:40	서울 착

0167

UR/서비스관련 韓.美 兩者協議 訓令(案)

- 지난 1.15일 經濟企劃院 對外經濟調整室長과 美側의 S.Kristoff 가 暫定的으로 合意한 바와 같이 兩國의 Offer List에 대한 疑問事項을 明瞭化하고 關心事項을 把握하는 線에서 兩者協議를 進行

  o 全般的인 서비스協商 進展速度 및 國內與件에 비추어 실질적인 R/O 協商의 進行은 어려움

- 다만 '90.6 我國에 대해 旣要請한 美國 Request에 대한 我國 立場을 說明

  o 同 list에 포함되어 있는 業種: 會計, 廣告, Audio/Visual, 建設 및 엔지니어링, 프렌차이징, 保險, 通信 컨설팅

0168

산업평화 이룩하여 경제난국 이겨내자

재 무 부

국금 22251-61 (503-9266) 1991. 2. 7.

수신 수신처 참조

제목 UR/서비스협상 관련 양자협의 참석

1. 재무부 국금 22251-35호('91.1.25)와 관련입니다.

2. '91.1.29~1.30간 개최예정이었던 UR/서비스 협상 관련 양자협의가 '91.2.11~12간 으로 연기 되었는 바, 동 협의에 참석할 당부대표를 아래와 같이 파견코자 하오니 필요한 조치를 취해주시기 바랍니다.

아 래

소 속	성 명	기 간
국제금융과 사무관	최 희 남	'91. 2. 9 ~ 2. 14
증권업무과 사무관	임 동 빈	'91. 2. 9 ~ 2. 14

끝.

재 무 부 장 관

국제금융국장 전결

수신처 : 경제기획원장관, 외무부장관.

0169

문　　화　　부

영 진　35171- 1690　　720-3821　　1991. 2. .

수 신　외무부 장관

참 조　통상국장

제 목　UR/한.미간 협상 참가에 따른 협조

1. 경제기획원 10502-4('91.1.24) 관련입니다.

2. UR/서비스협상 관련 '91.2.11 - 2.12 간 스위스 제네바에서 개최되는 한.미 양허협상에 정부대표단의 일원으로 다음사람이 참석하고자 하오니 필요한 조치를 취해주시기 바랍니다.

o 협상기간 : '91.2.11 - 2.12

o 장　　소 : 스위스 제네바

o 참 석 자 : (UR/시청각 서비스분야)

소　속	직　급	성　명	비　고
문화부 영화진흥과	행정사무관	곽 영 진	

o 출장기간 : '91.2.9 - 2.14

첨　부 : 1. 참석자 이력서 1부. 끝.

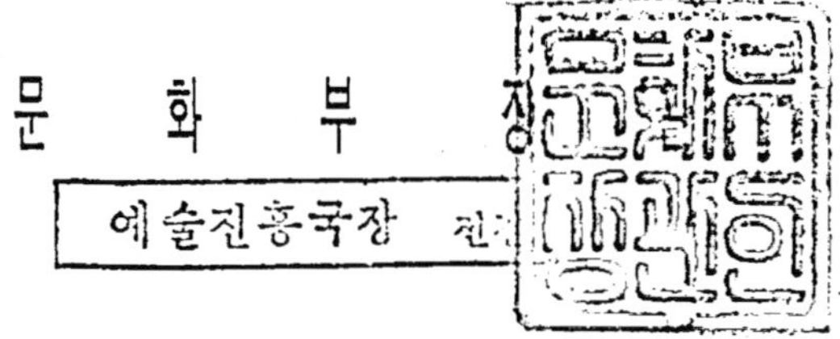

문　화　부　장

예술진흥국장 전결

0170

과 학 기 술 처

기제 16331- 1264 (503-7657) 1991. 2. 7.

수신 수신처참조

제목 UR/서비스 협상 관련 양자협의회의 참가

1. 표제회의에 정부대표로 참가할 당처직원을 아래와 같이 선정.통보하오니 적의 조치하시기 바랍니다.

가. 당처 참석자

소 속	직 위	성 명	비 고
과학기술처	기술제도담당관	노 홍 길	

끝.

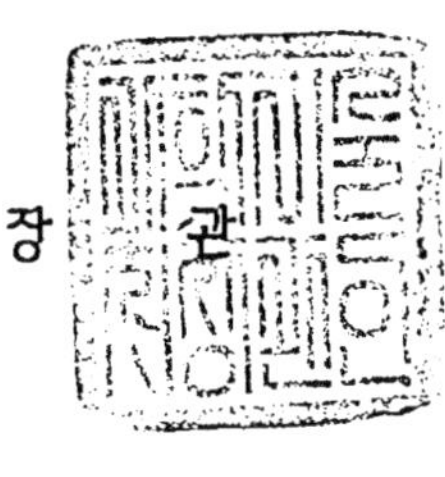

과 학 기 술 처 장 관

수신처 : 경제기획원장관, 외무부장관.

0171

6262

기 안 용 지

분류기호 문서번호	통기 20644-	(전화 :)	시 행 상 특별취급	
보존기간	영구·준영구. 10. 5. 3. 1.	장 관		
수 신 처 보존기간				
시행일자	1991. 2. 8.			

보조기관		협조기관	문 서 통 제
국 장			검열 1991. 2. 11
심의관			
과 장			발 송 인
기안책임자	안 성 국		1991. 2. 11 외무부

경 유 수 신 참 조	수신처 참조	발신명의	
제 목	UR/서비스협상 한.미간 양자협의		

91.2.11-12간 스위스 제네바에서 개최되는 UR/서비스협상 한.미간 양자협의에 참가할 정부대표가 "정부대표 및 특별사절의 임명과 권한에 관한 법률"에 의거 아래와 같이 임명되었음을 알려드립니다.

- 아 래 -

1. 회 의 명 : UR/서비스협상 한.미간 양자협의

2. 회의기간 및 장소 : 91.2.11-12. 스위스 제네바

// 계 속 ......

0172

1505-25(2-1) 일(1)갑 190㎜×268㎜ 인쇄용지 2급 60g/㎡
85. 9. 9. 승인 "내가아낀 종이 한장 늘어나는 나라살림" 가 40-41 1990. 2. 10.

3. 정부대표

ㅇ 경제기획원 제2협력관 장승우

ㅇ 경제기획원 통상조정3과장 강병일

ㅇ 상 공 부 유통산업과장 박갑록

ㅇ 과 기 처 기술제도담당관 노홍길

ㅇ 경제기획원 통상조정3과 사무관 신호현

ㅇ 재 무 부 증권업무과 사무관 임동빈

ㅇ 문 화 부 영화진흥과 사무관 곽영진

ㅇ 교 통 부 국제협력과 사무관 황성연

4. 출장기간 : 91.2.9(토)-2.14(목) (5박6일)

5. 소요예산 : 소속부처 소관예산.

6. 출장결과보고 : 귀국후 20일 이내. 끝.

수신처 : 경제기획원, 재무부, 상공부, 문화부, 교통부,

과학기술처장관.

0173

	분류번호	보존기간

발 신 전 보

번 호 : WGV-0198 910209 1115 DP 종별 :

수 신 : 주 제네바 대사, 총영사 대리

발 신 : 장 관 (통기)

제 목 : UR / 서비스협상 한.미간 양자협의

연 : WGV-0182

1. 91.2.11-12간 귀지에서 개최되는 표제 협의에 아래 대표를 파견하니 귀관 관계관과 함께 참석토록 조치바람.

   o 경제기획원 제2협력관 장승우
   o 경제기획원 통상조정3과장 강병일
   o 상 공 부 유통산업과장 박갑록
   o 과 기 처 기술제도담당관 노홍길
   o 경제기획원 통상조정3과 사무관 신호현
   o 재 무 부 증권업무과 사무관 임동빈
   o 문 화 부 영화진흥과 사무관 곽영진
   o 교 통 부 국제협력과 사무관 황성연

2. 금번회의에는 아래 입장으로 대처바람.

   o 아국 Offer List 설명 및 미측의 질의사항에 답변
   o 미측 Offer List에 대한 설명 요청 및 의문사항 질의
   o 필요시, '90.6 미국의 대 아국 Request에 대한 아국 입장 설명

끝. (통상국장 김삼훈)

보안 통제	

앙 고 재	91년 2월 8일	통기과	기안자 성명		과 장		국 장		차 관	장 관
			김봉주				전결			

외신과통제

0174

원 본

외 무 부

종 별 :

번 호 : GVW-0283 일 시 : 91 0212 1200

수 신 : 장 관(통기, 경기원, 재무부, 법무부, 상공부, 건설부, 보사부, 노동부, 교통부, 체신부, 문화부, 공보처, 과기처, 항만청)

발 신 : 주 제네바 대사대리

제 목 : UR/서비스 한.미 양자협의

2.11(월) USTR 제네바 사무소에서 개최된 표제협의 내용을 하기 보고함.

1. 협의 진행 개요

- 일시: 2.11 10:00-19:00

- 참석자

0 아측: 장승우 경기원 제 2 협력관 외 10명

0 미측: NANCY ADAMS USTR 부대표보외 2명

- 협의진행 방식

0 전체 UR 협상 및 서비스 협상 전망에 관한 간략한 의견 교환에 이어 양국

0 FFER LIST 의명료화를 위하여 분야별로 구체적인 의문사항에 대한 질의 응답 형식으로 진행되었으며, 실질적인 자유화 약속에 관한 협상은 하지않았음.

2. 일반토의

- 아측 논평요지

0 아측은 UR 협상의 성공적 타결을 위한 미측의 노력과 같은 맥락에서 서비스 무역확대에 기여할수 있는 OFFER 를 작성하기 위하여 노력하였음을 밝히는 한편 UR 전체협상과 관련 미국의 신속 처리 절차 문제의 처리전망과 향후 서비스 협상 진행 방식에 관한 미국의 복안에 대하여 문의하였음.

- 미측 논평 요지

0 미측은 신속처리 절차의 연장과 관련 적절한 시기를 모색하고 있으며, 의회의동의를 얻기 위하여는 농산물, 시장접근, 서비스에 있어서의 분명한 자유화 약속이 매우 중요하니 농산물 관련 EC 의 의도가 아직 불분명하다고 하는 한편 농산물에 있어서 아국이 신축적 입장을 표명한데 대하여 사의를 표명함.

0 서비스 협상과 관련 미측은 아국이 짧은시일내에 OFFER 을 제출한데 대하여

통상국	2차보	법무부	보사부	문화부	교통부	체신부	경기원	재무부
상공부	건설부	노동부	과기처	해항청	공보처	국이 미 1과 (2.14)		

PAGE 1 91.02.13 09:15 WG

외신 1과 통제관

0175

치하하는 한편 24 개국과 이와 같은 양자 협의를 진행하고 있으며, 본과정이 UR 협상 성과를 의회에 설득하기 위하여 필요하다고 언급함.

3. 분야별 토의

가. 아국 OFFER 에 대한 질의 답변

- 외국 서비스 공급기업의 자회사, 지사등의 설립에 있어서 등록, 인가등이 필요한 경우 주무부서 및 등록. 인가기준, STANDSTILL 이나 UNBOUND 로 표기된 분야에 있어서 현존 규제 조치, 각 서비스분야의 정의에 대한 질의 응답을 위주로 진행되었으며, 특히 미국은 보험분야와 관련 한.미간 합의 내용보다 낮은 수준의 BINDING과 MFN 원칙의 양립 문제에 의문을 제기하는 한편 양자 협정의 다자화 과정에서 자국이 얻은 기득권을 상실하지 않기를 바란다고 논평함.

- 또한 미국은 자국이 관심을 가지고 있으나 아국 OFFER 에 누락된 분야로서 법무서비스, 보건 서비스, LEASING, FRANCHISING, 보험중개등을 제기하였음.

나. 미국 OFFER 에 대한 질의 답변

- 아측 역시 회계사, 엔지니어등의 자격인가 제도와 FRANCHISING 의 정의 및 LEASING SERVICE 의 분류등에 대하여 질의하는 한편 서비스 분야의 통계와 관련 미측의 기술적 협력을 요청한바 미국은 자국 역시 서비스 통계에 대하여 많은 연구를 해왔음을 밝히고 별도의 협의 기회를 가지자고 제의하였음.

- 또한 아국은 서비스 협상 결과 아국 기업의 영업기회가 증대되었음을 국내에 설득할수있어야 한다고 전제하고 이와 관련 미국 OFFER에 항공 보조 서비스 및 해운 분야의 포함, 건설서비스에 있어서 인력이동 범위의 확대가 필요하다고 지적하였음.

4. 관찰 및 평가

가. 아국 OFFER 에 대한 평가

- 타국 OFFER 와는 달리 일부 추가 자유화 약속도 포함되었으며, 비교적 자세하게 기술되었다는 점에서 아국의 노력을 치하하였음.

나. 금번 협의 및 향후 협상 추진에 관한미측의도

- 금번 협의는 기본적으로 각국 OFFER 의 구체적 명료화를 위한 것임과 동시에 신속처리 절차의 연장에 대한 미국 의회 동의 획득을 위한 수단의 일환으로 추진되었으며, 미측은 금번같은 구체적 명료화를 위한 협의를 1-2 회더 가진후 이를 바탕으로 본격적인 자유화 협상을 추진할 의도인 것으로 판단됨.

0 이와 관련 미측은 지난주까지 EC, 스위스, 캐나다, EFTA 국가, 멕시코, 일본,

PAGE 2

0176

홍콩등과 1차협의를 완료하였으며, 2.12(화) 에 싱가폴 및 인니 (동 국가들도 OFFER 기 제출) 와 2.13(수)에 브라질 (2.13 에 OFFER 제출 예정) 및 알젠틴과 양자협의를 가질 예정이라고 함.

다. 아국의 향후 작업 방향

- 다음 사항에 대한 준비가 필요한 것으로 판단됨.

0 아국 OFFER 에 기 제시한 각 서비스 분야의 구체적 정의

0 각 서비스 분야별 통계 (각국의 국내 진출현황, 아국의 외국 진출 현황, 국경간 서비스무역 통계등)

0 구체적인 서비스 분야별 REQUEST LIST (건설분야에 있어서 아국이 요청할 인력의 종료및 범위등)

0 UNBOUND 및 STANDSTILL 로 표시한 분야의 현존규제 조치의 구체적 명시

0 법무, 보건, LEASING, FRANCHISING, 보험중계 등 OFFER 에서 누락된 분야의 협상 대응 방안마련

0 보험, 여행알선등 한.미 양자 협상에 의하여 기자 유화한 분야의 다자화 대응방안 마련

0 서비스 분야별 국내 규제 제도 (등록기준, 인가기준등)의 정비

(예: 사무실 면적 제한등 합리적 근거가 희박한 규제의 정비) 끝

(대사대리 박영우-국장)

문 화 부

영 진 35175-2121 720-3821 1991. 2 . .

수 신 외무부장관

참 조 통상국장

제 목 UR/서비스 한.미양자협의 참가결과 통보

1. 동기 20644-6262('91.2.11)의 관련입니다.

2. 위호관련, 스위스 제네바에서 '91.2.11 개최된 UR/서비스 한.미양자협의에 참가한 우리부 직원의 참가결과를 별첨과 같이 알려드리오니 업무에 참고하시기 바랍니다.

첨 부 : UR/서비스 한.미양자협의 참가결과 1부. 끝.

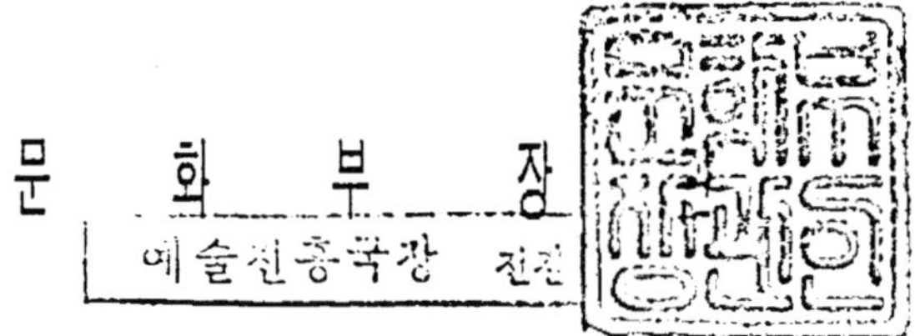

문 화 부 장

예술진흥국장 전결

0178

4917

UR/서비스 한.미 양자협의 결과

1. 협의개요

o 일 시 : '91.2.11(월), 10:00 - 19:00

o 장 소 : USTR 제네바 사무소 (스위스)

o 참 석

- 한국측 : 경제기획원 장승우국장등 8명 (6개부처)
- 미국측 : 무역대표부 부대표보 Nancy Adams등 3명

o 협의진행

- 전체 UR협상 및 서비스협상전망에 대한 의견교환

- 양국 OFFER LIST를 명확히 하기위해 분야별 구체적인 의문사항에 대한 질의응답

- 실질적인 자유화 (시장개방)에 대한 협상은 하지 않음.

※ 협상일정 및 참가자명단 별첨

0179

2. UR 협상전반에 대한 의견교환

ㅇ 우리측은 UR협상의 성공적 타결을 위해 서비스무역 확대에 기여할 수 있는 OFFER를 작성코자 노력하였음을 밝혔고

ㅇ 미국측은 우리측의 성의있는 OFFER 작성에 사의를 표명하며 향후 협상 진행 전망에 대한 의견을 개진

- 금번 협의는 각국 OFFER의 구체적 명료화를 위한것으로 현재 24개국과 양자협의를 추진중이고

- 동 협의결과를 의회에 보고후, UR 협상 신속처리(FAST - TRACKING) 기간 연장에 대한 의회의 동의를 얻고자 하며

- 이러한 협의를 1-2차례 가진후 본격적인 자유화 협상을 추진할 의도로 보임

※ 미국은 이미 EC, 스위스, 캐나다, 멕시코, 홍콩등과 1차 협의를 완료하였고, 한국에 이어 2.12 (싱가폴, 인도네시아), 2.13 (브라질) 및 아르헨티나와 협의예정이라 함.

3. 시청각서비스분야 협의 내용

가. 우리측 OFFER LIST에 대한 미측질의 및 답변

ㅇ 외국영화 수입프린트 벌수완화 시기 및 적용범위는

- '88 한.미 영화협상 합의사항대로 94년에 완전폐지 예정이며, 모든 나라에 적용될 것임.

0180

o 외국영화사 국내지사설치 등과 관련, 외국인투자인가 절차의 폐지계획은

- 영화배급업에 관한 외국인투자인가 절차는 존속될것이며, 이미 4개의 미국영화사가 동 절차에 의거 등록후 활동중임.

o <u>스크린쿼타제도 운영여부</u>

- 존속방침임.

* 동건은 낸시.아담스 자신이 처음 부여받은 임무이나 잘 처리되지 않고 있다는 코멘트가 있었음.

o <u>외국인이 영화관을 구입 또는 임대하여 운영할 수 있는지</u>

- 구입 및 임대운영은 허용되지 않고 있다고 답변

* 현행법상 부동산 매입은 허용되지 않고 있으나, 임대사용은 제한규정이 없는 실정임.

o 미국업계는 영화광고 제한에 따른 불평이 많은데 사실인지

- 내.외국인 공히 광고내용에 대한 심의를 거쳐 광고하고 있고 특별히 차등대우를 하지 않고 있음.

* 동건은 외국영화광고를 문화부의 수입추천 이전에 허용토록 요청한 사항으로 추측되나, 수입추천전에 광고를 허용할수는 없는 사항임.

0181

o '음반법'상 외국인투자제한 폐지 추진사항 및 음반.비디오 복제시 에도 동제한 규정이 적용되는지 문의

- '음반법' 상 외국인투자제한 규정은 '91.2.6일 국회에서 동법 개정안이 통과되어 폐지되었으며, 음반.비디오 복제시에도 적용되던 제한규정은 현제 삭제된 상태임.

- 그러나 동법의 시행은 우리측 OFFER 대로 '92.1월 이후에야 가능함.

나. 미국 OFFER LIST에 대한 우리측 질의 및 답변

o 영화, 음반, 비디오의 수입등 국경이동이 '상품'의 이동인지 '서비스'의 이동인지 개념이 명확치 않음.

- 상품과 서비스의 이동이 포괄된 개념으로 이해하고 있고 세부적으로는 생산, 배급(distribution), 상영(exhibition)의 방식으로 거래되고 있다고 보고있음.

o Sound Recording의 개념은

- 음반(디스크등)의 생산, 배급을 말하며 여기에는 음반의 복제권(Duplication License)도 포함된다고 봄.

o 영화제작과 관련, 국내 영화업자가 촬영을 위해 미국입국 비자 발급요청시 거절되고 있는데 그 이유는?

- 동 문제는 영화제작 서비스의 이동이라고 보기 어려우며, 미국내 영화관련 조합(UNION)의 요구에 따라 이민국에서 제한하고 있는 사항임.

0182

4. 평가 및 향후전망

o 미국측은 우리측 OFFER중 제한사항을 중심으로 개념과 범위를 재확인 하는 과정에서 예외적으로 호의적 반응을 보였으나,

o 미측 OFFER에는 있으나 우리측에는 거론치 않은 '출판'부분과 '영화관 임대운영' 문제등은 향후 1-2차 협의과정에서 구체적으로 재거론해 올것으로 전망됨.

o 따라서 동 분야에 대해서는 명확한 입장정립과 대응책 마련이 필요함.

0183

한.미 양자협의 참가자 명단

구 분	소 속	직 책	성 명	비 고
한국측	경제기획원	제2협력관	장 승 우	수석대표
	"	통상조정 3과장	강 병 일	
	"	통상조정 3과 사무관	신 호 현	
	상 공 부	유통산업과장	박 갑 록	
	과학기술처	기술제도담당관	노 흥 길	
	문 화 부	영화진흥과 사무관	곽 영 진	
	재 무 부	증권업무과 "	임 동 빈	
	교 통 부	국제협력과 "	황 성 연	
	대외경제정책 연구원	UR 협상전문연구위원 (경제학박사)	박 태 호	(통역)
미국측	무역대표부 (USTR)	Deputy Assistant	NANCY ADAMS	수석대표
	상 무 부	-	JAY BOWELINC	
	USTR제네바 사무소	Attache	CHRISTINA RUND	

0184

원 본

외 무 부

종 별 :

번 호 : GVW-0337 일 시 : 91 0221 1600

수 신 : 장관(통기),경기원,재무부,법무부,상공부,건설부,보사부,노동부,교통부, 체신부,문화부,과기처,공보처,항만청)

발 신 : 주 제네바 대사대리

제 목 : UR/서비스 주요국 비공식 협의

연: GVW-0324

2.21.(목) 11:00 DUNKEL 사무총장 주재로 개최된 30개국 (주로 각국의 주제네바 대사와 실무자 1인이참석) 협의 내용을 하기보고함. (박공사, 이경협관, 한경협관보 참석)

1. 표제 협의는 DUNKEL 총장이 협상 재개에대한 합의, 차기회의 일자, 향후 협상과제등만을 열거한 STATEMENT 만 낭독하고 곧바로 종결하였음.

2. 3.8 에 개최될 차기회의 역시 오늘과 같은 형태 (각국별로 2인씩 참가하는 30개국 협의)로 진행될 예정이며 회의 주제는 향후 협상일정에 대한 논의에 집중될 것으로 예상됨.

3. 따라서 구체적으로 3.8 이후 협상이 어떻게 진행될지는 미지수이나 향후 작업 과제를 고려할때 1) FRAMEWORK 및 분야별 부속서에 대한 공식 협상 (아울러 NATIONAL SCHEDULE 작성 방식에관한 토의도 병행될 것으로 예상)

2) NATIONAL SCHEDULE 의 형식 및 내용, 서비스분야의 분류, 서비스 공급 형태에 대한 정의등에 관한 복수국간 비공식 협의 3) 각국 OFFER 의 명료화 및 평가를 위한 양자 협의등이 병행하여 진행될 가능성이 많은 것으로 판단됨.

4. 이와관련 미국은 약 30개국 (당초 24개보다늘어남)과 1차 양자협의를 마쳤으며 3.19주부터 (구상단계에 불과하며 최종일정은 미정)2차 협의를 시작할 계획으로 있다고 함.

0 또한 미국은 일부국가와는 3.19 이전에 추가협의를 가질것을 계획하고 있는바, 일본에 대하여 3.19 부터의 협의이외에 3.8 동경에서 추가양자 협의를 가질 것을 금일 제의하였다고함.(일본의 입장은 미정)

첨부: 서비스분야 STATEMENT 1 부.

통상국	2차보	법무부	보사부	문화부	교통부	체신부	경기원	재무부
상공부	건설부	노동부	과기처	해항청	공보처			

PAGE 1

91.02.22 08:50 WG

외신 1과 통제관

0185

(GVW(F)-0072). 끝
(대사대리 박영우-국장)

PAGE 2

0186

SERVICES GVW(F)-372 10221100
GVW-337 관련

Thursday, 21 February 1991, a.m.

Note for Chairman

1. In his closing remarks at the Brussels Ministerial Meeting, Minister Gros Espiell requested me to pursue intensive consultations with the specific objective of achieving agreements in all the areas of the negotiating programme in which differences remain outstanding. These consultations will, he said, be based on document MTN.TNC/W/35/Rev.1, dated 3 December 1990, including the cover page which refers to the Surveillance Body and the communications which various participants sent to Brussels. He added that I would also take into account the considerable amount of work carried out at the Brussels meeting, although it did not commit any delegation.

2. While much intensive work was done in Brussels it is my understanding that the issues to be settled in the area of services remain, in general, those set out on pages 328 to 382 of W/35/Rev.1.

3. I suggest that we now make arrangements to restart negotiations on services. When doing so, I suggest that we ask ourselves what can usefully be done at the present stage. In this respect, it would appear that there is agreement among participants to undertake work in three specific areas: the framework, initial commitments and sectoral annexes. My own suggestion is that, at the next meeting of this group which will be held on Friday, 8 March starting in the morning, participants should first be given an opportunity (a) to take stock of the situation by assessing where we are in the negotiations on initial commitments, the framework text and on the annexes and (b) to tell us how you see further developments in this work in terms of priorities and interrelationships.

4. I suggest that participants should also identify technical work that can be done in the coming weeks in each of the three main elements of the negotiations on services - commitments, framework and annexes. Such technical work might relate for example to the clarification and evaluation of offers and to the establishment of appropriate negotiating procedures, to further examination of arrangements and agreements of a general character for which exceptions from m.f.n. provisions might be sought, and to specific modalities for the application of m.f.n. in particular sectors. 0187

TOTAL P.01

"노사 관계 안정"

노 동 부

고관32402-2483 (503-9749) 1991. 2. 22.

수신 외무부장관

제목 UR/서비스협상 관련 인력이동 참고자료 송부

1. 고관32402-15154('90.11.1)및 경제기획원 통조삼10502-61 ('91.1.24)의 관련입니다.

2. UR서비스협상의 양허협상에 대비, 국내에 상업적 주재를 하는 외국 서비스기업의 서비스 공급에 필수적인 인력의 이동허용범위를 각 부처에서 서비스 업종별로 설정함에 있어 참고토록 하기 위하여 별첨 자료를 송부하오니 참고 하시기 바랍니다.

첨부 : UR서비스협상 관련 인력이동허용범위 설정 참고자료 1부. 끝.

5045

노 동 부 장

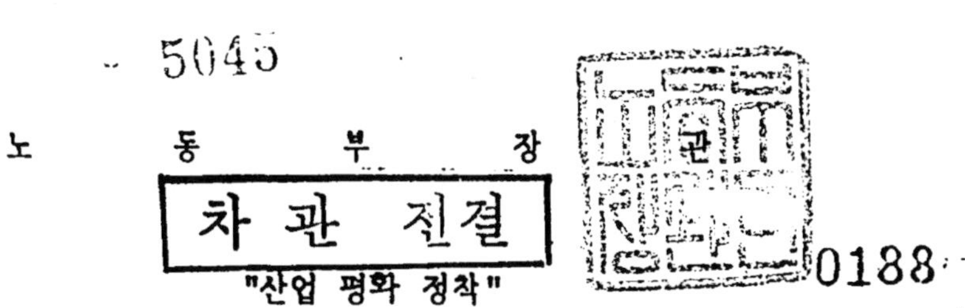

차관 전결

"산업 평화 정착"

0188

UR서비스협상관련 인력이동허용범위 설정 참고 자료

Ⅰ. 배 경

o UR/서비스협상의 양허협상에 대비, 국내에 상업적 주재를 하는 외국서비스 기업의 서비스공급에 필수적인 인력의 이동허용범위를 서비스업종별로 설정함에 참고토록 하기위하여 작성됨.

Ⅱ. 기본방향

o 우리나라는 인력이동에 관하여, 국내노동시장의 여건과 전망, 노동력이동에 따른 사회적 측면에 대한 고려등으로 서비스업종별로 필수인력에 한해 제한적인 이동만을 허용해야 한다는 입장에 있음.

o 서비스업종별 주무부처에서는 제Ⅲ항의 필수인력 예시목록을 참고하여 당해 서비스업종에 필수적인 인력의 허용범위를 설정.

- 예시목록 이외의 직종추가는 법무부 및 노동부와 협의하여 결정.
- 회계사등 전문가의 경우는 해당업종의 산업개방과 직결됨으로 주무부처의 신중한 검토 요망.

Ⅲ. 필수인력의 일반적 정의 및 예시목록

1. 일반적 정의

국내에 상업적 주재를 한 외국서비스기업의 종사자로서 다음에서 정의하는 관리자 또는 전문가에 해당하는 협정 체약국의 국민.

0189

1) 관리자 : 주로 조직 및 그 하부조직의 목표와 활동을 계획 · 조직 · 지휘 · 감독 하는자로서 조직의 주요한 의사 결정을 하거나 이에 참여하고, 다른 전문직 · 관리직 종사자들의 업무를 결정하고 이들을 지휘 · 감독하는 자.

이에는 전문직이 아닌 종사자에 대한 일선관리자가 제외되고 서비스의 생산에 필요한 업무를 주로 수행하는 자도 제외 됨.

2) 전문가 : 조직의 서비스 · 연구설비 · 기술 · 관리등에 관하여 고도의 전문적 · 독점적 지식과 경험을 가진 자.

0190

2. 예시목록

※ 한국표준직업분류(경제기획원 고시 제 74-1호, '74.11.11)에 의거하여, 주로 대분류 0/1전문, 기술 및 관련직종사자, 2. 행정및관리직 종사자에 해당하는 소분류 직종중에서 선정 · 열거하였음. 구체적인 직종의 정의등은 한국표준직업분류의 "해설"란 및 "항목 및 내용설명"란을 참조

011 화학자(Chemists)

012 물리학자(Physicists)

021 건축기술자 및 도시계획기술자(Architects and Town Planners)

022 토목기술자(Civil Engineers)

023 전기 및 전자기술자(Electrical and Electronics Engineers)

024 기계기술자(Mechanical Engineers)

025 화학기술자(Chemical Engineers)

026 금속기술자(Metallurgists)

027 광산기술자(Mining Engineers)

028 산업경영기술자(Industrial Engineers)

031 측량기사(Surveyors)

032 제도사(Draughtsmen)

041 항공기 조종사, 항공사 및 비행기관사(Aircraft Pilots, Navigators and Flight Engineers)

042 선박고급승무원 및 수로안내인(Ships Deck Officers and Pilots)

043 선박관리기술자 (Ships Engineers)

0191

051 생물학자 및 관련과학자(Biologists, Zoologists and Related Scientists)

052 세균학자, 약물학자 및 관련과학자(Bacteriologists, Pharmacologists and Related Scientists)

053 농경학자 및 관련과학자(Agronomists and Related Scientists)

081 통계학자(Statisticians)

082 수학자 및 보험수리사(Mathematicians and Actuaries)

083 체계분석가(Systems Analysts)

090 경제학자(Economists)

110 회계사(Accountants)

162 상업미술가 및 도안사(Commercial Artists and Designers)

163 사진사 및 촬영사(Photographers and Cameramen)

174 제작가, 연출가(Producers, Performing Arts)

192 사회학자,인류학자 및 관련학자(Sociologists,Anthropologists and Related Scientists)

194 인사 및 직업전문가(Personnel and Occupational Specialists)

195 언어학자,번역사 및 통역사(Philologists, Translators and Interpreters)

211 총괄관리자(General Managers)

212 생산관리자(농장관리자제외) (Production Managers, except Farm)

400 도소매 관리자(Managers, Wholesale and Retail Trade)

500 요식숙박업 관리자(Managers, Catering and Lodging Services)

0192

분류기호 문서번호	통기20644-	기 안 용 지 (전화 :)	시 행 상 특별취급	
보존기간	영구·준영구. 10. 5. 3. 1.	장 관		
수 신 처 보존기간				
시행일자	1991. 2.22.			

보조기관			협조기관		문 서 통 제
	국 장	전결			
	심의관				
	과 장				
기안책임자		김 봉 주			발 송 인

경 유 수 신 참 조	건 의	발신명의		
제 목	UR/서비스 협상 정부대표 임명건의			

91.2.27 스위스 제네바에서 개최되는 UR/서비스 협상회의에 참가할 정부대표를 "정부대표 및 특별사절의 임명과 권한에 관한 법률"에 의거 아래와 같이 임명할 것을 건의하오니 재가하여 주시기 바랍니다.

- 아 래 -

1. 회 의 명 : UR/서비스협상 복수국간 협의

2. 회의기간 및 장소 : 91.2.27, 스위스 제네바

// 계 속 ....

0193

1505-25(2-1) 일(1)갑 190㎜×268㎜ 인쇄용지 2급 60g/㎡
85. 9. 9. 승인 "내가아낀 종이 한장 늘어나는 나라살림" 가 40-41 1990. 2. 10.

3. 정부대표

○ 경제기획원 대조실 통상조정3과 사무관 김용준

○ 경제기획원 대조실 통상조정2과 사무관 이승길

4. 출장기간 : 91.2.25-3.1(4박5일)

5. 소요예산 : 소속부처 소관예산. 끝.

0194

1505-25(2-2) 일(1)을
85. 9. 9. 승인 "내가아낀 종이 한장 늘어나는 나라살림" 190㎜×268㎜ 인쇄용지 2급 60g/㎡
가 40-41 1990. 3. 15

■ 제 기 획 원

통조삼 10502- 133 503-9149 1991. 2. 21.

수신 외무부장관

제목 EC주최의 UR/서비스협상관련 복수국간 협의 참석

스위스 제네바에서 EC주최로 개최되는 제2차 UR/서비스협상관련 복수국간 협의(2.27)에 아국대표단의 일원으로 참석할 당원대표를 다음과 같이 추천합니다.

다 음

가. 출장자

소 속	직 위	성 명
경제기획원 대외경제조정실 (International Policy coordination Office)	통상조정3과 사무관 (Assistant Director, Multilateral Trade Division)	김 용 준 (KIM YONG JUN)
"	통상조정2과 사무관 (Assistant Director, GATT Division)	이 승 길 (LEE SEUNG GIL)

나. 출장기간: '91.2.25 - 3.2 (5박 6일)

다. 경비부담: 당원 부담

첨부: 1. 출장일정 1부.

2. 이력서 각 1부.

3. 협상대책자료 1부 (별도송부). 끝.

경 제 기 획 원 장

0195

출 장 일 정

'91. 2. 25(월)	12:40	서울 발 (KE 901)
	18:10	파리 착
	20:45	파리 발 (SR 729)
	21:45	제네바착
2. 26(화) ~ 2. 28(목)		UR/서비스협상관련 복수국간 협의 주요국 및 GATT사무국과 비공식협의
3. 1(금)	16:15	제네바 발 (SR 726)
	17:20	파리 착
	20:30	파리 발 (KE 902)
3. 2(토)	17:40	서울 착

0196

7h

원 본

외 무 부

종 별 :

번 호 : GVW-0315 일 시 : 91 0218 1830

수 신 : 장 관(통기,경기원,재무부,상공부,건설부,보사부,노동부,교통부,체신부, 문화부,공보처,과기처,항만청)

발 신 : 주 제네바 대사대리

제 목 : UR/서비스 비공식 협의

당지 주재 EC 대표부에서 UR/ 서비스 협상과관련, 2.27(수) 에 제 2차 비공식 협의를 개최하고자 하는 한편 NATIONAL SCHEDULE 작성에 관한 토론 자료를 보내왔는바, 동 자료를 별첨 FAX 송부하니 참고 바람.

첨부: EC 작성 토론자료 1부.

(GVW(F)-0065). 끝

(대사대리 박영우-국장)

통상국	2차보	보사부	문화부	교통부	체신부	경기원	재무부	상공부
건설부	노동부	과기처	해항청	공보처				

PAGE 1

91.02.19 09:06 WG

외신 1과 통제관

0197

1991-02-18 19:45 KOREAN MISSION GENEVA 2 022 791 0525 P.02
15 FEVR. '91 16:55 CCE GENEVE 022 7342331 P.2/5

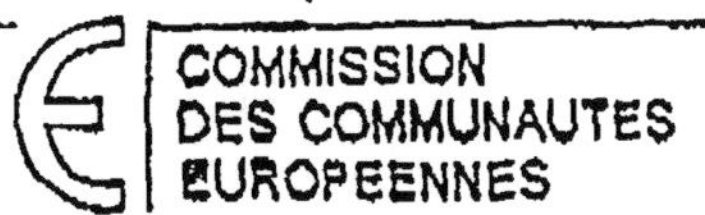

Délégation Permanente auprès des Organisations Internationales à Genève

Le Chef de Délégation

Genève, le 15/2/91

GVW(T)-0065 1021 1830
"GVW-0315 첨부"

Further to my note of 12 February, and in the light of the reactions of a number of participants, I would like to invite you to participate in an informal plurilateral meeting on trade in services at 10.00 a.m. on Wednesday 27 February. It will take place in the Commission Delegation's Offices, 2nd Floor, 37-39 rue de Vermont, Geneva.

To facilitate discussion, I attach a short paper setting out a certain number of issues which were raised in the discussion on 31 January.

I would be grateful if you could indicate to Ms Eliane BARBAGLIA (734.97.50, ext. 225) the names of those from your delegation who will be participating.

Trân Van-Thinh
Ambassadeur-Représentant Permanent auprès du GATT

0198

4-1

Adresse: Case Postale 195, 37-39, rue de Vermont, CH - 1211 GENEVE 20
- Tél: 734 97 50 - - Fax: 734 22 36 - Télex: 414165 et 414166 ECO CH

Brussels, 15 February 1991

INFORMAL PLURILATERAL MEETING ON TRADE IN SERVICES
(EC Delegation, Geneva, 10.00 a.m. 27 February 1991

ISSUES FOR DISCUSSION

(Note : This paper is an attempt to draw out some of the points raised in the first discussion on 31 January so that the second discussion can be more fruitful. It is not intended to reflect the particular position of any participant.)

1. FORMAT AND CONTENT OF SCHEDULES

The offers at present on the table vary substantially in their presentation, in the type of measure included, in the method of reference to specific types of measure and in the degree of detail. At the conclusion of the negotiating process, there should obviously be a common approach to scheduling in order to ensure that the contractual element represented by each party's schedule is as unambiguous as possible, so as to achieve security of commitments. This objective will inevitably also be affected by the degree to which the provisions of the framework itself do or do not contain ambiguities. Discussions on some of the issues raised in this note may highlight any such ambiguities.

A distinction is necessary between obligations on transparency and the commitments which result from negotiation. Is it accepted that the schedules are not intended to provide an encyclopedic description of the regulatory situation in any party? This seems to be the assumption behind the general approach of the framework. Is there then a case for distinguishing between information supplied in negotiations (desirable in order to obtain a clear picture of the nature of the commitment being offered) and the types of measure which are included in the schedule? What is the relationship between this distinction and the implicit recognition in Article VI of the draft GATS that certain types of regulation (based on "objective criteria") are not intended to be scheduled? What are the legal implications of a change in such regulations for the commitments undertaken - are we talking here about "non-violation cases"? If they are scheduled, are they bound and therefore not able to be modified in terms of the level of market access/national treatment?

Particular examples quoted in this context include : residence requirements, monopolies, qualification requirements, nationality requirements, non-discriminatory measures which limit access to or operation in the market (quantitative or qualitative), prudential measures, measures based on administrative discretion. What are the views on the types of measure which should be scheduled (and which are therefore implicitly negotiable)?

How much detail of measures should be included in the schedule? Is a broad description of the régime sufficient, or is there need for a detailed list of each and every element? Should legal references alone be enough, without any descriptive text?

/u/js/GNS/plurilat

0199

4-2

Most countries operate a certain number of measures which are not sector-specific (exchange controls, legislation on movement of personnel, restrictions on purchase of real estate etc.). Should these be scheduled on an "all sectors" basis? If so, what is the relationship between this part of the schedule and the sector-specific parts - are the two parts cumulative or alternative? What is the status of such generally applicable measures in sectors where no other binding is undertaken? Does the entry in the schedule only become operational when the specific sector is bound? Or is the general regulation itself bound for all sectors?

Should an analogous approach, separating in the schedule the different types of regulatory authority, be adopted for sub-national measures and/or measures of self-regulatory bodies? Or is it less ambiguous to schedule all measures, whatever the body which operates them, in the same sector-specific entry?

An examination of the offers makes clear that there is no common understanding of the distinction to be made between limitations on market access and qualifications on national treatment; some have opted to put a particular measure in one column, others to put a similar measure in the other. The distinction arises from the structure of the draft framework itself, which separates Articles XVI and XVII. To what extent is such a distinction meaningful and/or necessary in the schedule? Or in the framework? If it is believed to be necessary, does the distinction have to be unambiguous, or can we rely on the assurance that all measures which should be scheduled are scheduled, whichever column they appear in? In that case, what is the meaning of an entry which is "unbound" in one column, but which sets out a specific binding in the other? If it is felt necessary to maintain the two column format, is there need to develop some guidelines as to the column in which certain types of specific measure should be entered? Should these be binding or not?

There also appears to be some difficulty in distinguishing clearly between the four modes of delivery. Some participants have questioned whether a clear distinction can be made between cross-border supply and consumption abroad; the one may merely signify an alternative means of payment for the provision of an identical service. Similarly, the provision of a service through the temporary, short-term presence of a physical person (e.g. certain professional services) seems generally to have been considered as cross-border supply. At what point does such provision become provision through commercial presence? The relationship between the movement of physical persons and other modes of delivery (cross-border supply or commercial presence) was also underlined in the informal discussions. Although some of these questions also need to be examined in relation to the definition of "provision of a service", they also raise questions as the appropriateness and/or desirability of making a clear distinction between the different modes of delivery in the schedules themselves, irrespective of how the distinction may be made in the framework.

/u/js/GNS/plurlist ./.

4-3 0200

2. CLASSIFICATION OF SERVICE SECTORS AND DEFINITION OF PROVISION OF A SERVICE

A comparison of the different offers demonstrates the problems posed by the absence of a detailed agreed sectoral classification. While a number of participants have opted to utilise the Secretariat Reference List of sectors (MTN.GNS/W/50) as a basis for their proposal, almost every offer departs in some way from this list. Some offers do include, to a greater or lesser extent, clarifications on the coverage of the sectors in which offers have been made, but there is not in general an attempt to relate these clarifications directly to the basic reference list. In some areas the inadequacies of the present reference list are obvious (e.g. financial services, telecommunications).

To what extent do participants see it as necessary and/or desirable to obtain a greater degree of harmonisation of classification of sectors in the context of the negotiation of a first set of commitments? Should this harmonisation be seen as obligatory or only optional? How best should it be pursued? As a starting point, should an attempt be made to draw up a concordance of the different offers on a sector by sector basis? Would it be useful to draw up a numerical classification system, based on W/50, in order to clarify the relationship of different offers? Should we try to agree detailed descriptions of the sub-sectors, or simply seek to ensure clarity for each individual offer/schedule?

It has consistently been recognised in the negotiations that the provision of a service may in many instances involve more than one mode of delivery; examples include commercial presence with personnel, cross-border supply involving the temporary presence of physical persons. The draft framework has been formulated in an inclusive way, so that all forms of mode of delivery are considered to be covered by the Agreement. To what extent is it necessarily appropriate to maintain the clear distinction between modes of delivery when considering the commitments which are made? Can one talk in any meaningful way of provision of a service solely in relation to one of the four modes of delivery?

To what extent are we in fact creating disciplines on measures affecting the supply or the consumption of a service? Both types of measure can affect international trade in services. Similarly, are we only concerned with measures affecting the import of a service or should we also look at export restrictions (e.g. restrictions on the inward movement of tourists)? At first sight priority would seem to lie with import restrictions, since export restrictions could be seen essentially as self-inflicted wounds.

0201

4-4

TOTAL P.05

EC主催의 제2차 復數國間協議 對策資料

I. 會議 개요

- 일 시: '91. 2. 27(수) 10:00

- 장 소: 스위스 제네바 EC대표부

- 참석범위: Offer List를 기제출한 14개국가, 기타 관심국가등 25여개국가

- 의 제: ○ National Schedule의 작성방법에 대한 토의
○ 서비스분류 및 포괄범위에 대한 토의

II. 協商對策

1. 基本立場

- 各國의 National Schedule은 서비스市場의 開放에 대한 法的 權利 및 義務를 나타내는 文書이므로 國際間의 紛爭의 所持를 최소화하기 위하여 明瞭化되어야 함.

- 따라서 GNS協商그룹에서 貿易擔當者들이 暫定的으로 合意한 National Schedule의 各要素에 대한 槪念定義가 법적인 관점에서 再檢討해야 함.

- 이런 次元에서 EC가 주최하고 있는 復壽國間 協議는 基本的으로 매우 유익하다고 보며 非公式的이던 公式的이던 계속 해서 進行하는 것이 必要하다고 봄.

0202

- 특히 National Schedule의 作成方法은 Framework 및 附屬書의 內容과도 직접적인 관련이 있는 만큼 兩者를 병행해서 協議를 進行해야 할 것임.
  - ㅇ 다만 National Schedule의 作成方法에 대한 토의는 技術的인 協議이고 利害關係를 결정하는 實質的인 協商이 아닌 만큼 동 協議를 통해서 自國의 實利를 추구하는 자세는 不適合하다고 봄.

- 韓國政府는 동 協議에 적극적으로 참여하여 필요한 기여를 할 計劃임.

- 다만 協商過程에도 公開主義(Transparency) 原則이 적용되야 한다는 차원에서 매번 모든 GNS協商參加國이 동 協議에 參席하지 않는다 하더라도 적절한 時間間隔으로 中間報告書를 作成하여 復壽國間 協議에 참석하지 않은 各國에 配布하는 配慮를 할 필요가 있다고 생각함.

2. National Schedule의 作成

가. National Schedule에 기재된 Commitment의 性格과 公開主義 義務

- 韓國이 National Schedule을 作成하는 過程에서 適用한 基本 指針은 다음과 같음.
  - ㅇ 客觀的 基準에 기초한 規制는 기재하지 않되 市場接近 및 營業活動에 영향을 주는 중요한 規制制度(예: 면호, 등록, 자격인정)등에 대해서는 동 規制事實의 存在에 대해서만 言及하고 法的根據를 명시함.

0203

o 이렇게한 이유는 동 規制制度의 內部基準으로 客觀的인 事項도 있고 主觀的인 事項도 있는바 이것을 구분하는것 자체가 어려운 문제가 있고 또한 明確히 區分이 된다고 하더라도 동 主觀的인 事項을 National Schedule에 모두 등재하는 것은 너무 방대한 작업이 될 것으로 판단

- 이렇게 볼때 동 規制制度의 內部基準에 대한 사항은 公開主義 義務를 적절히 활용하는 方向으로 運用해야 할 것임.

나. 中央政府와 地方政府의 區分 必要性

- 우선 附屬書를 포함한 서비스一般 協定이 中央政府 뿐만 아니라 地方政府 및 政府의 權限을 대행하는 自律規制團體에 까지 適用된다고 하는 점이 명확히 되야 함.

  o 이런 次元에서 一部國家가 National Schedule을 利用하여 서비스一般 協定의 適用對象範圍에서 地方政府등을 除外 시키려 하는 것은 부당

- 各規制當局이 서비스一般 協定上에 負擔하는 法的義務의 차이가 없는 점에 비추어 各國의 National Schedule에는 各 分野別로 規制事項이 종합적으로 기재되야 할 것임.

다. 市場接近과 內國民待遇의 區分

- 韓國이 National Schedule을 作成하는 過程에서 적용한 基本指針은 다음과 같음.

  o 일단 內國民待遇란에는 外國人에 대한 制度的인 差別, 특히 營業範圍上의 제한등에 관한 사항을 등재하고 그외의 모든사항은 市場接近란에 수록하였음.

0204

○ 이렇게한 理由는 모든 국가가 이미 지적한 바와같이 市場接近과 內國民待遇의 槪念區分이 매우 어렵기 때문이었음.

- 이런관점에서 볼때 양개념은 明確히 구분하는 것은 커다란 意味가 있다고 보지는 않음.

  ○ 특히 內國民待遇의 槪念을 制度上의 內國民待遇 이상의 실질적인 것으로 擴大解釋할 경우, 市場接近의 免許, 登錄要件 등과 직접적으로 연관되기 때문임.

- 그러나 內國民待遇를 傳統的인 意味로 해석할 경우에는 다소 意味가 있을 것으로 생각

  ○ 이경우 내국민대우란에 일단 국내에 진입한 외국인, 외국 서비스공급 기업등이 영업활동을 하는데 있어서의 제도상의 차별적인 대우를 적고 그외에는 모두 시장접근란에 등재할 수 있음.

라. 4가지 공급형태의 구분필요성

- 한국정부도 Offer List를 작성하는 과정에서 다른 국가와 마찬가지로 많은 어려움을 겪음.

- 따라서 금번 복수국간 협의를 통하여 법적권리, 의무의 측면에서 동 4가지 공급형태의 구분 필요성 및 기준등에 대한 것이 구체적인 사례와 더불어 충분히 논의되기를 희망

0205

2. 서비스의 정의 및 분류

- 동 문제는 협상시한의 제약, 기술상의 어려움 및 서비스 정의 및 분류의 명료화의 필요성이 종합적으로 고려되야 함.
  - ㅇ 즉 초기 GNS협상 과정에서 이미 밝혀졌듯이 서비스의 정의 및 분류에 대한 문제는 장기과제로서 GNS협상 자체진행의 걸림돌이 되어서는 안됨.

- 이런관점에서 현재 생각할 수 있는 구체적인 방안은 다음과 같음.
  - ① GATT사무국이 작성한 참고목록(MTN/GNS/W/50)을 각국의 Offer List등을 참고로 하여 개선하는 작업을 조속히 진행
  - ② 서비스의 정의 및 분류와 관계되는 GATT사무국, UN통계국등 관련 국제기구와 관심있는 국가들이 발전의 대책기구를 설치하여 연구검토하고 궁극적으로는 예비적인 유권해석을 할수 있도록 하는 방안 검토
  - ③ 또한 Sector by sector 별로 각국의 Offer List를 일치시키는 작업을 진행

- 한국정부는 위와같은 작업에 적극적으로 참여할 용의를 갖고 있음.

0206

8846

기 안 용 지

분류기호 문서번호	통기 20644-	(전화 :)	시 행 상 특별취급	
보존기간	영구 · 준영구. 10. 5. 3. 1.	장 관		
수 신 처 보존기간				
시행일자	1991. 2.26.			

보조기관		협조기관		문 서 통 제
국 장	전결			
심의관				
과 장				발 송 인
기안책임자	안 성 국			

경 유 수 신 참 조	경제기획원장관	발신명의	
제 목	UR/서비스협상 정부대표 임명 통보		

91.2.27. 스위스 제네바에서 개최되는 UR/서비스 협상회의에 참가할 정부대표가 "정부대표 및 특별사절의 임명과 권한에 관한 법률"에 의거 아래와 같이 임명되었음을 알려드립니다.

- 아 래 -

1. 회의명 : UR/ 서비스협상 복수국간 협의

2. 회의기간 및 장소 : 91.2.27. 스위스 제네바

// 계 속 .....

0207

1505-25(2-1) 일(1)갑 190㎜×268㎜ 인쇄용지 2급 60g/㎡
85. 9. 9. 승인 "내가아낀 종이 한장 늘어나는 나라살림" 가 40-41 1990. 2. 10.

3. 정부대표

o 경제기획원 대조실 통상조정3과 사무관 김용준

o 경제기획원 대조실 통상조정2과 사무관 이승길

4. 출장기간 : 91.2.25-3.1(4박5일)

5. 소요예산 : 소속부처 소관예산. 끝.

0208

1505-25(2-2) 일(1)을
85. 9. 9.승인 "내가아낀 종이 한장 늘어나는 나라살림"

190㎜×268㎜ 인쇄용지 2급 60g/㎡
가 40-41 1990. 3. 15

분류번호	보존기간

발 신 전 보

번 호 : WGV-0240 910225 1626 AO 종별 :

수 신 : 주 제네바 대사. 총영사

발 신 : 장 관 (통 기)

제 목 : UR/서비스협상 2차 복수국간 회의

1. 91.2.27(수) 귀지에서 개최되는 표제회의에 아래 대표를 파견하니 귀관 관계관과 함께 참석토록 조치 바람.

   o 경제기획원 통상조정3과 사무관 김용준

   o 경제기획원 통상조정2과 사무관 이승길

2. 금번회의 훈령은 상기 대표가 지참할 예정인바, 회의 참석후 결과상세 보고바람.

끝.

(통상국장 김 삼훈)

보 안 통 제	

앙 고 재	91년 2월 25일	통기과	기안자 성명		과 장		국 장		차 관	장 관

외신과통제

0209

2h

원 본

외 무 부

종 별 :

번 호 : GVW-0365 일 시 : 91 0226 1730

수 신 : 장 관(통기, 경기원)

발 신 : 주 제네바 대사

제 목 : UR/ 서비스 복수국간 비공식 협의

대: WGV-0240

2.27(수) EC 대표부에서 개최 예정이던 표제협의는 UR 협상이 공식 재개됨에 따라 일단 취소되었으며, 3.8 DUNKEL 총장 주재 회의결과에 따라 향후 개최 시기가 결정될예정임.끝

(대사 박수길-국장)

통상국 2차보 경기원

PAGE 1

91.02.27 09:40 WG

외신 1과 통제관

0210

원 본

외 무 부

종 별 :

번 호 : GVW-0428 일 시 : 91 0308 1630

수 신 : 장 관(통기,경기원,재무부,법무부,상공부,건설부,보사부,노동부,교통부 ,체신부,문화부,공보처,과기처,항만청.

발 신 : 주 제네바 대사

제 목 : UR/ 써비스 주요국 비공식 협의

3.8(금) DUNKEL 총장 주재로 개최된 표제협의는 향후 협상 계획에 대하여 토의하였는바, 주요 내용 하기 보고함.(박공사,이경 협관, 한경협관보 참석)

1. DUNKEL 총장은 GNS 의장이 향후 적절한 시기에 서비스 협상을 주재할 것이라고 전제하는 한편 (인도가 지지의사를 표명하고 서비스 협상 기구는 오직 GNS 뿐이라고 강조함.) 우선적으로 다루어야할 협상의제로서 다음과 같은 기술적 사항들을 예시하고 각국의 의견을 구함.

0 NATIONAL SCHEDULE 의 형태 및 내용의 명확화(자유화 약속의 기재 방법)

0 어떤 분야에 특정되지 않은 수평적 협정(HORIZONTAL AGREEMENTS: OECD CODE, 투자 보장협정등)중 MFN 으로 부터 일반적 예외가 필요한 요소

0 각종 용어의 정의

0 분쟁해결, 세이프가드, 보조금, 정부 조달의 각종조문

0보다 자세한 서비스분야 분류 목적

2. 캐나다는 각국 OFFER 에 담긴 자유화의 내용파악, 각국의 국내 작업 촉진, NATIONAL SCHEDULE 작성방법의 명확화, 서비스 분야 분류 목록의 보완 발전등의 효과가있음을 들어 분야별 전문가 참석하의 각국 OFFER 에 대한 다자간협의를 조기에 개시할 필요가 있다고 하였는바, 일본, 스위스, 호주, 스웨덴, 이집트등이 지지의사를표명하 였으며, 미국 역시 OFFER 에 대한 협의를 통하여 FRAMEWORK 상의 시장 접근, 내국민 대우, 국내 규제 조항의 수정 필요성이 제기될 가능성이있음로 두가지에 대한 토의를 병행하는 것이 최상의 방법이라고 하는 한편, 지급 및 이전, 조화,서비스무역의 정의등을 추가 작업이 필요한부분으로 제시함.

3. 이씨는 FRAMEWORK 을 배제한체 OFFER 를 기초로 작업할수는 없으며, NATIONALSCHEDULE 작성방법등이 관한 이론적 토의가 우선하여야 한다고하였으며,

통상국	법무부	보사부	문화부	교통부	체신부	경기원	재무부	상공부
건설부	노동부	과기처	해항청	공보처	고자선			

PAGE 1

91.03.09 02:46 CT

외신 1과 통제관

0211

인도는 FRAMEWORK 을 우선 토의하는 순차적 접근 방법을 주장하는 한편, NATIONALSCHEDULE 작성방법에 관한 기술적 토의는 가능하나 이는 실제 자유화 약속협상과는 전혀별개로 취급되어야 한다고 강조함.

4. DUNKEL 총장은 협상 진행방법에 대한 논의로 시간을 소비하기 보다는 제기된모든 사항들이 향후 협상 과정에서 고려될수 있을것이라고 하고 4월 8일주를 차기 협의 일자로 제시하였으며, 동 협의시 의제로

(1) 자유화 약소의 기재방법

(2) 상기 작업이 FRAMEWORK 등 타분야에 미치는영향

(3) 보다 자세한 서비스 분야 분류 목록 개발

(4) MFN 으로 부터 예외가 필요한 수평적 협정

(5) 기타 협상 요소에 대한 향후 협상일정 수립을제의하였음.

또한 알젠틴의 요청에 따라 사무국에서 향후협상과제에 대한 CHECK-LIST 를 만들기로 하고협의를 종결하였음.

5. 관찰 및 평가

- 본 협의를 통하여 2.26 TNC 회의에서 거론된협상기구의 지위와 관련 GNS 가 계속하여 공식협상기구가 된다는것이 구체적으로 확인되었음.

- FRAMEWORK 과 OFFER 에 대한 협상의 우선순위와 관련 이씨가 다른 선진국과는달리 FRAMEWORK 및 NATIONAL SCHEDULE 작성에 관한 이론적 토의에 보다 비중을 두는것 은 농산물협상과 관련, 서비스 분야에 있어서 MFN 원칙적용에 관한 미국의 수세적 위치를 부각시키려는 의도가 있는 것으로 추측됨.

- 4.8 이전에도 비공식 양자 또는 복수국간 협의가있을 것으로 예상되며, 미국이추진하고 있는 양자협의와 관련, 일본은 UR 협상의 일환으로서의 양자 협의에만 응한다는 방침하에 3.9 동경에서의 협의 요청을 거절하고 제네바에서 다른 국가들과의 협의의 일환으로 개최하자고하였다고함.(구체적 일정은 미정). 끝

(대사 박수길-국장)

PAGE 2

0212

관리 번호	91-196

	분류번호	보존기간

발 신 전 보

번 호 : WUS-1073 910320 1641 FD 종별 :

수 신 : 주 미 대사 . 총영사

발 신 : 장 관 (통 기)

제 목 : UR/건설 서비스 분야 개방 요구서 작성

일반문서로 재분류 (1991 .12 .31)

1. UR 서비스 협상과 관련, 협상 참가국들은 대아국 Request List를 준비하고 있으며, 특히 미국은 '91.2. 개최된 UR/서비스 한.미 양자간 회의 이후 건설분야에 대하여 추가 질문을 보내오는등 ~~자대한~~ 관심을 보이고 있음.

2. ~~의에 아국도~~ 미국에 대한 충실한 내용의 Request List ~~작성이 요망되므로 동 List~~ 작성에 참고코자 하니 하기 사항 파악, 조속 보고바람.

가. Brooks Act (P.L. 92-582)에 따르면 공공 공사의 A-E(설계-엔지니어링) 계약은 기술경쟁력, 경험, 과거실적 및 특수공업등을 평가기준으로 함으로써 외국업체가 불리한 대우를 받는 경우가 있을 것으로 사료되는바, 본 법의 시행기간, 기본 목적, 외국업체에 불리한 조항의 유무 및 그 내용

나. 미 연방정부 및 미군 발주공사의 경우 1984.10월부터 시행하고 있는 미국의 특혜정책(American Preference Policy)에 의거 공사 금액 500만달러 이상의 공사에 있어 미국 국적 업체에 대한 20%의 우대 혜택을 부여하고 있는바 동 특혜정책의 근거(법령, 행정지시등), 시행기간, 특혜의 구체적 사례

검 토 필 (1991. 6.30.) 0

앙 고 재	91년 3월 20일	통기과	기안자		과 장	신예관	국 장		차 관	장 관
			김봉주		(서명)	(서명)	전결			(서명)

보안통제	외신과통제
(서명)	

0213

다. 기타 아국업체의 미국내의 건설활동에 장애요소가 되는 사례(각종 공사의 입찰.계약시 외국인에 대한 차별, 위 "나"항과 유사한 미국인 특혜정책등)

3. 대미 Request List 작성의 시급성을 감안, 상기 사항 파악 즉시 전문 보고하고 관련자료는 파편 송부바람. 끝. (통상국장 김삼훈)

0214

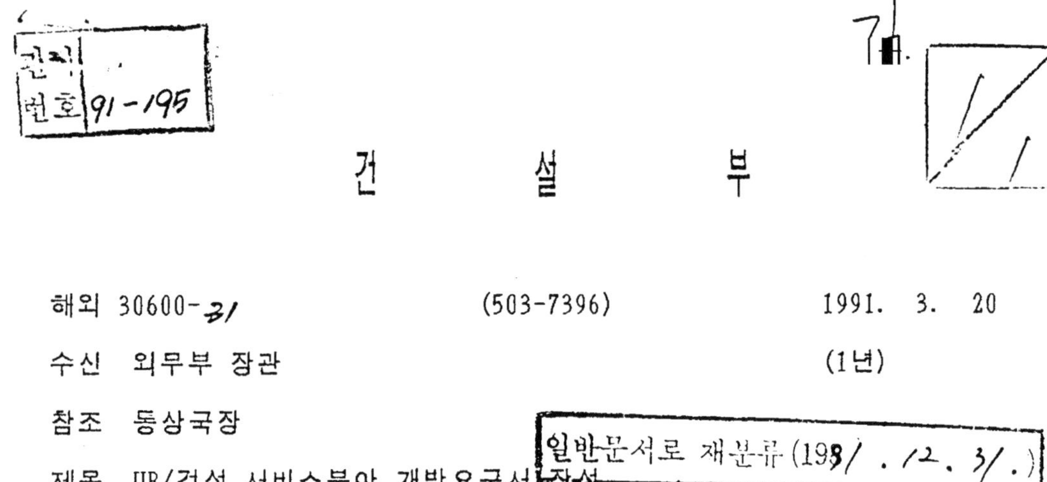

관리번호 91-195

기

건 설 부

해외 30600-31 (503-7396) 1991. 3. 20

수신 외무부 장관 (1년)

참조 통상국장

제목 UR/건설 서비스분야 개방요구서 작성

일반문서로 재분류(1991. 12. 31.)

1. 우루과이라운드 서비스협상과 관련 미국을 포함하여 각국은 해외 진출 민간기업, 재외공관을 통해서 아국에 대한 Request List (개방요구서)를 준비하고 있는바, 특히 미국은 '91. 2 개최된 UR/서비스 한.미 양자간 회의 이후 건설분야에 대하여 추가 질문을 보내오는등 지대한 관심을 보이고 있습니다.

2. 따라서 아국도 상대국(미국)에 대한 충실한 내용의 Request List 작성이 절실하게 요청됨에 따라 주재국 건설 서비스분야에 관한 다음 사항을 확인, 파악코자 하니 현지공관으로 하여금 조사후 회신토록 조치하여 주시기 바랍니다.

반송중 1991. 3. 20

가. Brooks Act (P.L. 92-582)에 따르면 공공공사의 A/E (설계-엔지니어링) 계약은 기술경쟁력, 경험, 과거실적 및 특수공법등을 평가기준으로 함으로써 외국업체가 불리한 대우를 받는 경우가 있을 것으로 사료되는바, 본 법의 시행기간, 기본목적, 외국업체에 불리한 조항의 유무 및 그 내용

나. 미 연방정부 및 미군 발주공사의 경우 1984년 10월부터 시행하고 있는 미국인 특혜정책(American Preference Policy)에 의거 공사금액 500만달러 이상의 공사에 있어 미국국적업체에 대한 20%의 우대 혜택을 부여

0215

2-1

/

해외 30600- 1991. 3. 20

하고 있는바 동 특혜정책의 근거(법령, 행정지시등), 시행기간, 특혜의 구체적 사례

다. 기타 아국업체의 미국내의 건설활동에 장애요소가 되는 사례 (각종공사의 입찰.계약시 외국인에 대한 차별, 위 "나"항과 유사한 미국인 특혜정책등)

3. 위 조사 의뢰사항은 대미 Request List 작성의 시급성을 감안 조사. 확인 즉시 전문 회신토록 하고 관련자료는 파편 송부되도록 아울러 조치하여 주시기 바랍니다. 끝.

전 건			전개(공람)		
접수일시	1991. 3. 20	번호 1026			
처리과					

검 토 필(1991. 6.30)

건 설 부 장

건설경제국장 전결

0216

2-2

김(요리)

원 본

외 무 부

종 별 :

번 호 : GVW-0516 일 시 : 91 0320 1530

수 신 : 장 관(통기,경기원)

발 신 : 주 제네바 대사

제 목 : UR/ 서비스 한.미 양자협의

1. 당지 USTR 제네바사무소에서는 별첨 (FAX 편송부)와 같이 서비스 OFFER 에 대한 양자협의를 위하여 4.10-4.19 기간중에 USTR JOSEPH PAPOVICH 를 수석대표로한 분야별 전문가 (금융, 증권제외, 보험, 통신, 노동력 이동 포함)들이 제네바에 올것임을 알려오면서 콩 기간중 하루 아국본부대표 파견 가능성을 문의하여 온바, 본부 대표파견 여부 및 양자협의 희망일자등을 조속 통보바람.

2. 미측 계획에 대한 여타국들의 동향은 추보예정임.

첨부: 관련 서한 1부.

(GVW(F)-0100). 끝

(대사 박수길-국장)

통상국 2차보 경기원

PAGE 1

91.03.21 09:22 WG

외신 1과 통제관

0217

20/00 '01 11:37 ☎700???? USTR GENEVA ☎002

GVW(T1) - 0/00
1.320 1530
" GVW-516 첨부"

UNITED STATES TRADE REPRESENTATIV
1-3 AVENUE DE LA PAIX
1202 GENEVA, SWITZERLAND
TELEPHONE: 732 09 70

March 20, 1991

The U.S. will be sending an interagency team to Geneva to conduct bilateral consultations on services offers. The interagency team headed by Joseph Papovich from USTR, Washington, D.C., will be address all service sectors, except banking and securities. (Banking and Securities will be the subject of separate consultations, at which both the U.S. Treasury and USTR will be present.) We would appreciate knowing if your government would be able to send a delegation from your capital any time during the period from April 10 through April 19. We expect the consultation to take half a day.

In addition to Joe Papovich, the U.S. delegation will include experts on insurance, telecommunications and labor mobility as well as other areas.

I would appreciate hearing from you as soon as possible, so we can prepare a more detailed schedule.

Please call me at 732 09 70 ext. 5310 or talk to my secretary Brita Lineburger ext. 5280 and let her know if a delegation from your country could be available during this period.

Sincerely,

Christina Lund

0218

1991-03-20 17:28 KOREAN MISSION GENEVA 2 022 791 0525 P.01

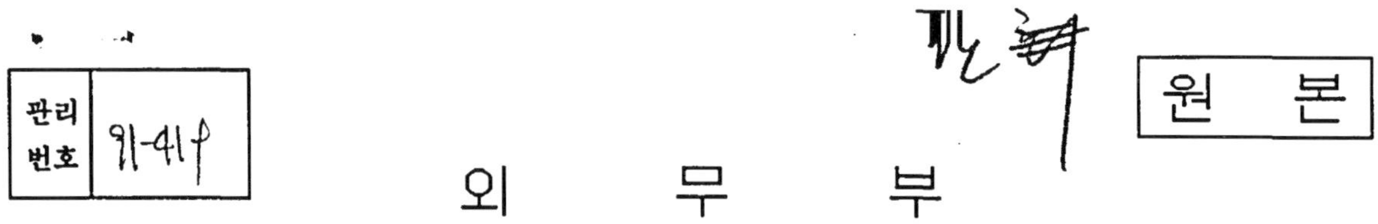

관리 번호 91-414

원 본

외 무 부

종 별 : 지 급

번 호 : USW-1359

일 시 : 91 0322 2017

수 신 : 장관(통기,통일,건설부)

발 신 : 주 미 대사

제 목 : UR/써비스

대 WUS-1073

연 USW-1303

1. 대호 BROOKS ACT 의 기본 목적은 별첨 동법의 LEGISLATIVE HISTORY(P.L.92-582, PP 4767-4775)에 표시된 바와같이, 연방 정부의 건설공사및 기술 용역 계약시 무자격 회사에 대한 수임으로 인한 부실 공사를 방지함에 있으며, 동법의LANGUAGE 상으로는 외국 회사에 대한 차별적 대우의 요소는 없는것으로 보임.

2. 또한 당지 법률 전문가들의 견해로는 집행기관(행정부)에서 동법 자체나동법의 LEGISLATIVE HISTORY 에 포함되지 않은 차별을 행하는것은 미국의 법제상 불가능할것이라함을 참고 바람.

3. 동 법의 시행 주체는 동법(별첨)SECTION 901 에 명기된바와같이 모든 연방 정부 기관장임.

4.AMERICAN PREFERENCE POLICY 관련 자료는 수집되는대로 추보 예정임.

첨부 USW(F)-0991

(대사 현홍주-국장)

91.12.31 까지

비밀해제됨(1991.6.30.) ⓘ

통상국 2차보 통상국 건설부

PAGE 1

91.03.23 11:35

외신 2과 통제관 CA

0219

번호: USW(F)
-0991
수신: 장관
(통기, 통일, 건설부)
발신: 주미대사
제목: 첨부(11 대)

"(e) Provisions of this section shall be effective only in the cases of members who, on or before June 30, 1975, execute the required written agreement to remain in active service."; and

(4) by inserting the following new item in the analysis:

"312a. Special pay: nuclear-trained and qualified enlisted members.".

Sec. 2. The provisions of section 7545(c) of title 10, United States Code, shall not apply with respect to any gift made after the date of enactment of this Act and prior to January 1, 1973, by the Department of the Navy to the city of Clifton Forge, Virginia, of a Baldwin steam locomotive (No. 606) which is no longer needed by the Navy and which has certain historical significance for the city of Clifton Forge, Virginia.

Approved October 27, 1972.

Brooks Act →

PUBLIC BUILDINGS—SELECTION OF ARCHITECTS AND ENGINEERS

For Legislative History of Act, see p. 4767

PUBLIC LAW 92-582; 86 STAT. 1278

[H. R. 12807]

An Act to amend the Federal Property and Administrative Services Act of 1949 in order to establish Federal policy concerning the selection of firms and individuals to perform architectural, engineering, and related services for the Federal Government.

Be it enacted by the Senate and House of Representatives of the United States of America in Congress assembled, That:

The Federal Property and Administrative Services Act of 1949 (40 U.S.C. 471 et seq.) [64] is amended by adding at the end thereof the following new title:

"TITLE IX—SELECTION OF ARCHITECTS AND ENGINEERS

"DEFINITIONS

"Sec. 901. As used in this title—

"(1) The term 'firm' means any individual, firm, partnership, corporation, association, or other legal entity permitted by law to practice the professions of architecture or engineering.

"(2) The term 'agency head' means the Secretary, Administrator, or head of a department, agency, or bureau of the Federal Government.

"(3) The term 'architectural and engineering services' includes those professional services of an architectural or engineering nature as well as incidental services that members of these professions and those in their employ may logically or justifiably perform.

"POLICY

"Sec. 902. The Congress hereby declares it to be the policy of the Federal Government to publicly announce all requirements for archi-

64. 40 U.S.C.A. § 471 et seq.

tectural and engineering services, and to negotiate contracts for architectural and engineering services on the basis of demonstrated competence and qualification for the type of professional services required and at fair and reasonable prices.

"REQUESTS FOR DATA ON ARCHITECTURAL AND ENGINEERING SERVICES

"Sec. 903. In the procurement of architectural and engineering services, the agency head shall encourage firms engaged in the lawful practice of their profession to submit annually a statement of qualifications and performance data. The agency head, for each proposed project, shall evaluate current statements of qualifications and performance data on file with the agency, together with those that may be submitted by other firms regarding the proposed project, and shall conduct discussions with no less than three firms regarding anticipated concepts and the relative utility of alternative methods of approach for furnishing the required services and then shall select therefrom, in order to preference, based upon criteria established and published by him, no less than three of the firms deemed to be the most highly qualified to provide the services required.

"NEGOTIATION OF CONTRACTS FOR ARCHITECTURAL AND ENGINEERING SERVICES

"Sec. 904. (a) The agency head shall negotiate a contract with the highest qualified firm for architectural and engineering services at compensation which the agency head determines is fair and reasonable to the Government. In making such determination, the agency head shall take into account the estimated value of the services to be rendered, the scope, complexity, and professional nature thereof.

"(b) Should the agency head be unable to negotiate a satisfactory contract with the firm considered to be the most qualified, at a price he determines to be fair and reasonable to the Government, negotiations with that firm should be formally terminated. The agency head should then undertake negotiations with the second most qualified firm. Failing accord with the second most qualified firm, the agency head should terminate negotiations. The agency head should then undertake negotiations with the third most qualified firm.

"(c) Should the agency head be unable to negotiate a satisfactory contract with any of the selected firms, he shall select additional firms in order of their competence and qualification and continue negotiations in accordance with this section until an agreement is reached."

Approved October 27, 1972.

0991-2

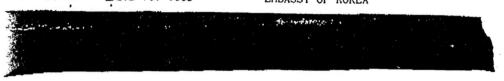

PUBLIC BUILDINGS
P.L. 92-582

PUBLIC BUILDINGS—SELECTION OF ARCHITECTS AND ENGINEERS

P.L. 92-582, see page 1486

House Report (Government Operations Committee) No. 92-1188, June 28, 1972 [To accompany H.R. 12807]

Senate Report (Government Operations Committee) No. 92-1219, Sept. 25, 1972 [To accompany H.R. 12807]

Cong. Record Vol. 118 (1972)

DATES OF CONSIDERATION AND PASSAGE

House July 26, 1972

Senate October 14, 1972

The Senate Report is set out.

SENATE REPORT NO. 92-1219

THE Committee on Government Operations, to which was referred the bill (H.R. 12807) to amend the Federal Property and Administrative Services Act of 1949, in order to establish Federal policy concerning the selection of firms and individuals to perform architectural, engineering, and related services for the Federal Government, having considered the same, reports favorably thereon without amendment and recommends that the bill do pass.

Purpose

The purpose of H.R. 12807 is to cast in statutory form the traditional system Government agencies have used for more than 30 years in the procurement of architect-engineer services. The bill would amend the Federal Property and Administrative Services Act of 1949 to establish a Federal policy for the selection of qualified architects and engineers to design and provide consultant services in carrying out Federal construction and related programs. The bill expressly declares it to be the policy of the Federal Government to negotiate contracts for such professional services on the basis of demonstrated competence and qualifications for the type of professional service required at fair and reasonable prices.

Background

On April 20, 1967, the Comptroller General of the United States requested Congress to clarify by legislation the procedure used in selecting architect and engineering services under Federal procurement statues. The Comptroller General subsequently recomendmed that the selection process for these services follow a competitive pricing procedure under which the amount of the fee to be paid would be considered a factor in the selection process. The Comptroller General has recom-

0991-3

0222

mended that the 6-percent limitation on architect-engineer fees should be repealed.

Legislation similar to H.R. 12807 was passed by the House during the 91st Congress and reported by this committee. However, Congress adjourned before the Senate could act on the measure.

A bill, S. 3156, was introduced in the 92d Congress by Senator McClellan and Senator Percy which is substantially similar to H.R. 12807.

There are several differences between H.R. 12807 and the measure reported by the committee in the 91st Congress. First, language was added to require public announcement of all requests for A/E services. This will assure that all interested A/E's have the opportunity to learn about the Government's requirements for design services. Such mandatory public announcement is designed to enhance further competition among A/E's for Government contracts.

H.R. 12807 also was modified to reflect the suggestion that discussions of anticipated concepts and the relative utility of alternative methods for furnishing required services should be taken into account in evaluating the relative competence and qualifications of A/E's and not wait until negotiations are already underway with the selected A/E.

Finally, at the suggestion of the General Services Administration, language was added to improve the selection procedure, should none of the originally selected firms agree to a satisfactory contract.

Explanation of the Bill

H.R. 12807 responds to the Comptroller General's request that Congress clarify the procedure for selecting architects and engineers. The bill retains the present practice of selecting the best qualified design professional, subject to the negotiation of compensation that is fair and reasonable to the Government.

The bill does not affect existing statutes which limit architect-engineer fees to 6 percent of the estimated construction cost. The 6-percent limitation, when applied to the preparation of designs, plans, drawings, and specifications as Congress intended, is a valuable safeguard to the public. While the limitation may pose some difficulty in negotiating fair compensation for small projects, renovation work and projects requiring exceptional design effort, the 6-percent fee limitation is deemed to be an equitable ceiling.

H.R. 12807 restates the selection procedure generally applied in the procurement of architectural and engineering services—a procedure which Federal, State, and local governments have been using for more than 80 years, and which is also followed to a large degree by the private sector. Under this selection procedure, architects and engineers compete on the basis of their respective capabilities, qualifications, and experience as they relate to a proposed project. A/E's are ranked by the procuring agency on the basis of their ability to perform the project. Negotiations are then conducted with the top ranking firm to arrive at the compensation for the project. Under H.R. 12807, the compensation paid must be "fair and reasonable to the Government." Furthermore, the architect engineer fee for the preparation of designs, plans, drawings, and specifications can be no more than 6 percent of the estimated construction cost of the project. The 6-percent limitation has been in existence since 1939 and is not changed by H.R. 12807.

0991-4

0223

As provided in the bill, architectural and engineering firms engaged in the lawful practice of their profession, are encouraged to submit annually a statement of qualifications and performance data to the agencies concerned with the procurement of such professional services. The agency head, for each proposed project after public announcement, must evaluate current statements of qualifications and performance data on file with the agency, together with those that may be submitted by other firms and then select in order of preference, no less than three of the firms deemed to be the most highly qualified to provide the services required, based upon criteria which he has established and published.

The agency head then enters into negotiations with the firm deemed most qualified, and a contract is let if a fee (comprising the architect's or engineer's cost of performing the services, plus his anticipated profit) that is fair and reasonable to the Government can be agreed upon. In making his determination, the agency head must take into account the estimated value of the services to be rendered and their scope, complexity, and professional nature.

In the event the most qualified architect or engineer is unwilling to perform the prospective services for a fee that is determined to be fair and reasonable to the Government, negotiations are terminated and the agency head must then enter into negotiations with the second most qualified firm. Failing accord with that firm, negotiations are commenced with the third most qualified firm.

If a contract with any of the highest qualified firms cannot be negotiated, additional firms must be selected in order of their competence and qualification, and negotiations continued until a contract is consummated.

Under this procedure, negotiations are conducted on the basis of a detailed analysis of the cost to perform the required service, plus a reasonable profit. Architects and engineers know that regardless of high ranking, their failure to agree to a fee that is fair and reasonable to the Government will deprive them of the opportunity to obtain the contract in question and that the Government will initiate negotiations with other firms.

In support of this procedure, the House Committee on Government Operations, which held hearings on the bill, makes the following pertinent observations in its report on H.R. 12807:

> The system favors selection of the most skilled and responsible members of these professions. Competition for Government contracts is based on qualifications and experience—terms of competition that qualified members of any profession or field of endeavor are willing to meet. Under this system, A/E's are under no compunction to compromise the quality of the design or the level of effort they will contribute to it in order to meet the lower "fee" quotations of other A/E's. They are free to suggest optimum design approaches that may cost more to design, but can save in construction costs and otherwise increase the quality of the building or facility to be constructed.
>
> This system protects the interests of the taxpayers. Having won the competition on the basis of capability, the winning A/E must then negotiate his fee. He must demonstrate on the basis of projected costs that his fee is fair and reasonable. He must accept whatever adjustments the Government de-

0991-5

0224

mands if he wishes to obtain the contract. He knows that if he holds out for an unfair or unreasonable fee, the Government will terminate the negotiations and award the contract to another A/E at a fair and reasonable price.

The procurement of architectural and engineering services has traditionally been recognized as presenting unique considerations. Like the medical and legal professions, the architectural and engineering professions demand abundant learning, skill, and integrity, requiring a broad spectrum of capabilities that for the best results must be closely matched with the needs and requirements of those who contract for them.

Miscellaneous Considerations

A question has been raised about the effect that H.R. 12807 may have on the antitrust laws of the United States. The question was raised because the Antitrust Division of the Justice Department had filed suits against the American Society of Civil Engineers and the American Institute of Architects aimed at deleting provisions in their codes of ethics prohibiting competitive bidding for professional services.

Realizing that such antitrust issue might be raised incident to this legislation, Mr. Brooks, chairman of the House Government Activities Subcommittee, which held hearings on H.R. 12807, addressed a letter to the Acting Attorney General on March 6, 1972, requesting that either he or a representative of the Department appear at a subcommittee hearing and state the position of the Department on the bill.

On April 18, Mr. Bruce Wilson, Acting Deputy Assistant Attorney General, Antitrust Division, representing the Department of Justice, appeared before the subcommittee.

During his testimony, Congressman Brooks asked:

> My question is, Does the bill as it is written, in its substance, violate the antitrust laws of the United States?

In his response, Mr. Wilson stated:

> No, Mr. Chairman; I don't think it does. Quite clearly, it is not a violation of the antitrust laws. What we are talking about here is not really antitrust laws as such. What we are talking about is competition policy and philosophy.

Another question raised concerning the bill relates to whether Congress should act on architect-engineer procurement before the Commission on Government Procurement reports to the Congress. This question also was considered by the House Government Operations Committee. It observed that:

> More than 5 years have passed from the time the Comptroller General originally requested Congress to clarify the legality of the traditional procedure the Government has used to procure A/E services. Subsequently, Congress established a Commission on Federal Procurement which, at this time, is making a broad evaluation of the Government's procurement policies for the purpose of submitting recommendations to the Congress as to how they might be improved.
>
> Were the procurement procedures reflected in H.R. 12807 an abrupt change or a new approach to the acquisition of A/E services, there might be reasonable justification for postpon-

0991-6

ing action on this bill until Congress had the opportunity to study the recommendations of the Procurement Commission. However, H.R. 12807 simply casts traditional A/E service procurement procedures into statutory form. This would clear up the uncertainty caused by the report of the Comptroller General that was submitted to Congress more than 5 years ago and end the confusion that has been caused by his efforts to establish his approach to A/E procurement as a substitute for the traditional time-tested procedures that are recognized in this bill.

Assurances of the Comptroller General that he will hold off enforcement of his interpretation of the law pending congressional and Procurement Commission review of the issue do not solve the problem. It is questionable, at best, whether Congress has authorized the Comptroller General, in his discretion, to withhold the imposition of such an interpretation of Federal statutes, once he has determined that Federal agencies are expending funds "illegally." Recognition of such discretionary authority could distort the relationship between congressional committees and the Office of the Comptroller General. It logically raises questions as to the circumstances in which the authority would be exercised and in what circumstances it would be withheld.

If the Commission should recommend a better procurement procedure, then Congress could amend the law to reflect the Commission's recommendations. Meanwhile, time continues to pass and the uncertainty as to A/E procurement procedures remains with us. Even assuming that the Procurement Commission were to render its final report within the next several months, a lengthy period of evaluation of the Commission's recommendations by the Congress would be essential. The time has come, therefore, to clarify existing law.

Although the Procurement Commission report will not be available for consideration by this Congress, the committee intends to expedite action on the Commission's recommendations pertaining to A/E services as early as possible next year. The committee also expects that upon its request, the Administrator of General Services, as well as other Federal agencies and departments, will furnish to the committee a full statement and explanation of any contract for A/E services negotiated pursuant to the provisions of this bill.

Differences Between House and Senate Bills

S. 3156 and H.R. 12807 are similar in their intent and substance. The primary difference between the two bills is that the Senate bill has a section applying the architect-engineer procurement requirements to the military services while the House bill has no such provision.

The committee believes the statement of policy contained in the House bill applies to all agencies of the Federal Government. Furthermore, Congress has made it clear on several occasions (e.g., H. Rept. 90-1860) that the traditional method of selecting architects and engineers is to be followed by the military agencies.

Since the military agencies are currently following the architect-engineer selection procedures as set forth in H.R. 12807, and would be

0991-7 4771

0226

LEGISLATIVE HISTORY
P.L. 92-582

expected to continue such procedures in accordance with the statement of policy contained in H.R. 12807, further amendment of the military procurement law is not deemed necessary.

Conclusion

The enactment of H.R. 12807 would insure the continuation of the Government's basic procurement procedure, with respect to architectural and engineering services, which has been in operation for more than 30 years. It is also the traditional system of procurement for similar services utilized by State and local governments.

It should be noted that architectural and engineering services are generally exempt under State and local statutes requiring public contracts to be awarded only after calling for bids. The practice of both professions is subject to regulation and licensing under the laws of the various States. Under the principles of common law, the relationship between the architect or engineer and his employer requires a higher level of trust and confidence, and good faith and loyalty than is normally imposed between parties to a simple contract.

The costs for architectural and engineering services in the construction of a structure or a facility generally represent a very small part of the total cost of construction, and yet those services are basic and essential to the quality of construction of the building or facility.

The Committee on Government Operations is always concerned with the element of cost in all Federal endeavors. In this instance, the committee feels that the Government's interest, which is the public interest, is best served by placing the emphasis on obtaining the highest qualified architectural and engineering services available. The bill makes ample provision for keeping costs under control by requiring negotiation for a fee that is fair and reasonable to the Government under the circumstances and by retaining the statutory 6-percent limitation on architect-engineer fees. Failure for any reason to provide the highest quality plans and specifications may well result in higher construction costs, a functionally inferior structure, or troublesome maintenance problems.

The bill is supported by the Administrator of General Services and is in keeping with the selection practices of those departments and agencies having construction and engineering responsibilities.

Estimate of Cost of H.R. 12807

As this proposal casts in statutory form the traditional system Government agencies have used for more than 80 years in the procurement of architect-engineer services, no additional cost can be anticipated as a result of enactment of H.R. 12807.

Section-by-Section Analysis

Section 901

This section contains definitions limiting and defining the scope of the bill. In subsection (1) the term "firm" is defined to mean an individual firm, partnership, corporation, association, or other legal entity permitted to practice the profession of architecture or engineering. This definition has a dual effect: first, it limits the scope of the bill to the procurement of services which members of these professions provide; and second, the definition would have the effect of

0991-8 4772

0227

PUBLIC BUILDINGS
P.L. 92-582

requiring members of these professions to be properly licensed under the appropriate registration laws of the States and other jurisdictions governing their practice. Thus, the bill relates to architects and/or engineers who are registered under statutes that require, on the basis of education, experience, and other appropriate criteria, a high level of professional capability.

This definition requires utilization of the method of selection provided in the bill for the procurement of architectural and engineering services, or also when the scope and the nature of the proposal, to a substantial or dominant extent, logically falls within the unique expertise of these professions.

Subsection (2) defines "agency head" as the Secretary, Administrator, or head of a department, agency, or bureau of the Federal Government. This definition does not rule out the submission of recommendations by subordinate officials or advisory committees, groups, or commissions of architects and/or engineers established by the agency head for the purpose of providing independent expert judgment in ranking the capability of architectural and engineering firms in relation to any proposed project.

This definition, of course, is subject to the exemptions in the Federal Property and Administrative Services Act set forth in 40 U.S.C. 474. These exemptions include any agencies falling within the jurisdiction of the Armed Services Procurement Act of 1947.

Subsection (3) defines "professional services" as those of an architectural or engineering nature, as well as ancillary services, that members of these professions or those in their employ may logically or justifiably perform. The purpose of this definition is to encompass all of the services which architects and engineers might logically or justifiably perform.

Section 902

This section declares as a policy of Congress that all agencies of the Federal Government shall negotiate contracts for architectural, engineering, and related professional services on the basis of a selection process based upon competence and capability and a price that is fair and reasonable to the Government.

This policy embodies the traditional methods of architect and engineer selection as reflected in this bill. And, further, it shows that Congress considers this selection method as an acceptable application of "competitive negotiation" for the procurement of these services.

This section expressly provides for public announcements of all requirements for architectural and engineering services, thus assuring the broadest publicity concerning Government A/E service procurements at a high level of competition in the award of A/E contracts.

Section 903

This section allows for the annual submission of statements of qualifications and performance data, which would avoid the cumbersome and costly administrative problem of dealing with these statements were they required to be submitted in response to each proposed project. Those architects and engineers who are interested in any proposed project but who had not previously filed such a statement would also be eligible for consideration upon submission of a current statement of qualifications and performance data. Section 903 provides for the establishment and publication by the agency head of criteria to be followed by him in the ranking of architects and engineers on the basis of their qualifications and capability to perform the proposed project.

This section does not require the submission of preliminary designs, plans, drawings, specifications, or other material relating to the proposed project. In unique situations involving "prestige" projects such as the design of memorials and structures of unusual national significance, when the additional cost justifies the approach, and when time allows, the agency head can rely upon design competition under the recognized procedures that have been traditionally applied to this type of procurement. Generally, however, it is expected that the agency head, through discussions with an appropriate number of the firms interested in the project, will obtain sufficient knowledge as to the varying architectural and engineering techniques that, together with the information on file with the agency, will make it possible for him to make a meaningful ranking. Under no circumstances should the criteria developed by an agency head relating to the ranking of architects and engineers on the basis of their professional qualifications include or relate to the fee to be paid to the firm, either directly or indirectly.

Section 904

Section 904(a) sets out the primary negotiation stage once the selection process has been completed. This section requires that the determination of the fee be fair and reasonable to the Government, taking into account the estimated value of the services to be rendered and the scope, complexity, and professional nature of the performance required of the architect or the engineer. The phrase "highest qualified" as used in this section relates back to the selection made in section 903. This phrase is not limited merely to the technical acceptability of the firm, but includes other meaningful, pertinent considerations which have been universally applied in determining relative qualifications of architects and engineers to perform a specific project, and which relate to the quality of the work the Government might reasonably expect from members of these professions.

Section 904(b) states the procedure to be followed should the highest ranking firm fail to agree to a fee the agency head determines is fair and reasonable to the Government. This section states that negotiations with the architects or engineers who are ranked first, second, and third, and so on be conducted independently and in a series. If the agency head determines that the highest ranking firm will not agree to a fee that is fair and reasonable to the Government, no further negotiations shall be conducted with that firm on the basis of that proposal. The agency head will then attempt to negotiate a contract with the next most qualified architect or engineer, and so on, until a contract is consummated at a fee that is fair and reasonable to the Government.

Section 904(c) would allow the agency head to select additional firms in order of competence and qualification and continue negotiations in accordance with earlier provisions of the act until an agreement is reached, should he be unable to negotiate a satisfactory contract with the firms originally selected.

0991-10

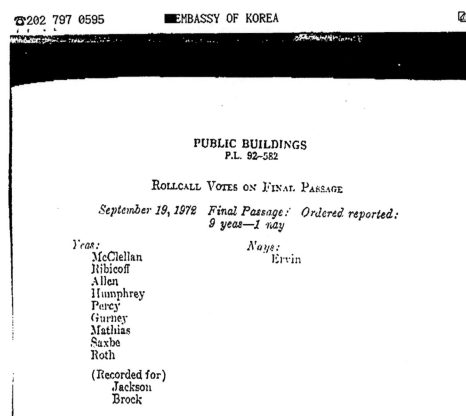

PUBLIC BUILDINGS
P.L. 92-582

ROLLCALL VOTES ON FINAL PASSAGE

September 19, 1972 Final Passage: Ordered reported: 9 yeas—1 nay

Yeas:
McClellan
Ribicoff
Allen
Humphrey
Percy
Gurney
Mathias
Saxbe
Roth

(Recorded for)
Jackson
Brock

Nays:
Ervin

September 20, 1972 Motion to Reconsider: Adopted: 8 yeas—6 nays

Yeas:
McClellan
Jackson
Ribicoff
Allen
Humphrey
Chiles
Javits
Ervin

Nays:
Percy
Mathias
Roth

(Proxy)
Gurney
Saxbe
Brock

September 20, 1972 Final Passage: Ordered reported: 9 yeas—2 nays

Yeas:
McClellan
Jackson
Ribicoff
Allen
Humphrey
Percy
Javits
Mathias
Roth

(Recorded for)
Metcalf
Gurney
Saxbe
Brock

Nays:
Ervin
Chiles

0991-11

4775

0230

관리번호	91-309

발 신 전 보

	분류번호	보존기간

번 호 : WUS-1140 910323 1321 AO 종별 :

WUK -0553 WJA -1328

수 신 : 주 미, 영, 일 대사. 총영사

발 신 : 장 관 (통 기)

제 목 : UR/해운 서비스 분야 개방요구서 작성

UR 서비스 협상과 관련, 협상 상대국에 대한 아국의 개방요구서 작성에 참고코자 하니 아래 사항에 관한 자료를 91.4.30한 수집 제출바람.

1. 해운시장 규제제도 및 관행

2. 자국업체에 대한 각종 보조 및 지원제도

3. 아국업체에 대한 차별사항등. 끝.

(통상국장 대리 최 혁)

일반문서로 재분류 (1991. 6 .30 .)

보안통제	

앙고재	년월일	과	기안자 성명		과 장		국 장		차 관	장 관

외신과통제

0231

원 본

외 무 부

종 별 :

번 호 : GVW-0566 일 시 : 91 0326 1840

수 신 : 장 관(통기,경기원,재무부)

발 신 : 주 제네바 대사

제 목 : UR/ 서비스 협상

연: GVW-0428, 0561

1. UR/ 서비스 주요국 비공식 협의

0 DUNKEL 총장이 주재하는 상기 협의는 별첨 (FAX 편 송부)과 같이 4.10(수) 및 4.11(목) 오전중 33개국 참석하에 개최될 예정임.

- 동 협의에 대비하여 갓트 사무국에서 NATIONALSCHEDULE 작성방법, 서비스 분야 분류목록, MFN적용의 예외가 필요한 수평적 협정에 관한 CHECK LIST 등 배경문서를 준비중에 있으나 동문서의 배포 여부 및 배포시기는 현재로서는 알수없는 상태임.

- 한편 상기 작업 과제가 기술적으로 복잡한 반면, 회의 개최 일자가 하루반에 불과하고 참서국이 33개국에 달하다는 점등에서 상기협에에서 본격적인 토의가 이루어지기 어려운 면이있다는 점을 고려할때, 동 협의 이외에 또다른 형태의 비공식 협의 개최 가능성도 있는 것으로 판단됨.

2. 미국이 추진하는 양자 협의

0 미국은 지난주에 EC, 북구등 유럽국가들과 각국 OFFER 의 명확화를 위한 2차양자 협의를 가졌으며, 4.10-4.19 주간에는 아시아.태평양지역 국가 및 터키, 이노, 파키스탄 등과 2차 협의를 가질 예정인바, 요청받은 대부분의 나라가 동 협의에 응할 계획이며, 구체적인 날짜를 교섭중에 있다고 함.

3. 금융분야에 관한 비공식 협의

0 카나다는 4.22 주간에 (4.23-24 로 예정) DUNKEL총장 주재 비공식 협의 참석국가를 대상으로 서비스 협상 담당자와 금융 전문가가 함께 참석하는 금융분야 부속서에 관한 비공식 협의를 계획하고 있다고 함.

첨부: UR/ 서비스 주요국 비공식 협의 개최 계획1부. 끝 (대사 박수길 - 국장)

(GVW(F)-106)

통상국 2차보 경기원 재무부

PAGE 1 91.03.27 08:41 WG

외신 1과 통제관

0232

1991-03-26 19:49 KOR MISSION GENEVA 2 022 791 P.01

GVW(H)-0106 10326 1840

GATT FACSIMILE TRANSMISSION

"GVW-566 첨부"

Centre William Rappard
Rue de Lausanne 154
CH-1211 Genève 21

Telefax: (022) 731 42 06
Telex: 412324 GATT CH
Telephone: (022) 739 51 11

TOTAL NUMBER OF PAGES 1
(including this preface)

Date: 25 March 1991

From: Arthur Dunkel
Director-General
GATT, Geneva

Signature: A. Dunkel

To:			
ARGENTINA	H.E. Mr. J.A. Lanus	Fax No:	798 72 82
AUSTRALIA	H.E. Mr. D. Hawes		733 65 86
AUSTRIA	H.E. Mr. F. Ceska		734 45 91
BRAZIL	H.E. Mr. R. Ricupero		733 28 34
CANADA	H.E. Mr. J.M. Weekes		734 79 19
CHILE	H.E. Mr. M. Artaza		734 41 94
CHINA	H.E. Mr. Fan Guoxiang		793 70 14
COLOMBIA	H.E. Mr. F. Jaramillo		791 07 87
COSTA RICA	H.E. Mr. R. Barzuna		733 28 69
EEC	H.E. Mr. Tran Van-Thinh		734 22 36
EGYPT	Mr. M.H. El-Falaky		731 68 28
HONG KONG	Mr. K. Broadbridge		733 99 04
HUNGARY	Mr. A. Szepesi		738 46 09
INDIA	H.E. Mr. B.K. Zutshi		738 45 48
JAPAN	H.E. Mr. H. Ukawa		733 20 87
KOREA	H.E. Mr. S.G. Park		791 05 25
MALAYSIA	Mr. Supperamanian Manickam		788 04 92
MEXICO	H.E. Mr. J. Seade		733 48 10
MOROCCO	H.E. Mr. M. El Ghali Benhima		798 47 02
NEW ZEALAND	H.E. Mr. T.J. Hannah		734 30 62
NIGERIA	H.E. Mr. E.A. Azikiwe		734 10 53
PAKISTAN	H.E. Mr. A. Kamal		734 80 85
PERU	Mr. C. Gutierrez		731 11 68
PHILIPPINES	H.E. Mrs. N.L. Escaler		731 68 88
SINGAPORE	H.E. Mr. See Chak Mun		45 79 10
SWEDEN	H.E. Mr. L.E.R. Anell		733 12 89
SWITZERLAND	H.E. Mr. W. Rossier		734 56 23
TANZANIA	H.E. Mr. A.H. Jamal		732 82 55
THAILAND	H.E. Mr. Tej Bunnag		733 36 78
UNITED STATES	H.E. Mr. R.H. Yerxa		799 08 85
URUGUAY	H.E. Mr. J.A. Lacarte-Muró		731 56 30
VENEZUELA	H.E. Mr. H. Arteaga		798 58 77
YUGOSLAVIA	H.E. Mr. N. Calovski		46 44 36

The next consultations on services, to which your delegation is invited, will be held in Room E of the Centre William Rappard on Wednesday, 10 April 1991, starting at 10 a.m., and will continue all day on Wednesday, and on Thursday, 11 April in the morning. Attendance is restricted to two persons per delegation.

Should I attend ?
Park

0233

PLEASE NOTIFY US IMMEDIATELY IF YOU DO NOT RECEIVE ALL THE PAGES

** OUR FAX EQUIPMENT IS HITACHI HIFAX 210 (COMPATIBLE WITH GROUPS 2 AND 3) AND IS SET TO RECEI

관리번호	91-226

외 무 부

종 별 : 지 급

번 호 : USW-1415 일 시 : 91 0327 1609

수 신 : 장관(통기, 통일, 경기원,건설부,상공부)

발 신 : 주 미 대사

제 목 : UR/건설 서비스 및 정부 조달

대:WUS-1073

연:USW-1303,1359

1. 대호 , 정부 발주 서비스 계약(건설포함)및 물자조달과 관련된 미국의 AMERICAN PREFERENCE POLICY 및 기타 전반적인 미국인 특혜 정책과 관련, 당지 PAUL WEISS 법률회사가 당관에 협조해 온 보고서를 별첨 송부함.

2. 동 보고서에 의하면, 미국인 특혜부여의 일반적 근거는 BUY AMERICAN ACT 로서 동법은 미 연방정부의 물자 및 건설자재 구매 계약시 통상 6 %(영세기업등에 대해서는 12 %)의 특혜를 부여토록 되어 있음.

3. 그러나, 1979 GOVERNMENT PROCUREMENT AND TRADE AGREEMENT ACT 에 의하여, 정부 조달 협정 가입국의 협정 대상품목에 대하여는 상기와같은 차별이 면제됨.(단, 88 종합 통상법 규정에 의하여 정부 조달협정 가입국이라 하더라도 협정의무를 성실히 이행치 않는 (NOT IN GOOD STANDING) 국가등에 대하여는 면제 부여를 중지하도록 규정)

4. 기타 국방관련 부문에서는 연례 국방성 예산 법안상 외국기업에 대하여 상기 2 항보다 심한 차별을 부과할수 있도록 되어 있다함.

5.PAUL, WEISS 사에서 작성한 최근 걸프전후의 미국 경제현황에 관한 보고서도 참고로 별첨 송부함.

첨부:USW(F)-1038 (42 매)

(대사 현홍주-장관)

예고:91.12.31 까지

김 도 필(1991.6.30.) 0

일반문서로 재분류(1991 .12. 31.)

통상국	장관	차관	1차보	2차보	통상국	청와대	경기원	상공부
건설부								

PAGE 1 91.03.28 07:55

외신 2과 통제관 BW

0234

주 미 대 사 관

보안 통제	

번호 : USW(F) - 1038

수신 : 장 관 (통기, 통일, 경기원, 건설부, 상공부)

발신 : 주미대사

제목 : 첨부. (표지 제외 42 매)

USW -1415의 첨부

0235

Re: <u>U.S. Government Procurement</u>

This memorandum discusses the existing barriers to the purchase of Korean products by the U.S. government and provides an analysis of possible courses of action to provide Korean products greater access to the U.S. government procurement market.

A. <u>United States Government Procurement</u>

The U.S. government is perhaps the largest purchaser of goods and services in the world, having spent $174.1 billion in 1988 alone. Approximately $85.5 billion, or about 49 percent of the total expenditure was for supplies and equipment.[1/] Other major expenditure categories included general services (25.7 percent), research and development (15.7 percent), construction (6.7 percent), automatic data processing (1.4 percent), and

---

1 A list of the types of equipment and supplies purchased by the U.S. government in fiscal year 1988 and the dollar amounts for each type are set forth in Exhibit A attached hereto. The list is published by the General Services Administration's Federal Procurement Data Center as part of its Federal Procurement Data System Standard Report, which is published every three months.

1038 - 1

0236

architecture and engineering (1.3 percent). The bulk of the U.S. government's purchases were made by the following agencies:

	Dollar Amount	Percentage of
Department of Defense	$134.9 billion	77.4%
Department of Energy	14.4 billion	8.2%
National Aeronautics and Space Administration	8.3 billion	4.7%
Department of Agriculture	2.28 billion	1.3%
General Services Administration[2]	2.14 billion	1.2%
Veterans Administration	2.03 billion	1.1%
Department of Transportation	1.5 billion	.9%

The sale of Korean products to this large market is impaired by (1) the Buy American Act,[3] which requires the U.S. government to give a preference to U.S. products in the procurement of supplies and construction materials, (2) the Trade Agreements Act of 1979,[4] which prohibits designated U.S. government agencies from purchasing certain products from nations, such as Korea, that have

---

2 The General Services Administration procures goods and services for agencies other than the Department of Defense.

3 41 U.S.C. §§ 10a-10d.

4 19 U.S.C. §§ 2511-2518.

1038-2

0237

not signed the Agreement on Government Procurement,[5] and (3) Annual Appropriations Acts for the Defense Department. The actual effect of these statutes will depend on several factors, including the particular product involved, the particular agency purchasing the product, and the particular type of contract. As noted below, the net effect of the Trade Agreements Act is to prevent Korea from supplying products under $20 to $30 billion worth of contracts.

B. Buy American Act

1. Supply Contracts

Under Section 2 of the Buy American Act, U.S. government agencies may purchase (1) unmanufactured articles, materials and supplies only if they are produced in the United States and (2) manufactured articles, materials and supplies only if they are manufactured in the U.S. substantially from U.S. produced articles, materials or supplies. Section 2 provides exceptions to this general rule if (1) the cost of the U.S. product is unreasonable, (2) the products are for use outside the

5 The Agreement on Government Procurement ("the Agreement"), negotiated under the General Agreement on Tariffs and Trade, is implemented in the United States by the Trade Agreements Act of 1979 (19 U.S.C. §§ 2511-2518 (1987)) and regulations issued thereunder. The purpose of the Agreement on Government Procurement is to open up government contracting opportunities for products from the signatory nations.

0238

1038 - 3

U.S., (3) the products are not manufactured in the U.S. in sufficient and reasonably available commercial quantities and of satisfactory quality, or (4) the agency determines that the domestic preference would be inconsistent with the public interest.[6]

The cost of a U.S. product will be considered "unreasonable" if it exceeds the cost of the foreign product by 6 percent (12 percent if the U.S. product is offered by a small business or a business in a labor surplus area).[7] For example, if a foreign product costs $100, the U.S. Government will purchase a U.S. product that costs up to $106, even though it is more expensive. For Department of Defense purchases, a substantial <u>50 percent</u> preference is given. Thus, under the previous example, the Department of Defense would purchase a U.S. product even if it costs up to $150, or 50 percent more than a foreign product.[8]

2. <u>Construction Contracts</u>

In connection with construction contracts, Section 3 of the Buy American Act similarly prohibits the

---

6 These products generally consist of raw materials, not manufactured articles, and are listed in 48 C.F.R. § 25.108, which is attached hereto as Exhibit B.

7 48 C.F.R. § 25.105.

8 Department of Defense Supplement to the Federal Acquisition Regulation § 25.105; 48 C.F.R. § 225.105.

1038 -4

0239

purchase of non-U.S. construction materials unless (1) the use of U.S. materials would be impracticable, (2) U.S. materials are unavailable in sufficient and reasonably available quantities and of a satisfactory quality, or (3) the use of U.S. materials would unreasonably increase the cost.

3. Amendments to the Buy American Act Under the Omnibus Trade and Competitiveness Act of 1988

The Buy American Act was recently expanded by amendments in the Trade and Competitiveness Act of 1988.[9] The new sections added to the Buy American Act prohibit the U.S. government from procuring products from (1) signatories "not in good standing" to the Agreement on Government Procurement, (2) signatories that discriminate against U.S. firms in the signatory government's procurement of products or services not covered by the Agreement,[10] and (3) nonsignatory countries whose governments discriminate against U.S. products or services in their procurement.

---

9 Pub. L. No. 100-418, § 7002, 102 Stat. 1545-47 (1988).

10 Since such signatory countries are in compliance with the Agreement, and thereby retain their "good standing" under the Agreement, Federal agencies would be prohibited from procuring only non-Agreement covered products from these countries; "eligible products" under the Agreement are exempt from the ban.

1038 - 5

0240

The Trade and Competitiveness Act applies the same prohibition in regard to contracts from a country discriminating against U.S. firms for the procurement of a <u>service</u> of any contractor or subcontractor that (1) is a citizen or national of a foreign country falling within one of these three categories listed above, or (2) is owned or controlled directly or indirectly by citizens or nationals of a foreign country falling within one of these three categories.[11] This prohibition would apply to

---

11 Under the statute, a contractor or subcontractor is deemed to be owned or controlled directly or indirectly by citizens or nationals of a foreign country if:

(A) 50 percent or more of the voting stock of the contractor or subcontractor is owned by one or more citizens or nationals of the foreign country;

(B) the title to 50 percent or more of the stock of the contractor or subcontractor is held subject to trust or fiduciary obligations in favor of one or more citizens or nationals of the foreign country;

(C) 50 percent or more of the voting stock of the contractor or subcontractor is vested in or exercisable on behalf of one or more citizens or nationals of the foreign country;

(D) the case of a corporation -

(i) the number of its directors necessary to constitute a quorum are citizens or nationals of the foreign country; or

(ii) the corporation is organized (footnote continued)

1038-6

0241

construction services.

The President must submit a report to Congress by April 30, 1990 identifying those countries which discriminate against U.S. products or services in government procurement.

C. Agreement on Government Procurement and Trade Agreements Act of 1979

The U.S., along with 45 other countries,[12/] is a signatory to the Agreement on Government Procurement. Under the Agreement, the signatory nations must (1) administer specific procurement programs in a manner whereby "eligible products," *i.e.*, products designated under the Agreement and suppliers of products from signatory nations, are treated no less favorably than domestic products or suppliers, (2) establish open procurement procedures, (3) adopt common rules of procurement practices, and (4) establish a dispute

(footnote continued from previous page)
under the laws of the foreign country or any subdivision, territory, or possession thereof; or

(E) in the case of a contractor or subcontractor who is a participant in a joint venture or a member of a partnership, any participant of the joint venture or partner meets any of the criteria in subparagraphs (A) through (D) of this paragraph.

12 A list of the signatory nations is attached hereto as Exhibit C. *See* 48 C.F.R. § 25.401.

1038-07

0242

settlement procedure.[13] Pursuant to U.S. implementation of the Agreement, the President has waived the Buy American Act restrictions with respect to eligible products of signatory nations, thereby allowing such products to compete on an equal basis with U.S. products. As a means of inducing non-signatory nations to sign the Agreement and in retaliation for the failure of non-signatory nations to give U.S. companies a fair opportunity to compete for government contracts, the U.S. prohibits designated agencies from purchasing any eligible products from non-signatory nations, such as Korea.

The Agreement, along with the waiver of the Buy American Act restriction for eligible products from signatory nations and the prohibition on purchases of eligible products from non-signatory nations, applies to a portion, but not all, of the U.S. government's procurement. First, the Agreement covers purchases by most U.S. agencies. Included under the Agreement are the Department of Defense (except for the Army Corps of Engineers), the National Aeronautics and Space Administration, the Veterans Administration, the Department of Agriculture, and the General Services Administration, which, together, accounted for approximately 84.5 percent of the U.S. government's

---

13 A copy of the Agreement is attached hereto as Exhibit D.

1038 —8

0243

purchases of goods and services in 1988. However, some agencies are excluded from the Agreement's coverage.[14]

Second, the Agreement does not cover various types of contracts, including (1) contracts below $156,000 (effective Feb. 14, 1988),[15] (2) construction contracts, (3) service contracts,[16] (4) research and development contracts, and (5) contracts for arms, ammunition or war materials or purchases indispensable for the national security or national defense.[17]

Third, the Department of Defense has excluded a number of items from the list of eligible products. The

---

14 A list of the designated agencies is set forth in Annex I to the Agreement in Exhibit D. Agencies which are not covered by the Agreement on Government Procurement include the Department of Transportation, the Department of Energy, the Bureau of Reclamation of the Department of Interior, the Army Corps of Engineers, the Tennessee Valley Authority, Comsat, Conrail, Amtrak, the U.S. Postal Service, and the GSA's Tools Commodities Division and Region Nine in California.

15 53 Fed. Reg. 3284 (Feb. 4, 1988).

16 Service contracts are included to the extent that such services are incidental to the purchase of eligible products; provided, that the value of the services is not greater than the value of the product. 48 C.F.R. § 25.403(f).

17 A list of the types of contracts not covered by the Agreement is attached hereto as Exhibit E. Any U.S. government agency may purchase Korean goods and services under such contracts. For example, the Department of Defense may purchase Korean products if the contract has a value less than $156,000. However, the contract would then be subject to the Buy American Act.

1038 — 9

0244

Department of Defense does not prohibit the purchase of such items from non-signatory nations, but does apply the 50 percent Buy American Act preference to these items. The excluded items include Federal Supply Classification Numbers 10 to 20 (primarily major weapons systems and war materials), 28 (engines, turbines and components), 31 (bearings), 51 (hand tools), 58 to 60 (communications and electronic equipment), 83 (textiles) and 84 (clothing). As shown in Exhibit A, during fiscal year 1988 the U.S. government as a whole spent about $56.6 billion on these items, or about 66 percent of the $85.5 billion spent on equipment and supplies. Since most of these items were weapons-related, it may be assumed that the bulk of the purchases were made by the Department of Defense. The exclusion of such items from the Agreement on Government Procurement leaves an estimated $29 billion in equipment and supplies to be covered by the Agreement.

In summary, if Korea were to sign the Agreement, it would gain three advantages.

1. The designated U.S. government agencies would be allowed to purchase Korean products for all of their contracts.

2. In purchasing eligible products, the designated agencies would not subject Korean products to the restrictions of the Buy American Act and would allow

1038 — 10

0245

Korean products to compete on an equal basis with U.S. products.[18]

3. Korean products could be sold more easily to the governments of other signatories to the Agreement.

The principal disadvantage in signing the Agreement is that Korea would have to open its own government procurement market to competition from U.S. products as well as products from other signatory nations.

D. Memoranda of Understanding

In accordance with Memoranda of Understanding ("MOUs") entered into between the U.S. and certain countries, including NATO participants, the U.S. has waived the Buy American Act restrictions for purchases of certain defense equipment.[19] The MOUs were entered into in order

---

18 The Buy American Act restrictions would still be applied by the designated agencies for contracts not covered by the Agreement, such as service contracts and construction contracts, and by the nondesignated agencies for all contracts.

19 Department of Defense Supplement to the Federal Acquisition Regulation, Subpart 25.74, 48 C.F.R. Subpart 225.74. In the event that a domestic offer, a participating country offer, and a nonqualifying country offer compete for defense equipment, the participating country offer shall be evaluated without applying the price differentials of the Buy American Act restrictions, whereas the nonqualifying country offer shall be subjected to the price differentials. However, in the event that the low domestic offer exceeds the evaluated price of the nonqualifying country offer, all foreign offers shall be evaluated as if no domestic offer was submitted. In the [illegible]

(footnote continued)

1038 - 11

0246

to increase the defense capabilities of NATO through more efficient cooperation in the field of research and development, production, and acquisition of defense equipment. The MOUs are designed to ensure that sources from participating countries are provided every opportunity to compete on a fair and equal basis with U.S. sources for research and development and for production contracts consistent with certain limitations.[20] A similar agreement applies to products of Egypt, Israel, and Canada. Korea may want to consider the possibility of negotiating a similar agreement. In such a case, however, Korea could be required to undertake certain reciprocal obligations with respect to U.S. products.

E. Annual Department of Defense Appropriations Legislation

Another mechanism used to limit the sale of foreign products to the U.S. market is special legislation enacted by Congress which restricts government procurement from foreign sources under specific circumstances. The annual Department of Defense appropriations legislation

---

(footnote continued from previous page)
against a nonqualifying country offer and no domestic offer is submitted, the participating country offer shall be evaluated on an equal basis with the nonqualifying country offer. 48 C.F.R. § 225.7403(a)(3)(ii).

20 A list of participating countries is attached hereto as Exhibit F.

1032-12

0247

imposes restrictions on the availability of funds for the acquisition of several products, including any article of food, clothing, cotton, wool, woven silk and woven silk blends, spun silk yarn for cartridge cloth, synthetic fabric, specialty metals, and hand or measuring tools.[21] Acquisition by the Defense Department of certain foreign buses and certain tools, is also restricted.[22]

Further, the Defense Department cannot appropriate its funds for the performance of research and development in connection with any weapons system or other military equipment if there is a U.S. corporation equally competent to carry out the research and development at a lower cost.[23]

Although MOUs may eliminate many or most of the restrictions imposed by both the Buy American Act and the Trade Agreements Act, imports for Defense Department procurement from countries having MOUs with the U.S. are

---

21 48 C.F.R. § 225.7002.

22 48 C.F.R. §§ 225.7006 and 225.7008.

23 48 C.F.R. §§ 225.7007. There are also restrictions for the construction of major components of the hull or superstructure of any naval vessel or the construction of any naval vessel in foreign shipyards (48 C.F.R. § 225.7005), and restrictions on the acquisition of manual typewriters which were manufactured by facilities located within states which are signatories of the Warsaw Pact (48 C.F.R. § 225.7004).

1038 — 13

0248

not exempt from these additional restrictions imposed by Congress.

F. Conclusion

The sale of Korean products to the U.S. government is impaired by the Buy American Act, the Agreement on Government Procurement and the related Trade Agreements Act of 1979. The existing barriers could be reduced by (1) signing the Agreement on Government Procurement, (2) negotiating a similar agreement solely on a bilateral basis with the U.S., or (3) entering an agreement covering products, such as certain defense-related equipment, that are not subject to the Agreement on Government Procurement. Any efforts to reduce such barriers would, of course, require an analysis of the existing markets, including a review of the specific products which Korea could supply, the specific barriers to those products, the potential U.S. government procurement market for such products, and the markets which the Korean government would be willing to open to competition from the U.S. and, possibly, other countries.

FEDERAL PROCUREMENT DATA SYSTEM

SUPPLIES AND EQUIPMENT – SUMMARY BY FSC GROUP

Actions Reported Individually on SF279

Fiscal Year 1988 Through Fourth Quarter

EXHIBIT A
Page 1

	Year to Date	
	Number of Actions	Dollars (000)
TOTAL FEDERAL SUPPLIES AND EQUIPMENT	171,316	85,495,551
10 Weapons	1,409	1,526,233
11 Nuclear Ordinance	103	335,187
12 Fire Control Equipment	1,584	1,209,770
13 Ammunition & Explosives	1,789	3,108,256
14 Guided Missiles	2,673	8,880,339
15 Aircraft & Airframe Structure	4,471	11,135,351
16 Aircraft Components & Accessories	5,539	2,622,138
17 Aircraft Launching, Landing & Ground Handling Equipment	684	291,851
18 Space Vehicles	404	1,526,080
19 Ships, Small Craft, Pontoons & Floating Docks	1,703	8,382,818
20 Ship & Marine Equipment	759	559,903
22 Railway Equipment	25	8,499
23 Ground Effect & Motor Vehicles, Trailers & Cycles	1,363	3,005,416
24 Tractors	218	60,559
25 Vehicular Equipment Components	1,660	654,381
26 Tires & Tubes	303	79,869
28 Engines, Turbines & Components	4,116	5,567,051
29 Engine Accessories	2,316	436,835
30 Mechanical Power Transmission Equipment	872	84,368
31 Bearings	799	91,209
32 Woodworking Machinery and Equipment	20	1,387
34 Metalworking Machinery	811	141,166
35 Service & Trade Equipment	308	40,046
36 Special Industrial Machinery	1,069	151,972
37 Agricultural Machinery & Equipment	148	5,226
38 Construction, Mining, Excavating & Highway Maint Equip	553	215,719
39 Materials Handling Equipment	845	448,240
40 Rope, Cable, Chain and Fittings	314	27,485
41 Refrigeration, Air Condition & Air Circulation Equipment	1,027	99,401
42 Fire-Fighting, Rescue & Safety Equipment	667	282,068
43 Pumps and Compressors	1,335	150,909
44 Furnace,Steam Plant & Drying Equip: Nuclear Reacto	672	1,187,380
45 Plumbing, Heating & Sanitation Equipment	293	45,417
46 Water Purification & Sewage Treatment Equipment	130	30,845
47 Pipe, Tubing, Hose & Fittings	1,181	82,904
48 Valves	1,757	124,115
49 Maintenance & Repair Ship Equipment	2,113	696,602
51 Hand Tools	2,150	77,579
52 Measuring Tools	200	11,388
53 Hardware & Abrasives	1,741	130,353

AS OF 02/02/89 10 1038-15

0250

FEDERAL PROCUREMENT DATA SYSTEM

EXHIBIT A
Page 2

SUPPLIES AND EQUIPMENT – SUMMARY BY FSC GROUP–Continued

Actions Reported Individually on SF279
Fiscal Year 1988 Through Fourth Quarter

	Year to Date	
	Number of Actions	Dollars (000)
54 Prefabricated Structures & Scaffolding	546	203,925
55 Lumber, Millwork, Plywood & Veneer	496	24,419
56 Construction & Building Material	1,012	141,447
58 Communication, Detection & Coherent Radiation Equipment	11,078	8,362,864
59 Electrical/Electronic Equipment Components	6,120	1,616,563
60 Fiber Optics Materials, Components, Assemblies & Accs	99	20,160
61 Electric Wire & Power Distribution Equipment	3,419	790,825
62 Lighting Fixtures & Lamps	716	102,726
63 Alarm & Signal Systems	348	81,695
65 Medical, Dental & Veterinarian Equipment & Supplies	14,809	1,145,034
66 Instruments & Laboratory Equipment	8,465	1,522,201
67 Photographic Equipment	1,109	88,223
68 Chemicals & Chemical Products	1,636	87,116
69 Training Aids & Devices	916	668,755
70 General Purpose ADP Equip, Software, Supplies & Support	24,187	3,321,575
71 Furniture	4,932	309,378
72 Household & Commercial Furnishings & Appliances	1,158	58,438
73 Food Preparation & Service Equipment	1,123	68,405
74 Office Machines & Visible Record Equipment	663	59,814
75 Office Supplies & Devices	4,333	162,436
76 Books, Maps & Other Publications	855	189,830
77 Musical Instruments, Phonographs & Home-type Radios	59	2,564
78 Recreational & Athletic Equipment	214	7,647
79 Cleaning Equipment & Supplies	1,494	70,730
80 Brushes, Paints, Sealers & Adhesives	1,327	63,535
81 Containers, Packaging & Packing Supplies	1,905	235,502
83 Textiles, Leather, Fur, Apparel, Shoe Find,Tents & Flags	448	192,101
84 Clothing, Individual Equipment & Insignia	1,854	1,067,894
85 Toiletries	861	64,557
87 Agricultural Supplies	280	31,408
88 Live Animals	57	8,381
89 Subsistence	16,652	2,493,290
91 Fuel, Lubricants, Oils & Waxes	2,558	5,108,783
93 Nonmetallic Fabricated Materials	495	98,369
94 Nonmetallic Crude Materials	18	1,215
95 Metal Bars, Sheets & Shapes	694	155,331
96 Ores, Minerals & Their Primary Products	227	342,339
99 Miscellaneous	3,985	2,995,943
E Real Property, Purchase	33	2,207

AS OF 02/02/89

11

1038 – 16

0251

EXHIBIT B
Page 1 of 3

List of Articles Not Subject to the Buy American Act Because They Are Not Mined, Produced or Manufactured in the United States in Sufficient and Reasonably Available Commercial Quantities of a Satisfactory Quality.

Acetylene, black
Agar, bulk
Anise
Antimony, as metal or oxide
Asbestos, amosite, chrysotile, and crocidolite
Bananas
Bauxite
Beef, corned, canned
Beef extract
Bephenium hydroxynapthoate
Bismuth
Books, trade, text, technical, or scientific; newspapers; pamphlets; magazines; periodicals; printed briefs and films; not printed in the United States and for which domestic editions are not available.
Brazil nuts, unroasted
Cadmium, ores and flue dust
Calcium cyanamide
Capers
Cashew nuts
Castor beans and castor oil
Chalk, English
Chestnuts
Chicle
Chrome ore or chromite
Cinchona bark
Cobalt, in cathodes, rondelles, or other primary ore and metal forms.
Cocoa beans
Coconut and coconut meat, unsweetened, in shredded, desiccated, or similarly prepared form
Coffee, raw or green bean
Colchicine alkaloid, raw
Copra
Cork, wood or bank and waste
Cover glass, microscope slide
Cryolite, natural
Dammar gum
Diamonds, industrial, stones and abrasives
Emetine, bulk
Ergot, crude
Erythrityl tetranitrate
Fair linen, altar

1038 - 11

0252

Fibers of the following types: abaca, abace, agave, coir, flax, jute, jute burlaps, palmyra, and sisal
Goat and kidskins
Graphite, natural, crystalline, crucible grade
Handsewing needles
Hemp yarn
Hog bristles for brushes
Hyoscine, bulk
Ipecac, root
Iodine, crude
Kaurigum
Lac
Leather, sheepskin, hair type
Lavender oil
Manganese
Menthol, natural bulk
Mica
Nickel, primary, in ingots, pigs, shots, cathodes, or similar forms; nickel oxide and nickel salts
Nitroguanidine (also known as picrite)
Nux vomica, crude
Oiticica oil
Olive oil
Olives (green), pitted or unpitted, or stuffed, in bulk
Opium, crude
Oranges, mandarin, canned
Petroleum, crude oil, unfinished oils, and finished products
Pine needle oil
Platinum and related groups metals, refined, as sponge, powder, ingots, or cast bars
Pyrethrum flowers
Quartz crystals
Quebracho
Quinidine
Quinine
Radium salts, source and special nuclear materials
Rosettes
Rubber, crude and latex
Rutile
Santonin, crude
Secretin
Shellac
Silk, raw and unmanufactured
Spare and replacement parts for equipment of foreign manufacture, and for which domestic parts are not available
Spices and herbs, in bulk
Sugars, raw
Swords and scabbards

1038 - 18

0253

EXHIBIT B
Page 3 of 3

Talc, block, steatite
Tantalum
Tapioca flour and cassava
Tartar, crude; tartaric acid and cream of tartar in bulk
Tea in bulk
Thread, metallic (gold)
Thyme oil
Tin in bars, blocks, and pigs
Triprolidine hydrochloride
Tungsten
Vanilla beans
Venom, cobra
Wax, carnauba
Woods; logs, veneer, and lumber of the following species: Alaskan yellow cedar, angelique, balsa, ekki, greenheart, lignum vitae, mahogany, and teak

1038 - 19

0254

EXHIBIT C

List of Nations Subject to
the Agreement on Government Procurement

Austria
Bangladesh
Belgium
Benin
Bhutan
Botswana
Burundi
Canada
Cape Verde
Central African Republic
Chad
Comoros
Denmark
Federal Republic of Germany
Finland
France
Gambia
Guinea
Haiti
Hong Kong
Ireland
Israel
Italy
Japan
Lesotho
Luxembourg
Malawi
Maldives
Mali
Nepal
Netherlands
Niger
Norway
Rwanda
Singapore
Somalia
Sweden
Switzerland
Western Somoa
Sudan
Tanzania U.R.
Uganda
United Kingdom
Upper Volta
Yemen

1038 — 20

0255

BUY AMERICAN RULES

EXHIBIT D

MISCELLANEOUS

AGREEMENT ON GOVERNMENT PROCUREMENT, AS AMENDED*

INDEX

*MTN Agreement, as modified by the Protocol Amending the Agreement on Government Procurement, effective February 14, 1988.

**Annexes II — IV are not included in this publication.

PREAMBLE

Parties to this Agreement (hereinafter referred to as "Parties"),

Considering that Ministers agreed in the Tokyo Declaration of 14 September 1973 that comprehensive Multilateral Trade Negotiations in the framework of the General Agreement on Tariffs and Trade (hereinafter referred to as "General Agreement" or "GATT") should aim, *inter alia*, to reduce or eliminate non-tariff measures or, where this is not appropriate, their trade restricting or distorting effects, and to bring such measures under more effective international discipline;

Considering that Ministers also agreed that negotiations should aim to secure additional benefits for the international trade of developing countries, and recognized the importance of the application of differential measures in ways which will provide special and more favourable treatment for them where this is feasible and appropriate;

Recognizing that in order to achieve their economic and social objectives to implement programmes and policies of economic development aimed at raising the standard of living of their people, taking into account their balance-of-payment position, developing countries may need to adopt agreed differential measures;

Considering that Ministers in the Tokyo Declaration recognized that the particular situation and problems of the least developed among developing countries shall be given special attention and stressed the need to ensure that these countries receive special treatment in the context of any general or specific measures taken in favour of the developing countries during the negotiations;

Recognizing the need to establish an agreed international framework of rights and obligations with respect to laws, regulations, procedures and practices regarding government procurement with a view to achieving greater liberalization and expansion of world trade and improving the international framework for the conduct of world trade;

Recognizing that laws, regulations, procedures and practices regarding government procurement should not be prepared, adopted or applied to foreign or domestic products and to foreign or domestic suppliers so as to afford protection to domestic products or suppliers and should not discriminate among foreign products or suppliers;

Recognizing that it is desirable to provide transparency of laws, regulations, procedures and practices regarding government procurement;

Recognizing the need to establish international notification, consultation, surveillance and dispute settlement procedures with a view to ensuring a fair, prompt and effective enforcement of the international provisions on government procurement and to maintain the balance of rights and obligations at the highest possible level:

Hereby agree as follows:

ARTICLE I

Scope and Coverage

1. This Agreement applies to:

(a) any law, regulation, procedure and practice regarding any procurement of products, through such methods as purchase or as lease, rental or hire-purchase, with or without an option to buy by the entities[1] subject to this Agreement. This includes services incidental to the supply of products if the value of these incidental services does not exceed that of the products themselves, but not service contracts *per se;*

(b) any procurement contract of a value of SDR 130,000 or more.[2, 3] No procurement requirement shall be divided with the intent of reducing the value of the resulting contracts below SDR 130,000. If an individual requirement for the procurement of a product of the same type results in the award of more than one contract or in contracts being awarded in separate parts, the basis for application of this Agreement shall be either the actual value of similar recurring contracts concluded over the previous fiscal year or twelve months adjusted, where possible, for anticipated changes in quantity and value over the subsequent twelve months, or the estimated value of recurring contracts in the fiscal year or twelve months subsequent to the initial contract. The selection of the valuation method by the entity shall not be used with the purpose of circumventing the Agreement.

In cases of contracts for the lease, rental, or hire-purchase of products, the basis for calculating the contract value shall be:

(i) in the case of fixed-term contracts, where their term is twelve months or less, the calculation should be based on the total contract value for its duration, or, where their term exceeds twelve months, its total value including the estimated residual value;

(ii) in the case of contracts for an indefinite period, the monthly instalment multiplied by forty-eight;

(iii) if there is any doubt, the second basis of calculation is to be used, namely forty-eight months.

In cases where a proposed procurement specifies the need for option clauses, the basis for application of this Agreement shall be the total value of the maximum permissible purchases, lease, rentals or hire-purchases, inclusive of optional purchases;

(c) procurement by the entities under the direct or substantial control of parties to this Agreement and other designated entities with respect to their procurement procedures and practices. Until the review and further negotiations referred to in the Final Provisions, the coverage of this Agreement is specified by the lists of entities, and to the extent that rectifications, modifications or amendments may have been made, their successor entities, in Annex I.

2. The Parties shall inform their entities not covered by this Agreement and the regional and local governments and authorities within their territories of the objectives, principles and rules of this Agreement, in particular the rules on national treatment and non-discrimination, and draw their attention to the overall benefits of liberalization of government procurement.

ARTICLE II

National Treatment and Non-Discrimination

1. With respect to all laws, regulations, procedures and practices regarding government procurement covered by this Agreement, parties to this Agreement shall provide immediately and unconditionally to the products and suppliers of other parties offering products originating within the customs territories (including free zones) of the parties to this Agreement treatment no less favourable than:

(a) that accorded to domestic products and suppliers; and

(b) that accorded to products and suppliers of any other party.

2. With respect to all laws, regulations, procedures and practices regarding government procurement covered by this Agreement the Parties shall ensure:

(a) that their entities shall not treat a locally-established supplier less favourably than another locally-established supplier on the basis of degree of foreign affiliation or ownership;

(b) that their entities shall not discriminate against locally-established suppliers on the basis of the country of production of the good being supplied, provided that the country of production is a Party to the Agreement in accordance with the provisions of paragraph 4 of this Article.

3. The provisions of paragraph 1 shall not apply to customs duties and charges of any kind imposed on or in connexion with importation, the method of levying such duties and charges, and other import regulations and formalities.

4. The Parties shall not apply rules of origin to products imported for purposes of government procurement covered by this Agreement from other Parties, which are different from the rules of origin applied in the normal course of trade and at the time of importation to imports of the same products from the same Parties.

ARTICLE III

Special and Differential Treatment for Developing Countries

Objectives

1. The Parties shall, in the implementation and administration of this Agreement, through the provisions set out in this Article, duly take into account the development, financial and trade needs of developing countries, in particular the least-developed countries, in their need to:

(a) safeguard their balance-of-payments position and ensure a level of reserves adequate for the implementation of programmes of economic development;

(b) promote the establishment or development of domestic industries including the development of small-scale and cottage industries in rural or backward areas; and economic development of other sectors of the economy;

(c) support industrial units so long as they are wholly or substantially dependent on government procurement;

(d) encourage their economic development through regional or global arrangements among developing countries presented to the CONTRACTING PARTIES to the GATT and not disapproved by them.

2. Consistently with the provisions of this Agreement, the Parties shall, in the preparation and application of laws, regulations and procedures affecting government procurement, facilitate increased imports from developing countries, bearing in mind the special problems of the least-developed countries and of those at low stages of economic development.

[1] Throughout this Agreement, the word entities is understood to include agencies.

[2] For contracts below the threshold, the parties to this Agreement shall consider, in accordance with paragraph 6 of Article IX, the application in whole or in part of this Agreement. In particular, they shall review the procurement practices and procedures utilized and the application of non-discrimination and transparency for such contracts in connexion with the possible inclusion of contracts below the threshold in the Agreement.

[3] This Agreement shall apply to any procurement contract for which the contract value is estimated to equal or exceed the threshold at the time of publication of the notice in accordance with Article V:4

1034-22

Coverage

3. With a view to ensuring that developing countries are able to adhere to this Agreement on terms consistent with their development, financial and trade needs, the objectives listed in paragraph 1 above shall be duly taken into account in the course of the negotiations with respect to the lists of entities of developing countries to be covered by the provisions of this Agreement. Developed countries, in the preparation of their lists of entities to be covered by the provisions of the Agreement shall endeavour to include entities procuring products of export interest to developing countries.

Agreed exclusions

4. Developing countries may negotiate with other participants in the negotiation of this Agreement mutually acceptable exclusions from the rules on national treatment with respect to certain entities or products that are included in their lists of entities having regard to the particular circumstances of each case. In such negotiations, the considerations mentioned in paragraph 1(a)-(c) above shall be duly taken into account. Developing countries participating in regional or global arrangements among developing countries referred to in paragraph 1(d) above, may also negotiate exclusions to their lists, having regard to the particular circumstances of each case, taking into account, *inter alia*, the provisions on government procurement provided for in the regional or global arrangements concerned and taking into account, in particular, products which may be subject to common industrial development programmes.

5. After entry into force of this Agreement, developing country Parties may modify their lists of entities in accordance with the provisions for modification of such lists contained in paragraph 5 of Article IX of this Agreement, having regard to their development, financial and trade needs, or may request the Committee to grant exclusions from the rules on national treatment for certain entities or products that are included in their lists of entities, having regard to the particular circumstances of each case and taking duly into account the provisions of paragraph 1(a)-(c) above. The developing country Parties may also request, after entry into force of this Agreement, the Committee to grant exclusions for certain entities or products that are included in their lists in the light of their participation in regional or global arrangements among developing countries, having regard to the particular circumstances of each case and taking duly into account the provisions of paragraph 1(d) above. Each request to the Committee by a developing country Party relating to modification of a list shall be accompanied by documentation relevant to the request or by such information as may necessary for consideration of the matter.

6. Paragraph 4 and 5 above shall apply *mutatis mutandis* to developing countries acceding to this Agreement after its entry into force.

7. Such agreed exclusions as mentioned in paragraphs 4, 5 and 6 above shall be subject to review in accordance with the provisions of paragraph 14 of this Article.

Technical assistance for developing country Parties

8. Developed country Parties shall, upon request, provide all technical assistance which they may deem appropriate to developing country Parties in resolving their problems in the field of government procurement.

9. This assistance which shall be provided on the basis of non-discrimination among developing country Parties shall relate, *inter alia*, to:

—the solution of particular technical problems relating to the award of a specific contract;

—any other problem which the Party making the request and another Party agree to deal with in the context of this assistance.

10. Technical assistance referred to in paragraphs 8 and 9 above would include translation of qualification documentation and tenders made by suppliers of developing country Parties from a GATT language designated by the entity, unless developed country Parties deem translation as burdensome, and, in that case, explanation shall be given to developing country Parties upon their request addressed either to the developed country Parties or to their entities.

Information centres

11. The developed country Parties shall establish, individually or jointly, information centres to respond to reasonable requests from developing country Parties for information relating to, *inter alia*, laws, regulations, procedures and practices regarding government procurement, notices about proposed procurements which have been published, addresses of the entities covered by this Agreement, and the nature and volume of products procured or to be procured, including available information about future tenders. The Committee may also set up an information centre.

Special treatment for least-developed countries

12. Having regard to paragraph 6 of the Tokyo Declaration, special treatment shall be granted to the least-developed country Parties and to the suppliers in those countries with respect to products originating in those countries, in the context of any general or specific measures in favour of the developing country Parties. The Parties may also grant the benefits of this Agreement to suppliers in least-developed countries which are not Parties, with respect to products originating in those countries.

13. Developed country Parties shall, upon request, provide assistance which they may deem appropriate to potential tenderers in the least-developed countries in submitting their tenders, selecting the products which are likely to be of interest to entities of developed countries as well as to suppliers in the least-developed countries and likewise assist them to comply with technical regulations and standards relating to products which are the subject of the proposed procurement.

Review

14. The Committee shall review annually the operation and effectiveness of this Article and after each three years of its operation on the basis of reports to be submitted by the Parties shall carry out a major review in order to evaluate its effects. As part of the three-yearly reviews and with a view to achieving the maximum implementation of the provisions of this Agreement, including in particular Article II, and having regard to the development, financial and trade situation of the developing countries concerned, the Committee shall examine whether exclusions provided for in accordance with the provisions of paragraphs 4 to 6 of this Article shall be modified or extended.

15. In the course of further rounds of negotiations in accordance with the provisions of Article IX, paragraph 6, the developing country Parties shall give consideration to the possibility of enlarging their lists of entities having regard to their economic, financial and trade situation.

1038 - 23

ARTICLE IV

Technical Specifications

1. Technical specifications laying down the characteristics of the products to be procured such as quality, performance, safety and dimensions, testing and test methods, symbols, terminology, packaging, marking and labelling, and conformity certification requirements prescribed by procurement entities, shall not be prepared, adopted or applied with a view to creating obstacles to international trade nor have the effect of creating unnecessary obstacles to international trade.

2. Any technical specification prescribed by procurement entities shall, where appropriate:

(a) be in terms of performance rather than design; and

(b) be based on international standards, national technical regulations, or recognized national standards.

3. There shall be no requirement or reference to a particular trade mark or name, patent, design or type, specific origin or producer, unless there is no sufficiently precise or intelligible way of describing the procurement requirements and provided that words such as "or equivalent" are included in the tenders.

4. Procurement entities shall not seek or accept, in a manner which would have the effect of precluding competition, advice which may be used in the preparation of specifications for a specific procurement from a firm that may have a commercial interest in the procurement.

ARTICLE V

Tendering Procedures

1. The Parties shall ensure that the tendering procedures of their entities are consistent with the provisions below. Open tendering procedures for the purposes of this Agreement are those procedures under which all interested suppliers may submit a tender. Selective tendering procedures, for the purposes of this Agreement are those procedures under which, consistent with paragraph 8 and other relevant provisions of this Part, those suppliers invited to do so by the entity may submit a tender. Single tendering procedures, for the purposes of this Agreement, are those procedures where the entity contacts suppliers individually, only under the conditions specified in paragraph 16 below.

Qualification of suppliers

2. Entities, in the process of qualifying suppliers, shall not discriminate among foreign suppliers or between domestic and foreign suppliers. Qualification procedures shall be consistent with the following:

(a) any conditions for participation in tendering procedures shall be published in adequate time to enable interested suppliers to initiate and, to the extent that it is compatible with efficient operation of the procurement process, complete the qualification procedures;

(b) any conditions for participation in tendering procedures shall be limited to those which are essential to ensure the firm's capability to fulfil the contract in question. Any conditions for participation required from suppliers, including financial guarantees, technical qualifications, information necessary for establishing the financial, commercial and technical capacity of suppliers, as well as the verification of qualifications, shall be no less favourable to foreign suppliers than to domestic suppliers and shall not discriminate among foreign suppliers. The financial, commercial and technical capacity of a supplier shall be judged both on the basis of that supplier's global business activity as well as its activity in the territory of the procuring entity, taking due account of the legal relationship between the supply organizations;

(c) the process of, and the time required for, qualifying suppliers shall not be used in order to keep foreign suppliers off a suppliers' list or from being considered a particular proposed procurement. Entities shall recognize as qualified suppliers such domestic or foreign suppliers who meet the conditions for participation in a particular proposed procurement. Suppliers requesting to participate in a particular proposed procurement who may not yet be qualified shall also be considered, provided there is sufficient time to complete the qualification procedure;

(d) entities maintaining permanent lists of qualified suppliers shall ensure that suppliers may apply for qualification at any time; and that all qualified suppliers so requesting are included in the lists within a reasonably short time;

(e) any supplier having requested to become a qualified supplier shall be advised by the entities concerned of the decision in this regard. Qualified suppliers included on permanent lists by entities shall also be notified of the termination of any such lists or of their removal from them;

(f) the Parties shall ensure that

(i) each entity and its constituent parts follow a single qualification procedure, except in cases of duly substantiated need for different procedures;

(ii) efforts be made to minimize differences in qualification procedures between entities;

(g) nothing in sub-paragraphs (a) to (f) above shall preclude the exclusion of any supplier on grounds such as bankruptcy or false declarations, provided that such an action is consistent with the national treatment and non-discrimination provisions of this Agreement.

3. Entities shall not provide to any potential supplier information with regard to a specific procurement in a manner which would have the effect of precluding competition.

Notice of proposed procurement and tender documentation

4. Entities shall publish a notice of each proposed procurement in the appropriate publication listed in Annex II. Such notice shall constitute an invitation to participate in either open or selective tendering procedures.

5. Each notice of proposed procurement shall contain the following information:

(a) the nature and quantity, including any options for additional quantities, of the products to be supplied and, if possible, an estimate of the timing when such options may be exercised; in the case of recurring contracts the nature and quantity and, if possible, an estimate of the timing of the subsequent tender notices for the products to be procured;

(b) whether the procedure is open or selective;

(c) any delivery date;

(d) the address and final date for submitting an application to be invited to tender or for qualifying for the suppliers' lists, or for receiving tenders, as well as the language or languages in which they must be submitted;

(e) the address of the entity awarding the contract and providing any information necessary for obtaining specifications and other documents;

(f) any economic and technical requirements, financial guarantees and information required from suppliers;

(g) the amount and terms of payment of any sum payable for the tender documentation;

(h) whether the entity is inviting offers for purchase, lease, rental or hire-purchase, or more than one of these methods.

1038 -24

0259

The entity shall publish in one of the official languages of the GATT a summary of the notice of proposed procurement containing at least the following:

(i) subject matter of the contract;

(ii) time-limits set for the submission of tenders; and

(iii) addresses from which documents relating to the contracts may be requested.

6. To ensure optimum effective international competition under selective tendering procedures, entities shall, for each proposed procurement, invite tenders from the maximum number of domestic and foreign suppliers,— consistent with efficient operation of the procurement system. They shall select the suppliers to participate in the procedure in a fair and non-discriminatory manner.

7. (a) In the case of selective tendering procedures, entities maintaining permanent lists of qualified suppliers shall publish annually in one of the publications listed in Annex III, a notice of the following:

(i) the enumeration of the lists maintained, including their headings, in relation to the products or categories of products to be procured through the lists;

(ii) the conditions to be filled by potential suppliers in view of their inscription on those lists and the methods according to which each of those conditions be verified by the entity concerned;

(iii) the period of validity of the lists, and the formalities for their renewal.

(b) Entities maintaining permanent lists of qualified suppliers may select suppliers to be invited to tender from among those listed. Any selection shall allow for equitable opportunities for suppliers on the lists.

(c) If, after publication of the notice under paragraph 4 above, a supplier not yet qualified requests to participate in a particular tender, the entity shall promptly start the procedure of qualification.

8. Suppliers requesting to participate in a particular proposed procurement shall be permitted to submit a tender and be considered provided, in the case of those not yet qualified, there is sufficient time to complete the qualification procedure under paragraphs 2-7 of this Article. The number of additional suppliers permitted to participate shall be limited only by the efficient operation of the procurement system.

9. If after publication of a notice of a proposed procurement but before the time set for opening or receipt of tenders as specified in the notices or the tender documentation, it becomes necessary to amend or re-issue the notice, the amendment or the re-issued notice shall be given the same circulation as the original documents upon which the amendment is based. Any significant information given to one supplier with respect to a particular proposed procurement shall be given simultaneously to all other suppliers concerned in adequate time to permit the suppliers to consider such information and to respond to it.

10. (a) Any prescribed time-limit shall be adequate to allow foreign as well as domestic suppliers to prepare and submit tenders before the closing of the tendering procedures. In determining any such time-limit, entities shall, consistent with their own reasonable needs, take into account such factors as the complexity of the proposed procurement, the extent of sub-contracting anticipated, and the normal time for transmitting tenders by mail from foreign as well as domestic points.

(b) Consistent with the entity's own reasonable needs, any delivery date shall take into account such factors as the complexity of the proposed procurement, the extent of sub-contracting anticipated, and the realistic time required for production, de-stocking and transport of goods from the points of supply.

11. (a) In open procedures, the period for the receipt of tenders shall in no case be less than forty days from the date of publication referred to in paragraph 4 of this Article.

(b) In selective procedures not involving the use of a permanent list of qualified suppliers, the period for submitting an application to be invited to tender shall in no case be less than twenty-five days from the date of the publication referred to in paragraph 4 of this Article; the period for receipt of tenders shall in no case be less than forty days from the date of issuance of the invitation to tender.

(c) In selective procedures involving the use of a permanent list of qualified suppliers, the period for receipt of tenders shall in no case be less than forty days from the date of the initial issuance of invitations to tender. If the date of initial issuance of invitations to tender does not coincide with the date of the publication referred to in paragraph 4 of this Article, there shall in no case be less than forty days between those two dates.

(d) The periods referred to in (a), (b), and (c) above may be reduced in the case of the second or subsequent publications dealing with contracts of a recurring nature within the meaning of paragraph 5 of this Article. In this case, the period for the receipt of tenders shall in no case be less than twenty-five days. The second or subsequent publication should include a reference to permit the identification of the first publication.

(e) The periods referred to in (a), (b), (c) and (d) above may be reduced where a state of urgency duly substantiated by the entity renders impracticable the periods in question but shall in no case be less than ten days from the date of the publication referred to in paragraph 4 of this Article.

(f) The Parties shall ensure that their entities shall take due account of publication delays when setting the final date for receipt of tenders or of applications to be invited to tender.

12. If, in tendering procedures, an entity allows tenders to be submitted in several languages, one of those languages shall be one of the official languages of the GATT.

13. Tender documentation provided to suppliers shall contain all information necessary to permit them to submit responsive tenders, including information required to be published in the notice of proposed procurement, except for paragraph 5(g) of this Article, and the following:

(a) the address of the entity to which tenders should be sent;

(b) the address where requests for supplementary information should be sent;

(c) the language or languages in which tenders and tendering documents must be submitted;

(d) the closing date and time for receipt of tenders and the length of time during which any tender should be open for acceptance;

(e) the persons authorized to be present at the opening of tenders and the date, time and place of this opening;

(f) any economic and technical requirement, financial guarantees and information or documents required from suppliers;

(g) a complete description of the products required or of any requirements including technical specifications, conformity certification to be fulfilled by the products, necessary plans, drawings and instructional materials;

(h) the criteria for awarding the contract, including any factors other than price that are to be considered in the evaluation of tenders and the cost ele-

1038 —25

0260

ments to be included in evaluating tender prices, such as transport, insurance and inspection costs, and in the case of foreign products, customs duties and other import charges, taxes and currency of payment;

(i) the terms of payment;

(j) any other terms or conditions.

14. (a) In open procedures, entities shall forward the tender documentation at the request of any supplier participating in the procedure, and shall reply promptly to any reasonable request for explanations relating thereto.

(b) In selective procedures, entities shall forward the tender documentation at the request of any supplier requesting to participate and shall reply promptly to any reasonable request for explanations relating thereto.

(c) Entities shall reply promptly to any reasonable request for relevant information submitted by a supplier participating in the tendering procedure, on condition that such information does not give that supplier an advantage over its competitors in the procedure for the award of the contract.

Submission, receipt and opening of tenders and awarding of contracts

15. The submission, receipt and opening of tenders and awarding of contracts shall be consistent with the following:

(a) tenders shall normally be submitted in writing directly or by mail. If tenders by telex, telegram or telecopy are permitted, the tender made thereby must include all the information necessary for the evaluation of the tender, in particular the definitive price proposed by the tenderer and a statement that the tenderer agrees to all the terms, conditions and provisions of the invitation to tender. The tender must be confirmed promptly by letter or by the despatch of a signed copy of the telex, telegram or telecopy. Tenders presented by telephone shall not be permitted. The content of the telex, telegram or telecopy shall prevail where there is a difference or conflict between that content and any documentation received after the time-limit; requests to participate in selective tendering procedures may be submitted by telex, telegram or telecopy;

(b) the opportunities that may be given to tenderers to correct unintentional errors between the opening of tenders and the awarding of the contract shall not be permitted to give rise to any discriminatory practice;

(c) a supplier shall not be penalized if a tender is received in the office designated in the tender documents after the time specified because of delay due solely to mishandling on the part of the entity. Tenders may also be considered in other exceptional circumstances if the procedures of the entity concerned so provide;

(d) all tenders solicited under open and selective procedures by entities shall be received and opened under procedures and conditions guaranteeing the regularity of the openings as well as the availability of information from the openings. The receipt and opening of tenders shall also be consistent with the national treatment and non-discrimination provisions of this Agreement. To this effect, and in connexion with open procedures, entities shall establish provisions for the opening of tenders in the presence of either tenderers or their representatives, or an appropriate and impartial witness not connected with the procurement process. A report on the opening of the tenders shall be drawn up in writing. This report shall remain with the entities concerned at the disposal of the government authorities responsible for the entity in order that it may be used if required under the procedures of Articles VI and VII of this Agreement;

(e) to be considered for award, a tender must, at the time of opening, conform to the essential requirements of the notices or tender documentation and be from suppliers which comply with the conditions for participation. If an entity has received a tender abnormally lower than other tenders submitted, it may enquire with the tenderer to ensure that it can comply with the conditions of participation and be capable of fulfilling the terms of the contract;

(f) unless in the public interest an entity decided not to issue the contract, the entity shall make the award to the tenderer who has been determined to be fully capable of undertaking the contract and whose tender, whether for domestic or foreign products, is either the lowest tender or the tender which in terms of the specific evaluation criteria set forth in the notices or tender documentation is determined to be the most advantageous;

(g) if it appears from evaluation that no one tender is obviously the most advantageous in terms of the specific evaluation criteria set forth in the notices or tender documentation, the entity shall, in any subsequent negotiations, give equal consideration and treatment to all tenders within the competitive range;

(h) entities should normally refrain from awarding contracts on the condition that the supplier provide offset procurement opportunities or similar conditions. In the limited number of cases where such requisites are part of a contract, Parties concerned shall limit the offset to a reasonable proportion within the contract value and shall not favour suppliers from one Party over suppliers from any other Party. Licensing of technology should not normally be used as a condition of award but instances where it is required should be as infrequent as possible and suppliers from one Party shall not be favoured over suppliers from any other Party. In the limited number of cases where offset procurement opportunities or similar conditions are required, these requirements shall be included in the notice of proposed procurement and tender documentation;

(i) options clauses shall not be used in a manner which circumvents the provisions of the Agreement;

(j) awards shall be made in accordance with the criteria and essential requirements specified in the tender documentation.

Use of single tendering

16. The provisions of paragraphs 1-15 above governing open and selective tendering procedures need not apply in the following conditions, provided that single tendering is not used with a view to avoiding maximum possible competition or in a manner which would constitute a means of discrimination among foreign suppliers or protection to domestic producers:

(a) in the absence of tenders in response to an open or selective tender, or when the tenders submitted have been either collusive or do not conform to the essential requirements in the tender, or from suppliers who do not comply with the conditions for participation provided for in accordance with this Agreement, on condition, however, that the requirements of the initial tender are not substantially modified in the contract as awarded;

(b) when, for works of art or for reasons connected with protection of exclusive rights, such as patents or copyrights, the products can be supplied only by a particular supplier and no reasonable alternative or substitute exists;

(c) insofar as is strictly necessary when, for reasons of extreme urgency brought about by events unforeseeable by the entity, the products could not be

1038 – 26

obtained in time by means of open or selective tendering procedures:

(d) for additional deliveries by the original supplier which are intended either as parts replacement for existing supplies or installations, or as the extension of existing supplies or installations where a change of supplier would compel the entity to procure equipment not meeting requirements of interchangeability with already existing equipment;[4]

(e) when an entity procures prototypes or a first product which are developed at its request in the course of, and for, a particular contract for research, experiment, study or original development. When such contracts have been fulfilled, subsequent procurements of products shall be subject to paragraphs 1-15 of this Article.[5]

17. Entities shall prepare a report in writing on each contract awarded under the provisions of paragraph 16 of this Article. Each report shall contain the name of the procuring entity, value and kind of goods procured, country of origin, and a statement of the conditions in paragraph 16 of this Article which prevailed. This report shall remain with the entities concerned at the disposal of the government authorities responsible for the entity in order that it may be used if required under the procedures of Articles VI and VII of this Agreement.

ARTICLE VI

Information and Review

1. Entities shall publish a notice in the appropriate publication listed in Annex II not later than sixty days after the award of a contract(s) under Article V:15 or 16. These notices shall contain:[6]

(a) nature and quantity of products in the contract award(s);

(b) name and address of the entity awarding the contract;

(c) date of award;

(d) name(s) and address(es) of winning tenderer(s);

(e) value of winning award(s) or the highest and lowest offer taken into account in the award of the contract;

(f) where appropriate, means of identifying the notice issued under Article V:4;

(g) the type of procedure used;

(h) where appropriate, justification according to Article V:16 for the use of such procedure.

2. Any law, regulation, judicial decision, administrative ruling of general application, and any procedure (including standard contract clauses) regarding government procurement covered by this Agreement, shall be published promptly by the parties to this Agreement in the appropriate publications listed in Annex IV and in such a manner as to enable other parties and suppliers to become acquainted with them. Parties to this Agreement shall be prepared, upon request, to explain to any other party their government procurement procedures. Entities shall be prepared, upon request, to explain to any supplier from a country which is a party to this Agreement their procurement practices and procedures.

3. Entities shall, upon request by any supplier, promptly provide pertinent information concerning the reasons why that supplier's application to qualify for the suppliers' list was rejected, or why that supplier was not invited or admitted to tender.

4. Entities shall promptly, and in no case later than seven working days from the date of the award of a contract, inform the unsuccessful tenderers by written communication or publication that a contract has been awarded, the value or values of the tenders and the name and address of the winning tenderer. It is understood that the criteria contained in paragraph 9 of this Article are also applicable to the information requirements above.

5. Upon request by an unsuccessful tenderer, the procuring entity shall promptly provide that tenderer whith pertinent information concerning the reasons why the tenderer was not selected, including information on the characteristics and the relative advantages of the tender selected, as well as the name of the winning tenderer.

6. Entities shall establish a contract point to provide additional information to any unsuccessful tenderer dissatisfied with the explanation for rejection of his tender or who may have further questions about the award of the contract. There shall also be procedures for the hearing and reviewing of complaints arising in connexion with any phase of the procurement process, so as to ensure that, to the greatest extent possible, disputes under this Agreement will be equitably and expeditiously resolved between the suppliers and the entities concerned.

7. The government of the unsuccessful tenderer, which is a Party to this Agreement, may seek, without prejudice to the provisions under Article VII, such additional information on the contract award as may be necessary to ensure that the procurement was made fairly and impartially. To this end, the procuring government shall provide information on both the characteristics and relative advantages of the winning tender and the contract price. Normally this latter information may be disclosed by the government of the unsuccessful tenderer provided it exercises this right with discretion. In cases where release of this information would prejudice competition in future tenders this information shall not be disclosed except after consultation with and agreement of the Party which gave the information to the government of the unsuccessful tenderer.

8. Available information concerning individual contract awards shall be provided, upon a request, to any other Party.

9. Confidential information provided to any Party which would impede law enforcement or otherwise be contrary to the public interest or would prejudice the legitimate commercial interest of particular enterprises, pub[illegible] private, or might prejudice fair comp[illegible]ion between suppliers, shall not be revealed without formal authorization from the party providing the information.

10. The Parties shall collect and provide to the Committee on an annual basis statistics on their procurements covered by this Agreement. Such reports shall contain the following information with respect to contracts awarded by all procurement entities covered under this Agreement:

(a) statistics on estimated value of contracts awarded, both above and below the threshold value on a global basis and broken down by entities;

(b) statistics on number and total value of contracts awarded above the threshold value, broken down by entities, categories of products according to a uniform classification system to be determined by the Committee, and country of origin of the product;

---

[4] It is the understanding that "existing equipment" referred to in Article V·16(d) includes software to the extent that the initial procurement of the software was covered by the Agreement.

[5] Original development of a first product may include limited production in order to incorporate the results of field testing and to demonstrate that the product is suitable for production in quantity to acceptable quality standards. It does not extend to quantity production to establish commercial viability or to recover research and development costs.

[6] It is understood that certain information on the contract award may not be published in cases of those contracts where release of such information would impede law enforcement or otherwise be contrary to the public interest or would prejudice the legitimate commercial interest of particular enterprises, public or private, or might prejudice fair competition between suppliers.

1038 – 27

(c) statistics, broken down by entity, and by category of product, on the number and total value of contracts awarded under each of the cases of Article V, paragraph 16 showing country of origin of the product;

(d) statistics, broken down by entities, on the number and total value of contracts awarded under derogations to the Agreement contained in Annex I.

ARTICLE VII

Enforcement of Obligations

Institutions

1. There shall be established under this Agreement a Committee on Government Procurement (referred to in this Agreement as "the Committee") composed of representatives from each of the Parties. This Committee shall elect its own Chairman and Vice-Chairman and shall meet as necessary but not less than once a year for the purpose of affording parties the opportunity to consult of any matters relating to the operation of this Agreement or the furtherance of its objectives, and to carry out such other responsibilities as may be assigned to it by the Parties.

2. The Committee may establish *ad hoc* panels in the manner and for the purposes set out in paragraph 8 of this Article and working parties or other subsidiary bodies which shall carry out such functions as may be given to them by the Committee.

Consultations

3. Each Party shall afford sympathetic consideration to, and shall afford adequate opportunity for consultations regarding, representations made by another Party with respect to any matter affecting the operation of this Agreement.

4. If any Party considers that any benefit accruing to it, directly or indirectly, under this Agreement is being nullified or impaired, or that the achievement of any objective of this Agreement is being impeded by another Party or Parties, it may, with a view to reaching a mutually satisfactory resolution of the matter, request in writing consultations with the Party or Parties in question. Each Party shall afford sympathetic consideration to any request from another Party for consultations. The Parties concerned shall initiate requested consultations promptly.

5. The Parties engaged in consultations on a particular matter affecting the operation of this Agreement shall provide information concerning the matter subject to the provisions of Article VI, paragraph 9, and attempt to conclude such consultations within a reasonably short period of time.

Dispute settlement

6. If no mutually satisfactory solution has been reached as a result of consultations under paragraph 4 between the Parties concerned, the Committee shall meet at the request of any party to the dispute within thirty days of receipt of such a request to investigate the matter, with a view to facilitating a mutually satisfactory solution.

7. If no mutually satisfactory solution has been reached after detailed examination by the Committee under paragraph 6 within three months, the Committee shall, at the request of any party to the dispute establish a panel to:

(a) examine the matter;

(b) consult regularly with the parties to the dispute and give full opportunity for them to develop a mutually satisfactory solution;

(c) make a statement concerning the facts of the matter as they relate to application of this Agreement and make such findings as will assist the Committee in making recommendations or giving rulings on the matter.

8. In order to facilitate the constitution of panels, the Chairman of the Commitee shall maintain an informal indicative list of governmental officials experienced in the field of trade relations. This list may also include persons other than governmental officials. In this connexion, each Party shall be invited to indicate at the beginning of every year to the Chairman of the Commitee the names(s) of the one or two persons whom the parties to this Agreement would be willing to make available for such work. When a panel is established under paragraph 7, the Chairman, within seven days, shall propose to the parties to the dispute the composition of the panel consisting of three or five members and preferably government officials. The parties directly concerned shall react within seven working days to nominations of panel members by the Chairman and shall not oppose nominations except for compelling reasons.

Citizens of countries whose governments are parties to a dispute shall not be eligible for membership of the panel concerned with that dispute. Panel members shall serve in their individual capacities and not as governmental representatives nor as representatives of any organization. Governments or organizations shall therefore not give them instructions with regard to matters before a panel.

9. Each panel shall develop its own procedures. All Parties, having a substantial interest in the matter and having notified this to the Committee, shall have an opportunity to be heard. Each panel may consult with and seek information from any source it deems appropriate. Before a panel seeks such information from a source within the jurisdiction of a Party it shall inform the government of that Party. Any Party shall respond promptly and fully to any request by a panel for such information as the panel considers necessary and appropriate. Confidential information provided to the panel shall not be revealed without formal authorization from the government or person providing the information. Where such information is requested from the panel but release of such information by the panel is not authorized, a non-confidential summary of the information, authorized by the government or person providing the information, will be provided.

Where a mutually satisfactory solution to a dispute connot be found or where the dispute relates to an interpretation of this Agreement, the panel should first submit the descriptive part of its report to the Parties concerned, and should subsequently submit to the parties to the dispute its conclusions, or an outline thereof, a reasonable period of time before they are circulated to the Committee. Where an interpretation of this Agreement is not involved and where a bilateral settlement of the matter has been found, the report of the panel may be confined to a brief description of the case and to reporting that a solution had been reached.

10. The time required by panels will vary with the particular case. Panels should aim to deliver their findings, and where appropriate, recommendations, to the Committee without undue delay, taking into account the obligation of the Committee to ensure prompt settlement in cases of urgency, normally within a period of four months from the date the panel was established.

Enforcement

11. After the examination is complete or after the report of a panel, working party or other subsidiary body is presented to the Committee, the Committee shall give the matter prompt consideration. With respect to these reports, the Committee shall take appropriate action normally within thirty days of receipt of

1038 - 28

the report unless extended by the Committee, including:

(a) a statement concerning the facts of the matter;

(b) recommendations to one or more Parties; and/or

(c) any other ruling which it deems appropriate.

Any recommendations by the Committee shall aim at the positive resolution of the matter on the basis of the operative provisions of this Agreement and its objectives set out in the Preamble.

12. If a Party to which recommendations are addressed considers itself unable to implement them, it should promptly furnish reasons in writing to the Committee. In that event, the Committee shall consider what further action may be appropriate.

13. The Committee shall keep under surveillance any matter on which it has made recommendations or given rulings.

Balance of rights and obligations

14. If the Committee's recommendations are not accepted by a party, or parties, to the dispute, and if the Committee considers that the circumstances are serious enough to justify such action, it may authorize a Party or Parties to suspend in whole or in part, and for such time as may be necessary, the application of this Agreement to any other Party or Parties, as is determined to be appropriate in the circumstances.

ARTICLE VIII

Exceptions to the Agreement

1. Nothing in this Agreement shall be construed to prevent any Party from taking action or not disclosing any information which it considers necessary for the protection of its essential security interests relating to the procurement of arms, ammunition or war materials, or to procurement indispensable for national security or for national defense purposes.

2. Subject to the requirement that such measures are not applied in a manner which would constitute a means of arbitrary or unjustifiable discrimination between countries where the same conditions prevail or a disguised restriction on international trade, nothing in this Agreement shall be construed to prevent any party from imposing or enforcing measures necessary to protect public morals, order or safety, human, animal or plant life or health, intellectual property, or relating to the products of handicapped persons, of philanthropic institutions or of prison labour.

ARTICLE IX

Final Provisions

1. Acceptance and accession

(a) This Agreement shall be open for acceptance by signature or otherwise, by governments contracting parties to the GATT and by the European Economic Community whose agreed lists of entities are contained in Annex I.

(b) Any government contracting party to the GATT not a Party to this Agreement may accede to it on terms to be agreed between that government and the Parties. Accession shall take place by the deposit with the Director-General to the CONTRACTING PARTIES to the GATT of an instrument of accession which states the terms so agreed.

(c) This Agreement shall be open for acceptance by signature or otherwise by governments having provisionally acceded to the GATT, on terms related to the effective application of rights and obligations under this Agreement, which take into account rights and obligations in the instruments providing for their provisional accession, and whose agreed lists of entities are contained in Annex I.

(d) This Agreement shall be open to accession by any other government on terms, related to the effective application of rights and obligations under this Agreement, to be agreed between that government and the Parties, by the deposit with the Director-General to the CONTRACTING PARTIES to the GATT of an instrument of accession which states the terms so agreed.

(e) In regard to acceptance, the provisions of Article XXVI:5(a) and (b) of the General Agreement would be applicable.

2. Reservations

Reservations may not be entered in respect of any of the provisions of this Agreement.

3. Entry into force

This Agreement shall enter into force on 1 January 1981 for the governments' which have accepted or acceded to it by that date. For each other government, it shall enter into force on the thirtieth day following the date of its acceptance or accession to this Agreement.

4. National legislation

(a) Each government accepting or acceding to this Agreement shall ensure, not later than the date of entry into force of this Agreement for it, the conformity of its laws, regulations and administrative procedures, and the rules, procedures and practices applied by the entities contained in its list annexed hereto, with the provisions of this Agreement.

(b) Each Party shall inform the Committee of any changes in its laws and regulations relevant to this Agreement and in the administration of such laws and regulations.

5. Rectifications or modifications

(a) Rectifications of a purely formal nature and minor amendments relating to Annexes I-IV to this Agreement shall be notified to the Committee and shall become effective provided there is no objection within thirty days to such rectifications or amendments.

(b) Any modifications to lists of entities other than those referred to in subparagraph (a) may be made only in exceptional circumstances. In such cases, a Party proposing to modify its list of entities shall notify the Chairman of the Committee who shall promptly convene a meeting of the Committee. The Parties shall consider the proposed modification and consequent compensatory adjustments, with a view to maintaining a comparable level of mutually agreed coverage provided in this Agreement prior to such modification. In the event of agreement not being reached on any modification taken or proposed, the matter may be pursued in accordance with the provisions contained in Article VII of this Agreement, taking into account the need to maintain the balance of rights and obligations at the highest possible level.

6. Review and negotiations

(a) The Committee shall review annually the implementation and operation of this Agreement taking into account the objectives thereof. The Committee shall annually inform the CONTRACTING PARTIES to the GATT of developments during the periods covered by such reviews.

(b) Not later than the end of the third year from the entry into force of this Agreement and periodically thereafter, the Parties thereto shall undertake further negotiations, with a view to broadening and improving this Agreement on the basis of mutual reciprocity having regard to the provisions of Article III relating to developing countries. In this connexion, the Committee shall, at an early stage, explore the possibilities of expanding the coverage of the Agreement to include service contracts.

7. Amendments

The Parties may amend this Agreement having regard, *inter alia*, to the

'For the purpose of this Agreement, the term "government" is deemed to include the competent authorities of the European Economic Community.

1038 -29

0264

Published by The Bureau of National Affairs, Inc.

experience gained in its implementation. Such an amendment, once the Parties have concurred in accordance with the procedures established by the Committee, shall not come into force for any Party until it has been accepted by such Party.

8. *Withdrawal*

Any Party may withdraw from this Agreement. The withdrawal shall take effect upon the expiration of sixty days from the day on which written notice of withdrawal is received by the Director-General to the CONTRACTING PARTIES to the GATT. Any Party may upon such notification request an immediate meeting of the Committee.

9. *Non-application of this Agreement between Particular Parties*

This Agreement shall not apply as between any two Parties if either of the Parties, at the time either accepts or accedes to this Agreement, does not consent to such application.

10. *Notes and Annexes*

The notes and annexes to this Agreement constitute an integral part thereof.

11. *Secretariat*

This Agreement shall be serviced by the GATT secretariat.

12. *Deposit*

This Agreement shall be deposited with the Director-General to the CONTRACTING PARTIES to the GATT, who shall promptly furnish to each Party and each contracting party to the GATT a certified copy thereof and of each rectification or modification thereto pursuant to paragraph 5 and of each amendment thereto pursuant to paragraph 7, and a notification of each acceptance thereof or accession thereto pursuant to paragraph 1 and of each withdrawal therefrom pursuant to paragraph 8, of this Article.

13. *Registration*

This Agreement shall be registered in accordance with the provisions of Article 102 of the Charter of the United Nations.

Done at Geneva this twelfth day of April nineteen hundred and seventy-nine in a single copy, in the English, French and Spanish languages, each text being authentic, except as otherwise specified with respect to the lists of entities annexed hereto.

NOTES

Article I, paragraph 1

Having regard to general policy considerations relating to tied aid, including the objective of developing countries with respect to the untying of such aid, this Agreement does not apply to procurement made in furtherance of tied aid to developing countries so long as it is practised by Parties.

Article V, paragraph 15(h)

Having regard to the general policy considerations of developing countries in relation to government procurement, it is noted that under the provisions of paragraph 15(h) of Article V, developing countries may require incorporation of domestic content, offset procurement, or transfer of technology as criteria for award of contracts. It is noted that suppliers from one Party shall not be favoured over suppliers from any other Party. When known, these requirements shall be specified in the notice of proposed procurement and tender documentation.

1038 - 30

0265

Annex I to Agreement on Government Procurement List of Entities Referred to in Part I, Paragraph 1(c)

The following entities are included in the coverage of this Agreement by the United States:

1. ACTION
2. Administrative Conference of the United States
3. American Battle Monuments Commission
4. Board for International Broadcasting
5. Civil Aeronautics Board
6. Commission on Civil Rights
7. Commodity Futures Trading Commission
8. Consumer Product Safety Commission
9. Department of Agriculture (The Agreement on Government Procurement does not apply to procurement of agricultural products made in furtherance of agricultural support programs or human feeding programs)
10. Department of Commerce
11. Department of Defense (Excludes Corps of Engineers)
12. Department of Education
13. Department of Health and Human Services
14. Department of Housing and Urban Development
15. Department of the Interior (Excludes the Bureau of Reclamation)
16. Department of Justice
17. Department of Labor
18. Department of State
19. Department of the Treasury
20. Environmental Protection Agency
21. Equal Employment Opportunity Commission
22. Executive Office of the President
23. Export-Import Bank of the United States
24. Farm Credit Administration
25. Federal Communications Commission
26. Federal Deposit Insurance Corporation
27. Federal Home Loan Bank Board
28. Federal Maritime Commission
29. Federal Mediation and Conciliation Service
30. Federal Trade Commission
31. General Services Administration (Purchases by the Tools Commodity Center, and the Region 9 Office in San Francisco, California are not included)
32. Interstate Commerce Commission
33. Merit Systems Protection Board
34. National Aeronautics and Space Administration

103A — 31

EXHIBIT D
Annex I
Page 2 of 4

35. National Credit Union Administration
36. National Labor Relations Board
37. National Mediation Board
38. National Science Foundation
39. National Transportation Safety Board
40. Nuclear Regulatory Commission
41. Office of Personnel Management
42. Overseas Private Investment Corporation
43. Panama Canal Commission
44. Railroad Retirement Board
45. Securities and Exchange Commission
46. Selective Service System
47. Smithsonian Institution
48. United States Arms Control and Disarmament Agency
49. United States Information Agency
50. United States International Development Cooperation Agency
51. United States International Trade Commission
52. Veterans Administration
53. Maritime Administration of the Department of Transportation
54. The Peace Corps

This Agreement will not apply to the following purchases of the DOD:

(a) Federal Supply Classification (FSC) 83 - all elements of this classification other than pins, needles, sewing kits, flagstaffs, flagpoles, and flagstaff trucks;
(b) FSC 84 - all elements other than sub-class 8460 (luggage);
(c) FSC 89 - all elements other than sub-class 8975 (tobacco products);
(d) FSC 2310 - (buses only);
(e) Specialty metals, defined as steels melted in steel manufacturing facilities located in the United States or its possessions, where the maximum alloy content exceeds one or more of the following limits, must be used in products purchased by DOD: (1) manganese, 1.65 percent; silicon, 0.60 percent; or copper, 0.06 percent; or which contains more than 0.25 percent of any of the following elements; aluminum, chromium, cobalt, columgium, molybdenum, nickel, titanium, tungsten, or vanadium; (2) metal alloys consisting of nickel, iron-nickel and cobalt base alloys containing a total of other alloying metals (except iron) in excess of 10 percent; (3) titanium and titanium alloys; or, (4) zirconium base alloys;

1038 -32

0267

EXHIBIT D
Annex I
Page 3 of 4

(f) FSC 19 and 20 - that part of these classifications defined as naval vessels or major components of the hull or superstructure thereof;
(g) FSC 51
(h) Following FSC categories are not generally covered due to application of Part VIII, paragraph 1: 10, 12, 13, 14, 15, 16, 17, 19, 20, 28, 31, 58, 59, 95.

This Agreement will generally apply to purchases of the following FSC categories subject to United States Government determinations under the provisions of Part VIII, paragraph 1:

22. Railway Equipment
23. Motor Vehicles, Trailers, and Cycles (except buses in 2310)
24. Tractors
25. Vehicular Equipment Components
26. Tires and Tubes
29. Engine Accessories
30. Mechanical Power Transmission Equipment
32. Woodworking Machinery and Equipment
34. Metalworking Machinery
35. Service and Trade Equipment
36. Special Industry Machinery
37. Agricultural Machinery and Equipment
38. Construction, Mining, Excavating, and Highway Maintenance Equipment
39. Materials Handling Equipment
40. Rope, Cable, Chain and Fittings
41. Refrigeration and Air Conditioning Equipment
42. Fire Fighting, Rescue and Safety Equipment
43. Pumps and Compressors
44. Furnace, Steam Plant, Drying Equipment and Nuclear Reactors
45. Plumbing, Heating and Sanitation Equipment
46. Water Purification and Sewage Treatment Equipment
47. Pipe, Tubing, Hose and Fittings
48. Valves
49. Maintenance and Repair Ship Equipment
52. Measuring Tools
53. Hardware and Abrasives
54. Prefabricated Structures and Scaffolding
55. Lumber, Millwork, Plywood and Veneer
56. Construction and Building Materials
61. Electric Wire, and Power and Distribution Equipment
62. Lighting Fixtures and Lamps
63. Alarm and Signal Systems

1038 -33

0268

EXHIBIT D
Annex I
Page 4 of 4

65. Medical, Dental, and Veterinary Equipment and Supplies
66. Instruments and Laboratory Equipment
67. Photographic Equipment
68. Chemicals and Chemical Products
69. Training Aids and Devices
70. General Purpose ADPE, Software, Supplies and Support Equipment
71. Furniture
72. Household and Commercial Furnishings and Appliances
73. Food Preparation and Serving Equipment
74. Office Machines, Visible Record Equipment and ADP Equipment
75. Office Supplies and Devices
76. Books, Maps and Other Publications
77. Musical Instruments, Phonographs, and Home Type Radios
78. Recreational and Athletic Equipment
79. Cleaning Equipment and Supplies
80. Brushes, Paints, Sealers and Adhesives
81. Containers, Packaging and Packing Supplies
85. Toiletries
87. Agricultural Supplies
88. Live Animals
91. Fuels, Lubricants, Oils and Waxes
93. Non-metallic Fabricated Materials
94. Non-metallic Crude Materials
96. Ores, Minerals and their Primary Products
99. Miscellaneous

General Notes:

1. Notwithstanding the above, this Agreement will not apply to set asides on behalf of small minority businesses.
2. Pursuant to Part I, paragraph 1(a), transportation is not included in services incidental to procurement contracts.

0269

1038 -34

EXHIBIT E

List of Contracts Not Subject to the Agreement on Government Procurement and the Trade Agreements Act of 1979

(a) Offers for eligible products below $156,000;
(b) Products of non-signatory countries;
(c) Purchases under small or small disadvantaged business preference programs;
(d) Purchases of arms, ammunition, or war materials or purchases indispensable for the national security or the national defense;
(e) Construction contracts;
(f) Service contracts (except those services incidental to the purchase of eligible products; provided, that the value of the services is not greater than the value of the product);
(g) Research and development contracts;
(h) Purchases by the U.S. Army Corps of Engineers;
(i) Purchases of items for resale;
(j) Purchases under Subpart 8.6, Acquisition from Federal Prison Industries, Inc., and Subpart 8.7, Acquisition from the Blind and Other severely Handicapped;
(k) Lease or rental agreements;
(l) Purchases for non-designated agencies; or
(m) Purchases of products that are excluded from duty free treatment for Caribbean countries under 19 U.S.C. § 2703(b).

1038-35

0270

EXHIBIT F

Countries Participating In Memoranda of Understanding With the United States

Canada
Federal Republic of Germany
Italy
United Kingdom of Great Britain and Northern Ireland (U.K.)
Norway
Kingdom of the Netherlands
Portugal
Belgium
Denmark
France
Turkey
Grand Duchy of Luxenbourg
Israel
Spain

1038 - 36

0271

PAUL, WEISS, RIFKIND, WHARTON & GARRISON
1615 L STREET, N.W. WASHINGTON, D.C. 20036-5694

DATE March 26, 1991

MEMORANDUM

Mr. Yong-Hyun Suh
Director

From Soon-Yub Kwon

Subject Status of the U.S. Economy

We provide below a general overview of the U.S. economic situation, and attempt to reconcile the divergent views among prominent economists about the likely duration of the current recession. Although recent economic indicators have created confusion about the short-term outlook, the Administration appears correct in its prediction that by the fourth quarter of 1991, the U.S. economy should be expanding once again.

A. The Current Situation

Of greatest concern at the present time is the value of the U.S. dollar relative to other currencies. Since the beginning of the year, the value of the dollar has risen by nearly nine percent, reaching a nine-month high, against a trade-weighted basket of currencies of the ten largest U.S. trading partners. The dollar's appreciation has occurred despite:

- o a two percent reduction in the U.S. gross national product ("GNP") during the fourth quarter of 1990 (after increasing 1.4 percent during the third quarter of 1990), with further reductions expected during the first and second quarters of 1991;

1038 - 37

0272

- an unemployment rate that now exceeds six percent and is likely to approach seven percent by mid-year;
- interest rates that have declined since early in 1990; and
- a .4 percent drop in January 1991 in the index of leading economic indicators (which is designed to predict economic activity about six months into the future) after a decline of .1 percent in December 1990.

B. Motor Vehicles

According to the Commerce Department, U.S. personal consumption expenditures for durable goods in the fourth quarter of 1990 declined 2.9 percent, following a 2.7 percent increase during the third quarter of 1990. Expenditures for motor vehicles and parts -- the principal cause of the wide swings in expenditures for durable goods throughout 1990 -- fell 18 percent to their lowest level since the fourth quarter of 1987. This reduction in new car and truck purchases resulted from both the recession and changes in the sales incentive programs offered by automakers: incentives in the fourth quarter were modest in comparison with those offered in the previous quarter, and new car prices increased sharply by the end of 1990.

C. The U.S. Dollar

On March 19, Undersecretary of Treasury David Mulford cited four reasons for the recent surge in the dollar's value: the perception that the U.S. economy is

1038 - 32

"stronger than was thought," political uncertainty in the Soviet Union, the economic crisis in the eastern part of reunified Germany, and the rapid success of U.S.-led coalition forces in the Persian Gulf. Mulford confirmed that U.S. officials at the Treasury Department and the Federal Reserve are "cooperating" with other central banks to slow the "very rapid movement" of the dollar in exchange markets. One U.S. dollar is now worth nearly 138 yen and 1.65 marks, while one pound costs $1.78.

Slower economic growth overseas may reduce foreign interest rates and place additional upward pressure on the dollar. Japan's Economic Planning Agency, for example, reported on March 19 that Japan's GNP during the fourth quarter of 1990 grew by .5 percent, compared to a one percent increase during the preceding quarter. The economies of Germany, Great Britain, France and Italy have also showed signs of weakness.

D. The U.S. Trade Deficit

The rising dollar will help keep U.S. inflation down, by reducing the cost of imported goods. But imports will increase in response and may displace sales of domestically-produced goods, making it more difficult to reduce the U.S. trade deficit and stimulate the economy.

Secretary of Commerce Robert Mosbacher has indicated that the Administration is "counting on" increasing exports to "fuel" U.S. economic growth in 1991, as they did in 1990. In 1990, U.S. exports increased eight percent to $394 billion (manufactured exports increased 9.7 percent). U.S. imports rose 4.7 percent to $495 billion, for a U.S. trade deficit of $101 billion (the lowest since the 1983 level of $52.4 billion), down seven percent from 1989. Preliminary trade data for January 1991, which were released on March 19, show U.S. exports to have risen 3.6 percent from December to $34.5 billion (the second-highest monthly figure on record). U.S. imports increased 4.8 percent to $41.5 billion, for a monthly deficit of $7 billion, up 10 percent from December. Some forecasters are predicting a reduction in the 1991 U.S. merchandise trade deficit of 25 percent to $75 billion, although this appears overly-optimistic in light of the dollar's recent strength.

E. Interest Rates

The Federal Reserve, at this point, appears unwilling to further reduce interest rates following the release on March 19 of new inflation figures, which indicated a "core" rate of increase for February (excluding the two highly-volatile categories of food and fuel) of .7 percent, or approximately eight percent on an annual basis. The overall consumer price index ("CPI") in February, including fuel and food, rose .2 percent, down from .4 percent in January. White House spokesmen described the

1038 - 40

higher rates of increase for some items in the inflation index as a "delayed reaction" to earlier increases in energy prices.

F. Prospects for an Early U.S. Recovery

The quick end to the Iraq war is also likely to cause an earlier end to the U.S. recession than many economists previously anticipated, for three reasons. First, the price of oil is now expected to remain around $20 per barrel throughout 1991. Bush Administration officials base their forecast of oil price stability on the elimination of uncertainty about the Persian Gulf situation, and Saudi willingness to maintain higher production rates out of gratitude for U.S. and European military assistance. Administration officials have also indicated that they expect the added stimulus to Japan's economy from lower oil prices to boost Japan's imports from the United States.

The second factor which should stimulate U.S. economic growth is rising consumer confidence. A variety of post-war surveys indicate that most consumers now believe the U.S. economy will begin improving by the second half of this year. Thirdly, the return home of several hundred thousand U.S. troops with six months of accumulated savings will almost certainly boost expenditures on automobiles and other durable goods.

1038-41

0276

Although an economic recovery therefore appears to be within sight, growth will probably be slow and steady, rather than explosive. The Federal Reserve will keep a careful eye on inflation, and consumers are expected to shop more responsibly in the future, with a higher emphasis on reasonable prices, quality and service. We would expect another look at interest rate reductions by the Federal Reserve if and when inflation appears safely under control.

If you would like further details on any of the issues addressed in this memorandum, please do not hesitate to let us know.

Best Regards,

S.K.

1038 - 42

0277

기안(경제부 inform)

원 본

외 무 부

종 별 :

번 호 : GVW-0575 일 시 : 91 0327 1600

수 신 : 장 관 (통기, 경기원, 재무부)

발 신 : 주 제네바 대사

제 목 : UR/ 서비스협상(금융분야)

연: GVW-0566

연호 카나다가 주관하는 금융분야 부속서에 관한 비공식 협의는 별첨 (FAX 송부)과 같이 4.23-24,GATT 에서 개최될 예정이며 캐나다측은 총 30개국에 대하여 초청시한을 발송하였음.

첨부:동서한 1부.(GVW(F)-0108)

(대사 박수길-국장)

통상국 2차보 경기원 재무부

PAGE 1

91.03.28 08:55 WG

외신 1과 통제관

0278

GVW(h)-0108 10327 1600

" GVW-0515 "

Permanent Mission of Canada to the United Nations

La Mission Permanente du Canada auprès des Nations Unies

UNCLAS / NONCLAS
UZ7D 5831
PAGE 3 OF/DE 4

1, rue du Pré-de-la-Bichette
1202 Geneva

March 26, 1991

Dear Colleague:

Please find, herewith, a letter of invitation to take part in informal discussions on financial services April 23rd and 24th, 1991. This session, which is open to all participants, will be held in the GATT building, with the exact location to be announced separately.

I trust you will share our interest and look forward to your participation.

Yours sincerely,

R.G. Wright
Minister

0279

The Permanent Mission of Canada
to the United Nations

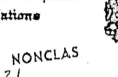

La Mission Permanente du Canada
auprès des Nations Unies

UNCLAS / NONCLAS
UZTD 5831
PAGE 4 OF/DE 4

1, rue du Pré-de-la-Bichette
1202 Geneva

March 26, 1991

Dear Colleague:

As part of the Uruguay Round discussions on financial services, Canada would like to host an informal meeting of financial experts in Geneva. The purpose of the meeting, which I will be chairing, is to exchange views on key elements for financial services. This includes - but is not limited to - prudential aspects, the "two track" application, the process of initial offers and the completion of schedules.

We would welcome participation of your government's experts in financial services. The meeting will take place on Tuesday April 23 and Wednesday April 24, as necessary in the Centre Rappard, Geneva.

On April 25 and April 26 and the following week, delegations will have, if they so desire, an opportunity to meet bilaterally at their own location and time of choosing to continue discussions.

Could we please have confirmation of participation by April 17 to François Nadeau in the Canadian Mission (tel: 733.90.00, fax 734.79.19) in Geneva or to me (fax number is 1-613-952-1596). Names of participants, with titles, phone and fax numbers would be appreciated.

I look forward to productive and informative meetings.

Frank Swedlove
Assistant Director
Financial Institutions Divisions
Department of Finance of Canada

0280

발 신 전 보

분류번호	보존기간

번 호 : WGV-0369 910328 1950 CV 종별 :

수 신 : 주 제네바 대사. ~~총영사~~

발 신 : 장 관 (통 기)

제 목 : UR/서비스 한.미 양자협의

대 : GVW-0516

대호 관련 아래 통보함.

1. 본부대표 파견 여부 : 노동력 이동 및 주요업종 담당부처 실무진으로 구성된 본부대표팀 파견 예정

2. 양자협의 희망일자 : 1991.4.16.(화) 오전 또는 오후. 끝.

(통상국장 대리 최 혁)

보안 통제	

앙고재	91년 3월 28일	통기과	기안자 성명	과 장	국 장	차 관	장 관
			김봉주		선결		대결

외신과통제

0281

경 제 기 획 원

통조삼 10502-209 503-9149 1991. 3. 25.

수신 외무부장관

참조 통상기구과장

제목 UR/서비스협상관련 제2차 한.미 양자협의

1. GVW-0516 ('91.3.20) 관련사항임.

2. USTR 제네바 사무소로 부터 UR/서비스 제2차 한.미 양자협의 개최와 관련 아국본부대표 파견여부 및 4.10-4.19중 양자협의 희망일자 선정등을 아국 제네바 대표부에 문의하여 온바, 당원 검토를 거쳐 다음과 같이 통보코자 하니 지급 조치하여 주시기 바랍니다.

다 음

가. 본부대표 파견여부: 노동력이동 및 주요업종 담당부처 실무진으로 구성된 본부대표팀 파견예정

나. 양자협의 희망일자: 1991.4.16(화) 오전 또는 오후 (USTR사무소의 예상소요시간은 half a day임)

끝.

경 제 기 획 원 장

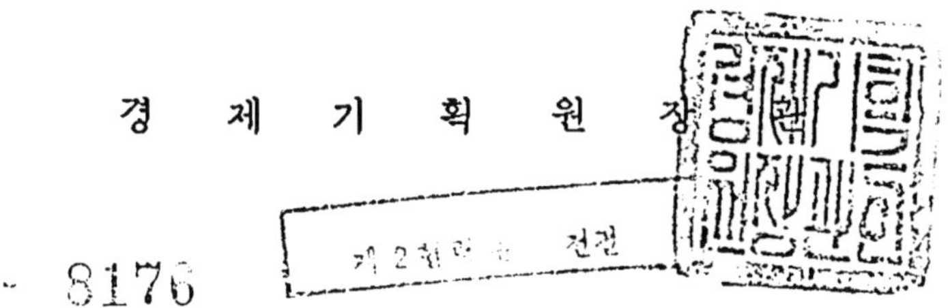

8176

0282

경 제 기 획 원

통조삼 10502-208　　503-9149　　1991. 3. 25.

수신 수신처참조 통상기구과.

제목 UR/서비스협상관련 양허협상책임자 및 자문관 명단통보

1. 통조삼 10502-61 ('91.1.24)와 관련입니다.

2. 금년 4월경부터 본격적으로 진행될 것으로 예상되는 UR/서비스 양허협상을 대비해서 각부처가 지정한 양허협상책임자 및 자문관 명단을 별첨과 같이 통보하니 매 현지 양허협상때마다 일관성있게 참석할 수 있도록 협조해 주기 바랍니다.

○ 특히 각부처는 소속연구기관 등과 협조하여 동 자문관이 국내 협상대책회의 및 현지협상에 최우선적으로 참여할 수 있도록 필요한 행정적 지원을 제공하기 바랍니다.

3. 아울러 동 양허협상책임자 및 자문관을 변경할 경우 당원에 즉시 통보해 주기 바랍니다.

별첨: UR/서비스협상관련 양허협상 책임자 및 자문관 1부. 끝.

경 제 기 획 원 장 관

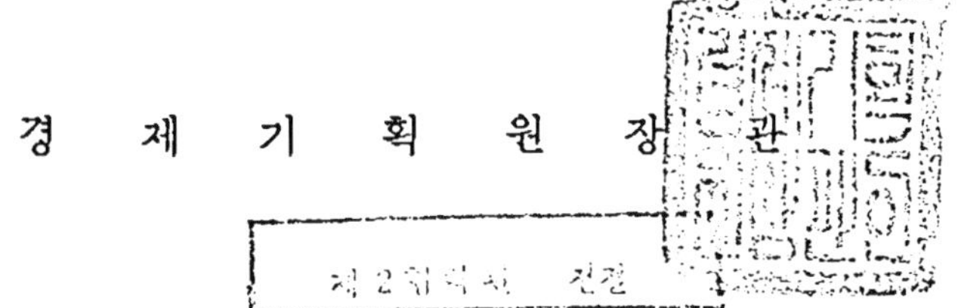

수신처: 외무부장관, 재무부장관, 법무부장관, 교육부장관, 농림수산부장관, 문화부장관, 상공부장관, 보건사회부장관, 건설부장관, 교통부장관, 노동부장관, 체신부장관, 과학기술처장관, 공보처장관, 해운항만청장, 특허청장, 대외경제정책연구원장, 김&장법률사무소장.

8175　　0283

UR/서비스협상관련 양허협상책임자 및 자문관

('91.3.22일 현재)

분 야	양허협상 책임자	자 문 관
<총괄반>		
- 서비스전반	경기원 대조실 제2협력관	대외경제정책연구원 박태호박사
		" 김태준박사
<분과반>		
- 정보통신	체신부 통신협력과장 김창곤	통신개발연구원 성극제박사
- 건 설	건설부 해외협력과장 이종호	국토개발연구원 김흥수박사
- 유 통	상공부 유통산업과장 박갑록	산업연구원 이영세박사
- 금 융	재무부 국제금융과장 진영욱	한국은행 이문호과장
- 운송분야 총괄 및 육운	교통부 국제협력과장 김규선	교통개발연구원 강승필박사
ㅇ 항공	교통부 국제항공과사무관 함영기	" 허 종박사
ㅇ 해운	항만청 진흥과사무관 이재균	해운산업연구원 김광태박사
ㅇ 관광	교통부 국제관광과사무관 최재길	교통개발연구원 현진권박사
- 보 건	보사부 국제협력담당관 신홍건	보건연구원 노인철박사
- 교 육	문교부 교육협력과장 유강하	세방종합법률사무소 정영철변호사
- 시청각서비스	문화부 영화진흥과장 서정배	중앙대학교 이승구 교수
- 노동력의 이동	노동부 고용관리과장 김영갑	한국노동연구원 박영범박사
- 사업서비스		
ㅇ 변호사	법무부 국제법무검사 김준규	태평양법률사무소 이정훈변호사
ㅇ 엔지니어링	과기처 기술제도담당관 노흥길	한국기술용역협회 배정련전무
ㅇ 회계사	재무부 증권업무과장 이우철	공인회계사협회 김종기부회장
ㅇ 세무사	재무부 소득세제과장 임지순	세무사협회 김성한이사
ㅇ 광 고	공보처 광고정책과장 김인철	한국ABC협회 신인섭전무
ㅇ 부동산중개업	건설부 토지관리과장 김동설	부동산중개업협회 이호일 회장
ㅇ 변리사	특허청 지도과장 류명현	유미특허법률사무소 송만호변리사

0284

정 리 보 존 문 서 목 록					
기록물종류	일반공문서철	등록번호	2019080103	등록일자	2019-08-14
분류번호	764.51	국가코드		보존기간	영구
명 칭	UR(우루과이라운드) / GNS(서비스협상그룹) 회의, 1991. 전5권				
생 산 과	통상기구과	생산년도	1991~1991	담당그룹	
권 차 명	V.2 4-5월				
내용목차					

0001

경 제 기 획 원

봉조삼 10502- 227 503-9149 1991. 4. 4.

수신 수신처참조 통상기구과

제목 UR/서비스협상관련 양허협상 대책자료 제출독려

1. 봉조삼 10502-61 ('91.1.24)와 관련입니다.

2. 서비스일반협상(GATS) 및 분야별부속서(Sectoral Annex)의 제정 작업과는 별도로 3월중순부터 미국은 30여개 주요협상국들과 양허계획표 (Offer List)를 바탕으로 한 제2차 양자협의를 추진하고 있으며 조만간 미국 이외의 타국가들도 본격적인 양자협의를 진행할 것으로 전망됩니다.

3. 이에 대비하여 '91.1.22 개최된 UR/서비스협상대책 회의에서 확정한 다음과 같은 양허협상 대책자료를 당원에 조속히 제출해 주시기 바랍니다.

- o 주요협상국가에 대한 개방요구서 (Request List)
- o 서비스교역 현황, 외국부자기업 현황등 양허협상에 필요한 통계자료
- o 각 업종별 노동력이동 허용범위
- o 아국의 Offer List에서 제외된 보건, 교육분야등의 협상대책

4. 아울러 각국이 제출한 Offer List (각부처에 기송부, 봉조삼 10502-819 ('90.12.14)중 소관사항을 요약.분석한 자료를 당원에 4.30까지 제출해 주시기 바랍니다. 끝.

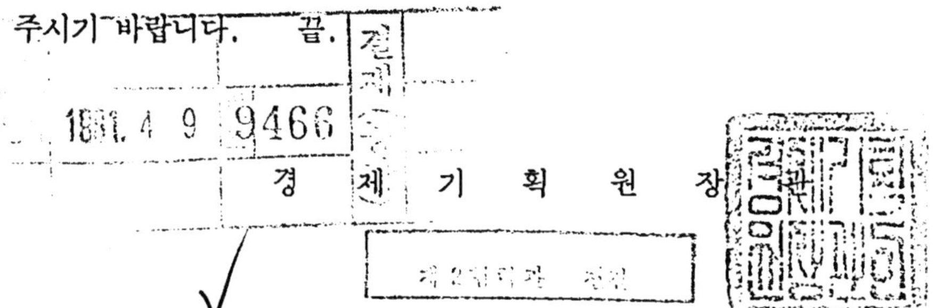

1991. 4. 9 9466

경 제 기 획 원 장

수신처: 외무부장관, 재무부장관, 법무부장관, 문화부장관, 농림수산부장관, 교육부장관, 상공부장관, 건설부장관, 보건사회부장관, 교통부장관, 노동부장관, 동력자원부장관, 체신부장관, 과학기술처장관, 공보처장관, 환경처장관, 해운항만청장, 특허청장, 대한무역진흥공사장.

0002

원 본

외 무 부

종 별 :

번 호 : GVW-0635 일 시 : 91 0408 1930

수 신 : 장 관(통기, 경기원)

발 신 : 주 제네바 대사

제 목 : UR/ 서비스 협상

연: GVW-0566

연호 4.10-11 간 개최 예정인 UR/ 서비스 주요국 비공식 협의 관련 갓트 사무국에서 작성한 CHECK-LIST 를 별첨(FAX) 송부함.

첨부: 사무국 작성 CHECK-LIST 1 부.(GVW(F)-116)

(대사 박수길-국장)

통상국 2차보 경기원 특허청. 재무부. 상공부

PAGE 1

91.04.09 09:15 WG

외신 1과 통제관

0003

GVW(F)-0116 10408 1430
GVW-635 324

3.4.91

CHECKLIST OF ISSUES RELATING TO A SERVICES CLASSIFICATION LIST AND THE SCHEDULING OF COMMITMENTS

The following checklist of issues and accompanying notes have been drawn up with a view to facilitating discussion at the meeting on 10-11 April. The list of issues is not intended to be exhaustive. Some delegations may wish to formulate some of these issues differently or to bring up other questions. For some other delegations, not all the issues listed below may need consideration. The list is not intended to limit the discussions in any way.

A. Services Classification List

In the services discussions so far there has been no agreed basis for a classification or nomenclature of services. This was possible because the discussions up to now were very much related to general principles and problems in connection with a framework agreement on trade in services.

A comparison of initial offers so far tabled by countries, however, has in the view of many demonstrated the necessity for a detailed common sector classification system which would enable countries to make, compare and record commitments in a consistent manner. Some participants advocate a common numerical classification system which would be based on the secretariat reference list contained in MTN.GNS/W/50 whereas others consider it more feasible, at least regarding the negotiation of initial commitments, to be able to use their own national classifications which would then be brought into concordance on a sector-by-sector basis.

Nature of Classification List

1. Should the services classification be based on the CPC classification?

Note:

(a) The reference list of the secretariat in MTN.GNS/W/50 was based on the CPC classification.

0004

(b) Most participating countries are moving to the CPC classification. Therefore consistency in national services classification is most likely through the adoption of the CPC classification.

2. If the CPC classification system is adopted as a basis for a refined classification list to be developed by the secretariat, how should the problem that in certain sectors the classification adopted for earlier sectoral discussions and for the making of offers differs from the CPC system be dealt with? Should such cases be addressed through adjustment or elaboration of the CPC classification, or should these cases be addressed through adjustment and elaboration of classifications adopted in individual offers by participants?

Note:

The CPC has a subcategory "other" for most of its categories. To the extent that it is felt that the CPC is not detailed enough or incomplete, additional services could be placed under the "other" subcategory for the purposes of the reference list. A first step could be to examine the offer lists that have already been submitted, as well as the reactions to the CPC based secretariat classification list made by certain countries in 1989, and determine to what extent the CPC may need to be augmented.

Use of Classification List

(a) In making their offers/requests, should participants be required to follow the classification list established by the secretariat, or should they cross-refer the items of the list which correspond to what is contained in their offers/requests?

(b) Should the final schedules of commitments be drawn up according to the classification list to be established by the secretariat, or would it be sufficient to have a concordance of the entries in schedules with their correspondents in the indicative list?

B. OTHER ISSUES RELATING TO THE SCHEDULING OF COMMITMENTS

A number of participants in the negotiations have submitted their initial offers on specific commitments. The process of consultations which has started among different delegations on the basis of such offers has revealed a number of technical issues that need to be resolved. Most of these issues concern the precise content of these offers and how they relate to the provisions in the draft framework on the negotiation of commitments and the consolidation of schedules.

1. Is it clear in every instance: what types of measures are covered under each of the four modes of supply, and what is the distinction between each of the four modes of supply?

2. What types of measures are considered to be restrictions on trade in services (i.e. limitations and conditions on market access and conditions and qualifications on national treatment) and therefore should be specified in the Parties schedule? What other measures do not constitute restrictions and fall under the provisions of Article VI (Domestic Regulation)?

3. How should information on regulations falling under Article VI which is exchanged during the process of negotiations be treated? Should it only be subject to transparency obligations of Article III, or should there be any additional requirements on the Parties to the Agreement with respect to its compilation? [Could this have any implications for the balance of rights and obligations under the Agreement?]

4. Is it necessary to make a clear distinction between the types of measures to be bound under market access and those which should be bound under national treatment? If so, what are the criteria on which such a distinction should be based?

5. Should measures which limit the activities of both domestic and foreign suppliers equally be listed under market access?

0006

6. How should horizontal restrictions such as restrictions on investment, real estate ownership or movement of persons which affect a certain mode of supply across all sectors be inscribed in schedules? Should they be tabled in the introductory part of each schedule and how would sector-specific entries in the schedule relating to such restrictions be treated? For example, would the currently used term "no limitations or conditions" be understood to mean "no sector-specific limitations or conditions"?

7. Would there be a need for an explanatory note that contains an agreed interpretation of the technical terms used in drawing up schedules (e.g. "not applicable", "standstill", " no limitations", etc.) in order to avoid any confusion or incompatibility between different schedules?

0007

3.4.91

Horizontal Agreements that Address Matters Pertaining to Services

1. As agreed in the March 8th consultations on services, the secretariat has prepared a background note on horizontal arrangements relevant to the negotiations. This note examines the main principles, obligations and commitments contained in bilateral horizontal arrangements such as treaties of friendship, commerce and navigation (FCNs), and bilateral investment treaties (BITs).[1]

2. This note does not deal with OECD instruments which are also horizontal in character, consisting of the Code of Liberalisation of Current Invisible Operations, the Code of Liberalisation of Capital Movements, and the National Treatment Instrument contained in the 1976 Declaration on International Investment and Multinational Enterprise. The principal features of these OECD instruments are described in MTN.GNS/W/16 of 6 August 1987. Some recent developments regarding the OECD codes of liberalisation are summarized in a separate note. The observations relating to the checklist of issues concerning the services classification list and the scheduling of commitments also apply to the list of questions relating to bilateral agreements and arrangements. Some of the questions raised with respect to the bilateral agreements and arrangements may also be relevant to the OECD instruments.

Background

3. Although FCNs have been used to facilitate bilateral commercial relations since the late 1700s, the investment-related provisions relevant to this discussion became common only after World War Two. Three factors may have contributed to a diminishing resort to FCNs and the increased use

---

[1]FCN and BIT are used here to refer generically to these types of agreements, whatever the formal title may be.

0008

of BITs from the 1960s onwards: (1) the availability of the GATT system to address, among a growing body of signatories, many central elements of FCNs; (2) the rising importance of overseas investment in international commerce; and (3) the need foreseen by industrialized countries for a legal framework to protect their investments in newly independent countries.

4. From the mid-1940s to the mid-1960s the United States concluded 22 FCN treaties that, in addition to other more traditional matters, sought to facilitate and protect investment. At the beginning of the 1960s, European countries began negotiating investment treaties, mostly with developing countries but also with some Eastern bloc countries. Germany, the United Kingdom, Netherlands, and Switzerland account for the majority of over 150 BITs concluded by European countries. The U.S. first began negotiating BITs with developing countries in the early 1980s. It reportedly sought stronger commitments to guard against foreign exchange restrictions, performance requirements, and expropriation than did the Europeans. A few BITs were also concluded among developing countries or between them and Eastern bloc countries. At the end of 1989, over 300 BITs had been negotiated worldwide. BITs may not have been equally critical for the regulation of investment among industrialized countries because of the establishment of the OECD instruments that deal with such matters among members.[2]

5. The bilateral agreements have developed standards for host-country treatment of foreign enterprises or investors, including those which provide services, at a time when multilateral disciplines in this area are limited. The contents of such bilateral agreements vary depending on the year they were concluded or the parties involved. However, the kinds of provisions that form the principal elements are briefly described below.

---

[2] In particular, the Code of Liberalization of Capital Movements and the "National Treatment Instrument" of the 1976 Declaration on International Investment and Multinational Enterprises.

0009

General description

6. FCNs, in particular, but also BITs, address a broad spectrum of bilateral commercial concerns. Thus, both cover issues and commerce significantly beyond the scope envisioned for the GATS. FCNs address, for example, basic rights of natural and juridical persons, acquisition and disposal of property, taxation, trade in goods, transfer of payments, business activities of persons or companies, shipping and customs formalities. BITs address investment and activities of investors generally and also include specific provisions dealing with conditions of entry, monetary transfers, protections against and compensation for nationalisation, expropriation or loss and dispute settlement procedures.

7. The bilateral agreements raise certain issues in the areas of coverage and principles which are relevant to the discussions on the framework on trade in services. First, the bilateral agreements cover certain kinds of services, in particular, those delivered via commercial presence. Second, they apply the concepts of national treatment and m.f.n.. However, the bilateral agreements frequently contain exceptions to the application of these concepts to certain services.

8. With respect to principles applied, in most BITs and in most post-war FCNs, the parties agree to extend national treatment and m.f.n. treatment with respect to entry and with respect to business operations in the domestic market for one another's firms or investors. The treaties fall short, however, of granting a "right of establishment", although the language of provisions on conditions of entry offers stronger guarantees in some accords than in others. There is an implication, however, that the parties should treat applications from foreign investors no less favourably than those from its nationals unless related to a sector or activity exempted under the terms of the agreement.

9. As regards coverage, the relevant provisions of post-WWII FCN treaties address the conduct of business by each party's persons or companies in the territory of the other party. Although not often explicitly mentioned,

services are usually considered to be included within the scope of such provisions of the FCNs. In BITs, investors who provide services are also implicitly, and in some cases explicitly,[3] covered by the agreement in the same way as other kinds of investment activities.

10. In most cases, the bilateral agreements contain exceptions to the application of national treatment and/or m.f.n.. For example, in BITs negotiated by the U.S. the application of national treatment is frequently limited for the following sectors or activities: air transportation, ocean and coastal shipping, maritime services and maritime-related services, banking and insurance, primary dealership in U.S. government securities, ownership and operation of broadcast or common carrier radio and television stations, provision of common carrier telephone and telegraph services, provision of submarine cable services, energy and power production, custom house brokers, ownership of real property, government grants, government insurance and loan programs, mining on the public domain, and use of land and natural resources. FCNs negotiated by the U.S. often employ more generic language making similar exceptions for: air transport, water transport, banking involving depository or fiduciary functions, communications, and land or other natural resources.

[3] E.g., one U.S. BIT states that investment means "every kind of investment, in the territory of one Party owned or controlled directly or indirectly by nationals or companies of the other Party, such as equity, debt, and service and investment contracts ... ".

0011

Checklist of questions relating to horizontal arrangements

- Are the main concepts and principles that form the basis of these arrangements compatible with those of the draft framework?

- Are the obligations contained in these arrangements more or less stringent than those in the draft framework?

- What role has the principle of reciprocity played in these arrangements?

- How do the commitments undertaken in these arrangements compare with market access and national treatment commitments envisioned under the GATS?

- How do the approaches taken with respect to to coverage, limitations on, or exemption of particular services transactions or sectors differ with the approach used in the GATS?

0012

Recent Developments in the OECD Code of Liberalization of Current Invisible Operations and the Code of Liberalisation of Captital Movements: Supplementary Information

1. Recent changes to the OECD Codes have resulted from an ongoing review that is being carried out by the OECD Committee on Capital Movements and Invisible Transactions (CMIT). As a result of this review, new liberalisation obligations have been adopted. Major changes since MTN.GNS/W/16 was drafted relate to banking and financial services and to audio-visual works. Work is also underway in a number of other sectors.

2. The review of the Current Invisibles Code was mainly to take account of technological changes that had contributed to the development of new service industries or to the growth of those only marginally important when the Code was first drafted. Updating of the Capital Movements Code was partly to extend coverage to new financial instruments and partly to cover other operations not previously subject to liberalization obligations.

3. Under Decisions adopted in May 1989, the liberalization mechanisms of the Codes apply to a full range of banking and financial services:

(a) Changes to the Current Invisibles Code include:

- a new section on banking and financial services covering cross-border services including payment services (e.g. the issuance and use of cheques, travellers'cheques and credit cards), banking and investment services (e.g. underwriting and broker/dealer services), asset management (e.g. protfolio management and pension fund management) and advisory and agency services (e.g. investment research and advice);

- new provision calling on members to ensure "equivalent treatment" under which requirements for establishment for branches and agencies of non-resident financial institutions shall be no more burdensome than those applying to domestic institutions;

0013

- additional specific provisions regarding authorization, representation, representative offices, self-employed intermediaries, membership of associations or regulatory bodies, prudential considerations, and financial requirements for establishment.

(b) Changes to the Capital Movements Code include:

- The extention of its coverage to virtually all capital movements including, money-market operations, forward operations, swaps and other activities not previously covered.

4. The Current Invisibles Code also adopted a much broader concept of audio-visual works in July 1988. It brought under coverage modern audio-visual products and activities, such as video-cassettes and television broadcasting by cable and satellite, as well as activities associated with audio-visual works involving the temporary presence of non-residents.

원 본

외 무 부

종 별 :

번 호 : GVW-0641 일 시 : 91 0409 1100

수 신 : 장관(통기),경기원,재무,법무,상공,건설,보사,노동,체신,

발 신 : 주 제네바대사 교통,문화,공보,과기,항만청)

제 목 : UR/ 서비스 비공식 협의

4.8(월) 호주대표부에서 개최된 14개국(아국,호주,알젠틴, 멕시코,뉴질랜드,홍콩,헝가리,싱가폴, 스웨덴,스위스,미국, 이씨,일본,캐나다) 비공식 협의 내용을 하기 보고함.(이경협관, 한경협관보 참석)

1. MFN 일탈 관련 수평적 협정

- 어떤 수평적 협정에 대하여 MFN 일탈이 필요한지에 대한 논의는 하지 않았으며 다만, 향후 작업 방향에 대하여 미국과 이씨가 완전한 목록 작성과 내용검토, 분야별 협정과의 구별이 필요하다고 지적함.

0 스웨덴은 갓트사무국 작성 CHECK-LIST 가 부자보장 협정과 OECD CODE 만을 다루고 있는바 이중과세 방지 협정도 추가 검토가 필요하다고 하였으나 다른 나라들은 무역에 미치는 영향이 작다는 이유로 반대입장을 견지함.

0 가타, OECD CODE 는 동 회원국들이 비회원국들에 대하여도 실제로 MFN 을 적용하고 있으나 국제적인 법적 의무로서 MFN 을 제공하고 있는 것은 아니므로 검토가 필요하며 노동력 이동에 관한 협정도 수평적 협정이므로 검토대상이 되어야 한다는 의견이 제시됨.

2. 서비스 분야 분류표

- 서비스 분야 분류표 작성의 중요성 및 기술적 어려움, 사무국의 목록 보완 작업 과정에서 각국의 협력 필요성, 각국별로 자국 OFFER상의 서비스 분야를 정의하는 문제등이 거론되었으나 구체적인 작업계획에 대하여는 특별한 논의가 없었음.

3. NATIONAL SCHEDULE 작성 방법

- 일본이 작성한 별첨(FAX 송부) 토론자료에 대한 일본측의 설명과 일부국가의논평이있었음.

0 일본은 동 자료중 제 3안(모든 차별적 조치는 내국민 대우란에 기재, 비차별적

통상국	2차보	법무부	보사부	문화부	교통부	체신부	경기원	재무부
상공부	건설부	노동부	과기처	해항청	공보처			

91.04.09 23:27 DN

외신 1과 통제관

0015

조치는 시장접근란에 기재하되 양허가 이루어지는 분야만 SCHEDULE 에 등재)에 대한 선호를 암시하였는바 미국은 무차별적인 인가 요건과 무차별적 시장접근에 관한 수량제한 또는 수요검사 요건(NEED TEST) 과의 구별이 어려운 점을 지적함. 이에대하여 일본은 양허협상을 통하여 합의가 이루어지는 쿼타는 SCHDULE 에 등재하여 거치되고합의가 이루어지지 않은 분야의 쿼타는 UNDOUND상태로 남게될 것이라고 한바 이 경우에는 실제로 시장접근이 얼마나 부여되는 것인지 알수없게 된다는 문제점을 대부분의 나라가 지적하였으며 미국은 서비스 무역에서는 국경의 실체를 파악하기 어려우므로 시장 진입이후에 내국민대우 개념을 적용하는 방식을 더이상 따를 필요가없다고 말함.

0 한편, 캐나다와 호주는 서비스 협상과정에서 시장접근과 내국민 대우를 개념적으로 구분해 온것이 사실이나 실제 SCHEDULE 작성과정에서는 두가지를 구분하지 않고 한란에 기재하는 방식을고려중이라고 언급함.

첨부: 일본작성 토론자료 1부

(GVW(F-0118). 끝

(대사 박수길-국장)

PAGE 2

0016

GVW(TI)-0118 104○9 1700

"GVW-0641 첨부"

1991. 4. 8

<일본작성>

Discussion Paper
on Market Access, National Treatment,
Structure and National Schedule

This discussion paper is drated in an attempt to clarify possible conceptual confusion concerning the manner in which specific commitments may be made in the national schedule. Japan noticed some of the conceptual confusion in the process of putting together its voluntary offer list. Through our discussion with some of the parties which have already submitted their offers, we found that many of those parties share the same concern about possible confusion.

This paper is not intended in any way to challenge the achievements of the negotiations so far. This is simply an attempt to provide our recognition of issues which have not been remedied and thus remain to be possible causes of conceptual confusion in negotiating commitments.

I. Issues

1. Through our negotiations on structure of the Framework Agreement, an agreement has been reached on the adoption of the so-called "hybrid" approach as a way of inscribing the national schedule. In other words, those sectors which are subject to commitments are listed in a positive manner, i.e. the Bottom-Up approach; and any limitations and conditions on Market Access and any conditions and qualifications on National Treatment are to be inscribed in the national schedule using the Top-Down approach. Those sectors and conditions for which a Party commits itself are to be agreed through negotiations (i.e., no predesignated obligations).

2. A national schedule formulated in this manner, however, raised some confusion in the following respects on the part of the parties which worked to submit their voluntary initial offers as well as parties which tried to understand the offers.

(1) Lack of common understanding as to the coverage in activities of a given sector. For instance, do people in Country A and Country B necessarily envisage the same range of activities as to what is being offered under, for instance, the "Telecommunication Sector"? (Issues of nomencrature).

- 2 -

(2) Are the four modes of delivery an appropriate way of classifying possible means of providing services?

(3) Lack of common understanding as to what is meant by Market Access and National Treatment and as to distinction between the two concepts.

3. In this discussion paper, we tried to give thought, namely, to the third issue alone, namely to the concepts of Market Access and National Treatment. In regard to modes of delivery, we have not tried to analyze the issue head-on, but possible hints to the manner in which this issue should be looked at will be indicated in the course of this discussion paper. (With regard to the issue of nomencrature, we have refrained from handling it in this paper.)

II. Market Access and National Treatment: Analysis of the Two Concepts in TNC/W/35

1. A Top-Down approach is adopted for the inscription of limitations and conditions on Market Access and conditions and qualifications on National Treatment with regard to a sector for which a party makes commitments. The sector is listed with the Bottom-Up approach. The obligation of the Party is not to introduce any measures, which are inconsistent with the limitations and conditions on Market Access and conditions and qualifications on National Treatment other than those in its national schedule. (Article XIX) However, for this method of inscribing commitment, to produce a national schedule with an unequivocal understanding for all, there must be a common understanding as to what is exactly meant by unconditional Market Access and unconditional National Treatment.

2. TNC/W/35 defines the concept of National Treatment in Article XVII. Therefore, a Contracting Party can understand what is being committed by unconditional National Treatment when this is being offered in national schedules of other Contracting Parties. However, Article XVI does not define the concept of Market Access. If we recall, the wording of Article XVI in TNC/W/35 is inherited from Article XVI of GNS/35. However, at the time when GNS/35 was drafted, there were two conflicting views on the manner in which limitations and conditions on Market Access and National Treatment should be inscribed in the National Schedule. Developed countries advocated adoption of the Top-Down approach, whereas developing countries prefered the Bottom-Up approach. GNS/35 was drafted in such a way that it could circumvent the conflict of the two approaches, and, as a result, no clear indication is

0018

given in Article XVI whether this Article adopts a Top-Down approach or the Bottom-Up approach. (If not for Article XIX, Article XVI would be interpreted to have adopted the Bottom-Up approach.)

3. (1) Our understanding is that many of the other parties which tabled their offer lists have tried to differentiate Market Access and National Treatment. Limitations on Market Access is, in many cases, defined as restrictions at the time of entry to the market by a foreign service provider, and National Treatment is called into question in regard to provision of services after entry into the market. We believe that these parties have classified restrictive measures in the following ways.

(a) Because there is no provision stipulating, in a concrete manner, how a national schedule should be inscribed, a party making an offer has to judge for itself how it should classify its restrictions in its offer list by interpreting the negotiating history. Many parties, we understand, inscribe "no restriction" under the column of Market Access when they do not maintain any restrictions which discriminate foreign service providers from domestic service providers. In other words, these parties consider unconditional Market Access to be tantamount to not imposing any restrictions which discriminate foreign service providers from domestic service providers.

(b) Interpretative Note on Paragraph 2 of Article VI provides that requirements which are not based upon objective criteria shall be considered as restrictions on market access and/or limitations on national treatment and, when a specific commitment is made, shall be inscribed, as appropriate, in the Party's schedule.

The logical consequence of the above is that non-discriminatory restrictions other than those which do not meet "objective criteria" are not, by definition, regarded as limitations on Market Access or National Treatment.

0019

10-13

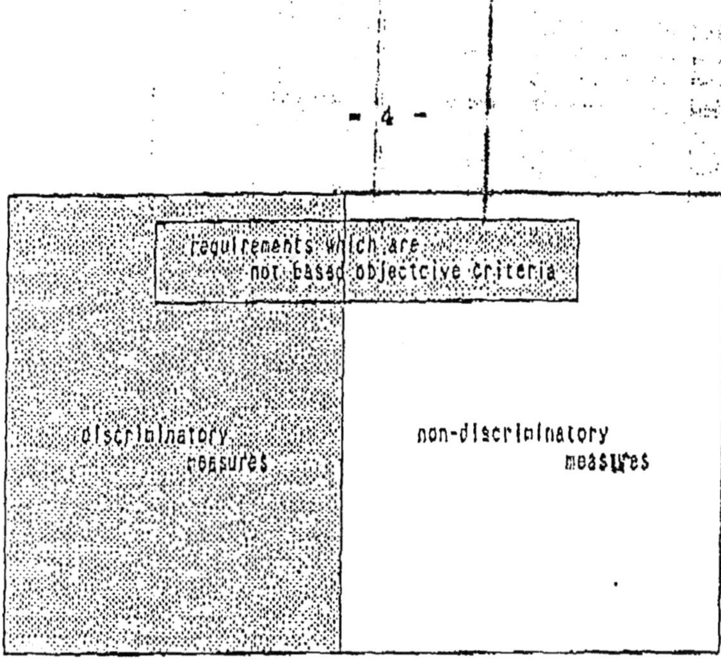

measures which will be negotiated under the concept of "Market Access".

(2) The approach in (1) above, however, leads us to the following problems.

(a) Provisions of Articles XVI and XVII do not indicate in any way that the former Article relates to the issues of entry into the market and that the latter Article is relevant to provision of services after the entry into the market.

(b) It is not possible to deduce directly from provisions of Article XVI that unconditional Market Access is equivalent to not imposing any discriminatory restrictions on foreign service providers.

(d) Some parties inscribed in their offers quantitative limitations. With the argument given above, how should non-discriminatory measures which impose quantitative limitations, other restrictions affecting the number of service providers and residency requirements be treated?

III. Possible Options for Solutions

We have come up with a number of approaches in order to alleviate the conceptual confusion. Here we list three options. Japan has no particular preference and is ready to consider other options which any party proposes.

In trying to come up with a solution, we tried to address the following three points.

0020

(1) Is difference between concepts of Market Access and National Treatment clear? In other words, is the distinction between the two concepts meaningful?

(2) Is it clear what commitments are undertaken in respect of Market Access?

(3) Is there no confusion in inscribing a national schedule? Can a national schedule be interpreted in an unequivocal manner?

Option 1

1. Structure

(1) Sectors are to be committed with the Bottom-Up Approach, whereas limitations and conditions on Market Access and National Treatment are to be committed with the Top-Down Approach.

(2) Unconditional Market Access means no discriminatory restrictions at the time of entry into the market. Unconditional National Treatment means no discriminatory restrictions with regard to provision of services after the entry into the market.

(3) In case non-discriminatory restrictions limit provision of services by foreign service providers, such non-discriminatory restrictions may be negotiated as Additional Commitments, but not as a part of liberalization process to achieve unconditional Market Access or unconditional National Treatment.

2. Intention behind this option.

This option aims at streamlining the method adopted by many of the parties which submitted offers. (This option tries to modify TNC/W/35 as little as possible.)

3. Problems

(1) It is difficult to judge whether a specific discriminatory restriction is with regard to the entry into the market or with regard to provision of services after the entry into the market. Hence confusion could arise as to whether the restriction should be inscribed in the Market Access column or in the National Treatment column.

10-5

0021

(2) If attainment of unconditional market access and national treatment means attainment of the situation where only non-discriminatory restrictions are imposed, is it meaningful to differentiate the two concepts, one regarding measures at the time of entry into the market and another concerning measures after entry into the market? The same goal seems to be served equally by eliminating Market Access column and dealing with all discriminatory measures under the single column of National Treatment. In other words, if the concept of Market Access only deals with discriminatory measures, there seems to be no need to maintain the concept which is independent of National Treatment.

Option 2.

1. Structure

(1) Market Access is the concept dealing with restrictions relating to entry into the market. National Treatment is the concept dealing with restrictions with regard to provision of services after entry into the market.

(2) Market access is to be defined in concrete terms in the Agreement as various forms of entry into market. In other words, "menu" of Market Access is to be defined. If a party wishes to impose restrictions on Market Access, the party should inscribe in its national schedule limitations and conditions according to the forms of entry into market defined as the "menu". (If no inscription is made in the national schedule, the party is regarded as committing itself to permit all forms of entry into market defined as Market Access in the relevant sector.)

(3) Full attainment of Market Access means removal of not only discriminatory measures, but also non-discriminatory measures which are convened by the defined concept of Market Access.

(4) A party may negotiate, as a matter of limitations and conditions on Market Access or National Treatment, removal or alleviation of any discriminatory measures as well as those non-discriminatory measures which are subject to the menu. With regard to other measures, they have to be dealt with as a part of Additional Commitment negotiations.

2. Intention behind this option :

(1) Define the concept of Market Access in concrete terms as a "menu", all the parties can share the same understanding as to what attainment of Market Access means.

0022

10-6

(2) A Party needs to inscribe all measures which restrict the "manu", and hence confusion with regard to inscription of the national schedule can be reduced.

3. Problems

Difficulty is anticipated in agreeing to an appropriate menu for all sectors.

For instance, residency of a service provider is necessary in some sectors from the viewpoint of e.g. consumer protection, whereas imposition of such requirement may not be necessary in certain sectors. Unless the menu is tailored for specific sectors (by annexs), it would be difficult to agree on the menu for sectors across-the-board.

Option 3.

1. Structure

(1) No differentiation is made from the viewpoint of whether a measure is related to entry into the market or to provision of service after entry into the market. All discriminatory measures are treated as limitations on national treatment.

(2) Other restrictions which inevitably are non-discriminatory measures shall be inscribed in the national schedule under the Market Access column only when concessions are agreed to through negotiations (bilateral or multilateral). (Market Access commitment thus necessarily becomes a Bottom-Up obligation.)

(3) No limitions are imposed on types of measures under Market Access negotiations.

2. Intention behind this option

(1) Distinction between National Treatment and Market Access is made clear. National Treatment addresses discriminatory measures, and Market Access addresses non-discriminatory measures.

(2) Since a Market Access obligation becomes a Bottom-up obligation, there is no need to agree on the definition of Market Access as in Option 2, hence controversial work of drafting a Market Accesse "manu" can be avoided.

0023

(3) With respect to Market Access, a Party needs to adhere only to the obligations inscribed in the Market Access column of its national schedule. This makes a Party's obligation clear.

3. Problems

The Top-Down approach is maintained for National Treatment, but the Bottom-Up approach is adopted for Market Access. This means a departure from what is agreed in TNC/W/35.

IV. Mode of Delivery

1. One of the reasons for confusion in inscribing a national schedule derives from the question of appropriateness of the four modes of delivery from the viewpoint of actual state of trade in services. Although we have not given in-depth thought to this question some suggestions may be obtained from the above process of considering thought on the Market Access and National Treatment issue.

2.

(1) If we adopt Option 2 or 3 for instance, a Contracting Party is required to inscribe in its national schedule conditions on National Treatment. This means that national schedule would contain lists of discriminatory measures maintained by a Contracting Party. Since those conditions are clearly provided for, are there any compelling reasons to classify those restrictions according to the four modes of delivery?

(The drafted National Treatment Instrument of OECD, for instance, does not classify exceptions to national treatment, which member countries are required to register.)

(2) If Option 2 is adopted (the "menu" of Market Access is defined in this case), a Contracting Party only needs to list those measures which restrict the attainment of the "menu". The purpose of this listing up is to clearly indicate which element of the "menu" is being constrained and in what manner. It should be noted that there is no need to define which mode of delivery the measure is classified into.

(cf. In the four-country draft of financial annex (MTN.TNC/W/50), the menu of market access commitment is defined. A Contracting Party needs to indicate, if any,

0024

10-8

the measures which limit full attainment of the listed obligations (menu), but not types of modes of delivery.)

(3) If Option 3 is adopted, the Contracting Party is to list its concessions with the Bottom-Up approach with regard to Market Access. In this system, there does not seem to be positive reason to divide up the concessions in the light of the four modes of delivery.

3. For these reasons, it may not be necessary to define modes of delivery as is provided in TNC/W/35, once the Market Access and National Treatment issue is solved, possibly by using the above-said options.

0025

10-9

Measures which will be negotiated under the concepts of "Market Access","National Treatment" and "Additional Commitment"

Option. 1.

discriminatory measures		non-discriminatory measures
National Treatment	Market Access	Additional Commitment

Option. 2.

discriminatory measures		non-discriminatory measures
National Treatment	Market Access	Additional Commitment

Option. 3.

discriminatory measures	non-discriminatory measures
Natinal Trearment	Market Access

0026

1-10

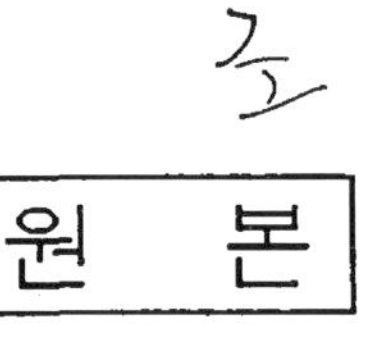

관리번호	P1-264

원 본

외 무 부

종 별 :

번 호 : UKW-0833　　　　일 시 : 91 0409 1500

수 신 : 장관(통기) 사본: 해운항만청

발 신 : 주 영 대사

제 목 : UR/해운 서비스분야 개방요구서 작성

대: WUK-0553

1. 해운시장 규제제도 및 관행

-주재국은 전통적으로 해운시장을 자율적인 시장경제의 기능에 맡기고 있는바 해운회사에 대한 면허나 해운시장의 자율적 기능에 대하 일체의 규제는 원칙적으로 없음

-단지 선박운항은 해상안전에 지대한 영향을 미치고 있는바 이러한 차원에서 선박건조 및 운항에 대한 각종 안전규정 제정 및 시행을 통하여 해상안전및 오염방지를 위해 국제해사기구(IMO)의 규정을 대부분 따르고 있음

2. 자국 업체에 대한 각종 보조 및 지원제도

-주재국의 해운정책은 해운산업은 시장경제질서에 맡긴다는 기본원칙에 따라 타산업과 차별적인 지원등을 시행하고 있지 않음

-해운업계는 선주협회를 중심으로 국방상 해운의 중요성등 해운산업의 특성을 들어 주재국 정부에 대해 조세감면 및 자유상각허용등 타 산업과 차별적 지원을 요구하고 있으나 주재국 정부는 아직 이를 받아들이지 않고 있음

-단지 해기사 양성은 업체 책임하에 기업체의 부담으로 되어 있는바 주재국정부는 해기사 양성 비용을 업체의 신청에 의해 약 50 프로 지원하고 있으나 아국은 국립해양대학을 통하여 전액 국비로 양성하는 것과 비교해 볼때 특별한 지원이라고 할수 없음

3. 아국에 대한 차별사항

-주재국은 전통적으로 해운 자유원칙에 따르고 있어 영업적 측면에서 외국선대에 다한 차별은 없음

-해운에 대한 100 프로 외국인 부자법인 설립 및 아국 선사의 지사 또는 사무소도

통상국　차관　2차보　해항청

PAGE 1　　　91.04.10 07:38

외신 2과 통제관 BW

0027

주재국 세법에 따른 절차만 거치면 자유로이 설립할 수 있음

-또한 국적선대의 영국 항구 기항 또는 화물적하에 하등의 제한은 없음

-단지 주재국 기항 선박의 IMO 협약이 규정한 각종 안전항해 설비를 갖추고있는지 여부를 심사하여 이에 미달할 경우 입출항 금지조치를 취할수 있고 이는 전 외국선대에 해당하며 국제법으로 인정됨

-또한 EC 와 공동으로 불공정경쟁 행위에 대한 제재조치로 외국선대가 정부지원등을 통한 비 상업적 이익을 얻어 운임을 덤핑하는 경우 보복관세를 부과할 수 있음

-그러나 아국과 주재국간에 한영 해운협정이 가서명 되어 발효를 앞두고 있는바 이에 따라 양국의 업체가 상호 공정경쟁 할 경우 별 문제점은 없는 것으로 판단됨

4. 상세사항 기보고한 주영(해무) 1572-115(91.1.29) 영국 해운정책 보고 참조.끝

(대사 이홍구-국장)

91.6.30 까지 H

일반문서로 재분류 (1991. 6.30.)

PAGE 2

0028

	분류번호	보존기간

발 신 전 보

번 호 : WGV-0436 910410 1110 FL 종별 : 지급

수 신 : 주 제네바 대사. 총영사

발 신 : 장 관 (통 기)

제 목 : UR/서비스 협상

대 : GVW-0635

대호 갓트사무국의 Check-list에 대한 검토 의견을 별첨 송부하니 4.10-11간 귀지에서 개최되는 UR/서비스 주요국 비공식 협의 참가시 참고바람.

첨 부(fax) : 상기 Check-list 검토 의견서. 끝.

WGV(F)-74

(통상국장 대리 최 혁)

보안 통제	

앙 고 재	91 년 4 월 10 일	통기 과	기안자 성명		과 장	심의관	국 장		차 관	장 관
						대결	전결			

외신과통제

0029

WGV(F)-74

10410 1110 (12매)

GATT事務局 Check List에 대한 檢討

(UR/서비스협상관련 비공식회의관련)

1991. 4

經濟企劃院

對外經濟調整室

0030

目 次

0031

1. 會議槪要

- 日　　時: '91.4.10 - 11

- 場　　所: 스위스 제네바 GATT 회의실

- 會議性格: GATT事務總長 주재의 주요 30여개 國家가 參席하는 非公式會議

- 會議議題: ㅇ 讓許計劃表(National Schedule)의 作成方法
  ㅇ 水平的協定(Horizontal Agreement)의 檢討등

2. GATT事務局 Check List의 要約

* 3.8 開催된 UR/서비스協商 主要國 非公式會議의 結果 GATT事務局은 4.3일 同 Check List를 作成

<서비스 産業의 分類>

- 서비스分類는 CPC(Central Product Classification) 分類에 따라야 하는가?

- 서비스分類에 問題가 發生한 경우 CPC 分類가 修訂.補完되어야 하는가 아니면 個別國家의 Offer List의 修訂.補完되어야 하는가?

<National Schedule (NS)에 關聯된 其他問題>

- 4가지 서비스供給 形態의 差異는 무엇이며 각각 어떤조치(measures)들이 해당되는가?

- 서비스交易의 障壁으로 간주되는 措置(measures)는 무엇이며 서비스交易의 障壁이 아니고 Framework 제6조(國內規制)에 해당되는 措置는 무엇인가?

0032

- 第6條에 해당되는 規制로서 讓許協商過程에서 相互交換된 情報를 어떻게 취급해야 하는가?
  ① 단지 公開主義(제3조)의 對象이 되는가?
  ② 또는 체약국단이 취합(compilation)을 해야하는가?

- 市場接近(MA) 란에 bound되는 措置와 內國人待遇(NT) 란에 bound되는 措置의 區分이 필요한가? 만약에 區分이 되야 한다면 그 基準은?

- 國內供給者와 外國供給者를 동일하게 제한하는 조치들을 MA 란에 수록해야만 하는가?

- 外國人投資, 不動産所有, 人力移動등 공통적인 制限事項을 어떻게 NS에 수록할 것인가?

- NS에 使用된 "該當없음(not applicable)", "凍結(stand-still)", "制限없음(no limitation)"등 技術的인 用語에 대한 說明書가 필요한가?

<水平的 協定 (Horizontal Agreement)>

- 水平的協定上의 槪念과 原則들이 서비스一般協定의 Framework과 일치하는가?

- 同協定上의 義務들이 Framework상의 義務들보다 엄격한가?

- 同協定上의 相互主義가 어떤 역할을 했는가?

- 同協定下에서의 自由化約束(commitment)을 GATS下의 自由化約束과 어떻게 비교할 수 있는가?

- 同協定이 包括範圍(coverage), 制限事項(limitation), 特定去來形態와 業種의 免除(exemption)에 대하여 취하고 있는 接近方式과 GATS의 接近方式이 어떻게 다른가?

0033

3. 檢討意見

가. 全般的인 意見

- GATT事務局이 작성한 Check List는 브랏셀 閣僚級 TNC會議 이후 雙務間, 複數國間 非公式會議에서 論議되었던 主要爭點들이 體系있게 정리되어 있다고 評價됨.

  o 특히 友好通商航海條約(Treaty of Friendship, Commerce & Navigation), 雙務投資協定(Bilateral Investment Treaty)등 水平的協定에 대한 개요와 質問事項은 協商의 進展에 커다란 도움이 될 것으로 기대

- GATT事務局의 Check List에 대한 項目別 檢討에 앞서 本格的인 實質協商에 앞서 技術的 問題를 討議하는 問題등에 대한 我國立場은 다음과 같음.

  o 各國의 National Schedule은 서비스市場의 開放에 대한 法的 權利 및 義務를 나타내는 문서이므로 國際間의 紛爭의 소지를 最小化하기 위하여 明瞭化되어야 함.

  o 이를 위하여 分野別專門家, 法律專門家등이 참여하는 多者間 協商을 통하여 技術的인 事項들이 충분히 討議되어야 함.

  o National Schedule의 作成方法은 Framework의 內容과도 直接的인 관련이 있는 만큼 양자를 병행해서 協議를 進行해야 할 것임.

0034

o 다만 National Schedule의 作成方法에 대한 討議는 記述的인 協議이고 利害關係를 決定하는 實質的인 協商이 아닌 만큼 同 協議를 통해서 자국의 실리를 추구하는 姿勢는 不適合하다고 봄.

o 技術的인 過程에도 公開主義(Transparency) 原則이 適用되야 한다는 次元에서 적절한 時間間隔으로 中間報告書를 作成하여 非公式協議에 參席하지 않은 國家에 配布하는 配慮를 할 필요가 있다고 생각함.

o 이러한 配慮가 서비스一般協定에 참가하는 國家의 數를 擴大하는데 도움을 줄것으로 기대

나. 서비스産業의 分類

- 우선 GATT事務局이 各國의 Offer List등을 바탕으로 하여 參考目錄(MTN/GNS/W/50)을 改善하는 作業을 조속히 할 것임.

- 同問題는 서비스分類의 明瞭化의 必要性, 各國의 分類體系의 相異 및 時間의 制約등이 종합적으로 고려되어야 함.

- 따라서 우선 各國 서비스分類體系를 우선으로 하여 National Schedule을 作成하되 中.長期的으로 UN 統計局, IMF등 관련 國際機構와 協調하여 各國의 서비스分類體系를 漸進的으로 統一시켜 나가는 것이 바람직할 것으로 판단

o 이런 차원에서 GATT事務局이 작성한 參考目錄(MTN.GNS/W/50)은 단순한 參考目錄에 불과하며 各國의 自由化約束의 內容을 判斷하는 法的 拘束力을 갖는 목록은 아님.

0035

- 한편 韓國은 CPC分類體系가 서비스産業에 채택되어야 한다고 보고 있음.

  o 다만 GATT事務局이 새로 作成할 參考目錄에도 不拘하고 서비스分類에 問題가 발생한 경우 最終的인 解釋의 基準은 各國의 서비스産業 分類表이므로 個別國家의 Offer List가 修訂.補完되야 할 것으로 판단

다. National Schedule에 關聯된 問題

(1) 서비스供給形態(Mode of Delivery)

- 韓國이 Offer List를 作成하는 過程에서 적용한 基本指針은 다음과 같음.

  o 國境間 서비스移動(Cross-border Supply): 生産要素의 移動을 수반하지 않은 서비스自體의 國境間移動으로 해석하였으나 會計事, 稅務事등 개별서비스 供給者의 일시적 이동에 의한 서비스供給의 경우도 同 國境間 서비스공급란에 기재

    . 왜냐하면 이러한 경우는 支社, 子會社등 企業을 설립하는 것도 아니고 또한 "勞動力의 移動"에 해당하는 規制措置가 없기 때문임.

  o 海外消費(Consumption abroad): 서비스에 대한 消費가 海外에서 이루어지는 경우로 解釋하였으며 이에따라 觀光, 敎育, 醫療등의 分野에 있어서 소비자가 相對國으로 物理的 移動을 하는 경우와 船舶등이 海外에서 修理를 받는 경우등을 상정

ㄴ. 그러나 外國에 所在하고 있는 金融機關에의 預金加入, 外國에 소재하고 있는 保險會社에의 保險加入등이 "國境間 서비스供給"인지 "海外消費"에 해당하는지의 구분이 不分明한바, 아국은 預金 및 保險金의 支給地를 基準으로 하여 國境間 서비스공급란에 기재

o 商業的駐在(Commercial presence): 合作投資會社, 子會社, 支社(지점, 출장소, 사무소)를 設立하는 것으로 해석하였으며, 다른 서비스供給形態에 비해서 비교적 구분이 용이

o 人力의 移動(Movement of personnel): 商業的 駐在에 수반되는 人力의 移動, 會計事등 個別的인 人力의 移動 뿐만아니라 出入國管理法上의 規制下에 있는 모든 人力의 移動을 포함하는 것으로 해석하고 있으나 아직 충분히 검토가 되지않아 我國의 Offer List에서 除外 시켰음.

- 다른국가와 마찬가지로 我國도 Offer List를 作成하는 過程에서 槪念의 不分明으로 混亂을 겪었으며 이러한 協議를 통하여 4가지 供給形態의 區分必要性, 基準 및 具體的인 事例들이 충분히 論議되기를 회망

(2) Framework 제6조(國內規制)에 해당되는 措置

- Framework 제6조는 各國이 國家政策目標(national policy objective)를 달성하기 위해서 서비스供給에 대한 규제를 할수 있는 權限을 認定

o 다만 동 規制가 서비스交易에 制限的으로 作用해서는 안되며 國家政策目標達成에 必要한 수준이상의 負擔을 強要해서는 안된다고 制限事由를 달고 있음.

- 따라서 國家政策目標의 達成을 위해서 인정되는 정당한 規制와 서비스交易에 제한적으로 작용하는 不當한 規制를 區分해야 할 필요성 존재

- 그러나 事前的으로 區分하여 協商參加國間에 合意에 도달하는데는 상당한 어려움이 있을 것으로 豫想
  - o 예를들면 經濟開發등의 國家目標에 대하여 先.開途國間에 立場의 현격한 차이 존재

- 따라서 事後的으로 紛爭解決節次(Framework 제23조)를 통해서 兩者를 區分하는 具體的인 事例를 축적한 후에 合理的인 區別基準을 만드는 實用的인 接近方式을 택하는 것이 바람직할 것으로 생각
  - o 다만 Framework 제4조(예외)에 明示되어 있는 例外事由들이 事後的인 判斷의 根據가 될 것임.

- 한편 讓許協商過程에서 알게된 各國의 規制는 서비스協定 체약국단이 사무국을 통하여 취합 各國에 배포하는 것이 유익할 것으로 사료됨.
  - o 同資料는 各國의 學習過程(learning process)에 도움을 주어 서비스産業 發展 및 貿易의 擴大를 가져올 것으로 예상

(3) 市場接近과 內國民待遇의 區分

- 韓國이 National Schedule을 작성하는 過程에서 적용한 基本指針은 다음과 같음.

  - o 內國民待遇의 槪念을 傳統的인 의미로 해석하여 內國民待遇란에는 外國서비스나 外國서비스供給者가 국경을 통과한 후 國內營業 活動에서 받게되는 制度上의 差別的인 事項을 등재하였으며 그외의 모든사항은 市場接近란에 수록하였음.

0038

- 이렇게한 理由는 모든국가가 이미 지적한 바와같이 市場接近과 內國民待遇의 槪念區分이 매우 어렵기 때문이었음.

  o 특히 內國民待遇의 槪念이 制度的인 差別措置의 撤廢 이상으로 外國서비스 供給者에 대하여 실질적으로 同等한 競爭機會(Equality of Opportunity)를 意味할 경우 兩者의 區分은 더욱 어려움.

- 그러나 實際 Offer List를 作成해본 結果에 비추어 볼때 兩者의 區分 必要性은 그렇게 크지않음.

  o 外換送金制限, 外國人土地所得制限등 모든 서비스業種에 적용되는 差別的인 待遇이외에 特定分野에만 적용되는 差別的인 待遇는 金融分野를 제외하고는 거의 존재하지 않음.

- 그러나 市場接近과 內國民待遇의 구분이 지난 4년간의 協商의 結果이며 비록 一部業種에 部分的이긴 하지만 外國人에 대한 差別的인 事項이 존재하므로 現在의 基本的인 體制를 維持하는 것이 바람직하다고 사료됨.

- 한편 國內供給者와 外國供給者를 同一하게 規制하는 措置들은 市場接近란에 기재되야 함.

  o 國籍要件 및 居住要件등도 市場接近에 실질적인 제한이 되는 경우 同 市場接近란에 기재해야 相對國이 進出 可能性에 대하여 판단할 수 있음.

라. 水平的 協定

(1) 我國이 締結한 水平的 協定의 槪要

- FCNs과 關聯해서는 1956년 締結한 韓.美通商 航海友好條約이 존재

  o 同條約은 市場進入(entry)에 대하여 內國民待遇를 規定하고 있으며 아울러 市場進入 이후의 營業活動등에 대해서도 內國民待遇와 最惠國待遇를 規定하고 있음.

  o 다만 運送, 커뮤니케이션, 金融, 沿岸海運등 一部業種을 유보하고 있으며 國際收支赤字 등의 理由로 制限을 가할 수 있다고 規定하고 있음.

- BIT와 關聯해서는 25개국과 投資增進 및 保護를 위한 協定을 締結

  o 西獨(1988), 스위스(1971), 베네룩스제국(1974), 네덜란드(1974), 튜니지아(1975), 英國(1976), 美國(1976), 프랑스(1977), 스리랑카(1980), 덴마크(1988), 헝가리(1988), 말레이시아(1988), 파키스탄(1988), 이탈리아(1989)등

  o 同 BIT의 內容은 대동소이한바 一般的으로 市場接近(外國人投資)에 대해서는 法的인 義務가 없으며 Best effort 義務만 부담하되 市場진입이후에는 內國民待遇(NT)와 最惠國待遇(MFN) 義務를 부담하며 조약발효이전의 旣存協約에 따른 待遇에는 MFN例外를 인정

0040

(2) 檢討意見

- 韓.美 FCN은 市場接近과 內國民待遇를 法的인 義務로 포함 시켰다는 점에서 서비스一般協定의 Framework에 비해서 매우 강한 義務條項을 담고 있으며 各國과 締結한 BIT도 內國民待遇를 法的인 義務로 하고 있다는 점에서 Framework 보다는 강한 協定이며 따라서 Framework의 構造와 一致하지 않는다고 볼수 있음.

  o 특히 市場接近을 義務條項으로한 韓.美 FCN은 交易 및 投資에 대하여 충분한 경험이 없는 상태에서 締結된 것으로 무리가 있다고 볼수 있음.

- 또한 BIT에 規定되어 있는 相互主義(兩國間의 MFN待遇 保障등)는 여러국가와 BIT를 締結한 締結한 關係로 特別한 意味를 갖고있지 못한 실정임.

  o MFN등의 침해를 이유로 이의가 제기된 사례가 없음.

- 한편 同 水平的인 協定은 일반적으로 모든 分野를 포괄하고 있으나 國家에 따라서 一部分野에 대하여 協定適用을 除外 시키고 있음.

  o 이경우 協定本文에 根據規定을 설정하고 부칙에 除外 시키는 分野를 具體的으로 열거하고 있음.

끝.

0041

조 · ·

원 본

외 무 부

종 별 :

번 호 : GVW-0662 일 시 : 91 0411 1700

수 신 : 장 관(통기,경기원,재무부,법무부,상공부,건설부,보사부,노동부,교통부, 체신부,문화부,공보처,과기처,항만청)

발 신 : 주 제네바 대사

제 목 : UR/서비스 주요국 비공식 회의(11)

4.10(수) DUNKEL 사무총장 주재로 개최된 표제협의 내용을 하기 보고함.

(본직, 이경협관, 한경협관보 참석)

1. 서비스 분야 분류표- 아국을 포함한 대부분의 나라가 서비스 분야공통 분류체계가 필요하다는 점과 CPC 를 기초로하여야 한다는 점에 대하여 견해가 일치하였음.

0 다만, 이씨는 CPC 가 국내 미시경제차원의 분류체계이기 때문에 조심스러운 접근이 필요하다고 유보적 입장을 표명함.

- 그러나 동 분류 체계의 성격에 대하여는 다음과같이 선.개도국간 견해를 달리하였음.

0 브라질, 알젠틴, 칠레등 개도국들은 각국의 NATIONAL SCHEDULE 을 공통 분류체계에 일치시켜야한다는 입장 (공통분류 체계가 기속적 성격)을 견지하고 실질 자유화 협상이 개시되기 전에 동분류 체계가 완성되어야 하며, 이와 아울러 통계개선 작업도 이루어져야 한다고 한 반면

0 대부분의 선진국 및 헝가리 및 멕시코는 각국 SCHEDULE 을 최대한 공통 분류체계에 일치시키는 것이 바람직하나 나라별로 서로 다른 규제제도를 감안한 신축성 (서비스분야 분류의 제한적인 조화)이 있어야 하며, 동 분류 체계의 기능도 각국SCHEDULE 의 상호 비교 (CROSS-REFERENCE) 를 위한 것이어야 한다고 함.

- 한편, 사무국 작성 분류표 (GNS/W/50) 보완, 발전작업 필요성에 합의가 형성되어 사무국이 동작업을 진행키로 하였음.

2. NATIONAL SCHEDULE 작성 관련 문제

- 일본은 시장접근 제한과 내국민 대우 제한의 구분이 곤란한 문제를 해결하는데 촛점을 맞춘 토론문서 (기송부)를 배부하고 각 대안을 설명함.

통상국	2차보	법무부	보사부	문화부	체신부	경기원	재무부	상공부
건설부	노동부	과기처	해항청	공보처	교통부			

PAGE 1 91.04.12 09:06 WG

외신 1과 통제관

0042

0 인도, 멕시코, 브라질등은 동 대안이 그동안의 협상경과를 완전히 무시하는 것이며 대부분의 경우 시장 접근 제한과 내국민 대우 제한을 구별할수 있다고 반박한 반 면

0 미국, 캐나다, 입시, 호주등은 시장접근 제한과 내국민 대우 제한을 구분할수 없는 경우가 많으며, 이를 구분하는 기준을 설정하기에는 너무많은 시간이 소요되며 동 구분기준이 아주 정확하지않을 경우에는 어떤 나라가 한쪽에는 COMMITMENT를하는 반면 진짜 의미가 있는 제한 조치는 다른쪽에 숨길수가 있다는 점등을 들어시장접근과 내국민 대우를 구분하지 않고 한란 (ONECOLUMN) 에 기재하는 방식에 대한 선호를 암시하였음.

- 또한 서비스 공급형태의 군분과 관련 어떤 서비스는 두가지 이상의 공급 형태가 결합된 상태로 공급되고 어떤 서비스는 4개 공급형태중 일부가 해당 사항이 없는 경우도 있다는데에는 견해가 일치하였으나, 인도, 멕시코, 브라질등은 대부분의 경우 4개 공급형태의 구별이 가능하며 동 4개 공급형태가 FRAMEWORK 에 계속 유지되어야 자본과 노동력의 이동간 균형이 이루어 질수 있다고함. (4개 공급형태가 구분되어야 노동력 이동 MODEOF DELIVERY 에 대한 양허 협상 추진이 용이해지며, 그렇지 않으면 각국의 인력이 동제한이 분야별로 이루어지는 것이 아니라 이민법이나 출입국관계법에 의해 이루어지므로 양허 협상에 의한 COMMITMENT 가 어렵게 될소지가 있는 것으로 추측됨.)

0 이에 반하여 선진국들은 4개 공급형태 군분이 불분명한 경우가 많으며, 중요한 것은 외국 서비스공급자가 어떤 형태로 서비스를 공급할수 있으며, 어떤 형태로는 안 되는지 아는 것이라는 점을 들어 4개 공급형태를 아에 구분하지 않거나 각국별로 자국의 해석에 따라 적절한 란에 제한 조치를 기재하면 된다는 입장을 취하였음.

- SCHEDULE 에 등재대상이 되는 제한조치에 관하여 선진국들은 내.외국인에게 똑같이 적용되는 무차별적 조치 (수량제한 포함)도 시장접근을 제한하는 경우에는 SCHEDULE 에 등재되어야 한다고 한 반면 개도국들은 무차별적조치는 제한 (RESTRICTIONS) 이 아니며 국내 규제 (REGULATIONS OR REQUIREMENTS) 이기 때문에 등재대상이 되지 않는 다고하여 이에 관한 공통접근방법의 필요성이 부각되었음.

- DUNKEL 총장은 기본적으로 이론적 토의를 중단하고 각국의 OFFER 를 비교하고 명료화하는 실용적 접근 방법과 제기된 문제들의 구체적 해결을 시작하는 접근 방법이 있을수 있다고 전제하고 후자에 입각하여 사무국으로 하여금 과제별 대안들을

개발하는 작업을 착수토록함.

3. 표제협의는 4.11(목) 속개하여 수평적 협정과 향후 협정 일정에 대하여 토의할 예정임. 끝

(대사 박수길-국장)

원 본

외 무 부

종 별 :

번 호 : GVW-0663 일 시 : 91 0411 1830

수 신 : 장 관(통기,경기원,재무부,법무부,상공부,건설부,보사부,노동부,교통부,체신부,문화부,공보처,과기처,항만청)

발 신 : 주 제네바 대사

제 목 : UR/서비스 주요국 비공식협의(2)

4.11(목) 속개된 표제협의 내용을 하기보고함.

1. MFN 일탈 관련 수평적 협정

- 수평적 협정 종류별로 그 성격 및 내용, MFN의 예외 허용 여부등에 대한 구체적 토의는 진행되지 않았으며, 다음 쟁점에 대하여 선개도국간 견해가 대립됨.

0 미국 및 일본은 서비스 협정에서는 설립권이 양허 협상에 의하여 부여되나 FCNS 나 BITS에는 설립권이 포함되어 있으므로 FREE-RIDER문제가 발생한다는데 반하여 인도등 개도국들은 비용을 지불하지 않고 실질적 이득을 얻는 것이 FREE-RIDER 이지 명목상 열린다고 해서 개도국들이 실질적 혜택을 보는 것은 아니라고함.

또한 미국은 갓트에도 기존 협정에 대한 조부 (GRANDFATHERING) 조항이 많이 있다고 지적하였으나 알젠틴등은 UR 이후에도 양자 협정 체결이 지속된다면 서비스 협정제정의 의미가 어디에있는지 의문을 표시하고 특정종류의 협정에 대한 일률적 예외 허용보다는 갓트 2조와 같이 MFN예외의 구체적 목록을 열거하는 방식을 지지함.

0 OECD CODE 와 관련, 미국과 일본은 동 CODE회원국들이 비회원국들에게도 MFN 을 적용해주고 있는 것이 사실이나 이를 서비스협정상의 의무로 규정하는 것은 전혀 다른문제이며, 이렇게 될경우 동 CODE 회원국들의 협상력이 상실된다고 한바 인도등은 구체적으로 과연 어떤 측면에서, 어떤 서비스분야에서 협상력이 상실되는지 검토되어야 한다고 반박함.

0 기타 일본은 많은 FCNS 에 상호주의 규정이있는바 FCNS 가 다자화되어야 한다면 동 상호주의 규정이 어떻게 무조건적 MFN 과 조화될수 있는지 문제를 제기하였으며, EC 는 노동력이동에 관한 협정의 검토 필요성도 제기함.

- 한편 많은 나라가 FCNS 나 BIT 뿐만 아니라 모든 수평적 협정을 총망라하여 분류표를 작성하고 법적인 측면에서 어떻게 MFN 이 적용될수 있으니 검토되어야

통상국	2차보	법무부	보사부	문화부	교통부	체신부	경기원	재무부
상공부	건설부	노동부	과기처	해항청	공보처			

91.04.12 09:11 WG

외신 1과 통제관

0045

한다고 함에 따라 사무국이 이에대한 추가 작업을 진행키로 함.

2. 향후 협상 일정

- DUNKEL 총장은 향후 약 2주내에 사무국에서 (1)서비스 분야 분류표, (2) NATIONAL SCHEDULE작성방법 (문제점열거, 분서, 공통접근 방법모색), (3) 수평적 협정에 관한 문서를 작성하겠다고 하고 각국이 서비스 분야 분류표에관한 서면의견 제출, 기존 협정에 관한 정보제공등 사무국의 작업에 협조해 줄것을 요청하였으며, 차기 회의 일정은 5.28주로정하였음.

- 캐나다는 하기 휴가전까지 작업과제를 사전에 정할 필요가 있다고 하고 동과제로서 (1) 각국OFFER 에 대한 다자간 검토, (2) '인력의 일시적이동'과 노동력 이동부 속서 및 FRAMEWORK 에 있어서 서비스 무역의 정의와의 관계

(3) FRAMEWORK 의 각조문

. 1차 논의대상: 제 1조, 5조, 6조, 7조, 8조, SCHEDULE작성방법의 변화에 따른 FRAMEWORK 의 변경

. 2차 논의대상: 협정 부적용 및 제도적 규정, MFN 과 관련 문제, 최초의 자유화 약속과의관계등을 제시하였으나 개도국들의 반대로 합의에 도달하지 못하였음.

3. 건의

- 향후 1-2 주간 진행될 사무국 문서작성 작업에 반영할 필요가 있는 사항, 즉, 아국이 희망하는 서비스 분야 분류 방식 (특히 통신, 금융 분야),아국이 맺고 있는 수평적 협정중 MFN 적용에 문제가 예상되는 부분등을 통보해 주기 바람. 끝

(대사 박수길-국장)

0046

	분류번호	보존기간

발 신 전 보

번 호 : WGV-0470 910413 1421 FN 종별 :

수 신 : 주 제네바 대사. 총영사

발 신 : 장 관 (통 기)

제 목 : UR 협상 참관

경제기획원 대조실 조정2과 이병화 사무관이 서비스 협상, 정부조달협정 가입 협상 참관 및 농산물협상, TPRM 관련 자료 수집차 4.14-24간 귀지 출장 예정임.

끝. (통상국장 대리 최 혁)

보안 통제	

앙 고 재	91년 4월 13일	통기 과	기안자 성명		과장	심의관	국장		차관	장관
						대결	전결			

외신과통제

0047

모사전송

경 제 기 획 원

봉조이 10520- 255 (503-9146) 1991.4.13.

수신 외무부장관

참조 영사교민국장

제목 UR 협상 분야별 회의참가

스위스 제네바에서 개최되는 UR/분야별회의에 아래와 같이 참가코자 하오니 해외출장에 필요한 조치를 취하여 주시기 바랍니다.

- 아 래 -

가. 출장자

소 속	직 위	성 명
대외경제조정실	사무관	이 병화

나. 출장지: 스위스 제네바

다. 출장기간: '91.4.14-4.24(10박 11일)

라. 출장목적:

- UR/농산물 및 서비스협상참가
- 정부조달협정가입 협상참가
- 국별무역정책검토기구회의참가

마. 여행경비: 당원부담. 끝.

경 제 기 획 원 장

0048

기 안 용 지

분류기호 문서번호	통기 20644-	(전화: 720 - 2188)	시 행 상 특별취급	
보조기간	영구. 준영구 10. 5. 3. 1.	차 관	장 관	
수 신 처 보존기간		전 결		
시행일자	1991. 4.16.			

보조기관	국 장		협조기관	제2차관보	문 서 통 제
	심의관				
	과 장				
기안책임자	조 현				발 송 인

경 유 수 신 참 조	건 의	발신명의		
제 목	정부대표 임명			

'91.4월중 아래 일정으로 개최되는 UR/서비스 협상에 참가할 정부대표를 "정부대표 및 특별사절의 임명과 권한에 관한 법률"에 의거, 아래와 같이 임명할 것을 건의하오니 재가하여 주시기 바랍니다.

- 아 래 -

1. 회의명, 회의기간 및 개최장소

가. 한.미 서비스 양자협의 : 91.4.19-20, 제네바 /계속/

0043

나. UR/금융 서비스 협상 : 91.4.23-24, 제네바

2. 정부대표

가. 한.미 서비스 양자협의

o 수석대표 : 경제기획원 대외경제조정실 장승우
제1협력관

o 대표 : 경제기획원 대외경제조정실 하동만 과장
경제기획원 대외경제조정실 신호현 사무관
재무부 보험정책과 임승태 사무관
공보처 광고정책과 정의영 사무관
주 제네바 대표부 관계관

o 자문관 : 대외경제정책연구원 박태호 박사

나. UR/금융 서비스 협상

o 수석대표 : 주제네바대표부 재무관 엄낙용

o 대표 : 재무부 국제금융과 최희남 사무관
재무부 보험정책과 임승태 사무관

/뒷면 계속/ 0050

o

o 자문관 : 한국은행 이문호 금융제도 과장

대외경제정책연구원 이장영 박사

3. 출장기간

o 경제기획원 대외경제조정실 장승우 협력관 : 91.4.17-22

o 경제기획원 대외경제조정실 하동만 과장 : 91.4.17-22

o 재무부 보험정책과 임승태 사무관 : 91.4.17-26

o 재무부 국제금융과 최희남 사무관 : 91.4.21-26

o 공보처 광고정책과 정의영 사무관 : 91.4.17-22

4. 소요예산 : 소관부처 예산

5. 훈 령

가. 한.미 서비스 양자협의

o 분야별로 구체적인 사항에 대한 질의응답 형식으로 진행하되, 협의(consultation)에 국한하며 본격적인 양허 협상은 유보

/뒷면 계속/

0051

o 아국의 유통소매업 개방 계획과 현행 규제사항 및
절차에 관하여 설명

o 아국의 offer list에 포함되지 않은 분야중 미국의
관심 표명 분야인 법무, 보건, lease, franchising,
보험중개업은 현 상황 및 규제상황을 설명

나. UR/금융서비스 협상

o 기존의 아국 입장이 반영된 SEACEN의 공동 입장 견지

o 금융부속서 작성시 고려토록 주장할 사항

- 금융 서비스 협상은 각국의 통상 신용 정책 및
금융제도의 안정성과 건전성을 보장하기 위한
정책 수행 권한을 존중해야 함.

- 금융분야에 부과되는 의무는 다른 서비스
분야에 대한 의무보다 과중해서는 안됨

- 금융서비스 자유화는 각국의 발전 단계 및
고유한 금융구조의 특수성을 고려하여
단계적인 자유화가 되어야 함. 끝.

0052

산업평과 이룩하여 경제난국 이겨내자

재 무 부

국금 22251-211 (503-9266) 1991. 4. 13.

수신 수신처 참조

제목 한·미 UR 서비스 양자협의 및 UR 금융서비스 회의참석

1. GVW-0516('91.3.20), GVW-0575('91.3.27)와 관련입니다.

2. UR 서비스협상과 관련 스위스 제네바에서 개최되는 한·미 서비스 양자협의(4.19) 및 UR 금융서비스회의(4.23~24)에 참석할 당부대표를 아래와 같이 파견코자 하오니 필요한 조치를 취해주시기 바랍니다.

아 래

소 속	성 명	기 간	비 고
보험정책과 사무관	임 승 태	'91. 4.17~26	한·미회의 및 금융회의 참석
국제금융과 사무관	최 희 남	'91. 4.21~26	금융서비스회의 참석
한국은행 금융제도과장	이 문 호	"	"
K I E P	이 장 영		"

첨부 : 회의참석 대책. 끝.

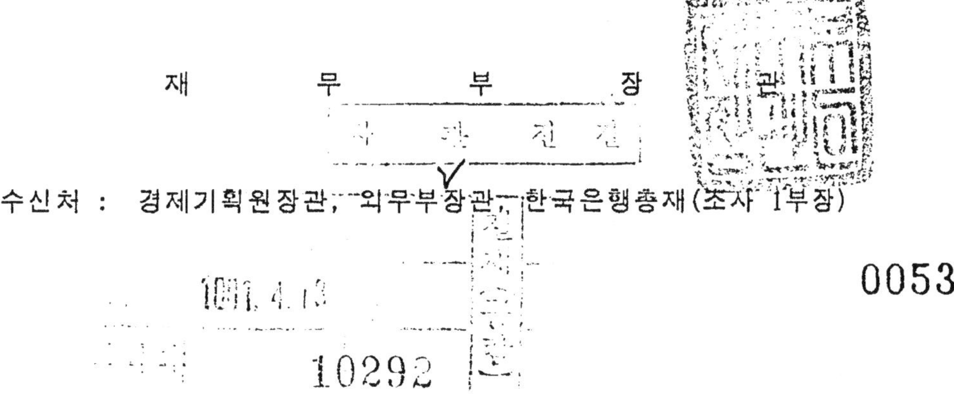

재 무 부 장 관

수신처 : 경제기획원장관, 외무부장관, 한국은행총재(조사 1부장)

0053

조

- 청결로 자연보호 질서로 사람보호 -

체 신 부

통협 34475-2792 750-2341 1991. 4. 15.

수신 외무부장관

제목 UR/서비스분야 제2차 한.미 양자 협의

1. 통조삼 10502-248 (91.4.11) 관련입니다.

2. 위 관련으로 4.19일 제네바에서 개최될 UR/서비스 분야 제2차 한.미 협의회에 우리부 대표를 아래와 같이 파견코자 하오니 필요한 조치를 취하여 주시기 바랍니다.

가. 참가대표

소 속	직 위	성 명 (영 문)	비 고
정보통신국	정보통신업무과장	구 영 보 (Koo,Yung-Bo)	

나. 파견기간 : 91.4.17-4.21(5일간)

다. 소요경비 : $2,678 (체제비 + 항공료). 끝.

발송 1991. 4. 15 체신부

체 신 부 장 관

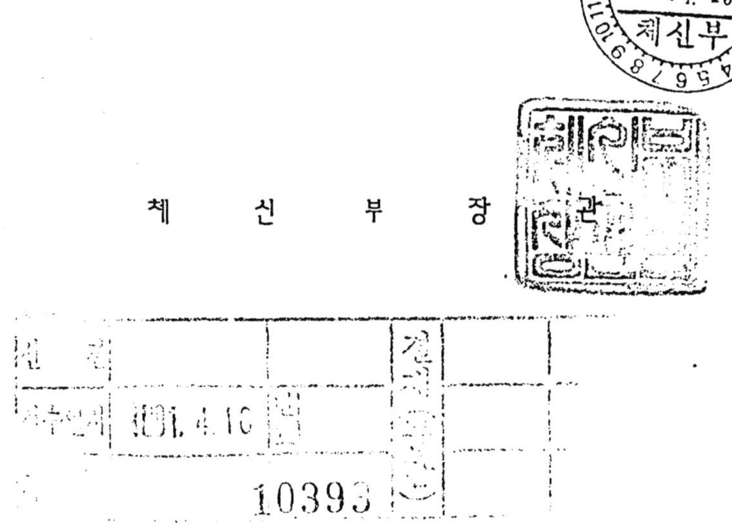

0054

경 제 기 획 원

봉조삼 10502- 763   503-9149   1991. 4. 16.

수신 외무부장관

제목 UR/서비스 한.미 양자협의 참석

1. 스위스 제네바에서 개최되는 제2차 UR/서비스 한.미 양자협의에 아국 대표단의 일원으로 다음과 같이 참석코자 하니 협조하여 주시기 바랍니다.

다 음

가. 출장자

소 속	직 위	성 명	비 고
경제기획원 대외경제조정실	제1협력관	장승우	수석대표
	통상조정3과장	하동만	
	통상조정3과 사무관	신호현	
대외경제정책연구원	연 구 위 원	박태호	자 문 역

나. 출장기간; '91.4.17-4.22 (5박 6일)

다. 경비부담: 당원, KIEP

첨부: 출장일정 1부. 끝.

경 제 기 획 원 장

0055

출 장 일 정

'91. 4. 17(수)	12:40	서울 발 (KE 901)
	19:10	파리 착
	20:45	파리 발 (SR 729)
	21:45	제네바착
4. 18(목)		UR/서비스 한.미 양자협의를 위한 사전대책 회의
4. 19(금)		UR/서비스 한.미 양자협의
4. 20(토)		주요협상국 및 GATT사무국과의 비공식협의
4. 21(일)	18:45	제네바 발 (SR 728)
	19:50	파리 착
	21:30	파리 발 (KE 902)
4. 22(월)	17;30	서울 착

0056

17696

기 안 용 지

분류기호 문서번호	통기 20644-	(전화 : 720 - 2188)	시 행 상 특별취급	
보조기간	영구. 준영구 10. 5. 3. 1.	장	관	
수 신 처 보존기간				
시행일자	1991. 4.16.			

보조기관		협조기관	문서통제
국 장	전 결		검열 1991. 4. 18
심의관			
과 장	대결		
기안책임자	조 현		발 송 인

경 유 수 신 참 조	수신처 참조	발신명의	발송 1991. 4 18 외무부
제 목	정부대표 임명 통보		

1. '91.4월중 아래 일정으로 개최되는 UR/서비스 협상에 참가할 정부대표가 "정부대표 및 특별사절의 임명과 권한에 관한 법률"에 의거, 아래와 같이 임명 되었음을 통보합니다.

- 아 래 -

가. 회의명, 회의기간 및 개최장소

o 한.미 서비스 양자협의 : 91.4.19-20, 제네바

o UR/금융 서비스 협상 : 91.4.23-24, 제네바 /계속/

0057

나. 정부대표

o 한.미 서비스 양자협의

- 수석대표 : 경제기획원 대외경제조정실 장승우

제1협력관

- 대표 : 경제기획원 대외경제조정실 통상조정3과

하동만 과장

경제기획원 대외경제조정실 신호현 사무관

재무부 보험정책과 임승태 사무관

공보처 광고정책과 정의영 사무관

주 제네바 대표부 관계관

- 자문관 : 대외경제정책연구원 박태호 박사

o UR/금융 서비스 협상

- 수석대표: 주제네바 대표부 재무관 엄낙용

- 대표 : 재무부 국제금융과 최희남 사무관

- 자문관 : 재무부 보험정책과 임승태 사무관

한국은행 이문호 금융제도 과장

대외경제정책연구원 이장영 박사

0058

다. 출장기간

o 경제기획원 대외경제조정실 장승우 협력관(4.17-22)

o 경제기획원 대외경제조정실 하동만 통상조정3과장 (4.17-22)

o 재무부 보험정책과 임승태 사무관(4.17-26)

o 재무부 국제금융과 최희남 사무관(4.21-26)

o 공보처 광고정책과 정의영 사무관(4.17-22)

o 한국은행 이문호 금융제도과장(4.21-26)

o 대외경제정책연구원 이장영 박사(4.21-26)

o 대외경제정책연구원 박태호 박사(4.17-22)

라. 소요예산 : 소관부처 예산

2. 상세 출장보고서는 귀국후 20일 이내에 당부로 제출하여 주시기 바랍니다. 끝.

수신처 : 경제기획원장관, 재무부장관, 공보처장관

0059

	분류번호	보존기간

발 신 전 보

번 호 : WGV-0495 910417 1912 FL 종별 : 암호송신

수 신 : 주 제네바 대사. 총영사 대리 (사본: 주미대사)

발 신 : 장 관 (통 기)

제 목 : UR/서비스 협상

귀지에서 개최되는 한.미 서비스 양자협의(4.19-20) 및 UR/금융 서비스 협상 (4.23-24)에 참가할 정부대표가 아래 임명 되었으니 귀관 관계관과 함께 참석토록 조치바람.

1. 정부대표 및 출장기간

가. 한.미 서비스 양자협의

- 경제기획원 대외경제조정실 장승우 제1협력관 (4.17-22) (수석대표)
- 경제기획원 대외경제조정실 통상조정3과 하동만 과장 (4.17-22)
- 경제기획원 대외경제조정실 신호현 사무관 (4.17-22)
- 재무부 보험정책과 임승태 사무관 (4.21-26)
- 공보처 광고정책과 정의영 사무관 (4.17-22)
- KIEP 박태호 연구위원(자문관)
- 주 제네바 대표부 관계관

나. UR/금융 서비스 협상

- 주 제네바 대표부 엄낙용 재무관(수석대표)
- 재무부 보험정책과 임승태 사무관

보안 통제	

앙 고 재	91년 4월 17일	통기 과	기안자 성명		과 장	심의관	국 장		차 관	장 관
			조현				전결			

외신과통제

0060

- 재무부 국제금융과 최희남 사무관 (4.21-26)
- 한국은행 금융제도과장 이문호(자문관)
- KIEP 이장영 연구위원(자문관)

2. 훈 령

가. 한.미 서비스 양자협의

o 분야별로 구체적인 사항에 대한 질의응답 형식으로 진행하되, 협의 (consultation)에 국한하며 본격적인 양허 협상 유보

o 아국의 현행 규제사항 및 절차와 유통소매업 개방 계획에 관하여 설명

o 아국의 offer list에 포함되지 않은 분야중 미국의 관심 표명 분야인 법무, 보건, lease, franchising, 보험중개업은 현 상황 및 규제상황을 설명

나. UR/금융 서비스 협상

o 기존의 아국 입장이 반영된 SEACEN의 공동 입장 견지

o 금융부속서 작성시 고려토록 주장할 사항

- 금융 서비스 협상은 각국의 통상 신용 정책 및 금융제도의 안정성과 건전성을 보장하기 위한 정책 수행 권한을 존중해야 함.
- 금융분야에 부과되는 의무는 다른 서비스 분야에 대한 의무보다 과중해서는 안됨
- 금융서비스 자유화는 각국의 발전 단계 및 고유한 금융구조의 특수성을 고려하여 단계적인 자유화가 되어야 함. 끝.

(통상국장 김삼훈)

0061

원 본

외 무 부

종 별 :

번 호 : GVW-0729 일 시 : 91 0422 1500

수 신 : 장관(통기),경기원,재무부,법무부,상공부,건설부,보사부,노동부,교통부,

발 신 : 주 제네바 대사대리 체신부,문화부,과기처,항만청) 사본:박수길 대사

제 목 : UR/서비스한.미 양자 협의

4.19 (금) USTR 제네바 사무소에서 개최된 표제협의 내용을 하기 보고함.

1. 회의 진행개요

- 서비스 분야별 구체적 자유화 약속에 관한협상은 하지 않았으며, 양국 OFFER 내용에대한 명료화와 논평, UR/서비스 협상 진행에관한 의견 교환에 국한하였음.

2. 일반토의

- 아측은 각국 OFFER 에 대한 명료화 작업도 추진할 필요가 있음을 인정하나 FRAMEWORK 과 분야별 부속서에 우선 순위가 주어져야 하며, 특히 전체 UR 협상 진전이 부진한 상태에서 관계부처 담당자를 양자협의에 참여시키는데 어려운 점이 많으므로 협의개최 직전에 미측대표가 변경되는등의 사례가 재발하지 않도록 주의를 촉구함.

- 미측은 UR 협상에 있어서 서비스 부분의 실질적 성과의 중요성을 재차 강조하고 FRAMEWORK과 분야별 부속서에 우선 순위가 주어져야한다는 데에는 동의하나 각국 OFFER 상의 시장접근 및 국내 규제 제도의 명료화등 해결해야 할 기술적 과제가 많으며 동작업과 FRAMEWORK 및 분야별 부속서의 상호 연계 검토의 중요성이 증대하고 있다고 답변 함.

- 한편, 아측은 미국이 최근에 가진 일련의 양자협의 동향에 대하여 문의한바 미측은 OFFER 를 제출한 나라뿐만 아니라 미제출국가와도 협의를가졌으며, (총 27개국, 나라별로 2회 또는 3,4 회)OFFER 미제출 국가중 브라질, 알젠틴은 초안은 마련되었으나, 제출시기는 결정되지않았고 (농산물 협상 진전과 연계 전략)노르웨이는 곧 자세한 OFFER 를 제출 예정이며, 필리핀, 태국, 인도, 파키스탄, 이집트, 동구권등도 준비중에 있으나 당해 국가내의 규제제도 변화, OFFER 작성상의 기술적 어려움등을 겪고있다고 함. 또한 미국은 아국 OFFER 가 비교적 충실하고 다른 개도국들의 OFFER 제출을 촉진하는 계기가 된점에 대하여 치하함.

통상국 2차보 구주국(대사) 법무부 보사부 문화부 교통부 체신부 경기원
재무부 상공부 건설부 노동부 과기처 해항청

PAGE 1 91.04.23 08:51 FN

외신 1과 통제관

0062

3. 아국 OFFER 에 대한 질의 답변

가. 총괄 분야

- 미측은 아국이 노동력 이동에 대하여 어떻게 접근하고 있는지 문의한바 아측은 각분야별로 SKILLED WORKER 의 범위를 정하는 작업을 추진중이나 구체적 입장은 미정이라고 하였으며, 미측은 인력이동에 있어서 내국민 대우의 의미등 노동력 이동 부속서가 더 보완되어야 할 것이라고 함.

나. AUDIO VISUAL 서비스

- 영화 수입 배급, 음반 및 비디오 수입, 광고등에 대하여 아국제도를 소상히 설명하였으나 미측은 수입허가가 거부된 펩시콜라 광고물이 거의 내용변경 없이 한국에서 재 재가된 것이 방송된 사례가 있음을 제기하고 과거 외국 광고물 수입신청 및 허가 실적에 관한 통계를 요청함.

- 또한 미측은 신문광고의 경우 예치금 (20억원)이너무 과중하다고 지적함.

다. 건설

- 미측은 건설분야 내국민 대우란에 아국이 UNBOUND 한데 대해 향후 도입을 고려하고 있는 규제 조치에 대하여 문의한바 아측은 중소 규모 기업보호를 위하여 외국 기업에 대한 공사 계약한도등을 고려하고 있다고 하였으며, 납입자본금 밑공사실적에 의한 수주 제한과 관련 외국 기업의 자본금 증액을 보장할수 있는지에 대하여 통화신용 정책상의 제한이 있을수 있다고 답변함.

라. 회계사

- 미측은 동 분야에 대한 논의가 개별 회계사의 자격 인정문제에 너무 치중하고 있으나 보다 중요한것은 회계 법인의 설립문제이며 이에 대한 개방계획이 있는지 문의한바 현재까지 고려된바 없다고 답변함.

마. 프랜차이징

- 프랜차이징이 독립된 서비스 분야가 될수 있는지, 또는 분야별 서비스 공급 형태의 하나 (즉, 국경간서비스 공급)가 될수 있는지 여부에 대하여 의견교환이 있었으며, 다자간 차원에서 추가 검토가 필요한 사항이라는데 견해가 일치함.

바. 법률 서비스

- 법률 서비스의 대부분이 자문 업무 분야보다는 소송에 치중하고 있는 아국의 실정에 비추어 동분야의 개방에는 좀더 시간이 필요하다고 언급하였음.

사. 리이스

- 미측은 금융 리이스는 금융 서비스의 일부로 취급될 문제이며, 주요 관심사는 운영 리이스라고한바 아측은 동 개념 자체가 아국의 불명확한 사업 실정에 비추어 추가검토가 필요한 사항이라고 언급함.

아. 보건 서비스

- 미국의 관심사항이 외국인이 소유하는 의료기관의 설립인지 아니면 의료기관의 경영관리 위탁인지 문의한바 미측은 주로 후자에 관심이 있다고 답변하였으며, 아측은 추후 검토하겠다고 함.

자. 보험

- 미측은 보험 전문가의 갑작스런 불참으로 미측의 관심사항을 파악할수 없었으며, 다만 기 제기된 미국의 의문사항과 아국 보험 시장 현황에 대하여 구체적으로 설명하였음.

- 또한 아측은 UR 협상 결과에 관계없이 양자적으로 합의된 사항은 계속 미측에 혜택이 부여될 것이라는 점을 확인하였으며, 동 사항에 대한 MFN 적용문제와 관련 이를 무조건적으로 타국에도 부여할수 없다는 점에서 양국의 이해가 일치하는바 이에 대해상호 협력하여 해결 방안을 강구하기로 함.

4. 미국 OFFER 에 대한 질의 답변

가. 분야별 질의.답변

- 보험, 콤퓨터컨설팅, 회계사등 각분야별 질의사항을 서면 또는 구두로 미측에 제시하였으며, 3차협의시 구체적으로 논의하기로 하였음.

- 또한 건설분야와 관련 정부 발주 공사와 인력이동이 제외된다면 UR/서비스 협상을 통하여 아측이 얻을수 있는 이익이 미미하고 국내업계의 설득이 어렵다고 지적한바 미측은 자국.건설시장에서 정부 발주공사 비중이 미미하다고 다변함. 건설분야에 자유화 약속이 필요한 인력이동의 범위에 대하여는 아국이 추후 LIST를 제시하고 재협의키로 함.

나. 일반 논평

- 아측은 지금까지 미국이 각국과 가진 2차 협의를 통하여 축적한 정보를 공유할것을 요청한바 미측은 비밀 정보를 제외하고는 공유할수 있을것이라고 하는 한편 다른 나라들도 자국과 같이 양자협의를 시작하여야 할 것이라고 함.

- 또한 아측은 과거 한.미 양자 협상으로 인하여 국내에서 많은 비판이 있었을 뿐 만 아니라 MFN문제 매문에 많은 곤란한 일이 발생하고 있음을 지적하고 향후 협상은

다자 협상으로서의 성격이 유지되어야 할 것이라고 언급함. 끝
(대사대리 박영우-국장)

원 본

외 무 부

종 별 :

번 호 : GVW-0762 일 시 : 91 0425 0930

수 신 : 장관(통기, 경기원, 재무부, 상공부)

발 신 : 주 제네바 대사대리

제 목 : UR/ 서비스(금융분야) 비공식 협의(1)

4.23(화) MR. FRANK SWEDLOVE (캐나다 재무부) 주재로 개최된 표제협의 내용을 하기 보고함.

1. 회의 개요

- 일시 및 장소: 4.23(화) 10:00-18:00 GATT ROOM E

- 참석국가 (31 개국): 아국, 미국, EC, 일본,카나다, 스위스, 북구 3국, 호주,뉴질랜드, 오지리,홍콩, 알젠틴, 브라질, 칠레, 콜롬비아, 페루,인도, 이집트, 멕시코, 모로코, 터키, 탄자니아, 헝가리,말련, 싱가폴, 인니, 필리핀, 유고, 파키스탄

- 회의 진행 개요: 대부분의 나라가 GNS담당관과 금융 전문가가 각 1인씩 참석하여 금융 감독 규제 (PRUDENTIAL REGULATIONS) 와 TWOTRACK APPROACH 에 대한 의견교환을 가졌으며,4.24(수)에는 각국 OFFER 에 대한 명료화등을 위한 의견 교환을 가질 예정임.

2. 금융 감독 규제

가. 금융 감독 규제를 반영할 조문

- EC 는 SEACEN 의 공동 제안(TNC/W/52) 에금융 감독 규제가 국내 규제(제 6조)항에 반영되어 있는 것과 관련 제 6조상의 국가정책 목표가 자세하고 분명하게 정의될수 있다면 금융 감독 규제가 제 6조에 반영되는 것이 적합하나 PRUDENTIAL REASON에 근거하여 외국은행 설립이 거부되는 경우 이는 예외 조항에 해당하는 것이며,(즉 국내규제가 부과된 것이아니라 시장접근이 거부된 것이므로) 금융 감독규제 권한의 한정적 적용을 위해서도예외조항(제 14조)상의 '자의적이거나 정당화 될수없는 차별' 및 위장된 무역 제한'등의 제한조건이 적용되는 것이 좋으므로 제 14조에 반영하는것이 타당하다고 함. ((1) 시장접근과 내국민대우에 대한 제한, (2)

차관 1차보 2차보 구주국 통상국 경기원 재무부 상공부

PAGE 1 91.04.25 20:30 FD

외신 1과 통제관

0066

국내 규제, (3) 국내 규제조항에서 포괄되지 못한 사항에 대한 예외허용등 3단계 규제 구조)

- 이에 대하여 싱가폴은 FRAMEWORK 제 14조 2항을들어 예외 조항에 반영할 경우 PRUDENTIAL MEASURE를 매번 서비스 협정 사무국에 통지해야 한다는부담이 있다고 한바 EC 는 모든 조치를 매번통지해야 하는 것은 아니라고 함.

나. 금융 감독 규제의 정의

- EC 는 SEACEN 제안과 관련, 예금자등의 보호와 금융 체제의 안정성 보장 이외에 어떤 다른 목적의 PRUDENTIAL REGULATION 이 있을수 있는지 의문을 제기하고 개방형의 (OPEN-ENDED)예외는 LOOPHOLE 의 우려가 있으며, 지금까지 서비스 협상에서의 경향은 극히 제한적으로 예외사유를 정의하는 것이었을뿐 만 아니라 특히 어떤정책(예: 환 경 보호 등)을 기준으로 하는 것이었다고함.

다. 개별 결정 (INDIVISUAL DECISION) 에 대한 분쟁해결 절차 적용여부

- 스웨덴, 미국, EC 등은 SEACEN 제안 6조3항의 개별 결정에 대한 분쟁해결 절차적용배제와 관련, 시장접근 약속을 한 분야에 있어서도 PRUDENTIAL REGULATION 을 이 유로 실제설립이 계속 거부된다면 당해국의 구제수단은 무엇인지 의문을 제기한바 말련은 설립인가는내.외국인 공히 받아야 하는 것으로서 설립권(QWPUF ESTABLISHMENT) 이란 존재하지 않는 것이며, 금융기관의 설립인가에는 중대한 책임이 따르게 되는것이므로 정책 당국 고유의 자유 재량에 의하여 결정되는 것이며, 분쟁해결 대상이될수 없다고 함.

- 이에 대하여 EC 는 분쟁해결 절차는 개별결정 자체를 재심사하는 법정이 아니며, 당해정부가 취하는 조치의 기준에 촛점을 맞추는 것이라고 하는 한편, 설립권과 관 련 EC 등많은 나라에 특정 조건하에 설립권이 인정되고 있으며, 객관적 기준에 합치하면 인가를 해주어야지 그 이상 자유재량을 행사할수 없다고함.

- 한편, 항가리는 규제 체계(REGULATORY FRAMEWORK)가 시장접근 약속을 무효화한다면 분쟁해결절차에 진칩하는 것이 당연하나 단일 사항은 자연인의 입국 비자 발급 거부와 똑같은 논리로 정당화 될수 있다고 함.

- 이에 이씨는 개별 결정의 경우 국내 사법상의구제 절차를 모두 소진한 이후 분쟁해결 절차에 진입하도록 하는 것이 하나의 대안이 될수 있을것이라고 한바 일본은 국내 사법절차를 경유하는데 너무 많은 시간이 걸리는 경우가 있으므로 주의하여야한다고 함.

3. TWO T5RACK APPROACH

가. 각국의 기본 입장

- 90년도 GNS 협상에서 제기되었던선.개도국간 찬.반 논리가 재연 되었음.

0 선진 국들의 옹호 논리: 많은 나라가 금융분야에서는 협정 발효시부터 의무를부담하는 NEGATIVE APPROACH 가 유용하다는 견해를 가지고 있었는바, POSITIVE APPROACH 를 주장하는 나라와의 타협의 산물이 TWO TRACK APPROACH 인바 어느나라든 둘중하나를 선택할수 있으므로 신축적이며, 각국의 자유화 약속 수준도 어떤 사전전제가있는 것이 아니기 때문에 FRAMEWORK 제18조 (자유화 협상)의 정신이 변질된바 없음.또한 정치적 이유 로서 야심적 목표를 설정해 놓고 장기적으로는 모든 나라가 NEGATIVE APPROACH 를 채택할수 있도록 할 필요가 있음.

0 개도국들의 반대 논리: 금융 분야도 FRAMEWORK에 따라 자유화 추진이 가능함. TWO TRACK APPROACH가 실질적으로 FRAMEWORK 과 다를바가 없고 융통성이 있는 것이라면 왜 두 종류의 서로 다른의무체계(SET OF OBLIGATION) 를 규정하는지 이해할수 없음. 개도국들이 곧 NEGATIVE APPROACH를 채택하도록 압력이 가해질 수 있음. TRACK선택과 관련 MFN 적용에 조건 부과가 우려됨. 부속서는 FRAMEWORK 규정의명료화.해석등에 한정하고 자유화 추진에 있어서는 중립적이어야 함.

- 한편, 스위스, 스웨덴, 일본, 카나다 등 TNC/W/50공동 제안국들은 NEGATIVE APPROACH 를 택한 나라들이 POSITIVE APPROACH 를 선택한 나라들에 MFN 적용에 조건을두지 않는 다는 것을 부속서에 명시할수도 있다고 하였으며, FRAMEWORK상의 분야별협정 부적용(SECTORAL NONAPPLICATION) 도 상대국의 자유화 약속 수준에 따라 발동되는 것이지 POSITIVE APPROACH 를 취했다는 그 자체로서 원용되는 것은 아니라고함.

나. TWO TRACK APPROACH 와 자유화 계획작성

- 미국은 각국이 FRAMEWORK 상의 방법에 따라 OFFER 를 작성하다 보니 많은 기술적 어려움을 겪게 되었으며, TNC/W/50 에 따르게 되면 NATIONAL SCHEDULE 작성이 용이해 진다고 하였으며,4개 공동제안국 역시 각국의 자유화 약속의 명료성, 정확성,법적 안정성이 증대된다고 하였고 특히 일본은 동 부속서 초안이 금융분야의 시장접근이 무엇 인지 정확하게 정의함으로써 자유화 계획 작성의 어려움을 덜었다고 함.

- 이에 대하여 아국은 FRAMEWORK 의 POSITIVEAPPROACH 자체가 SCHEDULE 작성을 기술적으로 어렵게 하는 것은 아니며 POSITIVE APPROACH 에의하더라도 각 서비스

분야별로 시장접근의 정의가 자세하게 규정된다면 각국의 자유화 약속의 명료성이 증대될수 있다고 지적하였으며,멕시코는 NEGATIVE APPROACH 에 의한다면 기재되지않은 사항은 구속되므로 각국의 약속 기재내용이 더 복잡해 질것이라고 함.

다. 새로운 서비스(NEW PRODUCTS) 문제

- 아국은 TNC/W/50 에 의할 경우 새로운 서비스공급 허용 의무에 대한 유보가 가능한지 문의한바,EC, 스위스 등은 동문제는 국내법 규정에 따른 국내 규제(내.외국인 에 공히 적용되는)나PRUDENTIAL REASON 에 의한 규제는 허용되나 그외에는 신청후합 리적 기간내에 허용해 주어야 할것이라고 하였으며, 카나다는 새로운 서비스 공급을 금지하는 사유가 PRUDENTIAL REASON 에 의한 것이외에는 찾기 어려울 것이라고 언급함. 끝

(대사대리 박영우-국장)

원 본

외 무 부

종 별 :

번 호 : GVW-0770 일 시 : 91 0425 1800

수 신 : 장 관(통기,경기원,재무부,상공부)

발 신 : 주 제네바 대사

제 목 : UR/ 서비스 (금융분야) 비공식 협의(2)

4.24(수) 속개된 표제회의는 기 제출된 OFFER에 대한 설명과 각국의 질의 답변으로 진행되었는바 주요 내용 하기 보고함.

1. 각국 OFFER 에 대한 질의 답변

가. 캐나다

- EC 는 캐나다 OFFER 가 동결 약속만 담고있는바, 구체적인 유보 목록이 필요하다고 지적하는 한편, 현존 규제 조치의 완화를 어느정도까지 검토하고 있는지 문의한 바 캐나다는 유보목록을 작성중에 있으며, 규제조치의 완화도 신중하게 검토하고 있다 고 함.

나. EC

- OFFER 의 구체적 내용에 대한 질의 답변은 없었으며, 다만 미국은 EC 의 OFFER 를 포함한 각국 OFFER 상의 상호주의 적용 단서와관련 상호주의는 MFN 과 양립할수 없다고 보는데 각국의 견해는 어떠한지 문제를 제기한바, EC 역시 상호주의는 MFN 원칙에 합치하지 않는다고 보며 자국의 경우 매우 제한적으로 분쟁해결 절차 완료후 보복조치시행시) 적용코자 하는 것이라고 함.

다. 스위스

- 스위스 역시 자국 OFFER 상의 상호주의 조건을 MFN 원칙 적용에 연계시키려는 의도는 아니나 상호주의의 폐기는 중대한 정책 변화를 의미하기 때문에 당분간 유지코자 하는 것이라고 밝혔으며, 외국인의 부동산 취득제한 조치가 금융 부속서초안 제 3부상의 의무 규정에 합치한다고 보는지에 대한 질문 (미국)에 대하여 절대적으로 합치하는 것은 아니나 당분간 유지코자 하며, EC 와의 유럽경제 공간 (EES)협의에서도 동 문제가 논의되고 있으나 최종 결과는 예단할수 없다고함.

0 또한 서비스 공급기업의 설립이 의미를 가질수 있도록 금융부속서 초안상의

통상국 2차보 경기원 재무부 상공부

PAGE 1 91.04.26 09:30 WG

외신 1과 통제관

0070

인력에 대하여 COMMITMENT 할 용의가 있는지 (미국)에 대하여 취업 허가에 총량 쿼타 제도가 있으나 KEY-PERSONNEL의 입국은 별제한이 없다고 함.

0 내국민 대우란에 ' SUBJECT TO MANDATORY LEGISLATION EXISTING ON 1. 1. 1986' 조건을 첨부한 사유 및 동단서가 '86년 이후에 자유화된 사항은 UNBOUND된다는 의미 인지 (미국, 스웨덴)에 대하여 OFFER 작성 과정에서 누락된 제한 조치에 대한 세이프 가드로서 의미가 있으며 '86년 이후에 자유화된사항은 BOUND 할 용의가 있다고 함.

0 항가리는 스웨덴의 경우 (내.외국인간)무차별적 제한도 기재했으나 스위스 접근 방법이 다른것 같다고 전제하고 차별적 조치만 기재했는지, 기속적 법률이 행정당국에 자유재량을 부여한 경우 동 자유재량 조치의 기재여부에 대하여 문의한바 자국의 경우 PRUDENTIAL RGULATION외에는 무차별적 제한이 거의 없으며, 기속적법률에 의하여 행정부에 자유재량이 부여되는 사례도 많지 않으며 객관적 기준만 충족하면자동적으로 인가되기 때문에 법적 안정성이 완전 하다고 답변함.

라. 일본

- EC 는 일본 OFFER 중 일부 분야에 UNBOUND로 기재된 것과 관련 금융분야 부속서 초안에 의하여 NEGATIVE APPROACH 를 택한 나라가 UNBOUND로 표기할수 있는지 의문을 제기하고 구체적인 유보 목록이 필요하다고 지적함.

0 또한 EC 는 내국민 대우란에 '제한없음'이금융 부속서 초안의 NT 개념에 의하는지, 은행.증권.선물.외환 부문등에서 소비자이동란에 '제한 없음'이 일본 소비자가 외국금융시장에 완전히 접근할수 있다는 것인지, 동 COMMITMENT 와 금융 부속서 초안 상의 CROSS-BORDERTRADE - 자유화와의 관계는 어떻게 되는지, 자유재량적 부자 관리 사업과 단순 부자 상담 사업이어떻게 다른지 질의함.

- 일본은 NEGATIVE APPROACH 에 의할 경우 UNBOUND라고 표기하는 것은 적절하지 않으며 구체적인 유보목록을 만들겠다고 하는 한편 금융 전문가는 부속서 초안상의 NT 개념을 수용한다고 밝힌반면 GNS 담당관은 유보의사를 표명함.

0 한편 단순 부자 상담은 상담 사업자가 위험부담을 하지 않는 것이며, 자유재량부자 관리는 모든 권한을 가지고 임의로 부자하는 사업이라고 정의함.

- 한편 미국 및 EC 는 일본 OFFER 중 많은부분에 인가 획득이 필요하다고 기재하고 있으나 인가를 받도록 하는 것은 서비스 협정과 금융부속서 초안에 어긋나는 제한이 아닌데도 이를 명시한 이유 및 동 FOOTNOTE 의 법률적 가치에 대하여 의문을표시함.

0 일본은 그에 대하여 참가국간 이견이 없다면 FOOTNOTE 를 철회할 용의가 있다고 하였으며, 미국 및 캐나다는 인가 요건이 PRUDENTIAL REGULATION에 기초한 것이아니라면 기재되어야 한다고 함.

마. 미국

- 캐나다는 INTER STATE BANKING 에 대한 (내.외국인) 무차별적 제한 조치의 폐지용의에 대하여 질의한 바 최종 OFFER 가 만들어지기까지는 알수 없다고 하였으며, 오지리는 외국보험사에 불리한 차별적 간접세부과에 대하여 질의한바 미국은 세금 부과 문제는 서비스 협정에 포함되지 않는다는 전제하에 OFFER 를 작성하였다고 함.

0 또한 EC 는 원 보험의 CROSS-BORDER TRADE 에대한 제한이 주별로 다른데 구체적 유보 목록을 작성하여야 할 것이라고 한바, 미국은 긍정적입장을 표명함.

- 한편, 항가리는 STATE-OWNED COMPANY 에 대한 제한이 원보험 업무에 한하는지, 동제한 사유가 반독금 정책 때문인지 아니면 소유주체가 STATE라는 사실 때문인지, 개별적으로 인가해주는 기준은 무엇인지, 동 제한이 FRAMEWORK 이나 금융부속서 초안에 합치하는지 (법적 근거 및 정당성)등에 대하여 질의한 바 미국은 모든 업무에 대하여 제한되며, 개별적인 인가 기준은 알수 없으며, 동제한이 FRAMEWORK 에는 위배되지 않는다고 보나실제 개별적 인가 체계가 어떠냐에 따라 달라질것이라고 함.

바. 아국

- EC 및 미국으로부터 다음과 같은 질문이있었음.(아측 답변 내용 생략)

0 한국의 OFFER 가 현존시장 접근 수준을 반여한 것인지, 아니면 보다 낮은 수준으로 OFFER한 것인지

0 은행. 보험등의 분야에서 설립이특정 기준하에 허용되는 것으로 되어 있는바 공식기준이 있고 동 기준이 공개되는지, 무차별적 규제라면 제한 조치가 아님.

0 은행 보조 서비스에 있어서 내국민 대우란에있는 업무만 허용되는지

0 증권 회사 지분 참여제한 (10 퍼센트미만)이 개별 외국 증권사당적용되는 것인지, 외국인 지분 전체에 대하여 적용되는것인지

0 증권 거래소 회원 가입문제가 자유재량으로 처리된다고 보는데 이에 대한 견해는

0 재보험에 대한 제한중 국내사 우선 출재의무란 (여상 EC 질문)

0 은행 사무소 및 지점 설치에 대한 기준은

0 은행의 현지 법인 설립이 가능한지 (이상미국질문)

2. 기타

- NATIONAL SCHEDULE 작성 방법과 관련 미국은 NEGATIVE APPROACH 가 스케쥴 작성에 보다 용이하고 DYNAMIC 하다고 전제하고 다음과 같이 자국이 고려화 있는 대안을 설명함.

0 시장접근 (ENTRY) 과 내국민 대우 (OPERATION)를 구분하기 곤란하므로 1차적으로 ' NO LESSFAVORABLE' 란에 내.외국인 차별 조치 (ENTRY 에대한 제한 포함)를 기재

0 두번째로 NEED TEST, 서비스 공급자수 제한, 독점등 내.외국인에 무차별적인 제한 조치 기재

0 세번째로 기타 사항에 대한 추가 자유화 약속 (ADDITIONAL COMMITMENT) 기재

- 이에 대하여 스위스는 자국도 그와 같은 접근방법을 고려하고 있다고 밝히고 동 방식을 금융분야에도 적용할 것인지 문의한바 미국은 꼭 그런것은 아니라고 함.끝

(대사대리 박영우-국장)

1 (사본: 통일-환)

경 제 기 획 원

통조삼 10502-275 503-9149 1991. 4. 25.

수신 수신처참조

제목 '91년도 UR/서비스관련 제2차 한.미양자협의 참석결과 송부

1. 스위스 제네바에서 개최된 '91년도 UR/서비스협상관련 제2차 한.미 양자협의 참석결과를 별첨과 같이 송부하니 관련부처는 이를 참조하여 앞으로 있게될 본격협상에 만전을 기해 주시기 바랍니다.

2. 특히 동 참석결과 보고서중 Ⅲ 2의 「향후 대응이 필요한 사항」은 현시점에서 각분야별로 즉각적인 대안의 마련과 대응논리의 개발이 필요한 사항인 만큼 해당부처는 소관사항에 대한 귀부의 검토의견을 5월10일까지 당원에 회신하여 주시기 바랍니다.

첨부: '91 UR/서비스 제2차 한.미 양자협의 참석결과 1부. 끝.

경 제 기 획 원 장 관

수신처: 외무부장관, 내무부장관, 재무부장관, 법무부장관, 교육부장관, 농림수산부장관, 문화부장관, 상공부장관, 보건사회부장관, 건설부장관, 동력자원부장관, 교통부장관, 노동부장관, 체신부장관, 체육청소년부장관, 과학기술처장관, 환경처장관, 공보처장관, 해운항만청장, 특허청장, 통계청장, 한국무역협회장, 대한무역진흥공사장, 전국경제인연합회장, 대한상공회의소장, 대외경제정책연구원장, 한국개발연구원장, 산업연구원장.

0074

UR/서비스協商
關聯資料

'91 UR/서비스 第2次韓·美兩者協議參席結果

1991. 4

經濟企劃院
對外經濟調整室

0075

目 次

I. 協議概要

1. 日 時 : '91.4.19 (金)

2. 場 所 : 스위스, 제네바 (USTR 代表部)

3. 參席者 :

- 我國代表團
  - ○ 經濟企劃院 第1協力官 장승우 (首席代表)
  - ○ 〃 通商調整3課長 하동만
  - ○ 〃 通商調整3課 事務官 신호현
  - ○ 財 務 部 保險政策課 事務官 임승태
  - ○ 公 報 處 廣告政策課 事務官 정의영
  - ○ 對外經濟政策硏究院 硏究委員 박태호
  - ○ 제네바 代表部 經協官 및 經協官補

- 美國代表團
  - ○ Ms. Bonnie Richardson(Head of Delegation)
    Coordinator for Uruguay Round
    Services Bilaterals
    US Trade Representative's Office
  - ○ Mr. Ian Davis
    Director, Korea
    Department of Commerce
  - ○ Ms. Christina Lund
    USTR Mission, Geneva

4. 協議進行 概要

가. 協議 進行方式

- 第1次 兩者協議('91.2.11)時와 마찬가지로 兩國 Offer 內容에 대하여 分野別로 具體的인 質疑·應答을 통한 明瞭化와 論評 및 UR/서비스 協商進行에 관한 意見交換에 局限
  - ○ 서비스 分野別 具體的인 自由化 約束에 관한 協商은 하지 않음.

나. 一般討議

- 我側은 各國 Offer에 대한 明瞭化 作業도 推進할 必要가 있음을 認定하나 Framework와 分野別 附屬書를 위한 協商에 優先順位가 주어져야 하며, 특히 全體 UR協商 進展이 不振한 狀態에서 兩者協議가 開催되고 있어 關係部處 擔當者를 協議에 參與시키는데 어려운點이 많으므로 協議開催 直前에 美側代表가 變更되는 등의 事例가 再發되지 않도록 注意를 促求함.
- 美側은 UR協商에 있어서 서비스部門의 實質的 成果의 重要性을 재차 强調하고 Framework와 分野別 附屬書를 위한 作業에 優先順位가 주어져야 한다는 데에는 同意하나, 各國 Offer上의 市場接近 및 國內規制制度의 明瞭化등 解決해야할 技術的 課題가 많으며 同 作業과 Framework 및 分野別 附屬書의 相互連繫 檢討의 重要性이 增大하고 있다고 言及

0078

— 한편, 我側은 美國이 最近에 가진 一連의 兩者協議 動向에 관하여 問議한바, 美側은 Offer를 提出한 나라뿐만 아니라 未提出 國家들과도 協議를 가졌다고 答辯함(總 27個國)

○ Offer 未提出國家중 브라질, 아르헨티나는 草案은 마련 되었으나 提出時期는 農産物 協商進展과 連繫戰略으로 말미암아 아직 決定되지 않았고,

○ 노르웨이는 今明間 자세한 Offer를 提出 豫定이며,

○ 필리핀, 泰國, 印度, 파키스탄, 이집트, 東歐圈 등도 準備中에 있으나, 當該國家內의 規制制度 變化, Offer作成上의 技術的인 어려움등을 겪고 있다고 함.

— 또한 美國은 我國 Offer가 比較的 充實하게 作成되어 있고, 他開途國들의 Offer提出에 자극이 됨으로써 全體 서비스協商에 寄與하게 된점을 言及함。

Ⅱ. 分野別 主要論議 內容

1. 我國 Offer에 대한 質疑·應答

가. 共通事項 (勞動力移動)

- 美側은 我國이 勞動力移動에 대하여 어떻게 接近하고 있는지 問議하였으며, 我側은 各 分野別로 熟練技術人力 (Skilled worker)의 範圍를 定하는 作業을 勞動, 法務, 建設, 保社部등 關聯部處와 協議中이며 具體的인 我國立場은 아직 未定이라고 答辯
  - ○ 我側은 이와關聯 最近의 鑛夫등 外國人力輸入에 있어 關聯部處間 열린 論爭事例를 紹介
- 美側은 人力移動에 있어서 內國民待遇의 意味등 勞動力移動 附屬書의 補完 必要性을 言及

나. 視聽覺 (Audio-Visual)서비스

- 我側은 外國人投資認可 指針上의 制限業種인 映畫輸入配給業 登錄時의 制限基準을 當分間 廢止할 計劃이 없음을 確認
- 映畫의 新聞廣告에 따른 現行 規制事項 및 節次에 관하여 說明
- 또한 音盤 및 비디오業에 대한 外國人 參與制限이 廢止됨에 따른 登錄可能 및 其他 關聯事項을 補完하여 說明

0080

다. 廣 告

- 海外에서 外國廣告業體에 의하여 製作된 廣告物의 輸入이 實質的으로 禁止되고 있다는 美側의 質疑에 대하여 我側은 廣告物 輸入時의 關聯節次와 放送 또는 映畫上映時의 廣告에 대한 審議節次, 그리고 廣告關聯機關(韓國放送廣告公社 및 韓國新聞協會 廣告協議會)의 性格 및 機能에 대하여 자세히 說明
- 我側은 지난 1次協議時 提起되었던 Coca-Cola 廣告의 경우 수차례의 審議後 우리의 倫理基準에 符合되게 修正되어 通過된 事例를 說明
- 그러나, 美側은 Pepsi-Cola 廣告의 例를들어 外國製作社가 만든 漫畫廣告의 경우 輸入許可가 拒否된 反面, 國內製作社가 同一하게 만든 廣告物은 廣告가 許容되고 있어 公演倫理審議委員會등의 審議基準 및 그 運營에 疑問을 提起함.

○ 美側은 公報處가 最近 外國廣告物의 許可, 修正通過 및 拒否 事例등을 記錄한 資料가 있다면 이를 參考로 提示해 줄것을 希望 ○ 我側은 이를 確認後 推後 通報키로 함.

- 한편, 我側은 放送廣告時間이 制限되어 있어 廣告에 대한 超過需要를 充足시키지 못해 廣告放映의 어려움에 따른 隘路를 認定하고 있으나 今年 9~10月頃 TV채널이 새로 追加될 것이므로 형편이 보다 改善될 것으로 展望된다고 說明함.

- 그러나 앞으로 繼續하여 韓國放送廣告公社와 韓國新聞協會 廣告協議會의 性格 및 機能에 대하여 兩國間 繼續 論亂이 될 것으로 展望됨.

○ 특히 美側은 framework의 非政府 規制 事項을 提起하며 上記 團體들의 機能에 强한 疑問提起

라. 建 設

- 美側은 我國 Offer의 內國民待遇에 Unbound로 記入한 理由에 대해 지난 1次 協議時 我側이 說明한 대로 現在 內國民待遇에 대한 制限事項이 없으나 向後 國內 中小業體 保護를 위해 一定制限 基準(最小基準制限)을 만들 것이라는 計劃을 理解하고는 있으나,

- 美國은 大規模企業뿐 아니라 많은 中小規模의 建設用役業體를 가지고 있기 때문에 이의 基準設定與否에 關心 및 憂慮를 表示함.

- 또한 美側의 建設業 免許取得要件에 대한 問議에 대하여 我側은 免許基準은 多樣한 業種別로 具體的基準이 相異하기 때문에 일일히 列擧 說明은 어려우나, 土木建築業의 例를들어 免許基準(資本金, 建設技術者, 營爲 實績등)을 說明

0082

- 美側은 建設部門 1次協議 要約中 外國企業의 國內建設 Project의 主契約者 役割 遂行 可能 與否에 대하여 補完 答辯을 希望하였으며 我側은 檢討後 追後 通報하겠다고 答辯

  ○ 向後 制定될 國內建設 認可基準에 대한 指針提示 檢討가 必要

- 또한 美側은 專門建設部門에 있어 外國企業의 Project 受注時 國內企業에 대한 技術移轉義務가 주어지는 事例가 있다고 言及하며 이의 是正을 希望

  ○ 我側은 私企業間의 契約上 發生하는 事例에 대하여는 政府가 介入할 事項이 아님을 說明

- 外國建設業體의 建設協會 加入義務 및 新規業體에 대한 都給限度額 策定에 관한 美側 追加 質問事項에 대하여

  ○ 我側은 國內 免許를 取得한 모든 建設業體들은 建設協會에 義務的으로 加入해야 하며, 新設業體의 경우는 拂入 資本金 만으로 算定되고, 法人 設立後 當該 現地法人 名義로 施工한 工事實績은 次年度 都給限度額 策定時 反映됨을 說明

마. 엔지니어링 디자인 서비스

- 科學技術處 登錄要件에 一定數의 技術者 雇傭條件이 있는 바, 外國企業의 韓國技術者 雇傭에 대한 制限與否에 대하여 我側은 아무런 制限이 없음을 說明
- 我側은 앞으로 技術用役育成法을 改正하여 外國企業의 國內 市場 參與機會를 擴大하기 위해 科學技術處에 登錄을 하지 아니한 外國企業도 主契約者가 될수 있도록 하는 方案도 檢討하고 있으나, 이와같은 改正方向에 대해 많은 民間企業이 反對意思를 表示하고 있기 때문에 적지 않은 어려움이 豫想됨을 說明함.

바. 會計·稅務

- 美側은 同 分野에 대한 論議가 個別 會計士의 資格認定 問題에 置重하고 있으나 보다 重要한 것은 會計法人의 設立 問題이며, 이에대한 우리의 開放計劃이 있는지 問疑 한바, 現在까지 考慮되고 있지 않다고 答辯
- 또한 美側은 美會計法人이 韓國CPA의 雇傭可能與否를 물어온 바, 이의 前提條件은 會計法人의 商業的 駐在인바, 이는 現在로서는 不可하다고 答辯
- 美側은 現在 同 分野에 대해서 어느나라와도 相互認定에 관한 協定을 맺고 있지 않다고 言及
- 稅務士의 경우 規制事項 및 節次에 관한 我國 立場을 1次 協議時의 答辯을 補完하여 說明 0084

사. 컴퓨터關聯 서비스

- 컴퓨터關聯 서비스의 包括範圍 및 制限事項에 관한 美側 問議에 대하여 我側은 現在 改正作業中인 韓國標準産業分類가 今年 8月中 完了豫定이며 現在 作業中인 改正(案)에 의하면 우리의 包括範圍가 美國의 範圍와 大同小異함을 說明
- 現在 컴퓨터關聯 서비스, 엔지니어링(技術用役育成法 改正時), 컨설팅 部門등은 새로운 分野이기 때문에 現在로서는 適切한 規制事項이 없으나 資格基準등 客觀的인 規制事項의 新設 必要性을 言及함.
  - ○ 向後 我國의 適正 規制事項 補完 分野로서 關聯部處의 追加 檢討가 必要

아. 觀 光

- 旅行斡旋業(Travel Agency)의 支社나 子會社 設立時 關聯 規制事項에 대한 美側質疑가 있었으며 我側은 檢討後 追後 通報 約束

- 海外旅行者에 대한 信用카드 使用限度 및 換錢限度 變更에 대하여 我側이 海外旅行의 直接經費에 대하여는 信用카드 使用에 制限이 없다고 하자 이를 'Offer에 binding할 用意가 있는지를 問議하여 왔으며, 我國은 檢討後 追後通報 하겠다고 함.

자. 流 通

- 我側은 流通業開放이 MFN 原則適用으로 因하여 無差別的으로 이루어질 境遇의 問題點에 對하여 說明

- 지난 4.11～12 韓・美 貿易實務小委時 化粧品 및 書籍의 2個 部門이 流通業 開放에서 除外되었는바 이들 部門에 대한 開放計劃이 있는지에 대한 美側質疑가 있었음. (本 質問은 Ian Davis 商務省 韓國 director 質問으로 이의 確認 및 檢討 必要)

- 美國의 關心 表明分野인 Franchising에 대하여 我側은 同 分野는 獨立된 서비스分野라기 보다는 多樣한 서비스 分野에서 事業을 展開하는 하나의 運營方式이라 할 수 있음을 言及하였으며, 美側도 이를 認定하고 있으며 Franchising이 Cross-border trade領域에 包含되기를 希望하며 兩者協議時 相對國들과 意思打診중이라고 說明함.

- 我側은 理論的으로 cross-border supply는 서비스의 國境間 移動을 意味하는 바 무슨 서비스가 移動하는지를 問議한바, 美側은 企業의 know-how 및 商標 또는 商號(good name)등 이라고 說明함.

  O 프랜차이징은 연쇄점뿐 아니라 family hotel, fast food restaurant, 自動車 修理, Car-rental등 多樣한 分野를 包含하고 있는 Royalty를 條件으로한 技術導入契約 形態이므로, 실제로 商業的 駐在없이 know-how만 國內企業에 移轉이 可能하므로 이의 深層的인 檢討가 要求됨

0086

차. 法務서비스

— 我側의 現行 規制事項에 대한 說明이 있었으며 美側은 外國法諮問(foreign legal consultant)에 대한 關心表明

○ 我側은 向後 協商段階를 對備하여 美側에게 關心分野에 國內法 實務까지 包含되는지 與否를 問議한 바 國內法 實務分野에 대하여는 特別한 關心事項을 보이지는 않음.

카. 리스

— 美側은 金融리스는 金融서비스의 一部로 取扱될 問題이며 主要關心事는 運營리스라고 言及한바, 我側은 同 槪念의 分類 自體가 不明確한 我國實情에 비추어 追加檢討가 必要한 事項이나, 現在 리스會社가 飽和狀態에 있기 때문에 過當競爭의 副作用을 막기 위해 追加設立은 地方리스社로 制限하고 있는 實情을 說明

타. 保 健

— 美國의 關心事項이 外國人이 所有權을 保有하는 醫療機關의 設立인지 아니면 醫療機關의 經營管理 委託인지를 問疑한 바, 美側은 主로 後者에 關心이 있다고 答辯하였으며,

○ 我側은 追後 檢討할 事項이나 現在로서는 醫療部門이 外國人 投資認可指針上 禁止業種에 該當되며, 國內法人이라도 醫療法人은 非營利法人으로 運營되고 있음을 說明

파. 保 險

(1) 原保險 (Cross-border supply)

- 海上積荷保險에 대한 Cross-broder Supply를 許容하는 韓國側 Offer는 外國 保險社가 韓國政府의 免許없이 이를 受保할 수 있다는 意味인가라는 美側의 質問事項에 대하여,

  ○ 我側은 海上積荷保險에 대해서는 對外貿易을 支援한다는 觀點에서 外國 保險社들도 韓國政府의 免許없이 受保할 수 있도록 許容하고 있음을 說明하고,

  ○ 海上積荷保險의 附保는 輸出·入業者間 貿易條件 (F.O.B. 또는 C.I.F.등)과 關聯하여 決定되는 事案인 만큼, 이를 韓國政府로 부터 免許를 取得한 保險社에게만 附保토록 制限하는 것은 現實的으로 意味가 없다고 答辯함.

- 韓國側 Offer는 輸入海上積荷保險에 대해서는 왜 輸出海上積荷保險과 달리 '95.1.1부터 Cross-border Supply를 許容한다고 猶豫期間을 設定하였는가라는 美側 質疑에 대하여,

0088

○ 我側은 國內 損保社들이 外國 大型 損保社와 同等하게 競爭할 수 있는 基盤을 다질 수 있도록 一定期間 履行 留保期間('95.1.1부터)이 必要하다고 說明함.

(2) 原保險(商業的 駐在)

- 美側은 支店, 合作社, 子會社등 進出形態에 關係없이 美國 原受 保險社가 韓國市場에 參與할 수 있다는 韓·美間의 諒解가 있었는 바, 今番 韓國側 Offer는 子會社 設立을 不許하고 있고 合作社 設立도 보다 嚴格한 制限을 두고 있음을 指摘하면서 韓國政府는 어떻게 한편으로 韓·美間의 이러한 約束을 지키면서 다른 한편으로 MFN原則을 遵守할 것인가에 대한 疑問을 提起

- 我側은 既存 韓·美間의 保險兩者 協商結果는 UR協商 結果와 關係없이 앞으로도 繼續 遵守될 것이라고 說明하였으며

  ○ 다만, 美國 保險社가 우리市場에 進出할 境遇, 生命·損害保險을 莫論하고 進出形態(支店, 合作社, 子會社)에 關係없이 一定資格 具備時 이를 許容할 것이나,

○ 國內 生保市場은 短期間에 많은 保險社가 設立됨에 따라 이미 飽和狀態에 있다고 判斷되어 向後 우리 生保產業이 이를 受容할 수 있는 時間的 餘裕를 가질 수 있도록 進出許容 時期를 合理的으로 調整할 것임을 言及함.

○ 損保市場의 境遇는 美國 損保社로 부터 아직까지 支店을 除外하고는 合作社 또는 子會社로의 進出 需要가 없었기 때문에 이에 대한 指針도 없는 狀態이며, 向後 美側으로부터 具體的인 申請이 接受될 경우 指針을 마련하여 이의 許容 與否를 審査할 豫定임을 밝힘.

- 한편, 我側은 過去 韓·美間 保險協商 結果를 MFN 原則에 따라 多者化할 수는 없다는 立場임을 說明함.

○ 卽, 我國이 大規模 貿易黑字를 보이고 있는 國家를 爲해 만든 特惠的 性格의 Guideline을 我國이 慢性的 大規模 貿易赤字를 示顯하고 있는 國家에게 同一하게 適用할 수는 없음을 言及

- 또한 我側은 韓·美間 保險協商 結果와 MFN 原則 遵守 問題에 관하여 아래 方案등을 提示하고 向後 多者間 協商에서의 受容可能性에 대하여 美側과 論議를 가짐.

0090

(第1案) 過去 韓·美間 保險協商 結果를 兩國間 Harmonization Arrangement로 看做하여 MFN原則으로 부터 逸脫할 수 있는 方案

(第2案) 韓·美間 保險協商 結果의 MFN化를 長期的인 目標로 삼고 今番 및 以後 連續되는 協商등을 통해 漸進的으로 達成해 나가거나 MFN原則 適用에 대한 履行 留保期間을 設定하는 方案

(第3案) 國別로 進出許容 保險社 數에 대한 Quota를 設定하는 方案

— 美側은 同 事項에 대한 MFN適用問題와 關聯 이를 無條件的으로 他國에도 賦與하기는 어려울 것이라는 點을 理解하고 이를 위해 相互協力하여 解決方案을 講究해 나가기로 함.

(3) 再保險 (Cross-border Supply)

— 大韓再保險 (KRIC)에 대한 義務出財制度의 廢止與否 및 國內 出財義務의 內容에 대한 美側質問에 대하여,

○ 我側은 '90.4.1부터 典型的인 企業保險인 火災, 機械, 船舶 및 積荷등 4個 種目에 適用하였던 大韓再保險 대한 20% 義務出財制度는 完全히 撤廢되었음을 確認함.

- 또한 國內社 優先出財制度란 損害保險事業者로 하여금 自社의 保有超過分을 國內의 다른 損害保險事業者에게 優先的으로 出財토록 하는 制度임을 說明하고 各 原保社의 保有超過分에 대한 海外出財는 國內 他會社의 再保險 保有能力을 充足시킨 以後에야 可能함을 說明

- 外國 保險社에 대한 情報와 直去來 經驗이 不足한 우리 保險社 立場을 勘案할 때, 國內社 優先出財 制度의 必要性을 言及함.

○ 國內社 優先出財制度는 우리業界가 海外再保險 去來에 대한 充分한 經驗과 知識이 蓄積되고 資本金의 大型化등을 通해 相當水準의 國際競爭力이 갖추어질 때까지 不可避한 制度

○ 同 制度는 우리나라에서만 運營되는 것이 아니고 相當數의 國家가 國內 保有 極大化를 爲해 이와 類似한 直接的인 規制 措置를 取하거나 國內社間 自律協定 등의 間接的인 制限이 있다는 點을 說明

0092

(4) 保險仲介 서비스

- 美側은 過去 韓·美間 雙務 會談時 保險代理店 許可 Guideline을 生命保險分野까지 適用시켜 줄 것과 保險 Broker 制度의 導入을 위한 Timetable을 要請

- 我側은 現行 專屬代理店 許可 Guideline은 生命保險分野까지 適用되고 있음을 說明

- Broker 制度의 導入과 關聯, 現行料率 및 商品構造下에서는 이를 導入키 困難한 立場임을 言及

  ○ 卽, 各 保險社가 販賣하는 保險商品이 相互 類似하여 Broker나 獨立代理店에 대한 消費者의 需要가 채 形成되지 않고 있는 實情임을 밝힘.

0093

2. 美國 Offer에 대한 質疑·應答

가. 保 險

- 美國의 Offer에 의하면 11個 州에 대한 Port of entry 制度가 있는바, 同制度는 外國企業이 支社나 子會社를 設立하고자 할때 優先的으로 이들 port of entry로 指定되어 있는 州에서의 免許取得이 前提되고 있음.

 o Port of entry (11 states) : 앨러버마, 알라스카, 콜로라도, 플로리다, 일리노이스, 미시간, 매리랜드, 뉴멕시코, 뉴욕, 네바다, 몬타나

- 我側은 同 免許節次가 外國保險社들에게는 너무 複雜한 制度라고 指摘함. 즉 外國保險社가 어느 特定州에서 事業을 營爲하고자 할때, 이 會社는 먼저 port of entry state로 부터 免許取得을 한 後에나 可能함을 言及하고 이는 外國企業體에 대한 事實上의 市場接近上 制限을 意味하는 것이라고 함.

 o 美側은 關聯 部處로 하여금 檢討後 알려주겠다고 答辯

- 我側은 또한 美 Offer상의 "blue water ocean marine"에 대한 意味를 問議하였으며, 美側은 現在 保險專門家가 參席치 못했기 때문에 檢討後 이를 通報해 주겠다고 約束함.

 * 保險分野는 我側이 많은 質問을 準備하였으나, 美側의 갑작스런 保險專門家 不參으로 말미암아 向後 協議時를 對備하여 其他 質問들을 留保함.

0094

나. 建 設

- 我側은 政府發注工事가 政府 調達協定 加入國에만 局限되고 建設 人力移動이 制限된다면 UR/서비스協商을 통하여 我國이 얻을 수 있는 利益이 微微하고, 國內業界의 說得이 어렵다는 點을 指摘한 바, 美國은 自國建設 市場에서의 政府發注工事 比重이 微微하기 때문에 政府調達 協定에도 不拘하고 韓國이 얻을 수 있는 利益은 많을 것이라고 說明함.

  ○ 지난 1次協議時 我側이 提示한 建設部門 熟練勞動力(Skilled labor)의 美 Offer상 Specialist範疇 包含 考慮 要請에 대하여는 美側은 case-by-case로 決定될 事項이나, 美國內에서 充當이 可能한 人力에 대해서는 勞動力移動을 許容하기 어려우며, 我側이 提示한 技術人力도 充當可能 人力으로 볼 수 있다는 見地의 否定的인 追加答辯을 해 왔음.

- 建設分野에 自由化約束이 必要한 人力移動의 範圍에 대하여는 我國이 追後 list를 提示하고 再協議를 가지도록 合意함.

- 我側은 美國이 政府調達의 發注時 選定基準으로서 都給限度額 같은 制度가 있는지 問議하였으며, 美國은 檢討後 追後 通報하겠다고 答辯

0095

다. 公認會計士

- 我側은 美國이 韓國의 公認會計士에 대한 資格認定을 하고 있는지 與否 및 認定하고 있다면 그 節次 및 規制事項들은 무엇인지를 質議

- 美側은 現在까지는 어느나라와도 相互認定協定을 맺고 있지는 않다고 言及하고, 美國內 公認會計士 資格取得時 아무런 制限이 없다고 言及

- 我側이 美國의 州別 公認會計士 資格節次에 관하여 1次協議時 要請한 事項에 대하여 美側은 我側代表團에게 現 州別 公認會計士 關聯規程集을 傳達하였으며, 我側은 關聯部處로 하여금 檢討케 하겠다며 感謝를 表示.

- 또한 我側은 캘리포니아, 뉴욕, 일리노이스, 텍사스, 매사추세츠 동에서의 學歷評價(academic evaluation)基準의 提示를 要請했으며 美側은 檢討後 追後 通報하겠다고 答辯

라. 컴퓨터 컨설팅

- 我側은 컴퓨터部門 컨설팅이 美 Offer 상에 記載되어 있지 않음을 指摘한데 대하여 美側은 이를 認定하고 檢討後 追後 答辯하겠다고 言及

0096

마. 프랜차이징

ㅡ 美側이 我國 流通部門에 대한 質疑·應答時 旣論議 하였으며 詳細事項은 書面傳達로 代置

○ 我側은 프랜차이징을 獨立된 서비스部門으로 보지 않으며 一種의 經營方式이라는 見解表明. 美側도 이에 대해 否定은 하지 않으나 프랜차이징을 cross-border supply 供給樣式의 範疇內에 包含시키려는 意圖로 보여짐.

바. 一般論評

ㅡ 我側은 지금까지 美國이 各國과 가진 2次協議를 통하여 蓄積한 情報를 共有할 것을 要請한 바 美側은 秘密情報를 除外하고는 共有할 수 있을 것이라고 하는 한편 다른나라들도 自國과 같이 兩者協議를 始作하여야 할 것이라고 함.

ㅡ 또한 我側은 過去 韓·美兩者協商으로 인하여 國內에서 많은 批判이 있었을 뿐만 아니라 MFN問題 때문에 많은 困難한 일이 發生하고 있음을 指摘하고 向後 協商은 多者協商으로서의 性格이 維持되어야 할 것이라고 言及함.

Ⅲ. 協議結果評價 및 向後 對應方向

1. 協議結果 評價

- 美側은 我國 Offer가 一部 追加自由化 約束도 包含하여 比較的 充實하게 記述되어 있고 他開途國들의 Offer 提出에 刺戟이 되었다는 點에서 我國의 努力을 肯定的으로 評價함.

- 今番 協議는 第1次 兩者協議時와 같이 兩國 Offer의 具體的 明瞭化를 위한 것임과 동시에 美 行政府의 迅速處理節次(Fast Track Authority)의 延長에 대한 美國 議會의 同意 獲得을 위한 手段의 一環으로 推進되었음.

- 美側은 向後 具體的 明瞭化(clarification)를 위한 協議를 1~2回 더 가진後 이를 바탕으로 相互制度改善을 위한 自由化 協商을 推進할 計劃인 것으로 判斷됨.

2. 向後對應이 必要한 事項

(向後 協議 및 讓許交換協商에 對備하기 위해 다음 事項에 대한 徹底한 準備 必要)

① 我國 Offer에 旣提示한 各 서비스分野의 具體的 定義 및 包括範圍의 明瞭化 (關聯 全部處)

0098

〈例〉 컴퓨터關聯서비스

② Unbound 및 Standstill로 表示한 分野의 現存 規制措置의 具體的 明示 및 把握으로 不必要한 誤解의 素地를 拂拭 (關聯 全部處)

- 國內規制 및 外國進出業體에 대한 規制內容 把握

③ 서비스 分野別로 具體的인 Request list 作成(關聯 全部處)

- 協議가 進行됨에 따라 基礎的인 概念등에 대한 質疑는 消盡되고 있으며, 現存 規制事項들에 대한 徹底한 硏究를 통한 關聯部處의 質疑 開發이 切實히 要請

〈例〉

○ 建設分野에 있어 我國이 要請할 必須人力의 種類 및 範圍

○ 建設部門 技術人力 또는 管理人力이 美國 Offer의 必須人力에 속하는 Specialist의 範疇에 包含되기 위한 論理開發 必要

④ 勞動力移動에 대한 我國立場 定立(法務, 勞動, 建設, 保社部등)

- 勞動力移動의 範疇에 包含될 業種의 list開發이 時急

⑤ 新分野인 컴퓨터 및 通信部門 컨설팅에 대한 適切한 資格規定 마련등이 時急히 要請(商工部, 遞信部, 科技處)

- 例를 들어 現在 科學技術處에서 推進中인 技術用役育成法의 改正時 特別法에 必要 資格規定의 新設 檢討 必要

⑥ 保險, 旅行斡旋業등 韓·美 兩者協商에 의하여 이미 自由化된 部門의 MFN 適用에 對한 多者化 對應方案 마련(財務部,交通部)

⑦ 法務서비스, 保健서비스, Leasing, Franchising, 保險仲介業등 我國 Offer List에서 漏落되어 있는 分野의 對美 協商對應 方案마련 및 點檢

- 保健서비스의 경우 醫療法人의 設立에 대한 對應方案에 置重되어 있으나 病院管理 專門人力이 就業入國하여 國內 病院을 運營하는 경우(保健社會部)
- 法務서비스의 경우 美側의 關心事項은 豫想대로 外國法諮問 (foreign legal consultant)인바 이에 대한 對應方案 點檢(法務部)
- 프랜차이징은 서비스 國境間 移動과 關聯하여 再檢討(商工部)
  - ㅇ 技術導入契約의 重要性이 增大되고 있으며 UR/TRIPS와도 關聯事項임

⑧ 서비스 分野別 國內規制制度 整備의 持續的 推進(關聯 全部處)

- 컴퓨터關聯 서비스, 소프트웨어開發業등 關聯制度 未備分野
- 映畫輸入·配給業, 海外廣告物輸入, 流通, 旅行斡旋業등 開放對備 未洽 分野
- 技術用役育成法, 建設業法등 現實態에 比하여 法令制度가 落後된 分野

0100

⑨ 今番 韓·美 2次 協議時 美側에 提示키로한 資料整備

- 外國廣告物의 輸入 및 公倫審議 現況(公報處)
- 外國企業의 國內建設 Project에 대한 主契約者로서의 遂行 可能 與否(建設部)
- 旅行斡旋業의 支社나 子會社 設立時 關聯 規制事項(交通部)
- 海外旅行의 直接經費에 대한 信用카드의 使用이 無制限이라는 事實을 Offer에 binding할 用意가 있는지의 與否(財務部)
- 醫療機關의 經營管理 委託 可能性(保社部)

〈參考〉 我國이 美側에 答辯 要請한 事項

① 保險分野의 免許取得에 있어 Port of entry state制度의 外國企業에 대한 市場接近上 制限 與否

② 保險部門 Offer중 "blue water ocean marine"의 意味

③ 政府調達의 發注時 選定基準으로서 都給限度額 같은 制度가 있는지의 與否

④ 公認會計士 部門에 있어 캘리포니아등 5個州의 學力評價基準 提示

⑤ 컴퓨터 컨설팅이 現在 美國 Offer에 記載되어 있지 않음을 指摘하고 이를 確認 要請

別　　添

1. 韓國代表團 首席代表의 Opening Speech (英文)

2. GATT 事務局 Gary Sampson 서비스 擔當局長과의 面談結果 要約

Speech by Mr. Seung Woo Chang
Director General
Economic Planning Board
Republic of Korea
April 19, 1991

I have some brief remarks to make before we start today.

First of all, I would like to say that I am very happy to meet you here today, Ms. Bonnie Richardson, Mr. Ian Davis and Ms. Christina Lund.

I have learned that Ms. Nancy Adams has moved to another position and thus could not be here today with us. And, to make matters worse, I will also be moving to another position shortly. However, in my new position, I will be responsible for overall international issues, including the Uruguay Round negotiations. Thus, although I will no longer be directly involved in the trade talks, I will still remain involved in an indirect capacity. Taking my position will be a new Director General from the Economic Planning Board, Mr. Yoon Jae Lee, who unfortunately could not be here today. Furthermore, Mr. Byung Il Kang will also be moving to another position with me. Thus, a new Director Dong Man Ha, who is here today, will resume the responsibilities for the services negotiation.

I would like to now briefly introduce our delegation who are here today.....

As to today's meeting, I would like to follow the procedure

taken during our first meeting last February. Namely, we will first respond to your questions and then we will make our questions to you.

I understand that last time you submitted written questions and that we responded to some of them in written form to Ms. Nancy Adams. So, today, starting with Audio-Visual sector, we would like to continue to answer the questions you may have.

However, before we do so, I would like to make a couple of a points regarding our bilateral consultation process.

First, you should understand that in Korea there are about twenty different ministries involved in preparing the UR services negotiations. Currently, as you are all well aware, the Uruguay Round negotiations are virtually at a standstill, including the services negotiations. However, we are now holding our second consultative meeting on services with the United States. As the coordinating ministry, the Economic Planning Board have received some pressure from the other ministries who are concerned that Korea is following the U.S. leadership far too closely, especially compared to other advanced developing countries. We would like to hear your comments regarding this.

The second point I would like to make is regarding the scheduling of our meetings. During the scheduling of the first meeting as well as this one, there were either last minute changes in participants and/or dates for the meeting. The very short notice of these changes by the U.S. side has made it very

0104

difficult for the EPB to prepare for the meetings. I think that we should avoid such last minute ad hoc changes as much as possible as they can raise a credibility problem regarding our talks.

I hope that you understand that these comments were made to facilitate our talks and to avoid any misunderstandings.

Thank you very much.

2. Gary Sampson과의 面談

(我國 代表團 : 首席代表외 3名 參席)

가. Sampson局長의 韓國에 對한 評價

- GNS會議때나 分野別 註釋書 制定過程에 韓國이 積極的으로 參與하고 있어 매우 肯定的으로 評價됨

- 韓國의 Offer List(지난 1月 15日提出)는 매우 廣範圍한 Sector를 Cover하였으며 Covernote등 形式上에서도 先進國 못지 않게 매우 整理가 잘 되어있다고 評價하고 이는 앞으로 開途國 offer 作成에 重要한 參考 資料로 利用될 것임.

- 美國과의 bilateral 協議등 最近의 協商過程에서도 積極 參與하고 있는 것은 韓國의 位相을 매우 높여주고 있음.

나. Offer 提出과 最近 協商參加 國家의 範圍

- 先進國(EC, 美國, 日本, 카나다, 濠洲, Nordic등) 뿐아니라 韓國, 中國, 南美의 主要國, 아세안 國家들이 거의 다 提出하였으며 印度, 파키스탄까지도 거의 準備가 完了된 狀態이어서 參與國家의 Coverage는 매우 크다고 봄. 이들 國家들만 考慮한다고 해도 全世界 서비스交易의 90%以上이 Cover 되는 것임.

0106

다. 앞으로의 日程

- 美國의 雙務協議는 繼續될 것으로 보이나 이는 事務局의 所管事項은 아니고 앞으로 複數國間 協議(Plurilateral)가 몇번 열릴것 같으며 여기서는 지금까지 兩者 協議와 一般協定 및 分野別 註釋書 制定過程에서 나타난 問題點들을 다룰 것으로 豫想

- 美國의 Fast-Track Authority 延長問題가 5月末이 되어야 確定될것 같으므로 政治的 결단이 必要한 分野는 6月이 되어야 本格的으로 論議될것 같음. 그러나 8月 여름休暇등을 考慮한다면 9月에 가서야 協商進展이 本格的으로 再開될 可能性도 있음(이것은 서비스分野에만 局限된 것은 아님)

- 따라서 6, 7月 또는 8月까지는 各 分野에서 技術的으로 어려운 事項들이 繼續的으로 論議될 것이며 協商의 本格的 進展이 있게될 境遇를 對備하게 될 것임.

- 서비스協商에서 一般協定制定은 專門家 Group에 의해 의외로 빨리 끝날 수 있다고 豫測되는 반면, 讓許協商은 今年末까지 걸릴것 같다고 一般的으로 展望함.

○ 分野別 註釋書는 金融, 勞動力移動등의 分野가 아직은 未解決 issue가 많은것 같음. 그러나 이달 24日에 열리는 金融分野 會議는 앞으로의 金融分野 註釋書와 讓許協商의 向方에 대한 重要한 會議가 될 것임.

라. 韓國의 準備必要 事項

- 무엇보다도 各國들이 旣存에 맺고 있는 모든 雙務, 地域協定 등이 이번 UR協商에서 어떻게 다루어질 것인가 하는것 등이 조만간에 論議될 豫定이므로 이에 對備해야 할 것임.

  ○ 卽 美國과의 FCN(韓美 友好條約), 雙務間 投資協定 (Bilateral Investment Treaty), 韓·美間(分野別) 合意 등을 모두 整理해서 이들이 MFN條項으로부터 一時的으로나마 derogation될 수 있는지 등을 事務局과 協議할 準備를 해야 할 것임.

- 또한 美國과의 兩者會議뿐 아니라 EC, 日本등과의 兩者協議 내지 協商에 準備해야 함.

- 앞으로 열리게될 複數間 會議에 積極 參與하여 韓國이 안고 있는 여러問題, 특히 美國에 열어준 保險, 廣告, 旅行斡旋業등 分野를 모든 나라에 열어주어야 하는 어려움(MFN原則때문에) 등을 다른 나라들과 같이 協議해야 할 것임.

0108

원 본

관리번호 91-308

외 무 부

종 별 :

번 호 : USW-1966 일 시 : 91 0424 1813

수 신 : 장관(통기, 해운항만청장)

발 신 : 주 미 대사

제 목 : UR/ 해운 서비스 분야 개방 요구서 작성

대 WUS-1140

1. 미국의 해운 시장 규제는 기본적으로 미국 대외교역 관련 항로에서 불공정관행 제거 및 미선사의 해외 영업활동 제약에 적극적인 대처를 위한 명목하에 준사법적 독립기관인 연방해사위원회 9FEDERAL MARITIME COMMISSION)를 중심으로외국 선사들에 대한 각종 의무 부과와 광범위한 조사. 처벌권 및 강력한 대항조치 발동을 비롯 소위 USER FEE 명목의 제반 부과금 등으로 구분할수 있는바 분야별 구체적 사례 다음과 같음

가. 미국 대외 교역 관련 항로 취항 외국선사에 대한 규제 내용

0 SHIPPING ACT 1984 에 의거 미국 취항 정기선사들은 FMC 에 제반 협정 요율등의 FILE 및 각종 보고와 회계관계 자료 제출 의무가 부과되어 있으며 FMC 가요구시 법령 준수 각서를 제출 해야됨.

0 또한 SHIPPING ACT 및 이에 따른 각종 명령 위반시 최고 건당 일일 25,000 불까지의 막대한 벌금 부과 가능

0 1990 NON- VESSEL- OPERATING COMMON CARRIER ACT 에 의거 미교역 참여 무선반 운항 사업체(NON-VESSEL- OPERATING COMMON CARRIER:NVOCC) 는 유사시 손해배상 또는 벌칙금 관련 재정적 책임을 질수 있도록 5 만불의 성실 의무 이행 보증금(BOND) 을 FMC 에 예치해야 하며 미국내에서의 사법. 행정정 업무 대행을 위한 법정 대리인 지정이 의무화 되어있음(91.4.15 시행)

나. 강력한 대항 조치

0 MARCHANT MARINE ACT 1920 및 FOREIGN SHIPPING PRACTICE ACT OF 1988 에의거 외국에서의 해운관련 불공정 관행 또는 제약에 대해 FMC 에 광범위한 조사권 인정 및 강력한 제재 권한 부여

통상국 차관 1차보 2차보 해항청

PAGE 1

91.04.25 09:14

외신 2과 통제관 CA

0109

0 주요 체재 내용으로는

-당해국 선박의 미항만 입항 제한 또는 수송화물량 제한

- FMC 에 신고한 운임 요율의 전부 또는 일부 적용 중지(영업 중지 효과)

- FMC 에 등록된 협정 규정에 따른 선대운영권리 의 전부 또는 일부 금지

-선박항차당 최고 100 만불의 벌금 부과

다. 각종 USER FEE 부담가중 및 관세

0 100 톤 이상 입항 선박에 대해 입항시마다 397 불의 CUSTOMS USER FEE 부과(년간 5,955 불 이내)

0 미주요 항만 준설 및 수로 유지 비용 보전을 목적으로 수출입 화물 에 대해 100 불당 0.12 퍼센트 의 HARBOR MAINTENANCE TAX 부과

0 100 톤 이상 선박 입항시 544 불의 ANIMAL AND PLANT HEALTH INSPECTION SERVICE (APHIS) USER FEE 부과(년간 최고 15 번 납부: 91.5.13. 부터 종전 150불 수준을 인상 시행 예정)

0 미국적 선박의 외지 수리에 대한 50 퍼센트 의 종가세 부과(AD VALOREM TAX)

VE 연안 해운법 미국적 선박 유보

0 MERCHANT MARINE ACT 1920 의 의거 미연안 해운업 참여를 미국적 시민 소유 미국내 건조. 등록 선박에 한정

2. 자국업체에 대한보조 및 지원은 선박확보 및 운항과 관련된 보조금 지급및 지급 보증제도등과 주요 화물 해송의 미국적 선박 유보 제도 등임.

가. 선박 확보 지원 제도

0 MERCHANT MARINE ACT OF 1936 에 의거 미국내 선박건조 비용과 외국에서의 건조 비용 차액에 대해 50 퍼센트 범위내에서 보조금 을 지급, 미조선산업 및상선대 육성 지원책을 펴왔으나 1982 년 폐지

-0 상기 1936 상선법 TITLE XI 에 근거 미국적 선박의 건조 및 개조를 위한자금조달을 용이하게 하도록 선박 건조 자금조달 채무자가 지급 불능상태에 처하였을때 연방 정부가 부채의 원금 . 이자를 지급 보증하는 연방정부의 선반담보보험제도 실시중

(FEDERAL SHIP MORGAGE INSURANCE PROGRAM)

0 MERCHANT MARINE ACT OF 1970 에 근거한 자본형성 기금 제도(CAPITAL CONSTRUCTION FUND :CCF) 의 의거 미 해운업체가 선박 건조, 개조 및 구매를 목적으로

PAGE 2

0110

일정한 구좌를 만들어 자체 기업내 기금을조상할 경우 연방법인세를 유보하고 있음.

나. 선박 운항 채액 보조금 제도(OPERATING DIFFERENTIAL SUBSIDY: ODS)

0 MERCHANT MARINE ACT OF 1936 TITLE VI 근거로

0 미국내 건조. 미국선원 승선 미국적 선박으로 미국 대외교역에 필수적인 항로에 취항시 외국적선과의 경쟁력을 유지하도록 외국적 선박보다 높은 운항비의 차액을 연방정부가 보조금으로 지급

0 운항비에 포함되는 항목은 주로 선원비, 선박수리 유지비등이며 년평균 3 억불 규모의 ODS 가 지급 되고 있음.

다. 주요 화물 수송관련 미국적 선박 우선 이용제도(CARGO PREFERENCE)

0 THE CARGO PREFERENCE ACT OF 1904 에 의거 군관련기관 소유 . 조달화물의 경우 전량 미국적 선박 수송 의무 부과

0 PUBLIC RESOLUTION 17 (1934 년) 의 의거 미수출입 은행 자금에 의해 유발된 화물은 모두 미국적 선박에 의한 수송 의무 부과, 단 수혜국 선박의 경우 미 해사청(MARITIME ADMINISTRATION) 으로부터 웨이버를 발급 받아 50 퍼센트까지 수송 참여 가능하나 참여 기회 제한

0 THE CARGO PREFERENCE ACT OF 1954 에 으거 정부 기관 관련 화물(GOVERNMETN-GENERATED CARGO)의 경우 최소 50 퍼센트 이상은 공정하고 타당한 요율을 제시하는 미국적 선박이 있을 때는 반드시 미국적 선박에 수송토록 의무 부과.

3. 아국 업체에 대한 특별한 차별 사항은 없으나 FMC 의 태평양 항로에 대한 집중적인 불공정 관행 조사(89 년 이래 계속) 와 미선사의 해외 영업 활동 제약에 대처한 외국 해운 불공정 관행 조사 및 대항 조치 활동이 아시아 지역 국가(아국을 포함 일본, 중국, 대만등) 및 동지역 국가 소속 선사에 집중되고 있어 미국. 구주선사에비해 상대적인 영업활동 제약 요소로 할수 있으며 , 국내법 제정을 통한 대외국선사 영업활동 규제. 감시 확대 추세는 향후 미국관련 대외 교역 수송참여 외국선사에 대한 간접적인 경쟁 제약 요소로 작용할 우려가 있다고 판단됨(관련 자료는 별도 파편 송부 계획임)

(대사 현홍주- 국장)

91.6.30. 까지

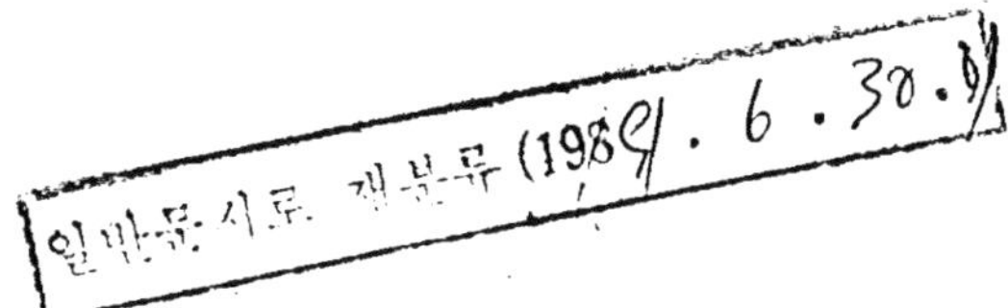

PAGE 3

0111

관리번호 91-324

주 일 대 사 관

일본(해)1500-318 91. 5. 1

수신 : 장관(통기)

참조 : 해운항만청장

제목 : UR 해운서비스분야 개방요구서 작성

대 : WJA-1328

대호관련 자료를 별첨과 같이 수집조사 보고합니다.

첨부 : 1. 일본의 해운시장 제도 현황 1부.

2. 관련자료 3부. 끝.

주 일 대 사

0112

일본의 해운시장 제도현황

(해운시장규제, 지원제도 및 외국선사에 대한 차별정책을 중심으로)

1. 일본의 해운시장 규제 제도

1) 일반규제 개요

사 업 명		근 거	규 제 내 용		비고
			참 여 규 제	운 임 규 제	
여객운송	일반여객정기항로사업	해상운송사업법	면 허	인 가	
	여객부정기항로사업	"	허 가	인 가	
화물운송	화물정기항로사업	"	사 전 신 고	인 가	
	부정기항로사업	"	신 고	—	
	내항운송업	내항해운업법	허가 또는 신고	—	
	내항선박대도업	"	"	—	
	자동차항송화물정기항로사업(페리)	"	허 가	인 가	
기타해운업	선박대 사업	해상운송사업법	신 고	—	
	해상운송취급업	"	"	—	
	해운중립업	"	"	—	
	해운대리점업	"	"	—	
기타	창 고 업	창고업법	허 가	사 전 신 고	
	철 도 사 업	철도사업법	면 허	인 가	
	항만운송사업	항만운송사업법	면 허	인 가	

* 관련참고자료(별첨 1) : 운수사업별 참입규제 및 운임규제현황
(운수사업의 운임요금제도 p222)

0113

2) 외국인의 사업참여 규제 여부

ㅇ 일본의 경우 법인설립이 원칙적으로 완전개방되어 업종별 규제가 없이 외국인도 자유롭게 법인을 설립 영업 가능함

ㅇ 따라서 외국선사의 지점설치에 있어서도 자본 및 인적규제가 없이 법인 설치가 자유이므로 실제 다수선사가 현지법인 설치 운영중임

- 아국의 경우 현대상선, 조양상선등이 현지 법인을 설치 영업하고 있음

ㅇ 다만 내항운송업 및 내항선박 대도업은 Cabotage(연안항해무역)로서 대내직접 투자 제한이 있음

2. 자국업체에 대한 지원제도

1) 외항해운대책에 의한 지원제도

(1) 대책개요

(가) 외항선박의 정비 계획(계획조선)

ㅇ 외항해운의 경영기반의 강화 및 국제경쟁력있는 선대확보위해 근대화선등으로의 대체 선박건조를 중심으로한 외항선박 정비 및 해운업의 경영다각화를 도모하기 위한 외항객선의 정비촉진

('90년도 지원조건)

- 외항화물선의 정비

. 대출금리 : 6.9%(1991.1현재)

. 융자비율 : LNG 및 초성력화선 60%, 기타 선박 50%, 개조 30%

. 융자기간 : 3년거치 10년 상환

- 외항객선의 정비

. 금 리 : 7.1%

. 융자비율 : 50%

0114

(나) 이자보급관계 재도

o 기체결된 이자보급 계약에 의한 외항선박 건조융자 이자보급금 지급 및 '87년 이후 일본개발은행에 의한 이자보급금 상당액의 유예조치(3년거치 5년 상환 조건) 계속에 의한 일본 개발은행 교부금 교부 시행

(2) 지원 예산의 추이

(단위 : 백만엥)

년 도	외항선박의 정비계획(계획조선)	이 자 보 급 관 계	
		이 자 보 급 금	이자유예특별교부금
80	97,000	6.634	—
81	117,000	6.630	—
82	134,500	6.920	—
83	118,000	6.990	—
84	109,500	6.869	—
85	100,000	6.863	—
86	90,000	6.889	—
87	70,000	25.897	119
88	45,000	716	483
89	40,000	398	738
90	42,000	168	2.251
91	43,000	43	3.239

※ '91년도는 정부예산(안)에 의함.

0115

(3) 최근의 지원실적

ㅇ 외항선박 건조실적(일본개발 은행 융자)

年度	建造量						建造資金(百万円)				融資比率(%)			
	貨物船		油送船		合計									
	隻数	千総トン	隻数	千総トン	隻数	千総トン	自己	財政	市中	総額	公団	復金	見返	開銀
'69	45	1,412	12	1,062	57	2,474	15,189	96,990	44,516	156,695	—	—	—	(定期船)66.5(定期船以外)63
'70	33	1,234	12	1,390	45	2,624	15,824	107,230	52,078	175,132	—	—	—	(定期船)66.5(定期船以外)63
'71	29	1,827	12	1,392	41	3,218	37,093	115,390	64,408	216,891	—	—	—	(コンテナ)61.75(定)58.5(その他)52
'72	22	1,483	15	1,822	37	3,304	46,618	135,820	77,756	260,194	—	—	—	(コンテナ)61.75(定)58.5(その他)52
'73	11	351	14	1,634	25	1,985	32,975	85,440	57,211	175,626	—	—	—	(コンテナ)61.75(定)58.5(その他)52
'74	12	555	13	1,384	25	1,939	33,384	96,770	55,521	185,675	—	—	—	(コンテナ)61.75(定)58.5(その他)52
'75	11	593	3	352	14	945	18,192	74,260	25,380	117,832	—	—	—	(コンテナ)70(その他)60
'76	9	117	1	48	10	165	7,820	23,200	7,474	38,494	—	—	—	(コンテナ)70(その他)60
'77	11	224	1	34	12	258	10,268	28,170	9,232	47,670	—	—	—	(コンテナ)70(その他)60
'78	5	88	4	214	9	302	6,111	21,000	7,089	34,200	—	—	—	(コンテナ)70(その他)60
'79	14	638	18	989	32	1,627	19,610	102,170	31,941	153,721	—	—	—	(コンテナ・LNG)75(その他)65
'80	18	932	13	907	31	1,839	22,553	182,300	58,305	263,158	—	—	—	(コンテナ・LNG)75(その他)65
'81	18	1,238	7	564	25	1,802	52,524	165,990	43,693	262,207	—	—	—	(コンテナ・LNG)70(その他)60
'82	12	367	4	312	16	679	24,967	70,930	35,494	131,391	—	—	—	(コンテナ・LNG)60(その他)50
'83	18	974	1	24	19	998	24,880	58,290	29,178	112,348	—	—	—	(コンテナ・LNG)60(その他)50
'84	19	994	6	571	25	1,565	39,082	80,170	40,119	159,371	—	—	—	(コンテナ・LNG)60(その他)50
'85	12	533	5	682	17	1,215	22,759	66,910	22,710	112,379	—	—	—	(コンテナ・LNG 超省力化船)60(その他)50
'86	11	636	5	644	16	1,280	22,070	79,600	31,042	132,712	—	—	—	(コンテナ・LNG 超省力化船)60(その他)50
'87	1	51	—	—	1	51	1,170	3,510	1,170	5,850	—	—	—	(コンテナ・LNG 超省力化船)60(その他)50
'88	2	168	—	—	2	168	2,430	7,290	2,430	12,150	—	—	—	(LNG・超省力化船)60(その他)50
'89	6	427	1	147	7	574	9,544	24,282	9,525	43,351	—	—	—	(LNG・超省力化船)60(その他)50

出所：運輸省国際運輸・観光局

(注) ①'47～'48年度の財政には旧船舶公団持分と復興金融金庫融資額を含む。②'54年度の建造資金の財政には利子補給持り融資を含み、市中には除かれている。③'56年度から'68年度までの市中には若干の自己資金、延払を含む。④融資比率は建造要領による。⑤'59年度の不定期船、油送船の開銀融資比率はスクラップ船を付けた場合は10%アップ。⑥建造量欄の油送船にはLPG船及びLNG船を含む。

ㅇ 이자 보급금 예산(보정후) 및 지급 실적

(単位：千円)

年度	予算(補正後)			支給実績			国庫納付額
	開銀	市中	計	開銀	市中	計	
1971	11,576,472	3,345,644	14,922,116	11,526,969	3,271,656	14,798,625	—
1972	11,731,716	3,822,945	15,554,661	11,624,243	3,722,965	15,347,208	—
1973	11,161,314	3,934,859	15,096,173	11,121,213	3,926,862	15,048,075	19,136
1974	10,380,260	4,046,242	14,426,502	10,211,759	3,833,681	14,045,440	2,966,395
1975	9,350,123	3,934,126	13,284,249	9,190,337	3,777,452	12,967,789	2,171,308
1976	7,820,529	3,564,523	11,385,052	7,820,523 (△173)	3,564,521 (△254)	11,385,044 (△427)	38,623
1977	6,164,723	2,946,359	9,111,082	6,100,272	2,924,453	9,024,725	167,378
1978	4,548,729	2,206,648	6,755,377	4,518,535	2,190,178	6,708,713	56,526
1979	3,329,890	1,704,671	5,034,561	3,230,983	1,674,039	4,905,022	57,511
1980	4,522,999	1,777,323	6,300,322	4,260,214	1,680,412	5,940,626	615
1981	5,148,505	1,481,919	6,630,424	5,033,589	1,451,070	6,484,659	1,998
1982	5,447,761	1,472,471	6,920,232	5,362,465	1,449,483	6,811,948	2,266,458
1983	5,445,562	1,396,759	6,842,321	5,445,562	1,396,758	6,842,320	5,797
1984	5,483,399	1,342,319	6,825,718	5,483,399	1,342,318	6,825,717	—
1985	5,438,036	1,383,720	6,821,756	5,438,035	1,383,720	6,821,755	1,757
1986	5,534,091	1,306,126	6,840,217	5,534,091	1,306,126	6,840,217	—
1987	21,303,086	4,594,272	25,897,358	21,225,290	4,577,607	25,802,897	—
1988	—	699,623	699,623	—	682,712	682,712	—
1989	—	397,920	397,920	—	376,499	376,499	—
1990	—	167,847	167,847	—	—	—	—
累計	179,146,055	72,571,988	251,718,043	177,740,847	70,899,286	248,640,133	8,316,659

出所：運輸省国際運輸・観光局

(注) ①△印は、船価低減等による返納額（歳入）である。
②国庫納付額は、改正前の法第12条又は第13条および改正後の法第9条に基づく船主の国庫納付額である。
③利子補給は1953年度から実施されたが紙面の都合上一部省略した。(海運統計要覧 1971 P218～219参照)
④累計は1953年度以降の分である。
⑤支給実績は3月末のため未掲載。

0116

2) 내항해운대책에 의한 지원제도

(1) 지원개요

(가) 내항선박 건조지원

o 근대적 경제선의 정비를 위해 노후 내항선 및 비경제선을 해철 또는 수출하여 자동화된 대체선을 선박정비 공단과 공유방식으로 건조

- 건조대상 : 100총톤이상 12,000총톤미만 내항선
- 공단분담비율 및 년리('90년 경우)

<table>
<tr><th colspan="3">구 분</th><th>공단분담비율</th><th>년 리</th></tr>
<tr><td>여객선</td><td colspan="2">- 이 도 대 책 선
- 근 대 화 선</td><td>80%
70%</td><td>6.75%(중장거리 카훼리)
6.8%</td></tr>
<tr><td rowspan="4">화물선</td><td colspan="2">일 반 화 물 선</td><td>80%</td><td rowspan="4">6.8%</td></tr>
<tr><td colspan="2">유 조 선</td><td>70%</td></tr>
<tr><td rowspan="2">세멘트 전용선, 특수 탱커선, 자동차 전용선 사리, 석재 전용선</td><td>근대화선</td><td>70%</td></tr>
<tr><td>상기이외</td><td>80%</td></tr>
</table>

0117

(나) 선박 개조융자— 원

- ㅇ 내항선의 경제성향상 및 유통코스트합리화를 추진하기 위한 자동화, 합리화등 선박 주기환장치를 위한 자금의 일부를 선박정비 공단에서 융자하는 것임.
  - 융자비율 및 상환기간 : 공단인정 공사비의 50%이내에서 1년 거치 6년 상환조건 (다만 능력증가 개조공사, 공해방지 개조공사 및 해상오염방지 설비공사는 70%이내, 1000만엥미만 공사는 40%임)
  - 융자금리 : 년 7.8%

(2) 내항해운대책 지원추이

(단위 : 백만엥)

	대체건조	개조융자
'80	27,100	600
'81	31,600	600
'82	32,600	700
'83	34,100	700
'84	30,900	700
'85	30,900	700
'86	33,200	700
'87	35,900	1,000
'88	30,400	1,500
'89	33,200	1,500
'90	32,500	1,500
'91	35,900	1,200

* '91년은 정부예산안임

0118

3) 이도항로 보조제도

(1) 지원개요

ㅇ 이도항로의 유지, 정비를 위해 「이도항로 정비법」에 의거 이도 항로사업자에 대해 그 결손의 일부를 보조함

(2) 지원예산 추이

(단위 : 백만엥)

년도	'80	'81	'82	'83	'84	'85	'86	'87	'88	'89	'90	'91
예산액	2,720	3,719	3,806	3,869	3,889	3,936	3,514	3,220	3,243	3,737	3,764	3,804

* '91년은 정부예산(안)임

(3) 90년 지원실적

사업자수	항 로 수	보 조 율	보 조 금 액
128	135	3/4	백만엥 3,764

* 관련참고자료(별첨 2) : 해운대책과 선박정비 계획
(해운통계요람('91) p254-291 관련 내용)

0119

4) 해운업에 대한 주요세제 지원제도

(1) 선박에 대한 특정설비등의 특별 상각제도
(조세 특별조치법 제43조)

o 대장성이 정하는 합리화장치를 구비한 300총톤이상의 선박을 건조, 사업용으로 사용하는 경우 외항근대화선은 취득가액의 18/100 그이외 선박은 12/100에 상당하는 금액을 특별상각 가능함(적용기한 1993년 3.31일)

* 91년도 정부세제 개정안으로 기간 연장 추진중

(2) 선박의 교체 구매의 경우 과세의 특례(압축 기장제도)
(조세특별조치법 제65조의 7)

o 선박에 관해서 특정의 대체구매 자산의 하나에 압축기장여 인정되는바 그 압축한도액은 대체 선박의 가액, 처분선박의 가액중 적은가액에 대하여 차익비율을 곱한 금액의 80/100에 상당하는 금액
(적용기한 : '96.3.31)

* '91년 정부세제 개정안으로 기간연장 추진중

(3) 특정의 외항선박등에 대한 등록면허세의 경감조치
(조세특별조치법 제79조)

o 외국 항로에 취항하는 특정의 신조선박(계획조선에서 B 단계 이상의 근대화선에 한정)의 보존등기 및 저당권 설정등기 경우 등록면허세의 세율을 경감

- 소유권 보존등기 : 선박가액의 4/1000을 3/1000으로 경감
- 저당권 설정등기 : 채권금액의 4/1000을 3/1000으로 경감

(4) 선박에 대한 고정자산세의 과세표준액의 특별 조치
(지방세법 제 349조의 3 제5항)

o 선박에 대한 고정자산세의과세표준액은 특례조치로서 내항선박은 가격의 1/2, 외항선박은 가격의 1/6, 더욱이 외항선박중 전년중에 외국항로에 취항한 일수가 전취항 일수의 1/2을 초과한 소위 외국무역선에 대해서는 가격의 1/12이 됨

0120

(5) 외국선의 나용선료에 관한 소득세의 원천징수의 불적용 조치

(조세특별조치법 제42조)

- 외항해운업에 있어서 이직선원의 고용을 촉진하기 위해 설립되었다고 운수대신의 증명을 득한 내국법인(사업회사)가 나용선하는 외국선박에 대하여 일정요건하에 나용선료에 관한 소득세의 원천징수(세율 20%)을 불적용하는 조치(적용기한 92.3.31)

  * 관련참고자료(별첨 3) : 운수사업의 세제조치현황

  (운수사업의 운임요금제도p243-253)

5) 마루쉽(일본선박의 해외대여방식)에 의한 혼승제도의 도입확대

- 혼승제도의 내용

  - 외항해운에 있어 일본선의 국적해외유출(Flaging out)를 방지하기 위하여 '89년 노사합의가 성립,'90년 3월부터 마루쉽에 일본선원 9명에 외국선원의 혼승이 도입되었음

  - 혼승도입시 국제경쟁력 비교(척당년간 선원비)

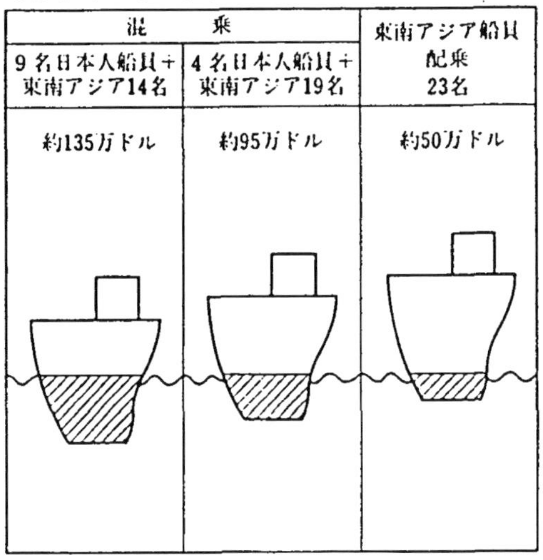

混乘		東南アジア船員配乘
9名日本人船員＋東南アジア14名	4名日本人船員＋東南アジア19名	23名
約135万ドル	約95万ドル	約50万ドル

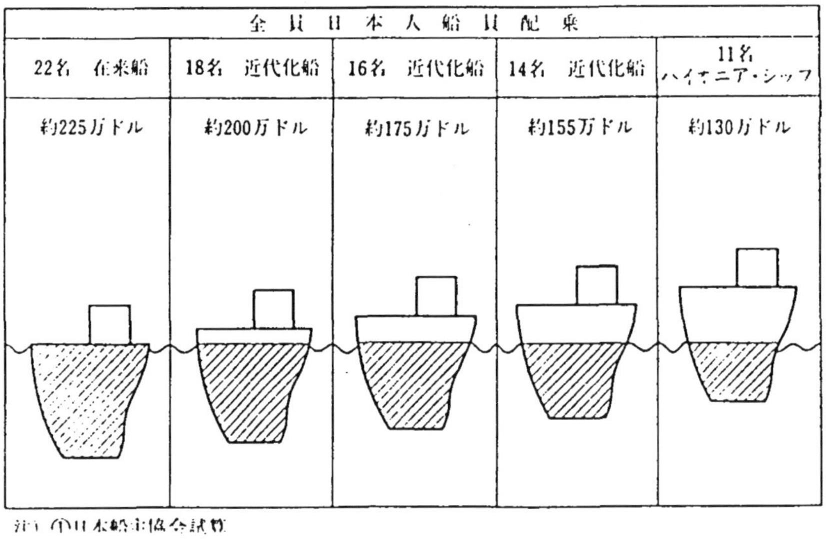

全員日本人船員配乘				
22名 在来船	18名 近代化船	16名 近代化船	14名 近代化船	11名 パイオニア·シップ
約225万ドル	約200万ドル	約175万ドル	約155万ドル	約130万ドル

注) ㈳日本船主協会試算

0121

ㅇ 일본의 혼승도입 현황(91.2.4 현재)

20条特例承認日	外航近海	船舶所有者	船名	船種
H2. 2.19	外航	日本郵船	北野	コンテナ船
〃	〃	〃	神成丸	自動車運搬船
H2. 5. 9	〃	大阪商船三井船舶	筑波山丸	原油タンカー
* 〃	〃	太洋海運	ぐろーばるはいうえい	自動車運搬船
H2. 8.27	〃	大阪商船三井船舶	えるべ	コンテナ船
H2.11.20	〃	〃	コスモディオーネ	原油タンカー
〃	〃	川崎汽船	みかさ	撒積船
H3. 2. 4	〃	飯野海運	泰邦丸	原油タンカー
〃	〃	ナビックスライン	ルビンエンブレム	撒積船
* 〃	〃	共栄タンカー	コスモマーキュリー	原油タンカー
* 〃	〃	神戸汽船	信濃川丸	〃
外航船小計 11隻 (*印既存船)				
H2. 3.22	近海	津島海運	吉海	貨物船
〃	〃	井村汽船	豊井丸	〃
〃	〃	神原汽船	天和丸	〃
〃	〃	細川海運	公海丸	〃
〃	〃	臼井海運	宮城丸	〃
〃	〃	小西海運	雄昌丸	〃
〃	〃	奥地汽船	第八義宗丸	〃
〃	〃	桑名海運	クルタウ	〃
H2. 3.22	近海	芸州海運	新州丸	貨物船
〃	〃	伸幸海運	公益丸	〃
〃	〃	丸高汽船	鶴豊丸	〃
〃	〃	佐藤国汽船	吉兆丸	〃
〃	〃	東日マリン	東照丸	〃
〃	〃	〃	安芸津丸	〃
〃	〃	〃	幸輝丸	〃
H2. 5. 9	〃	山本汽船	山興丸	〃
〃	〃	〃	山洋丸	〃
〃	〃	大阪造船所	福崎丸	〃
〃	〃	〃	江戸丸	〃
〃	〃	大洋海運	大洋丸	〃
〃	〃	友和船舶	友和華丸	〃
〃	〃	〃	友和喜丸	〃
H2. 8.27	〃	邦和海通	山邦丸	〃
H2.11.20	〃	山本商船	晴山丸	〃
〃	〃	〃	幸和丸	〃
〃	〃	愛知汽船	サンライズ	〃
近海船小計 26隻				
合計 37隻				

0122

각국의 해운강화(지원) 대책

국 명	건조융자	상각제도					해운강화책
		상각방법	잔존가액	내용년수	특별상각	자본이익과세	
영 국	-한도액:선가 80% -금리 : 7.5% -상환 : 8.5년	정액법(산업용 건물)과 정률법(기계설비)에 있어 선박은 25%의 정률법에 의함	0까지 상각	25%의 정률법은 8년 정도에 해당됨	초년도 상각은 '86.4이후 폐지	- 매각액이 취득액 상회분을 자본이익으로 인식 - 자본이익에 대한 세율은 법인세율과 같은 세율의 35% - 사업용자산의 자본이익은 압축기장 인정	- 선원의 소득세면제 : 년간 3/4이상 해외에 있는 경우 소득세면제 본인에 환급 - 선원의 파견, 귀국비용 보조 : 표준에코노미 항공운임의 35% 보조 - 선원의 훈련비 보조 : 젊은 선원£ 20/2주, 기타선원£ 50/주 - 만도선적제도의 이용에 의해 선원의 코스트 삭감 가능 · 직원중 4명은 영국선원, 기타선원은 외국인 선원 배승 가능

0123

국명	건조융자	상각제도					해운강화책
		상각방법	잔존가액	내용년수	특별상각	자본이익과세	
노르웨이	-한도액 : 선가 80% -금리 : 8% -상환 : 8.5년	정률법(최대한 장부가의 25%까지)	0까지 상각	법정되지 않음(25%의 정률법은 8년정도에 해당됨)	계약상각(건조계약이 있는 경우 년간 계약 가격의 15%을 한도로 25%의 사전상각 가능)	- 자본이익은 통상소득으로 과세 - 사업용자산의 양도이익은 4년간(선박은 8년간)이내에 신자산을 구입한 경우에는 압축기장 인정	- 노루웨이 국제선박등록제도(NIS)의 도입(87.7) • 선장이외는 외국인 선원을 출신국의 임금수준으로 고용가능 • NIS선에 승무한 외국인선원의 소득세 면제 - 선원의 소득세경감 : 선원의 과세소득의 23%공제
독일 (서독)	한도액 : 선가 80% 금리 : 8% 상환 : 12년	정액법, 정률법(정액법의 3배 또는 년률 30%중 적은율 한도) 생산고비례법	①1000총톤 미만선박: 1LDT당 125 마르크	법정되지 않고 세무당국이 공표하는 표준감가 상각표에 준거함	①공해방지기기등	- 자본이익은 통상소득으로 과세	- 선가보조 : 서독국적은 가진 전선박을 대상으로 장부가의 0.575%을 선주에 직접 보조

0124

국 명	건조융자	상각제도					해운강화책
		상각방법	잔존가액	내용년수	특별상각	자본이익과세	
			②1000총톤 이상선박: 1LDT당 175 마르크		②정액법적용 선박은 취득시부터 5년간 취득선가의 40% 한도	- 6년이상 사용한 선박을 양도시, 6년이내에 대체구매시 양도익의 50% 상당액에 대해 압축기장 인정	- 도이치국제선박 등록제도(ISR)의 도입 (1989.5) • 3항기이하의 직원 및 부원에 대해 일정수의 외국선원을 출신국의 임금으로 고용가능
프랑스	—	정액법, 정률법(내용년수의 다수에 따라 정액법 상각율의 일정배수로함)	0까지 상각	법정되지 않고 세무당국과의 교섭에 의해 내용년수 및 정액법에 의한 상각율을 결정 (실제 12년 정도 상각)	83년이후 85년도 사이 신규투자 산업용, 상업용 자산에 정액법의 상각방법을 적용하는 자산에 관하여 초년도에	- 단기 자본이익은 통상 소득에 포함과세 - 장기자본이익은 손익 상계하나 15%의 경감세율적용	- 케르케렌도 선적제도에 의해 코스트등 절감 - 정부가 금후 5년이상 기간 최저년간 4억프랑 합계 20억프랑의 원조계획 발표

0125

국 명	건조융자	상각제도					해운강화책
		상각방법	잔존가액	내용년수	특별상각	자본이익과세	
					통상의 상각에 하기의 특별상각을 더할수 있음. 내용년수 9년이하40% 10년 42% 11년이상42%에 내용년수 1년당 4%를 가산하여 80%를 한도로 한율 적용		

0126

국명	건조융자	상각제도					해운강화책
		상각방법	잔존가액	내용년수	특별상각	자본이익과세	
미국	—	조기부하자본회수제도(ACRS)정액법	0까지 상각	조기부하자본회수제도(ACRS)중 선박은 10년의 상각년수 Class에 분류됨	—	- 통상의 세율로 과세	- 운항차액보조(ODS) : 260백만불('91예산)
일본	-한도액 : 선가 60-50% -금리 : 6.9% -상환 : 3년거치 10년 상환	정액법 정률법 운항거리 비례법 (선별선택)	취득가액의 10%(상각가능한도액 95%)	- 법정내용년수 • 유조선 2000총톤 이상13년, 2000총톤 미만11년 • 유조선이외 15년 • 카훼리 11년 • 기타선박 14년	특정설비등의 특별상각 상각비율 : 외항근대화선은 취득가액의 18/100 300총톤이상의 합리화 선박은 12/1000	- 자본이익은 통상소득에도 포함 과세 - 선박에 관해 특정의 대체 구매시 압축 기장 인정	- 마루쉽(해외대여방식)에 의한 혼승의 도입 • 일본선원 9명이외에 외국인선원 혼승 인정

0127

3. 외국선사에 대한 규제제도 및 관행

1) 사전협의 제도

(1) 사전협의 내용

- 항만노동자의 고용과 취로에 영향을 미치는 항만운송 수단의 변화 즉 혁신선의 취로 및 콘네이너 선석에 관한 노동문제는 항만노사간에 사전협의하는 제도

  * 혁신선 : 풀콘선, 로로선, 다목적선등의 특수구조선

(2) 근 거

법적근거는 없고 1986.3.25 일본항운협회(하역, 창고회사등 항만사용자 단체)와 전국항만노동조합협의회(항만노동자단체)간에 체결한 "사전협의 제도에 관한 협정서", 일본항운협회와 선주항만협의회 및 외국선협회간의 "사전협의제도에 관한 확인서/각서"에 근거함

(3) 협의대상

° 혁신선의 신규서비스 개시

° 공사 콘테이너 선석에 풀콘선이외의 선박배선

° 신규공사 콘테이너 부두운영 개시에 따른 작업체제

° 사용 콘테이너 부두의 이동

° 콘테이너 부두의 작업체제의 변경

° 선사의 공동배선의 참가, 변경, 탈퇴등 작업체제의 변경에 관한 사항

° 선박대형화, 기항지변경 사항

° 기타 항만노동자의 고용 취로에 직접 영향을 미치는 사항

(4) 협의수속 절차

° 해당선사는 2개월전 직접 또는 선주항만협의회 또는 외국선박협회를 통해 일본항운협회에 사전협의 신청하면 일본항운협회는 중앙노사에 의해 구성된 "사전협의에 관한 협의회" 에 상정 협의결과를 해당선사에 회신

0128

- 선사의 사전협의 신청시 첨부내용
  . 선명, 선적, 선형, 하역방식등 본선의 내용
  . 운항선사, 항로명, 기항지, 기항회수등 본선운항계획
  . 항명, 사용선석, 취급화물, 작업개시일등 작업사항

o 해당선사와 일본항운협의회는 협의결과에 대해 확인서를 작성 서명한다
  - 확인서의 유효기간은 서명일로부터 만 2년간이며 기간만료 3월이전에 연장 가능

o 사전협의는 주요/경미사항을 구분하여 주요사항은 중앙협의, 경미사항은 지구협의에 각각 협의함

(5) 사전협의제도의 문제점

o 사전협의제도는 어디까지나 항만수송의 변화에 따른 항만노동자의 고용과 취로의 불안에 대처하기 위한 제도임에도 현재는 일본항운협회가 선사에 대해서 효율적이고 자율적인 배선을 규제하고 선사가 사용하는 항만업자에 대해서도 사전협의를 강요하여 선사의 자유로운 거래처 선택을 제한하는등 본래의 취지를 벗어나는 제도로 운영되고 있는 실정으로 특히 외국선사에 대해 악용될 소지가 있는 제도임
  - 선사의 약점은 만약 사전협의가 원만히 이루어지지 않을 경우 예상되는 선박운항정지등의 불안이며 작업회사의 선정에 대해서도 일본항운협회의 동의를 받아야 하는 입장임

2) 일본항운협회의 항만운영기금 부과

(1) 현 황

o 배 경
  - 일본지역의 급증하는 수입화물을 처리키 위한 Distribution Center 건립 및 노동력공급의 안정화 명목으로 일본항만기항 선사로부터 징수(일본항만운송협회)

0129

- 당초 30억엔 기금목표로 89.10-90.3까지 한시적으로 징수키로 하였으나 90.4-91.3까지 1년간 기간 연장하고 현재까지도 징수하고 있는 제도임

o 대상선사 : 일본항만에 기항하는 내.외국선사

o 부과대상 및 요율

대	상	요율(엔)
콘 테 이 너	TEU	830
	FEU	1,205
자동차전용선	대	120
벌 크 선	싸이로 곡물 (톤당)	23
	" 시멘트 (톤당)	8
	기계화하역벌크 (톤당)	75

(2) 문제점

o 민간기관에서 세금성격을 띤 기금거출은 부당(일본유일의 제도임)

o 기금거출의 강제성(미동의시 하역거부의사 표현등)

o 기금에 대한 선사의 수혜는 전혀없음

- 따라서 일본항만의 시설현대화, 노동력공급 명분등 일본 국내사정 및 부담분을 외국선사에 전가하는 것은 곤란

o 동기금 거출의 제도화시 결과적으로 일본수입상품의 가격을 인상시키는 결과가 됨

(3) 최근의 동향

o 일본정부(운수성)의 입장은 일본항운협회와 외국선사간의 합의에 의한 민간차원의 상관행으로 정부 불간여 입장임

0130

o 그러나 한국을 비롯 일본취항 선사관련 제국가는 불공정해운 관행으로서 이의 철폐를 요구중에 있음

- 관련 15개 국가의 동기금 철폐를 요청한 공한서한을 외무부에 제출(91.2.5)

  * 미국의 FMC, EC집행위도 동기금에 대한 불공정해운관행 여부 조사중

3) 세또내해의 외국선박 통항 규제 움직임

(1) 현 황

o 세또내해 해난방지를 위해 동해역을 통과만하는 외국적 선박에 대하여 일정기간 통항금지 지도 계몽후 통항금지 실시움직임이 있음(현재는 지도 계몽중)

- 규제배경 : 세또내해에서 증가일로의 외국선박에 의한 해난사고방지 및 내해해양환경 보존

- 지도계몽개시일 : 90. 8. 10.

- 대상선박 : 세또내해 해역을 통과만 하는 모든 외국적 선박(사실상 한국선박 대부분임)

- 규제사항 : 세또내해를 통과만하는 선박에 대하여 일정기간 순시선을 통한 지도 계몽후 통항금지시행 의도

(2) 문제점

o 동 규제조치가 지도기간 경과후 시행시 한일항로 취항선사(상선 및 어선)에 심각한 영향 초래

- 세또내해항만(고베, 오사카, 이미바리등)에 기항없이 나고야, 관동방면(요코하마, 도쿄항등)항해선박은 동해역 통과 불가로 큐수남단 우회항행이 불가피하여 운항코스트 상승 및 정기선 운항스케쥴 변경 불가피 예견(150-200마일 항해거리 추가됨)

0131

- 수송코스트 상승은 수출입 가격인상에 연결 한.일 양국간 원활한 교역에 지장 초래 예상
- 총톤수 1000톤이하 소형선박은 황천시 안정항해우려 소지

(3) 추진사항 및 최근동향

° 일본당국에 대해 동규제시 문제점 및 대안 설명으로 현재는 특별한 움직임이 없으나 완전히 단념한 것으로 볼수는 없음

- 제15차 한일정기 각료회의(90.11), 한.일수산청장관 회담(91.1)에서 거론
- 해난방지 지도단속은 강화하되, 한국선사도 해난예방을 위한 제반지도 감독 철저 수행

0132

조(요권)

원 본

외 무 부

종 별 :

번 호 : GVW-0822 일 시 : 91 0503 1830

수 신 : 장 관(통기,경기원,재무부,법무부,상공부,건설부,보사부)

발 신 : 주 제네바대사

제 목 : UR/GNS 비공식 협의

5.3(금) 오전 JARAMILLO GNS 의장 주재로 33개국 참석하에 개최된 표제 협의는 차기회의 진행계획에 대하여 협의하였는바 주요 내용 하기보고함.

(이경협관, 한경협관보 참석)

1. 협의내용

가. JARAMILLO 의장은 5.27주에 개최예정인 GNS회의와 관련 3개 기술적 과제(서비스분야분류표, 수평적 협정, NATIONAL SCHEDULE 작성방법) 및 FRAMEWORK 중 일부 조문(분쟁해결,국내규제,용어의 정의등)에 대한 토의와 아울러 지난 회의에서 캐나다가 제의하였던 각국 OFFER에 대한 토의와 아울러 지난 회의에서 캐나다가 제의하였던각국 OFFER 에 대한 다자간 검토문제를 제기하고 동 다자간 검토의 개최시기,기간 및 검토방법(분야별로 할것인지 나라별로 할것인지) 에 대한 토의를 제의함

나. 이에대하여 선진국들은 각국 OFFER 의 명료화 작업을 통하여 서비스 분야 분류표 및 NATIONAL SCHEDULE 작성방법등 기술적 과제의 해결이 용이해 질수 있음을 지적하고 5.27 주간 및 동 주간을 전후하여 2-3주간 분야별로 각국 OFFER의 다자간 검토를 병행할 것을 주장한 반면(특히 EC 는 5.20 주간에 통신분야 회의개최를 제의)브라질, 이집트,인도,알젠틴등은 각국 OFFER 에 대한 검토 이전에 3개 기술적과제에대하여 어느정도 성과가 선행되어야 한다고 맞섰으나 MATHUR 사무차장이 다음과 같이 중재하여 합의함.

- 5.23-24: 통신분야 AD HOC 그룹회의(각국 OFFER에 대한 검토)

- 5.27 주간:

0 제 1일: 서비스 분야 분류표 및 NATIONAL SCHEDULE작성방법

통상국	2차보	법무부	보사부	문화부	체신부	경기원	재무부	상공부
건설부	노동부	과기처	해항청	공보처	교통부			

PAGE 1

91.05.04 07:54 WH

외신 1과 통제관

0133

0 제 2일 이후: 각국 OFFER 에 대한 검토, 모든분야에 적용되는 수평적 규제, 인력이동등에 대한 일반토의를 먼저 한 이후 분야별검토(통신,금융분야 제외)

- 6.3주간: FRAMEWORK 규정(분쟁해결, 국내규제,용어의 정의) 에 대한 토의

다. 한편 많은 나라들이 3개 기술적 과제에 대한 사무국 문서작성의 조속한 완료를 촉구하였는바 MATHUR 사무차장은 5.13.주 말쯤에 동 문서가 완료될 것이라고 하였으나 수평적 협정은 사무국 단독으로 작업을 추진하기에 어려움이 많으며 각국의 정보제공이 필요하다고 하여 5.27주간에는 수평적 협정에 대한 논의는 하지 않기로 하였음.

2. 관찰 및 건의

- 금번 협의부터는 GNS 의장이 서비스협상회의를 직접 주재하게 되었으며 5월말부터는 각종 GNS 공식.비공식 회의가 상시 개최될 전망됨.

- 5.23.-24 의 통신분야 AD HOC 그룹 회의에는 통신 전문가의 참석이 필요하며 차기 회의시 금융분야(보험포함)는 논의되지 않을 전망이나 6월중에 예상되는 본격적인 각국 OFFER 는 논의되지 않을 전망이나 6월중에 예상되는 본격적인 각국 OFFER에 대한 검토 및 향후 양허협상등에 대비하여 금융서비스 각 세부분야별로 구체적인규제조치를 목록작성이 시급한 것으로 판단됨.끝

(대사 박수길-국장)

PAGE 2

0134

공 보 처

광정 20644- 4729 720-4138 1991. 5. 3.

수신 외무부 장관

제목 UR서비스 제2차 한.미 양자협의 결과보고

1. 통기 20644-17696 ('91. 4. 18)의 관련입니다.

2. UR서비스협상과 관련, 4.19 스위스 제네바에서 개최된 한.미 양자협의 참가 결과를 별첨과 같이 제출합니다.

첨부 : UR서비스 제2차 한.미 양자협의 결과보고 1부. "끝"

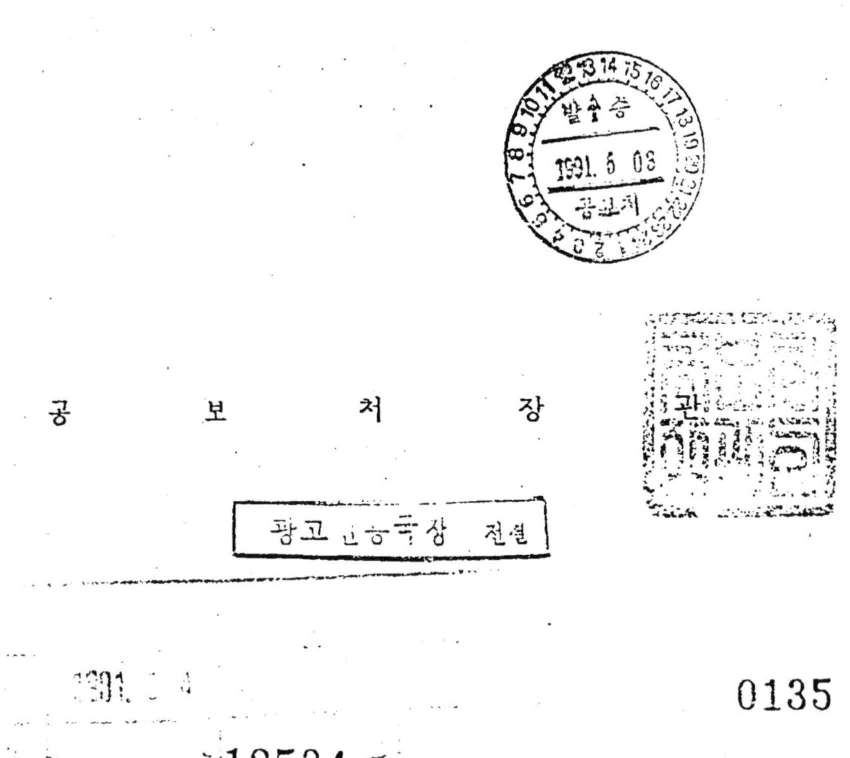

공 보 처 장

0135

UR서비스 제2차 한·미 양자협의 결과보고

1. 협의개요

o 일 시 : '91. 4. 19(금) 10:00-19:00

o 장 소 : 미국 무역대표부(USTR) 제네바 사무소

o 참 석 자

- 미국측 : BONNIE RICHARDSON (USTR서비스과장)
  IAN.M.DAVIS (미상무성 한국과장)
  CHRISTINA LUND (USTR 제네바 사무소 주재관)

- 한국측 : 장승우 (경제기획원 제1협력관)외 2명
  이종화 (제네바 한국대표부 경제협력관)외 1명
  임승태 (재무부 보험정책과 사무관)
  정의영 (공보처 광고정책과 사무관)
  박태호 (KIEP 연구원)

o 진행개요

- 한·미 양국 대표는 상대국이 제출한 자유화계획(Initial Commitment)의 내용에 대한 질의 답변을 통해 상호 의견교환
- 미국대표는 우리나라의 서비스분야중 시청각, 광고, 건설, 회계, 특허, 보험, 법률, 리이스 등의 세부 관심업종에 대하여 질문
- 우리나라 대표는 미국의 서비스분야중 보험, 컴퓨터컨설팅, 회계등의 각분야에 대한 질의사항을 서면 또는 구두로 제시
- 양국대표는 이번 제2차 한·미 양자협의시 협의하지않은 분야나 추가질문사항에 대하여는 제3차 협의시 다시 논의키로 합의

0136

2. 주요협의내용

가. 총 괄

ㅇ 양국대표들은 제1차 한·미 양자협의('91. 2. 11)시 설명이 미진한 분야에 대하여 상호 의견교환

- 건설업 및 기술용역과 관련한 회사설립 절차 및 요건
- 외국제작 광고물의 수입절차 및 심의기준등
- 공인회계사, 변호사, 세무사 등 전문직업 서비스부문의 자격요건 및 회사설립 절차
- 소매업 개방계획('91. 7)에 관한 현행규제사항 및 회사설립 절차 등

ㅇ 미국대표는 우리측 대표의 질문에 대하여 다음과 같은 사항을 설명

- 특허(Franchising)의 개념에는 상품의 유통이나 상표 또는 경영기술 등을 포함되며, 동 새로운 분야에 대한 자유화계획 제출 가능성을 각국에 타진하고 있음을 설명
- 공인회계사에 대한 각국의 상이한 자격요건을 설명
- 병원관리 용역 및 리스업등에 대한 시장접근 허용에 관하여 설명
- 미국연방 및 주정부의 공공분야 건설규모가 상대적으로 적으므로 정부조달 협정에도 불구하고 우리건설업의 미국진출 가능성에 관하여 설명

ㅇ 양국 대표는 UR서비스협상의 효과적인 추진을 위해 새로운 서비스분야 (예 : 컴퓨터컨설팅, 보험중개업, 특허사무소등)에 대한 개념규정 및 자유화방식등에 대하여 지속적으로 의견을 교환하고, 미국이 이제까지 20여개국과 양자협의한 정보를 가능한 범위내에서 우리측에 제공키로 하며, 제3차 협의는 필요시 별도 결정키로하고 2차협의를 종료

0137

나. 광고 관련 사항

o 우리측에서는 미측이 제1차 한·미 양자협의('91. 2. 11)시 제기한 사항과 추가 질문한 내용에 대하여 서면 답변 및 구두로 설명

- 미측 질문사항

  . 외국광고회사가 외국에서 제작한 광고물의 국내 사용에 관한 제한 (광고물제작시 외국인모델 출연 제한등)

  . 외국제작 광고물의 국내수입·사용허가의 절차 및 기준

  . 외국제작 광고물에 대한 KOBACO의 방송광고 금지 조치 여부

  . 신문협회가 일정규모의 거래실적을 신문광고대행사인정기준으로 하는 이유 (동 기준은 외국광고회사의 시장참입을 저해하고 있음)

  . 외국광고회사의 지사, 자회사의 국내 활동에 관한 특별한 제한 여부

  . 광고대행사 인정 과정 (조건)

- 우리측 답변내용 : 별첨 (UR서비스협상관련 대책보고시 기 보고)

o 이번 제2차 한·미 양자협의에서 양측은 다음사항에 관하여 상호 의견교환

- 미측 질문사항

  . 국내광고대행업이 현재 외국인투자 제한업종인지의 여부

  . 미국광고회사가 제작한 만화광고(Pepsi-Cola)에 대한 국내 수입·사용 거부 건수 및 사유를 알려주기 바람(이와관련 미측은 공연윤리위원회등의 심의기준 및 그 운영에 의문을 제기)

  . KOBACO의 방송광고에 관한 독점적 기능 및 대행사인정기준등의 규제 규정과 광고방송의 어려움에 대한 우리측 견해

  . 외국제작 광고물의 수입·사용 절차와 심의기준 및 광고대행사 인정 기준을 운영하고있는 민간단체들의 기능에 강한 의문제기

  . 비정부적 민간단체들의 자율규정에 의한 시장접근(Market Access) 규제에 대한 UR협상 추진 견해

- 우리측 답변내용 : 별첨

0138

3. 종합평가

o 이번 제2차 한·미 양자협의는 양국이 제출한 서비스 자유화계획에 관한 이해를 상호 구체화 하는 계기가 되었다고 생각되나, 이와같은 양자협의를 통하여 각국의 서비스시장 접근 및 국내 규제제도의 명료화, 서비스협정의 구조설정(Framework) 및 분야별 부속서의 작성등 작업과 상호 연계하여 앞으로 검토, 해결해야 할 기술적인 과제가 남아있다고 판단됨.

o 미측은 앞으로 개최될 한·미 양허협상시 외국광고회사의 국내시장 접근 및 활동에 관한 비정부적 민간단체의 규제사항까지도 UR서비스협상의 대상에 포함하여야 한다는 논리를 내세워 KOBACO와 한국신문협회광고협의회 및 공연윤리위원회등 민간단체들의 성격 및 기능에 대하여 계속 논란을 제기할 것이 예상되므로 우리측은 이에대한 구체적인 대응논리를 개발, 대처해 나가야 할 것으로 사료됨.

0139

UR 서비스협상관련 미측 질문사항에 관한 답변요지(서면제출)

(제1차 한·미 양자협의('91.2.11)시 제기사항)

미 측 제 기 사 항	검 토 의 견	비 고
o 외국광고회사가 외국에서 제작한 광고물의 국내 사용에 관한 제한(예 : CoCa-Cola) - 외국제작광고물의 국내 수입·사용 허가절차 및 기준	o 해외에서 외국광고회사에 의해 제작된 광고물을 국내에 수입 또는 복제 사용하고자 하는 경우에는 국내법에의거 주무부장관의 허가 필요 - 영화법 제10조 - 음반및 비디오물에 관한 법률 제13조 ※ 외국광고회사제작광고물의 수입허가(예) - 레인소프트정수기 TV-CM ('90. 6. 14) - 인터메조 TV-CM ('91. 1. 29) - 쉬크어드벤티지 TV-CM 등 ('91. 2. 26) o 방송광고와 영화광고를 국내에서 방영 또는 상영하고자 하는 때에는 국내법에 의해 방송위원회와 공연윤리위원회의 광고물내용 심의를 받아야 함 - 방송법 제17조제3항 - 영화법 제12조 및 제13조 - 음반 및 비디오물에 관한 법률 제16조	내국민대우

0140

미 측 제 기 사 항	검 토 의 견	비 고
	o 광고물제작시 외국인 모델의 출연은 광고시장 개방 계획에따라 89년부터 허용되고 있음	내국민대우
	o 방송광고물을 TV에 방영하고자 하는 경우에는 방송법에의거 방송위원회의 사전심의를 받도록 되어 있으며, 이 경우에 방송위원회는 방송광고물심의규정에 의거 방송광고물의 내용을 주로 윤리성의 측면에서 심의하고 있음	
o 한국방송광고공사의 법적기능 및 방송광고 관련 규정의 구속성 여부	o 한국방송광고공사는 한국방송광고공사법에 의거 방송국의 방송광고영업을 대행하고, 그 수수료 수입의 일부를 재원으로하여 방송, 문화·예술 진흥사업을 지원함으로써 국민의 건전한 문화 생활과 방송문화의 발전 및 방송광고진흥에 기여함을 목적으로 설립된 특수법인 임	내국민대우
	o 따라서 국내방송국에 방송광고를 하고자 하는 자는 한국방송광고공사법에 의거 한국방송광고공사를 반드시 통하여야 하며,이에 관한 동 공사의 관련규정을 준수하여야 함	

0141

미 측 제 기 사 항	검 토 의 견	비 고
o 신문협회가 일정규모의 광고거래실적을 신문광고 대행사 인정기준으로 하는 이유 (동 기준은 외국광고회사의 시장참입을 저해)	o 민간단체인 한국신문협회광고협의회에서는 광고회사가 신문광고를 대행하고자 하는 경우에는 계약이행 지급보증 등의 필요에 따라 일간지와의 거래실적 등의 자격요건을 갖춘 건실한 광고회사를 신문광고대행사로 인정하고 있음 o 한국신문협회광고협의회의 신문광고대행자격요건은 건전한 신문광고거래질서를 확립하기 위해 자율적으로 정한 것으로서 동 기준은 국내외 신문광고대행사들에게 동등하게 적용되고 있으므로 외국대행업체에 대하여 부당한 차별대우는 없음	내국민대우
o 외국광고회사의 지사, 자회사의 국내활동에 관한 특별한 제한 여부	o 외국광고회사의 지사나 자회사의 국내활동에 대하여는 특별한 제한은 없으나 외국광고회사는 국내광고회사와 동등하게 국내법규와 제도를 준수하여야 함 - 방송광고대행의 경우에는 한국방송광고공사법 및 동 시행령과 한국방송광고공사의 방송광고대행규정 준수 - 신문광고대행의 경우에는 한국신문협회광고협의회의 자율규정인 신문광고대행규칙 준수 - 출판(월간, 주간잡지) 광고대행의 경우에는 한국출판광고협의회의 자율규정인 출판광고대행규정 준수 - 기타 법률에 의한 광고물심의에 관한 규정 준수 . 방송위원회의 방송광고물심의규정(방송법)	내국민대우

0142

미 측 제 기 사 항	검 토 의 견	비 고
	. 공연윤리위원회의 영화광고심의에 관한 규정 (영화법)	
o 광고대행사 인정 과정(조건)	o 방송광고를 대행하고자 하는 자는 한국방송광고공사의 방송광고대행규정에 정해진 아래와 같은 방송광고대행자격요건을 구비하여 한국방송광고공사의 인정을 받아야 함 - 상법상의 회사로서 자본금 5천만원 이상 - 비계열광고주 3개이상 보유 - 방송광고대행계약 이행지급보증 o 신문광고를 대행하고자 하는 자는 한국신문협회광고협의회의 신문광고대행규칙에 정해진 아래와 같은 신문광고대행자격요건을 구비하여 한국신문협회광고협의회의 인정을 받아야 함 - 상법상의 회사로서 자본금 5천만원 이상 - 광고주 5개이상 보유 - 연간 20억원이상의 신문광고 거래실적 - 신문광고대행계약 이행지급보증	내국민대우 0143

제2차 한·미양자협의시 미측 질문 및 우리측 답변요지

o 국내광고대행업은 현재 외국인투자 제한업종으로 되어있지 않은가?

- 국내광고대행업은 광고시장개방 계획에 따라 88년부터 외국인투자를 제한적으로 허용하여 왔으며, '91. 1이후 부터는 외국인투자 자유업종으로 전환하였음.

o 미국광고회사가 제작한 만화광고(Pepsi-Cala)의 국내 수입·사용은 허용하지 않고 있는반면, 한국광고회사가 이와 똑같이 제작한 만화광고는 방영을 허용하고있다고 하는데 이러한 외국제작광고물 심의신청 사례중 거부 건수 및 그 사유를 참고로 알려주기바람.

- 외국제작 광고물을 국내에 수입·사용하고자 할 때에는 1차적으로 공연윤리위원회의 수입 심의를 받아 문화부장관의 수입 허가를 받도록 되어있으며,

- 수입광고물을 복사 또는 재편집하여 제작한 광고물을 TV에 방영하고자 할 때에는 방송법에 의해 방송위원회가 그 내용을 심의하고 있으므로 동 질문사례에 대하여는 방송위원회에 사실여부를 확인한 후 알려주겠음.

o KOBACO의 방송광고에 관한 독점적 기능 및 대행사인정기준 등의 규제규정과 광고방송의 어려움에 대하여 정부에서는 어떻게 생각하고 있는가?

- KOBACO의 법적기능이나 위상에 관하여는 '87-'88년 기간동안 한·미실무협의를 통해 상호 의견을 충분히 교환하였기 때문에 미측의 관심과 불만의 요소가 무엇인지 잘 알고 있으며 당시 미측도 우리의 KOBACO제도에 관하여는 기본적으로 이해하였다고 생각함.

0144

- 다시 설명하면, KOBACO는 한국방송광고공사법에 의해 설립된 특수법인 임. KOBACO는 법률의 규정에 따라 모든 방송매체의 방송광고영업을 대행하고있으며 이를 통해 매체사로 부터 방송광고수탁수수료를 받아 이 수수료 수입의 일부를 재원으로 하여 방송, 문화·예술 진흥사업을 지원함으로써 국민들의 문화생활과 방송 및 광고산업 발전에 기여하고 있음.

- KOBACO의 법적기능과 위상에 관하여는 그동안 국회와 민간차원에서도 많은 연구 검토가 있었으며 그 결과 현행 KOBACO의 기능과 위상에 대하여는 국민 다수가 찬성하고 있는것으로 판단되므로 현재 KOBACO의 위상을 재검토하는 문제는 생각하고 있지 않음.

- 현재 국내 방송채널수의 제한때문에 야기되고있는 광고방송시간 확보의 어려움은 국내방송구조의 개편에 따라 민간방송채널이 신설될 예정이므로 앞으로 이러한 문제점은 개선될 수 있을것임.

o 외국제작 광고물의 수입·사용절차와 심의기준은 무엇이며, 이와관련되어 있는 방송위원회, 공연윤리위원회, KOBACO, 신문협회광고협의회 등은 무슨기능을 하고있는가?

- 외국제작 광고물을 수입·사용하고자 할 때에는 외국영화와 마찬가지로 영화법과 음반 및 비디오물에 관한 법률에 의거 문화부장관의 수입허가를 받도록 되어 있으며, 이 경우에 수입업자는 우선 공연윤리위원회의 수입광고물심의를 받아 그 결과를 문화부장관에게 제출하여야 함.

- 또한 문화부장관으로부터 수입허가를 받은 광고물을 복사 또는 재편집하여 방송광고를 하고자 하는 경우에는 방송법에 의거 방송위원회의 방송광고물 심의를 받아야 함.

- 공연윤리위원회와 방송위원회는 각각 자율적인 광고물심의규정에 의거 광고물의 내용을 주로 윤리성의 측면에서 심의하고 있음.

0145

- KOBACO는 앞서 설명한 바와같이 한국방송광고공사법에 의거 모든 방송매체를 대행하여 방송위원회의 심의를 받은 방송광고물의 광고방송시간을 광고주에게 판매하고 있음.

- 신문협회광고협의회는 신문사를 회원으로 하여 설립된 자율민간단체로서 광고대행사가 신문광고를 대행하고자 하는 경우에는 협회가 자율적으로 정한 일정한 요건을 갖춘 광고대행사를 신문광고대행사로 인정하고 있음.

o 미측은 서비스 시장개방과 관련하여 비정부적 민간단체(예 : 공사, 협회등)들이 그들의 자율규정에 의해 시장접근(Market Access)을 규제하고 있는 경우 이를 UR협상의 대상에 포함시켜야 한다는 견해를 제기

0146

경 제 기 획 원

통조삼 10502- 2?7　　　503-9149　　　1991. 5. 9.

수신 외무부장관 (통상기구과)

제목 UR/서비스협상관련 자료제출 요청

1. '91.4.25일 개최된 TNC회의에 따라 UR/서비스협상이 공식적으로 재개되어 5.27-31까지 제네바에서 '91년도 제1차 UR/서비스협상 회의가 개최될 예정으로 있으며 6월이후 부터는 Framework상의 주요쟁점 및 각국 Offer List, National Schedule의 작성방법등에 대한 공식.비공식회의가 계속될 것으로 전망됩니다.

2. 이에따라 당원은 각서비스업종별 대책자료를 포함한 종합대책자료를 기존의 자료(UR/서비스 무역협상대책자료<88.10>, 서비스시장의 개방과 제한<89.5>)를 개정.보완하여 작성코자 하니 별첨 참고자료를 활용하여 별첨1과 같은 양식으로 '91.5.16까지 제출하여 주시기 바랍니다.

3. 아울러 금융, 통신등 분야별 부속서를 제정중인 관련부처는 해당 부속서의 주요쟁점에 대한 아국입장을 별첨2를 참고하여 '91.5.16까지 제출하여 주시기 바랍니다.

첨부: 1. 업종별 대책자료의 목차 1부.

<참고자료> ① 종합대책자료의 목차 및 업종별현황(89.10월자료)

② 서비스시장의 개방과 제한자료의 목차 및 업종별현황 (89.5월자료)

2. 분야별 부속서에 대한 아국입장(안) 1부. 끝.

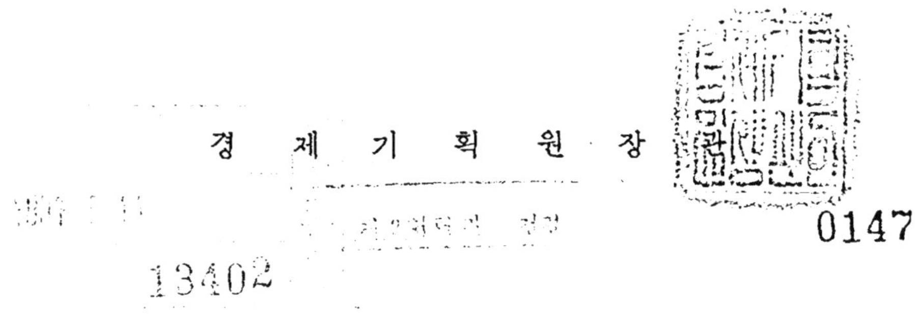

경 제 기 획 원 장

0147

(별첨 1)

業種別對策 資料의 目次

1. 産業現況

가. 業種別 細部分類
- 韓國標準産業 分類 및 個別法上 分類를 고려
- 다른나라의 Offer List에 나타난 分類와 비교

나. 國內業體 現況
- 業體數 및 規模, 資格者數
- 生産, 雇傭, 交易規模
- 國內産業의 競爭力水準

다. 國內 및 海外市場 動向

2. 國內 規制現況

가. 市場進入上 制限
- 外資導入法에 의한 外國人投資制限 事項
- 外換管理法에 의한 支店設置制限 事項
- 기타 個別法에 의한 制限事項

나. 國內營業上 制限
- 外資導入法에 의한 制限事項
- 外國換管理法에 의한 制限事項
- 기타 個別法에 의한 制限事項

0148

3. 對外 開放現況

- 韓.美協商에 의한 開放 內容

- 我國의 Initial Offer List에 포함시킨 내용

- 産業構造調整 計劃에 의해 이미 확정된 向後 開放計劃

- 다른나라의 Offer List에 나타난 開放計劃과 비교

4. 對外開放에 따른 影響

가. 肯定的 效果

나. 不正的 效果

다. 綜合的인 評價

5. 開放政策 方向

가. 基本方向

나. 開放政策方向

- 세부업종별 開放優先順位
- 市場接近制限事項 緩和計劃
- 營業活動制限事項 緩和計劃

다. 海外進出方案

- 我國企業의 海外進出에 대한 상대국의 交易障壁 撤廢方案
- 국제서비스산업의 國際競爭力强化 方案

라. 國內補完對策

0149

경 제 기 획 원

통조삼 10502-322 503-9149 1991. 5. 17.

수신 수신처참조 통상기구과.

제목 UR대책 서비스 실무소위원회 구성 통보

1. 당원 통조삼 10502-285 ('91.5.4)와 관련입니다.

2. 상기 사항과 관련하여 서비스분야 UR대책 실무소위원회를 별첨과 같이 재구성.운영키로 하였음을 통보하니 관련부처는 향후 업무추진에 참조하시기 바랍니다.

첨부: UR대책 서비스분야 실무소위원회 구성 및 운영안 1부. 끝.

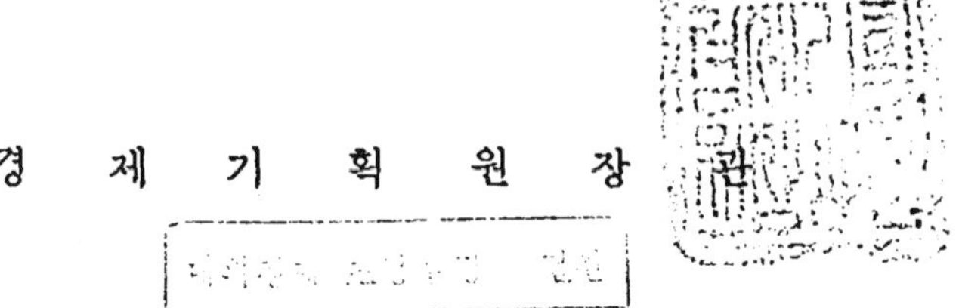

경 제 기 획 원 장 관

수신처: 외무부장관, 내무부장관, 재무부장관, 법무부장관, 교육부장관, 문화부장관, 상공부장관, 보건사회부장관, 건설부장관, 교통부장관, 노동부장관, 체신부장관, 과학기술처장관, 환경처장관, 공보처장관, 해운항만청장, 특허청장, 한국개발연구원장, 대외경제정책연구원장, 대한무역진흥공사장, 김&장법률사무소장.

0150

(별첨)

UR對策 서비스分野 實務小委員會 構成 및 運營

1. 目的: UR協商 그룹회의의 調整과 함께 향후 서비스協商이 本格 進行될 것이 예상되는바, 이에 效果的으로 對處해나가기 위하여 UR/서비스分野 實務小委員會를 擴大改編하고 機能을 強化

2. 構成

- 위원장: 경제기획원 제2협력관
- 간 사: 경제기획원 통상조정3과장
- 위 원: 경제기획원 산업3과장

경제기획원	산업3과장
"	제도개선과장
외 무 부	통상기구과장
내 무 부	지적과장
재 무 부	국제금융과장
법 무 부	국제법무심의관실 검사
"	입국심사과장
교 육 부	교육협력과장
문 화 부	영화진흥과장
상 공 부	유통산업과장
보건사회부	국제협력과장
건 설 부	해외협력과장
교 통 부	국제협력과장
노 동 부	고용관리과장
체 신 부	통신협력과장

0151

과학기술처　　기술협력2과장
환　경　처　　정책조정과장
공　보　처　　광고정책과장
항　만　청　　진흥과장
특　허　청　　지도과장

- 諮問委員: K I E P　　　　박태호 박사
　　　　　　"　　　　　　김태준 박사
　　　　K D I　　　　　김지홍 박사
　　　　K O T R A　　　국제경제과장
　　　　김&장법률사무소　신희택 변호사
　　　　기타 서비스分野別 專門家

3. 委員會 運營

가. 委員會의 機能

- 實務小委員會 委員長은 委員會 所管業務를 綜合.調整

- 서비스分野의 協商對策을 수립하고 懸案發生時 關係部處間 協議 및 意見調整

- UR/서비스협상 관련 國內制度改善 施策의 發掘.檢討

나. 細部 運營方針

- 各部處 委員은 所管部處 業種에 대한 協商資料 準備 및 協商參與

- 委員會는 필요시 수시로 開催하여 議題에 따라 參席範圍 및 民間專門家의 參與範圍를 伸縮的으로 運用

0152

경 제 기 획 원 2

통조삼 10502-321 503-9149 1991. 5. 17.

수신 수신처참조 〈통상기구과〉

제목 UR/서비스협상관련 각국의 Offer List 검토사항 제출요청

1. 통조삼 10502-297 ('91.5.9)과 관련입니다.

2. 스위스 제네바에서 5.27-31간 개최되는 '91년도 제1차 UR/서비스협상 회의에서는 각국의 Offer List를 검토할 예정으로 있읍니다.

ㅇ 각부처에 17개국가의 Offer List는 기송부 (통조삼 10502-819<'90.12.14>, 10502-274<'91.4.25>)

3. 이와관련하여 각부처는 소관업종에 대한 각국의 Offer 사항을 별첨1의 참고자료를 활용하여 별첨2와 같은 양식으로 검토하여 5.22(수)까지 당원에 제출하여 주시기 바랍니다.

ㅇ 동 검토자료는 향후 양허협상과정에서 필요한 아국의 단계적인 협상안과 상대국에 대한 요구사항을 작성하는 기본자료로 활용

첨부: 1. 주요국가의 Initial Offer List 검토 1부.

2. 소관업종별 각국의 Offer 검토목차 1부. 끝.

경 제 기 획 원 장

수신처: 외무부장관, 재무부장관, 법무부장관, 문화부장관, 농림수산부장관, 교육부장관, 상공부장관, 건설부장관, 보사부장관, 교통부장관, 노동부장관, 동력자원부장관, 체신부장관, 과학기술처장관, 공보처장관, 환경처장관, 해운항만청장, 특허청장, 대한무역진흥공사장, 대외경제정책연구원장.

0153 14625

(별첨)

소관업종별 각국의 Offer 검토목차

Ⅰ. 각국 Offer의 개요 및 배경

Ⅱ. 각국 Offer의 비교검토 내용

- 포괄업종
  * 개조식으로 1P가량 서술
  * 다음과 같은 표로 요약

국가 세부업종	미 국	E C	. . . .
a b : :	o x		

* o (동업종을 제시), x (동업종을 미제시)

- 자유화약속 수준
  * 개조식으로 1P가량 서술
  * 다음과 같은 비교표로 요약

국가 공급형태	미 국	E C	. . . .
국경간이동 소비자이동 상업적주재 노동자이동	NL NA RS UB		

* NL(No Limitation), NA(Not Applicable), RS(Restrictions), UB(Unbound)

- 종합평가

Ⅲ. 각국 Offer에 대한 질문사항

0154

2/

원 본

외 무 부

종 별 :

번 호 : GVW-0916 일 시 : 91 0517 1950

수 신 : 장관(통기,경기원,재무부,법무부,상공부,건설부,보사부,노동부,교통부,

체신부,문화부,공보처,과기처,항만청)

발 신 : 주 제네바 대사

제 목 : UR/GNS 협상

'91.5.27 개최예정인 표제협상 의제 및 NATIONAL SCHEDULE 작성관 련 사무국작성 문서를 별첨 (FAX) 송부함. 동 회의는 각국 OFFER 에 대한 토의는 비공식회의로 진행하는 한편 기타의제는 GNS 공식회의로 진행될 예정임.

첨부: 1. GNS 회의 의제 1부

2. 사무국작성 문서 1부

(GVW(F)-0165).끝

(대사 박수길-국장)

통상국	2차보	법무부	보사부	문화부	교통부	체신부	경기원	상공부
상공부	건설부	노동부	과기처	해항정	공보처	재무부		

PAGE 1

91.05.18 09:31 WG

외신 1과 통제관

0155

GVW(F)-0P16 10517 1P50
GVW-P16 첨부

GATT/AIR/ MAY 1991

SUBJECT: URUGUAY ROUND: GROUP OF NEGOTIATIONS ON SERVICES

1. THE GROUP OF NEGOTIATIONS ON SERVICES WILL HOLD ITS NEXT MEETING IN THE WEEK OF 27-31 MAY 1991, STARTING ON MONDAY, 27 MAY 1991, AT 11 A.M. IN THE CENTRE WILLIAM RAPPARD. AS CONSIDERED NECESSARY, THE MEETING WILL CONTINUE IN THE WEEK OF 3 JUNE 1991.

2. THE FOLLOWING ITEMS ARE ON THE AGENDA:

2.1 MATTERS RELATING TO THE SCHEDULING OF COMMITMENTS. A SECRETARIAT NOTE ON THIS SUBJECT MATTER WILL BE AVAILABLE.

2.2 MATTERS RELATING TO THE CLASSIFICATION OF SERVICES. A SECRETARIAT NOTE ON THIS SUBJECT MATTER WILL BE AVAILABLE.

2.3 HORIZONTAL AGREEMENTS. REQUEST FOR INFORMATION FROM PARTICIPANTS.

2.4 MATTERS RELATING TO THE INITIAL OFFERS TABLED SO FAR BY PARTICIPANTS (THE GROUP OF NEGOTIATIONS ON SERVICES WILL DISCUSS THIS ITEM IN INFORMAL SESSION).

2.5 MATTERS RELATING TO FRAMEWORK ISSUES, E.G. DISPUTE SETTLEMENT, DOMESTIC REGULATION, DEFINITION OF TERMS.

2.6 PROCEDURAL GUIDELINES FOR THE CONDUCT AND FINALIZATION OF THE NEGOTIATIONS ON INITIAL COMMITMENTS. A SECRETARIAT NOTE ON THIS SUBJECT MATTER WILL BE AVAILABLE.

2.7 OTHER BUSINESS.

3. THE FOLLOWING DOCUMENTS ARE OF RELEVANCE FOR THE DISCUSSION:

MTN.TNC/W/35/Rev.1;
MTN.GNS/W/109; MTN.GNS/W/112; MTN.GNS/W/113/Rev.1; MTN.TNC/W/51;
MTN.TNC/W/53/Rev.2; MTN.TNC/W/54; MTN.TNC/W/55; MTN.TNC/W/58;
MTN.TNC/W/59 and Add.1; MTN.TNC/W/61; MTN.TNC/W/62/Rev.1;
MTN.TNC/W/63 and Add.1; MTN.TNC/W/64; MTN.TNC/W/65 and Corr.1;
MTN.TNC/W/66 and Add.1; MTN.TNC/W/67; MTN.TNC/W/70-74.

4. PARTICIPANTS ARE REQUESTED TO INFORM ME AS SOON AS POSSIBLE OF THE NAMES OF THEIR REPRESENTATIVES.

A. DUNKEL

0156

2-1

Z-MISC2

16.5.91

SCHEDULING OF COMMITMENTS: EXAMPLES TAKEN FROM INITIAL OFFERS

This informal note relates to the consultations held on 10 and 11 April by the Director-General regarding the issue of the scheduling of commitments. Its purpose is to provide an illustration, by way of examples taken from initial offers, of the ways countries have dealt with some of the scheduling issues that have been raised. In this respect, the note summarises how countries have: categorized the types of measures which may be considered to be restrictions; distinguished between market access and national treatment restrictions; approached the issue of listing the modes of supply; and, finally, to what extent they have included a definition of terms used in their offers.

A. Types of measures to be considered restrictions

- Scheduling of discriminatory v. non-discriminatory restrictions

Sweden notes that in its offer restrictive regulations have been listed irrespective of whether they discriminate against foreign service suppliers or not and that depending on the eventual scope of Article VI some of the measures listed might not require scheduling as commitments.

In general, countries have listed their restrictions mainly under market access and these include the following:

- license for restaurants based on a needs test (CH)
- requirement for government employees to use national airline (CH)
- nationality restrictions re. broadcasting licenses for commercial presence and management (US)
- needs test for establishment of foreign health care facilities in some states (US)

- specific state-wide educational requirements e.g. bar examination for attorneys (US)
- prohibition of commercial activity for official tourism representations (US)
- issuance of trucking licenses based on public convenience, needs tests, regulation of rates (US)
- reciprocity requirement for foreign banks seeking commercial presence (JAP)
- conditions of nationality for accountants, doctors, public works surveyors, tourist guides, casino directors (EC-F)
- requirement for travel agencies to have permanent corporate base (EC-B)
- 20% limit on non-EC participation in French language publishing companies (EC-F)
- needs test for number of hospital beds and heavy equipment (EC-B,F,L)
- restriction of foreign share-holdings in "banks of national interest" (EC-I)
- right of establishment excludes establishment of representative offices of foreign banks (EC-IRL) or foreign insurance companies (EC-GR,IRL,E)
- residency requirement for access to actuarial profession (EC-E)
- 15% limitation on foreign ownership of radio and TV (NZ)
- restriction on use of radio spectrum by foreign governments (NZ)
- establishment of representative offices of overseas banks subject to authorization by Reserve Bank (NZ)
- citizenship and residence requirements to become a lawyer (waiver possible) (SWE)
- government monopoly for labour exchange agency and prohibition of temporary work agency (SWE)
- postal services, audiovisual services: publicly owned monopoly (SWE)

I-INIT 0158

2/-3

- education services, health related services; public service function (SWE)
- authorisation for import and use of foreign made advertising materials (KOR)
- prohibition of data transmission services (KOR)
- foreign equity participation requirements for the securities business and for direct insurance (KOR)
- cargo preference system for international deep sea shipping (to be phased out by 1995) (KOR)
- foreign equity requirement for joint ventures re. auxiliary shipping services (KOR)
- prohibition of commercial presence (except joint ventures) for international maritime transport (INDO)
- commercial presence in radio/TV broadcasting limited to Indonesian companies (INDO)
- hotel investments limited to certain categories (INDO)
- prohibition on foreign investment to establish private schools for nationals (TUR)

- Coverage of Article VI

US, JAP, HK: It is stated that certain existing non-discriminatory requirements e.g. prudential or professional competency considerations have not been listed as as limitations, conditions or qualifications to market access or national treatment.

- Entering a binding: reference to relevant regulation or description of restriction?

For Sweden, the term "bound" is used when the offer is to bind an existing regulatory situation. In its schedule, Sweden lists both the relevant laws and regulations and a description of existing restrictions in

0159

21 - 4

I-INIT

the case of horizontal measures; regarding sector specific commitments, the binding generally refers to a description of the restriction.

Many country offers consist of a standstill commitment. For example, in its offer, the EC is prepared to bind the regime in force (on a particular date) without referring to a particular law or regulation.

B. <u>Distinction between market access and national treatment restrictions</u>

<u>JAP</u>: Measures with regard to entry of financial service providers are listed in limitations and conditions on market access, and measures after such entry are listed in limitations and conditions on national treatment.

<u>SWE</u>: most measures that appear are listed under MA because they are considered to affect entry into a market (as compared to a totally unrestricted market access situation) rather than national treatment. When measures listed in the market access column discriminate against foreign suppliers that is stated in the column. No indication means that a given measure is considered to have the same effect on domestic and foreign suppliers and the corresponding entry in the national treatment column reads "no limitations", also indicating that no additional measures apply to the operations of foreign suppliers as compared to domestic suppliers of a like service. Should more restrictive measures apply to the operations of a foreign supplier an entry to that effect is made in the national treatment column.

In presenting their offers, most countries have not justified a distinction between market access and national treatment. As shown above, where restrictions are listed, they mainly fall under the market access heading.

J-INIT

0160

21-5

In some cases, however, entries are made under both headings, e.g.:

Sector: Production of audiovisual works

	Market access	National treatment
Switzerland	(1) No limitations (2) No limitations (3) No limitations (4) Unbound	Subsidies for motion-picture production are only granted for films produced by Swiss companies, where foreign participation is less than 50%.
New Zealand	(1) Unbound	(a) Payment of subsidies for production/distribution/-exhibition and broad-casting of audio-visual works are limited to NZ persons and companies.
	(2) No limitations or conditions	(b) 100 per cent deduction against NZ income tax may be claimed for investment in production of NZ films.
	(3) Radio and television: . maximum foreign ownership . restrictions on the use of the radio spectrum by foreign governments. . controls on shortwave and satellite broadcasting.	(c) Local TV and radio quotas.

0161

21-6

I-INIT

	Market access	National treatment
	(4) Unbound	(d) Controls on broadcasting by overseas persons (Broadcasting Act).

Sector: Air Transport Ground Handling Service

EC	(1) No limitation (subject to infrastructure capacities). STANDSTILL	(1) No limitation other than: E, IRL, NL: foreign airlines are not entitled to supply ground handling services to other air companies. STANDSTILL
	(2) No limitation STANDSTILL	(2) No limitation other than: DK: airport taxes are higher for non-European destinations. IRL: passengers handling charges are higher for non-European destinations. STANDSTILL
	(3) No limitation (subject to infrastructure capacities) other than: F, IRL, I and NL: foreign airlines are not entitled to set up their own airport infrastructure. GR: to be completed STANDSTILL	(3) No limitation other than: E, IRL and NL: foreign airlines are not entitled to supply ground handling services to other air companies. GR: to be completed STANDSTILL

21-7

I-INIT 0162

C. Modes of supply

- Format used in scheduling commitments

Most of the offers list three or four modes for each sub-sector or offer.

Four modes: CH, US, JAP, Australia, HK, NZ, Indonesia, Singapore, Colombia, Mexico, Turkey.

Three modes: EC, KOR (commitments relating to personnel movement still under consideration).

None: SWE, FIN, ICE.

Sweden argues that it is more meaningful to present an offer that gives a descriptive account of measures in force that affect market access and national treatment without sub-dividing them into "modes of delivery". Separate commitments for movement of consumers and cross-border supply would e.g. require that the targeted transactions could be identified and separated by a panel to avoid legal inconsistency. Separate commitments for different "modes of delivery" might also risk to reduce the flexibility of the Agreement to accommodate trade flows with dynamic developments.

- Treatment of horizontal measures

Some countries summarise the horizontal measures affecting trade in services across all sectors, others focus on some horizontal measures and others do not mention them at all.

AUSTRL: It is stated that nothing in the schedule affects the right of the government to regulate foreign investment in accordance with relevant legislation and policies applicable from time to time. In addition, reference is made to regulations relating to temporary residence and competition law.

KOR: Offer summarises limitations, conditions and qualifications applicable to all service sectors with respect to commercial presence, acquisition and usage of land, foreign exchange control and movement of personnel.

JAP: Acquisition by foreigners or foreign juridical persons of rights pertaining to land may ... be prohibited or made subject to (defence related) conditions or restrictions (Alien Land Law).

NZ: The reference to horizontal measures covers investment (whereby an "overseas person" requires approval by the Overseas Investment Commission for certain categories of investment), taxation, immigration policies and equipment.

SWE: Offer includes a summary of horizontal measures applicable to all sectors with respect to establishment, conduct of commercial operations, movement of personnel, current payments and capital movement, taxation regulations, and non-regulatory measures.

FIN: Reference to horizontal measures covers investment, establishment,capital movement and movement of personnel.

MEX: Offer contains a summary of the main laws and regulations concerning conditions and limitations on both market access and national treatment for cross.border mobility of services, consumer mobility, investment mobility (commercial presence) and mobility of personnel.

TURK: Horizontal measures relate to foreign investment, monopolies, and real estate.

- Personnel movement

CH, JAP, HK, NZ, SING.: Unbound for all sectors on offer.

USA: Where offered, bound only for essential personnel (managers, executives, specialists) on a temporary basis.

I-INIT

0164

ALA, INDO: For all services offered, subject to national immigration regulations and procedures.

EC, KOR: Subject to further consideration i.e. no offer as yet on this mode of delivery for sectors covered by initial commitments.

- Clarity of modes of supply

In the case of HK, cross-border trade unbound for all service sectors on offer because, apparently, it is not clear what this mode of delivery refers to.

D. Technical Terminology

MEX, SWE and JAP have included a definition of terms in their offers. The main terms that have been used in all offers are:

- "Bound"

MEX: "Bound" means the binding of all conditions, qualifications and restrictions regarding market access or national treatment existing on 1 January 1991. As far as mobility of personnel is concerned, this does not mean that the Regulations of the General Population Act are bound because, as mentioned above, they are currently being amended.

MEX: Bound: (...) means that the text in the market access or national treatment columns is bound. For example, if the following text appears in the commercial presence line of the market access column: "Bound: foreign investors can hold a share of up to 49 per cent of the equity of enterprises", this means that for this particular activity binding only signifies that foreign investors can participate up to the percentage mentioned in the capital of an enterprise. Likewise, where a single law or regulation is mentioned in the text, the other laws and regulations governing the activity in question are not bound.

SWE: Term used when the offer is to bind an existing regulatory situation. When the offer is to bind a liberalized regime not yet in place, the text explicitly says so and gives an indicative date for when the binding would take effect. In most such cases the exact regulatory content of a new measure is not known at this stage.

- "Not Bound"

MEX: This means that the Government of Mexico has not undertaken any commitment regarding the mode or modes of delivery concerning market access or national treatment for the activity in question.

SWE: The Swedish government reserves the right to introduce new or more restrictive measures in only a few exceptional cases. No binding is then offered and the term UNBOUND is used.

The term "not bound" has been used in particular in the case of the movement of personnel e.g. for CH, JAP, HK, NZ, and SING this mode is not bound (or "unbound") for all sectors on offer.

- "No limitations or conditions"

Most countries use this term.

MEX: "None". This means that no condition, qualification or restriction regarding access to markets or national treatment applies, but it does not mean that there are no laws and regulations governing the activity in question. In the case of consumer mobility, it does not mean that immigration laws and other relevant regulations will not apply.

JAP: "No restrictions" means that no restrictions are currently applied and are intended to be introduced in the future.

I-INIT 0166

21-11

- Other terms

JAP: "Standstill" means that certain restrictions are currently applied but are not intended to be strengthened in the future in such a manner as to enlarge the inconsistency with the requirements set forth in the Framework Agreement and its Sectoral Annex.

JAP: "Rollback and Standstill" means that certain restrictions have been eased since September 1986 or will be eased from now on, and no new restrictions are intended to be introduced in the future.

JAP: "Not Applicable" means that the mode of delivery of the designated service is not practical.

I-INIT 0167

21-12

16.5.91

SCHEDULING OF COMMITMENTS

Points Raised in Informal Discussions

1. In the consultations held by the Director-General on 10 and 11 April 1991, a number of issues relating to the scheduling of commitments were discussed. This note presents a number of these issues under the headings identified in the informal Secretariat note of 3 April 1991 (attached). The note also discusses a number of questions which participants may wish to address in future meetings.

2. The intention of the secretariat in preparing this informal note has not been to be exhaustive with respect to all the points or questions raised in the discussion, and the note can be modified as considered appropriate by participants.

Issues relating to the scheduling of commitments

3. What types of measures are considered to be restrictions on trade in services (i.e. limitations and conditions on market access and conditions and qualifications on national treatment) and therefore should be specified in the Parties' schedule?

Points raised by delegations:

(i) A country's offer should make clear the actual market access conditions. Thus, all measures which affect market access and national treatment for inscribed services could be scheduled.

(ii) Regarding which measures should be scheduled, two broad categories are relevant:

- all measures which discriminate between nationals and foreigners;

- all measures which impose quantitative restriction, (government monopolies, number of licences etc.), irrespective of whether there is discrimination between foreign and domestic suppliers.

(iii) A uniform approach is needed with respect to non-discriminatory measures: for example, to make them all subject to negotiation and inscribe them into schedules. To consider only certain types of non-discriminatory measures, such as quantitative restrictions, as suggested under (ii) above, would create problems.

(iv) If a regulation treats foreign and domestic suppliers alike, is it necessary to inscribe anything in the schedule as long as the objective criteria in Article VI are fulfilled?

(v) It is important to agree on what should be covered by Article VI:

- there has to be an appropriate test or criteria in Article VI to identify measures that do not restrict trade (e.g. a regulation that is not serving as a means to apply an additional restriction on trade);

- measures falling under Article VI should be categorised into different types so that the question of their scheduling could be considered.

(vi) If regulations falling under Article VI are not scheduled, how would information relating to these regulations which is required and exchanged during the process of negotiations be treated?

O-INIT - 0169

2/-14

- This issue is partially addressed under transparency; a transitional period for notification of such measures might be considered, or there may be an annex or footnote to the schedules; but it would be of a different character from measures that can be scheduled and do not fall under Article VI.

4. Is it necessary to make a clear distinction between the types of measures to be bound under market access and those which should be bound under national treatment? If so, what are the criteria on which such a distinction should be based?

Points raised by delegations:

(i) Except in those cases where a regulation is clearly covered by Article VI and thus does not require to be scheduled, it is necessary to have columns dealing with both national treatment and market access.

(ii) In most cases it is not difficult to make a distinction between entry and operation conditions. Examples of measures that deny market access to foreigners include restrictions of a numerical nature where the law explicitly states that there will be limitations on the number of operators.

(iii) Market access needs to be more clearly defined as the distinction between market access and national treatment is not clear. For example, is a quantitative limit for a specific portion of a national banking market a market access or a national treatment restriction? It would be possible for the country maintaining this restriction to put a commitment in either column.

21-15

O-INIT

0170

(iv) In the market access column, should only quantitative restrictions be listed and all other conditions and limitations listed under national treatment?

(v) Where "additional commitments" are being sought, they would have to be dealt with on an ad hoc basis.

5. What types of measures are covered under each of the four modes of supply, and what is the distinction between each of the four modes of supply?

Points raised by delegations:

(i) The distinction between modes of supply is crucial and fundamental to the agreement because:

- it is essential to maintain the distinction between trade in services and investment;

- there are many service sectors where more than one mode of supply is necessary in order to provide a meaningful market access concession;

- all services cannot be delivered through all modes of supply;

- the movement of personnel needs to be specified separately; it may be linked to establishment, but it is also an independent mode of supply which needs to be reflected in the schedules.

(ii) While a standard format with standard expressions indicates whether a particular mode is relevant for the supply of a particular service, all columns may not be relevant for all parties or for all services.

O-INIT 0171

21-16

(iii) Even if Article I provides for four modes of supply, it may not be necessary to list all the modes in the schedule. In this respect:

- there seems to be no need to specify all modes where there are only some mode specific regulations;

- it may not be necessary to list all the modes in the schedule i.e. a sector or sub-sector would be bound according to the available modes of supply even if the schedule does not indicate a particular mode.

(iv) In practice, negotiating partners need to know which modes of supply are not allowed. If there are restrictions, they should be mentioned in national schedules without a separate listing of available modes of supply.

(v) How is cross-border trade to be defined?

- No movement of personnel is involved.

- Movement of personnel in order to supply a service must be included.

- If the movement of personnel is involved, the duration of stay should determine if the trade is cross-border trade or not.

(vi) Regulations prescribing particular modes of supply may apply on a horizontal or sector-specific basis:

- where they apply on a horizontal basis, they should be specified in a generic way in the schedule;

21-7

O-INIT

- in general, measures concerning personnel movement are totally different from those governing establishment.

6. Would there be a need for an explanatory note that contains an agreed interpretation of the technical terms used in drawing up schedules?

Point raised by delegations:

- It is necessary to draw up a common terminology to ensure that when comparing entries in schedules, the same term means the same thing. This also applies to the description of restrictions inscribed in the schedules.

Questions and comments

7. In order to deal with the points raised in the preceding paragraphs, the following issues need to be addressed:

(i) In sectors where specific commitments are assumed, what are the types of regulatory measures which are considered to fall under Articles XVI (limitations and conditions on market access) and XVII (conditions and qualifications on national treatment), and therefore should be scheduled. What is the precise border line between such measures and other regulatory measures that conform with Article VI and therefore need not be scheduled? To resolve this question, it is necessary to have a clear understanding as to what the present Article VI is intended to cover.

(ii) Article VI indicates that requirements to be met by foreign services suppliers should not discriminate between parties or constitute a means to restrict international trade in services. Does this mean that only those measures that discriminate between domestic and foreign services or service providers

O-INIT 0173

21-18

constitute a limitation on market access for the purposes of Article XVI? Or, could a restriction on international trade in services also exist when there is a limitation or qualification which applies to both domestic and foreign services or service providers. Correspondingly, are the only regulations that need to be identified under these articles those that constitute a limitation or qualification on the foreign service or service provider, or should regulations that constitute a limitation or qualification on both domestic and foreign services or service providers also be identified?

(iii) Article XVII is clear insofar as it sets out a "no less favourable" standard for the treatment of foreign services and service providers. In the case of Article XVI, however, there is a problem in the light of the issues set out in paragraph 7(ii) above as to what measures would be covered under this article as against those that would be covered by Article VI. The basic point here is to determine the treatment of measures for the purposes of Article XVI which do not discriminate, but none the less restrict access for foreign suppliers (e.g. non-discriminatory numerical limitations).

(iv) As to the need for a distinction between market access and national treatment, if the qualifications or limitations to be dealt with under Articles XVI and XVII are only those that apply to the foreign service provider, a distinction between measures falling under Article XVI and those falling under Article XVII could be based on limitations that apply at the point of entry to the market, and those that apply at the stage of operation after entry. Alternatively, the distinction between national treatment and market access could be eliminated, and all limitations or qualifications with respect to the foreign supplier identified in one column.

0174

21-1P

O-INIT

(v) If, however, Article XVI also refers to measures which relate to both domestic and foreign services or service providers, then a distinction between the scheduling of commitments under Articles XVI and XVII would be necessary. An alternative basis for making such a distinction would be to list under Article XVI all measures which apply both to domestic and foreign services or service providers and under Article XVII only those which apply to foreign services and service providers.

(vi) It must be recognized that if Article VI is interpreted to mean that a restriction on international trade in services does not exist where a limitation or qualification applies to both the domestic and foreign service and service provider, the regulations permitted under that article could bear on the possibility of market access even in the absence of discrimination between domestic and foreign services or service providers. It may, therefore, in any event be necessary to make such regulations subject to additional transparency requirements in those cases where commitments are being undertaken. There may also be a need to consider introducing a provision into the agreement to deal with situations where due to subsequent changes in regulations (which apply to both domestic and foreign suppliers) there is a change in benefits which a foreign supplier would expect, or in the concession being offered.

(vii) If it is decided to maintain two separate columns for market access and national treatment, it may also be desirable, in view of the difficulties in distinguishing in every case between what needs to be scheduled under each column, to provide for an understanding that the mere listing of a measure under one column or the other will not have implications for any dispute settlement cases involving breach of commitments.

O-INIT

0175

21-20

(viii) Insofar as the specification of modes of supply is concerned, is a useful purpose served by the current schedule format which requires the identification of the four modes of supply in every instance?

(ix) If the schedule format is to be maintained, there would appear to be need for a clearer common understanding of what is covered by each particular mode of supply, including the extent to which movement of personnel is covered.

(x) A question also arises as to how the binding of a horizontal measure, which may be mode specific, should be entered in the schedule. Should it be entered in the introductory part of the schedule?

(xi) The need to draw up a common terminology in order to have the required degree of precision has been emphasized. A number of participants in making their offers have indicated the use made by them of certain terms, notably, "bound", "not bound", "no limitations or conditions", "not applicable" and "standstill". Complete agreement on what the terminology covers may be possible only in the light of the understanding reached regarding the scheduling of commitments, etc.

0176

21-21

O-INIT

TOTAL P.05

기 안 용 지

분류기호 문서번호	통기 20644-	(전화 : 720 - 2188)	시 행 상 특별취급	
보존기간	영구. 준영구 10. 5. 3. 1.	차 관	장 관	
수 신 처 보존기간		전결		
시행일자	1991. 5.22.			
보조기관 국 장		협조기관	기획관리실장	문 서 통 제
심의관			제2차관보	
과 장			총무과장	
기안책임자	조 현		기획운영담당관	발 송 인
경 유 수 신 참 조	건 의	발신명의		
제 목	UR/서비스 협상 정부대표 임명			

91.5.27(월)-31(금)간 제네바에서 개최되는 UR/서비스 협상에 참가할 정부대표단을 "정부대표 및 특별사절의 임명과 권한에 관한 법률"에 의거 아래와 같이 임명할것을 건의하오니 재가하여 주시기 바랍니다.

- 아 래 -

0177

1. 회 의 명 : UR/서비스 협상

2. 회의기간 및 장소 : 1991. 5.27(월)-31(금), 제네바

(필요시 6.3부터 협상 계속 실시)

3. 정부대표 (본부대표 2명 및 주 제네바 대표부 관계관)

o 본부대표

- 외무부 통상기구과 서기관 조 현

- 경제기획원 통상조정3과 사무관 김용준

o 자 문 : 대외경제정책연구원 연구관 김태준

※ 외무부 통상기구과 조현 서기관은 5.29-30간

개최되는 갓트/이사회에 별도 참석

4. 출장기간 : 1991. 5.26(일)-6.2(일) (7박8일)

(경제기획원 대표는 협상 연장시 6.3주간까지 출장기간 연장)

5. 소요경비

가. 외무부 대표 : 통상기구과 조현 서기관

o 금 액 : $3,062

- 2 -

0178

o 내 역 :

- 항공료 : $2,104 (서울-제네바 2등왕복)

- 체제비 : $958

. 숙비 : $66X7박=$462

. 일식비 : ($20+$42)X8일=$496

o 지변항목 : 경제활동, 국외여비

나. 경제기획원 대표 : 경제기획원 소관예산

6. 훈 령

o UR/서비스 협상에 제출한 각국의 Offer list를 명료화하기 위한 협의에 적극 참여, 향후 아국의 Offer list 개정 및 상대국에 대한 Request list 작성에 필요한 정보를 수집할것

o National Schedule 작성 방식 및 서비스 산업의 분류 공식에 관한 협의에 적극 참여하고 관련 정보를 수집, 향후 서비스 일반협정에 대한 실질협상 및 양허협상에 대비토록 할것.

첨 부 : 최근의 UR/서비스 협상 동향. 끝.

최근의 UR/서비스 협상 동향

1. 브랏셀 각료회의 결과

○ 서비스 협상 그룹 의장은 서비스 일반협정 초안(분야별 부속서 포함)을 브랏셀 각료회의에 보고

- 노동력 이동, MFN 문제등 미합의된 사항은 괄호로 묶고 대안을 병기

○ 농산물 협상의 교착으로 전체 브랏셀 각료회의에서 실질적 논의가 이루어지지 않음에 따라 서비스 일반협정에 포함된 쟁점사항에 대해서도 실질적인 논의의 진전은 달성치 못함.

- 다만, 미국은 상대국으로부터 실질적인 자유화 약속을 얻는다면 MFN 문제에 대해 협상할 용의가 있다고 신축적인 입장을 표명

○ 양허협상과 관련, 선진국들의 적극적 공세로 스위스, 미국, 일본, 호주, EC, 홍콩, 카나다, 스웨덴, 뉴질랜드등 9개국이 자국의 Offer List를 제출

- 동 국가들이 세계 서비스 교역에서 차지하는 비중은 약 80% 수준

2. 브랏셀 TNC 회의 이후의 동향

○ 전체 UR 협상에서 실질적 협상이 진행되지 않음에 따라 서비스 일반협정에 대한 논의는 일단 유보

○ Offer List를 제출한 국가들을 중심으로 양허협상에 대한 논의만을 활발하게 진행

※ 현재까지 Offer List를 제출한 국가 : 19개국

한국, 미국, EC, 일본, 카나다, 스위스, 호주, 뉴질랜드, 노르웨이, 핀랜드, 스웨덴, 오스트리아, 홍콩, 싱가폴, 인도네시아, 콜롬비아, 멕시코, 터키, 체코

o 특히 미국은 '91.1월 중순이래 아국을 포함한 약 30여개국과 비공식으로 개별적 양자협의를 계속 추진

- 91.2.11. 제1차 한.미 양자협의 개최
  . 양국의 Offer List를 명료화하는 선에서 토의
  . 미국은 자국의 추가적인 관심분야로서 법무서비스, 보건서비스, Leasing, Franchising, 보험중개업등을 제시
- 91.4.1. 제2차 한.미 양자협의 개최
  . 양국의 Offer List에 관한 상호의견 교환
  . 아국은 보험, 컴퓨터 컨설팅, 회계등 미국의 관심분야에 대한 아국 입장 개진

o GATT 사무총장은 91.2월부터 4월까지 30여개 주요국가간 비공식 회의를 연속적으로 개최

- 서비스 산업의 분류, 협상 일정, Offer List의 작성방법과 동 방법이 Framework에 미치는 영향등을 주로 토의

3. 평가 및 전망

o 서비스 협상은 선.개도국의 적극적인 참여로 비교적 순조로운 진전을 달성

- 서비스 교역의 자유화 추진방식을 포지티브시스템(Positive System)으로 채택
- 개발(Development) 개념을 많은 조문에 반영
- 분야별 부속서를 전체 Framework의 일부로 편입

o 그러나 막바지 단계에서 MFN 원칙을 개별서비스 분야에 구체적으로 적용하는 문제가 대두되면서 협상은 답보상태에 도달

- 특히 미국은 해운, 항공, 기본 통신분야등에 대하여 포괄적인 MFN 일탈을 주장하여 EC와 첨예한 입장 대립

o 한편 Offer List 제출 동향에 비추어 상당수의 국가가 서비스 일반협정에 가입할 가능성 증대

- 8개 개도국을 포함하여 19개국가가 자국의 Offer List를 제출하고 양허협상을 위한 기초협의에 적극적으로 참여

o 향후 서비스 협상의 성패는 전체 UR 협상 진전상황과 밀접히 관련되나, MFN 문제의 원만한 타결여부가 관건이 될 것으로 전망

- 농산물 협상에서 미국 및 케언즈그룹과 EC가 절충점을 찾는다면 서비스 협상은 큰 어려움없이 타결될 것으로 예측

o 서비스 일반협정에 대한 실질협상과 본격적인 양허협상은 미 의회의 신속처리권한에 대한 심의가 끝나는 6월이후에 진행될 전망

- 다만 각국 Offer List의 명료화, National Schedule의 작성방식, 서비스 산업의 분류등에 대한 회의는 활발하게 계속될 전망. 끝.

경 제 기 획 원

통조삼 10502- 278 503-9149 1991. 5. 23.

수신 외무부장관

제목 UR/서비스협상회의 참석

스위스 제네바에서 개최되는 UR/서비스협상회의(5.27-6.7)에 참석할 본부 대표단(자문역포함)을 다음과 같이 송부하니 조치해 주기 바랍니다.

다 음

가. 출장자

소 속	직 위	성 명
경제기획원 대외경제조정실 (Int'l Policy Coordination Office)	통상조정3과 사무관 (Assistant Director, Multilateral Trade Division)	김 용 준 (KIM YONG JUN)
대외경제정책연구원(KIEP) (자문역)	연구위원 (Fellow)	김 태 준 (KIM TAE JUN)

나. 출장기간: '91.5.26 - 6.4 (9박 10일)

다. 경비부담: 당원 및 KIEP 부담

첨부: 1. 출장일정 1부.

2. 협상대책자료 1부 (별도송부). 끝.

경 제 기 획 원 장

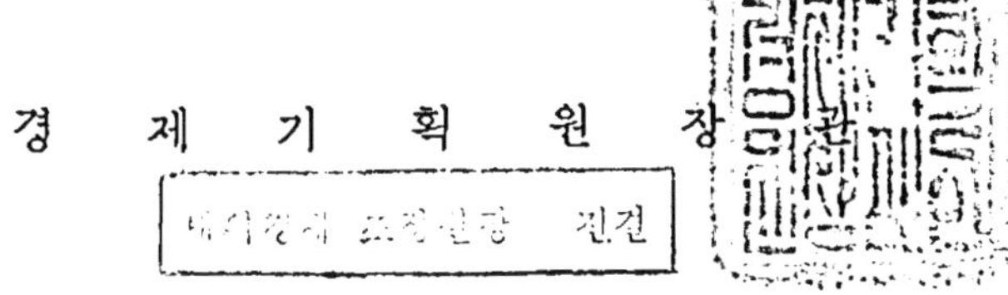

0183

출 장 일 정

'91. 5. 26(일)	12:40	서울 발 (KE 901)
	19:10	파리 착
	20:45	파리 발 (SR 729)
	21:45	제네바착

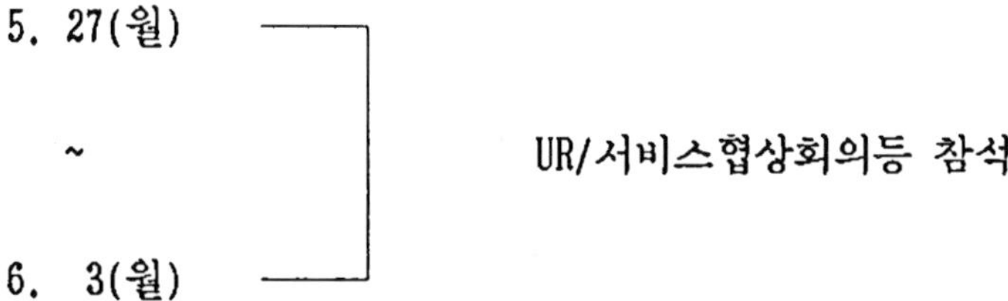

5. 27(월) ~ 6. 3(월) UR/서비스협상회의등 참석

6. 3(월)	18:45	제네바 발 (SR 728)
	19:50	파리 착
	21:30	파리 발 (KE 902)
6. 4(화)	17:30	서울 착

0184

기 안 용 지

분류기호 문서번호	통기 20644-	(전화 : 720 - 2188)	시 행 상 특별취급	
보존기간	영구. 준영구 10. 5. 3. 1.	장 관		
수 신 처 보존기간				
시ㅂ일자	1991. 5.24.			

보조기관	국 장	전 결	협조기관		문서통제
	심의관				검열 1991. 5. 24 통제관
	과 장	대결			
기안책임자		조 현			발 송 인

경 유 수 신 참 조	경제기획원장관	발신명의		발송 1991. 5. 24 외무부
제 목	UR/서비스 협상 정부대표 임명 통보			

91.5.27(월)-31(금)간 제네바에서 개최되는 UR/서비스 협상에 참가할 정부대표가 "정부대표 및 특별사절의 임명과 권한에 관한 법률"에 의거 아래와 같이 임명 되었음을 통보합니다.

- 아 래 -

1. 회 의 명 : UR/서비스 협상

/뒷면 계속/

0185

2. 회의기간 및 장소 : 1991. 5.27-31, 제네바

(필요시 6.3부터 협상 계속 실시)

3. 정부대표(본부대표 2명 및 주 제네바 대표부 관계관)

o 본부대표

- 외무부 통상기구과 서기관 조 현

- 경제기획원 통상조정3과 사무관 김용준

o 자 문 : 대외경제정책연구원 연구관 김태준

4. 출장기간 : 1991. 5.26(일)-6. 2(일) (7박8일)

(경제기획원 대표는 협상 연장시 6.3주간까지 출장기간 연장)

5. 소요경비 : 해당부처 소관예산. . 끝.

0186

	분류번호	보존기간

발 신 전 보

번 호 : WGV-0671 910524 1505 CT 종별 : 암호송신

수 신 : 주 제네바 대사. 총영사

발 신 : 장 관 (통 기)

제 목 : UR/GNS 협상

대 : GVW-0916

91.5.27부터 개최되는 표제 협상에 참가할 본부대표가 아래 임명 되었으니 귀관 관계관과 함께 참석 조치바람.

1. 본부대표 (괄호안은 출장기간)

   o 외무부 통상기구과 조현 서기관 (5.26-6. 1)

   o 경기원 조정3과 김용준 사무관 (5.26-6.4)

   o 대외경제정책연구원 김태준 박사 (자문, 5.26-6.4)

2. 훈 령

   o UR/서비스 협상에 제출한 각국의 Offer list를 명료화하기 위한 협의에 적극 참여, 향후 아국의 Offer list 개정 및 상대국에 대한 Request list 작성에 필요한 정보를 수집

   o National Schedule 작성 방식 및 서비스 산업의 분류 공식에 관한 협의에 적극 참여하고 관련 정보를 수집, 향후 서비스 일반협정에 대한 실질협상 및 양허협상에 대비. 끝. (통상국장 김 삼 훈)

보 안 통 제	

앙 고 재	91년 5월 23일	통기과	기안자 성명		과 장	심의관	국 장		차 관	장 관
			조현				전결			

외신과통제

0187

24.5.91

SERVICES SECTORAL CLASSIFICATION LIST

Informal Note by the Secretariat

In the consultations held by the Director-General on 10-11 April 1991, a number of participants were of the view that there was a need for a detailed common sector classification system that would enable countries to make, compare and record commitments in a consistent manner. The Director-General concluded that, in the light of the views expressed, the Secretariat could be entrusted with the detailed work of establishing a classification list. He indicated that for this purpose, written suggestions from participants and consultations between the secretariat and delegations on a bilateral or multilateral basis would be necessary.

The attached informal secretariat note presents a draft services classification list which, to the extent possible, takes into account the written and oral suggestions made by participating countries.

The basis of the proposed classification list remains the reference list as contained in MTN.GNS/W/50; the reference list has, however, been reorganised, further elaborated and disaggregated in accordance with suggestions. The sub-sectoral classification to a large extent draws on the Common Product Classification (CPC) as developed by the United Nations Statistical Office in collaboration with member countries of the U.N. Concordance between the sub-sectoral classification in the secretariat list and the corresponding sub-sectors in the CPC has been indicated.

The secretariat stands ready to modify the proposed draft classification list in accordance with suggestions made by participating countries. In this respect, the secretariat invites written comments from participating countries to be submitted to the secretariat by Friday, 14 June 1991. The intention of the secretariat would be to incorporate these comments to the extent possible, and to make available to governments a final version of the classification list at the end of June or as soon thereafter as possible.

The classification list could, of course, be subject to further modification in the light of developments in the services negotiations and ongoing work elsewhere.

0188

SECTORS AND SUB-SECTORS[1]	CORRESPONDING CPC Section B	RELATIONSHIP TO MTN.GNS/W/50 AND OTHER LISTS[3]
1. BUSINESS SERVICES		1. BUSINESS SERVICES
A. Professional Services		- Section A on professional services shortened to include only activities listed in the CPC considered to be accredited professions; this list corresponds in large measure to the list provided in MTN.GNS/PROF/W/1.
a. Legal Services	861	- Item A.h-j were moved from section 7, "health-related services", of MTN.GNS/W/50.
b. Accounting, auditing and certification services	862	- Sections B,C,D and E correspond to two-digit items in the CPC.
c. Taxation Services	863	- Section F on other business services is an aggregate of items at the three and four digit level in the CPC and correspond in large measure to activities listed under item B of MTN.GNS/PROF/W/1.
d. Architectural services	8671	- Items "biotechnology" and "exhibition management" have been included under item 1.F.u.
e. Engineering services	**8672**	- Under Section F, services incidental to manufacturing (items 884 and 885 of the CPC) have not been included since these services refer to the actual manufacturing of goods - i.e. an activity which presumably should be subsumed under trade in goods and not services. It remains to be examined whether there are any services incidental to manufacturing which could be covered by such an item.
f. Integrated engineering services	**8673**	- Services which could be specified under Section F or subsumed under item 1.F.u. include bankruptcy trustee services, pest control services, convention services, interior design.
g. Urban planning and landscape architectural services	**8674**	
h. Medical and dental services	**9312**	
i. Veterinary services	**9320**	
j. Other health-related professional services	**n.a.**[2]	
k. Other		
B. Computer and Related Services (other than those provided over public telecommunications transport networks)	**84**	
a. Consultancy services related to the installation of computer hardware	**841**	
b. Software implementation services	**842**	
c. Data processing services	**843**	
d. Data base services	**844**	
e. Other	**845+849**	
C. Research and Development Services	**85**	
D. Real Estate Services	82	
a. Involving own or leased property	821	
b. On a fee or contract basis	822	
E. Rental/Leasing Services without Crew	83	
a. Relating to ships	**83103**	
b. Relating to aircraft	**83104**	
c. Relating to other transport equipment	**83101+83102+ 83105**	
d. Relating to other goods		
F. Other Business Services		
a. Advertising services	871	
b. Franchising		
c. Market research and public opinion polling services	864	
d. Management consulting service	865	
e. Services related to man. consulting	**866**	
f. Technical testing and analysis serv.	**8676**	

[1] Changes from MTN.GNS/W/50 (i.e. additions or relocation of sub-sectors) are indicated in bold letters.

[2] n.a. (i.e. not available) indicates that a corresponding CPC classification does not exist.

[3] Informal submissions by participating countries have not been indicated.

0189

g. Services incidental to agriculture hunting and forestry	**881**
h. Services incidental to fishing	**882**
i. Services incidental to mining and oil-field serv.	**883**
j. Placement and supply services of Personnel	**872**
k. Investigation and security	**873**
l. Related scientific and technical consulting services	**8675**
m. Installation and assembly work (other than construction)	n.a.
n. Maintenance and repair of equipment (not including fixed structures, **maritime vessels, aircraft or other transport equipment)**	633+845+ 886+6112+ **6122**
o. Building-cleaning services	874
p. Photographic services	**875**
q. Packaging services	876
r. Translation and interpretation services	87905
s. Sewage and refuse disposal, sanitation and similar services	**940**
t. Printing, publishing	n.a.
u. Other	

2. COMMUNICATION SERVICES

A. Postal services	7511
B. Courier services	7512
C. Telecommunication services	752
a. voice telephone services	**7521**
b. packet-switched data transmission services	**7523**
c. circuit-switched data transmission services	**7523**
d. telex services	**n.a.**
e. telegraph services	**7522**
f. facsimile services	**n.a.**
g. private leased circuit services	**n.a.**
h. electronic mail	**n.a.**
i. voice mail	**n.a.**
j. on-line information and data base retrieval	**n.a.**
k. electronic data interchange (EDI)	**n.a.**
l. enhanced/value-added facsimile services, incl. store and forward, store and retrieve	**n.a.**
m. code and protocol conversion	**n.a.**
n. on-line information and/or data processing (incl.transaction processing)	**n.a.**
o. other	**n.a.**

2. COMMUNICATION SERVICES

- Section C provides a more comprehensive list of telecommunication services than its counterpart section in MTN.GNS/W/50.

0190

D. **Audiovisual services**		- Section D groups items found at the four-digit level in the CPC under "recreational, cultural and sporting services". It did not appear as a separate item under MTN.GNS/W/50. Audiovisual services appeared in "other personal services" in the joint OECD-EUROSTAT proposal to the Voorburg Group on Services Statistics.
a. **Motion picture and video tape production and distribution services**	**9611**	
b. **Motion picture projection service**	**9612**	
c. **Radio and television services**	**9613**	
d. **Sound recording**	**n.a.**	
e. Other		
E. Other communication services		
a. New and press agency services	962	
b. Library and archives services	9631	
c. Other		
3. CONSTRUCTION **AND RELATED ENGINEERING SERVICES**		3. CONSTRUCTION AND RELATED-ENGINEERING SERVICES
A. **Project design, planning, contracting, management, supervision and inspection (see also business and professional services)**	**n.a.**	- There has been a restructuring of the counterpart division in MTN.GNS/W/50 to reflect more precisely the break-down appearing under Division 51 of the CPC. It corresponds in large measure to the break-down in the joint OECD-EUROSTAT proposal to the Voorburg Group on Service Statistics. The main difference is the inclusion of Section A and B.
B. **Feasibility studies**	**n.a.**	
C. **General construction work for buildings**	**512**	
D. **General construction work for civil engineering**	**513**	
E. Installation and assembly work	514+516	
F. Building completion **and finishing work**	517	
G. Maintenance and repair of fixed structures	n.a.	
H. **Other**	**511+515+518**	
4. DISTRIBUTION SERVICES		
A. Commission agents' services	621	
B. Wholesale trade services	622	
C. Retailing services	631+632	
D. Countertrade	n.a.	
E. Other		
5. EDUCATIONAL SERVICES	921+929	
6. ENVIRONMENTAL SERVICES	n.a.	

7. FINANCIAL SERVICES

	CPC
A. All insurance and insurance-related services	812
a. life, accident and health insurance. services	8121
b. non-life insurance services	8129
c. reinsurance and retrocession	n.a.
d. services auxiliary to insurance	8140
B. Banking and other financial services (excl. insurance)	
a. Acceptance of deposits and other repayable funds from the public	81115-81119
b. Lending of all types, incl., *inter alia*, consumer credit, mortgage credit, factoring and financing of commercial transaction	81113
c. Financial leasing	81112
d. All payment and money transmission services	81339(?)
e. Guarantees and commitments	81199
f. Trading for own account or for account of customers, whether on an exchange, in an over-the-counter market or otherwise, the following:	
- money market instruments (cheques, bills, certificate of deposits, etc.)	81339
- foreign exchange	81333
- derivative products incl., but not limited to, futures and options	81339(?)
- exchange rate and interest rate instruments, inclu. products such as swaps, forward rate agreements, etc.	81339(?)
- transferable securities	81321
- other negotiable instruments and financial assets, incl. bullion	81339
g. Participation in issues of all kinds of securities, incl. under-writing and placement as agent (whether publicly or privately) and provision of service related to such issues	8132
h. Money broking	81339(?)

7. FINANCIAL SERVICES

- Unlike MTN.GNS/W/50, the break-down adopted includes insurance under financial services.

- Section A corresponds in large measure to the break-down in the CPC. Items 1.A.3 and 1.A.4 of MTN.TNC/W/50 are considered to be covered by item 6.A.d.

- While the break-down adopted in Section B draws on MTN.TNC/W/50, it reflects in large measure the broad categories of section 6 of MTN.GNS/W/50 but at a higher degree of specificity. Not all the concordances with the CPC have been identified.

i. Asset management, such as cash or portfolio management, all forms of collective investment management, pension fund management, custodial depository and trust services	8119+ 81323
j. Settlement and clearing services for financial assets, incl. securities, derivative products, and other negotiable instruments	81339(?) or 81319(?)
k. Advisory and other auxiliary financial services on all the activities listed in Article 1B of MTN.TNC/W/50, incl. credit reference and analysis, investment and portfolio research and advice, advice on acquisitions and on corporate restructuring and strategy	8131(?) or 8133(?)
l. Provision and transfer of financial information, and financial data processing and related software by providers of other financial services	8131(?)

8. HEALTH RELATED SERVICES

A. Hospital services	9311
B. Other	9319

9. TOURISM, TRAVEL AND LEISURE SERVICES

A. Hotels and restaurants (incl. catering)	**641-643**
B. Travel agencies and tour operators services	**7471**
C. Tourist guides services	**7472**
D. Entertainment services (not covered under audiovisual services)	**9619**
E. Sporting and other recreational services (not incl. radio/TV/film)	**9640**
F. Other	

8. HEALTH RELATED SERVICES

- It differs from MTN.GNS/W/50 in that medical and dental services have been moved to professional services.

9. TOURISM, TRAVEL AND LEISURE SERVICES

- The whole division is new. Section A corresponds to Section 8 of MTN.GNS/W/50 on hotels and restaurants, Section B has been moved from professional services as contained in MTN.TNC/W/50. Sections C,D and E correspond to four-digit level items in the CPC.

- Certain tourism activities not included elsewhere (e.g. local sightseeing, inter-city tour services) might be addressed through item F, "other".

ꭗ' consumption restriction of customers

0193

10. TRANSPORT SERVICES

A. International Maritime Transport Services	721
a. Passenger transportation	7211
b. Freight transportation	7212
c. Rental of sea-going vessels with crew	7213
d. Maintenance and repair of vessels	n.a.
e. Supporting services for international MTS	745
B. Internal Waterways Transport	722
a. Passenger transportation	7221
b. Freight transportation	7222
c. Rental of vessels with crew	7223
d. Maintenance and repair of vessels	n.a.
e. Pushing and towing services	7224
f. Supporting services for internal waterway transport	745
C. International Air Transport Services	73
a. Passenger transportation	731
b. Freight transportation	732
c. Rental of aircraft with crew	734
d. Maintenance and repair of aircraft	n.a.
e. Supporting services for international ATS	746
D. Internal Air Transport Services	n.a.
a. Passenger transportation	n.a.
b. Freight transportation	n.a.
c. Rental of aircraft with crew	n.a.
d. Maintenance and repair of aircraft	n.a.
e. Supporting services for international ATS	746
E. Space Transport	733
F. International Rail Transport Services	711
a. Passenger transportation	7111
b. Freight transportation	7112
c. Pushing and towing services	7113
d. Maintenance and repair of rail transport equipment	n.a.
e. Supporting services for rail transport services	743
G. Internal Rail Transport Services	
a. Passenger transportation	n.a.
b. Freight transportation	n.a.
c. Pushing and towing services	n.a.
d. Maintenance and repair of rail transport equipment	n.a.
e. Supporting services for rail transport services	743

10. TRANSPORT SERVICES

- The division is re-structured in accordance with each individual transport sector rather than in accordance with the purpose of the transport (e.g. passenger, freight). Maritime, air, rail and road transport are further divided into international and national/cabotage services.

- Auxiliary services appear both under each individual transport mode and in section (K) covering services common to all modes of transport.

- The division corresponds in large measure to the break-down appearing in the CPC. The main difference is that the CPC does not divide air, rail and road transport into international and national/cabotage services.

- Item 9.H.d might be partly covered by item 6112 of the CPC, maintenance and repair services of motor vehicles.

- Separation between rental of transport equipment with crew (transport services), or without crew (business services), follows from the CPC classification.

0194

H. International Road Transport Services	712
a. Passenger transportation	7121+7122
b. Freight transportation	7123
c. Rental of commercial vehicles with operator	7124
d. Maintenance and repair of road transport equipment	n.a.
e. Supporting services for road transport services	744
I. Internal Road Transport Services	
a. Passenger transportation	n.a.
b. Freight transportation	n.a.
c. Rental of commercial vehicles with operator	n.a.
d. Maintenance and repair of road transport equipment	n.a.
e. Supporting services for road transport services	744
J. Pipeline Transport	713
a. Transportation of fuels	7131
b. Transportation of other goods	7139
K. Services auxiliary to all modes of transport	740
a. Cargo-handling services	741
b. Storage and warehouse services	742
c. Freight transport agency services	748
d. Other	749
L. Other Transport Services	

11. OTHER SERVICES NOT INCLUDED ELSEWHERE

11. OTHER SERVICES NOT INCLUDED ELSEWHERE

- Section 12 of MTN.GNS/W/50, Sales of Intangible Assets, has not been included since the corresponding two-digit section in the CPC does not relate explicitly to services.

0195

송 ㄱ건

원 본

외 무 부

종 별 :

번 호 : GVW-0962 일 시 : 91 0524 1830

수 신 : 장관(통기, 경기원, 재무부, 상공부, 교통부, 체신부)

발 신 : 주 제네바 대사

제 목 : UR/GNS 통신분야 비공식 협의

5.23(목) 및 5.24(금) 오전 TRITT 의장(캐나다체신부 통상 정책과장) 주재로 개최된 표제협의 내용을 하기 보고함.

1. 회의 진행 개요

- 대부분의 나라에서 통신전문가가 참석하였으며 13개국(EC, 스웨덴, 핀랜드, 노르웨이, 아국, 스위스, 일본, 뉴질랜드, 호주, 홍콩, 캐나다) OFFER에 대한 질의 답변에 국한하여 진행되었음.

2. 주요 회의 내용

- 기본 서비스와 고도 서비스의 구분에 대한 의견교환

0 EC 는 통신서비스 중에서 전화, 전신, TELEX를 제외한 것을 고도 서비스로 규정

0 미국은 보다 넓은 고도 서비스 정의를 위하여 다음 요건중 하나라도 해당할 경우에는 고도 서비스로 취급하는 접근방법 선호

I) 이용자가 제공한 정보의 형식, 내용, CODE또는 PROTOCOL 등의 변화

II) 이용자 정보에 추가정보, 다른정보 또는 재구성된 정보의 제공

III) 이용자 정보와 축적 정보간의 상호 작용

- 서비스 공급 형태별 시장접근 제한 사항과 서비스제공 사업개시에 필요한 인가, 등록, 신고 절차의 유무 및 그 기준

0 스웨덴, 핀랜드, 노르웨이등은 고도서비스분야에 인가, 등록절차 자체가 없으나 이에관한 제도를 마련중에 있다고 하였으며, 동국가를 포함한 모든 나라가 등록, 인가 기준은 내.외국인간 무차별적으로 적용되고 있거나 또는 적용될 것이라고 함.

- CEILING BINDING 과 MFN

0 홍콩이 국내 서비스만 OFFER 한 것과 관련 아국은 홍콩이 일부국가와 국제 VAN 에 관한 양자 협정을 체결하고 있는바, 이를 어떻게 MFN과 조화시킬 것인지

통상국 2차보 교통부 체신부 경기원 재무부 상공부

PAGE 1 91.05.25 09:27 DQ

외신 1과 통제관

0196

문제를제기함.

0 또한 멕시코는 자국 통신법에 기본 통신 서비스제공사업에 외국인의 지분 참여를 49 퍼센트 까지 허용하는 반면 OFFER 에는 30 퍼센트 이하로 표기한 것과 관련,아국은 멕시코 내에 실제로 30퍼센트 이상 외국인 지분 참여가 허용된 사례가 있는지 질의하고 만약 그러한 사례가 있다면 비록 OFFER 에 30 퍼센트로 제시하였다 하더라도 MFN침해가 될 것이라고 지적함.(멕시코는 자국의 실제상황을 알수는 없으나 30 퍼센트 이상 허용된 사례가 있다면 MFN 문제가 제기될것이라고 함)

3. 기타 특기사항

- 아국은 아국 OFFER 설명과정에서 UR/서비스협상이 서비스 교역의 자유화를 목표로 하고있는 만큼 각국의 현행 규제를 단순히 OFFER에 옮겨 놓는 작업이 되어서는 곤란하다고 전제하고 아국의 경우 경쟁의 촉진과 기간통신망 보호 사이의 균형을 취하는 가운데 자유화 약속을 담았으며, 다른 나라도 실질적 자유화내용이 담긴 구체적 OFFER 가 제출 되기를바란다고 언급하였음.

- 아국, 이씨, 미국, 캐나다 등 많은 나라가 각국 OFFER 의 실질적 가치 평가를용이하게 하기 위하여 통신 서비스 분류 체계를 정비할 필요성을 지적하였음.

- 금번 협의와 같은 성격의 제 2차 협의 개최여부는 언급되지 않았으나 금번 협의가 예상보다 활발하게 진행되지 못한점을 고려할때 GNS전체 차원에서 스케쥴 작성 방법, 서비스 분야 분류표등에 대한 논의가 어느정도 진전된 이후에라야 2차 협의 문제가 제기될 것으로 판단됨. 끝

(대사 박수길-국장)

원 본

외 무 부

종 별 :

번 호 : GVW-0975 일 시 : 91 0528 1100

수 신 : 장관(통기,경기원,재무부,이하배부처참조)

발 신 : 주 제네바 대사

제 목 : UR/GNS 회의(1)

5.27 (월) JARAMILLOGNS 의장 주재로 개최된 표제회의 내용을 하기보고함.(이경협관, 외무부 조서기관, 경기원 김사무관, 한경협관보 참석)

1. 회의 진행 계획

- 5.27(월) 스케쥴 작성 방법 (공식회의)

- 5.28(화)-5.31(금): 분야별 각국 OFFER 명료화(비공식 회의)

0 5.28 오전: 전문직업, 사업서비스

0 5.28 오후: 건설, 노동력 이동

0 5.30 오후: 분배 서비스 (5.29 및 5.30 오전은 GATT 이사회 개최로 GNS 회의는 휴회)

0 6.1 오전: 관광, AUDIO VISUAL 서비스

0 6.1 오후: 운송 서비스

- 6.3 주 : 서비스 분야 분류표, FRAMEWORK 조문(분쟁해결, 국내 규제, 용어의 정의), 양허 협상절차

2. 주요 회의 내용

가. 시장 접근과 내국민 대우의 구분

- 미국, 이씨, 일본, 카나다, 북구, 스위스, 뉴질랜드등 선진국들은 시장접근과내국민 대우 군분의 어려움, 스케쥴에 제시된 자유화 약속의 법적명료성, 안정성 확보 필요성등을 이유로 첫번째란 (NO LESS FAVORABLE 란)에 내.외국인차별 조치(ENTRY 에 대한 제한과 OPERATION 에대한 제한 포함)를 기재하고 두번째란(시장접근란)에 내.외국인간 무차별적 규제(서비스공급자 수 제한, NEED TEST, 독점등)를 기재하는방법을 제시함.

- 인도, 멕시코, 말련, 칠레등 개도국들은 시장접근과 내국민 대우를 구분하기 어

통상국 2차보 법무부 보사부 문화부 교통부 체신부 경기원 재무부
상공부 건설부 노동부 과기처 해항청 공보처

PAGE 1 91.05.28 20:57 DN

외신 1과 통제관

0198

려운 사례가 일부 있으나 시장접근과 내국민 대우 개념에 대한 이론 체계가 유지되어야 하며 스케쥴 작성국가가 시장접근란과 내국민 대우란을 선택할 권리를 유보하여야 한다고하여 시장진입 (ENTRY) 이 허용된 이후에 국내 영업(OPERATION)에 대한 내국민 대우 여부를 가리는 지금까지의 접근 방법을 견지함.

- 아국은 시장진입과 동 진입 이후의 내국민대우를 구분하는 방식으로 OFFER 를작성하였으나 스케쥴 작성방법의 개선 필요성에 동의하고 동 작성 방법이 자유화 협상 과정에 중립적일 것을 조건읍 선진국 들의 제안을 검토할 용의가 있다고 언급함.

나. 내.외국인간 무차별적 규제의 기재 여부(제6조와 16조의 관계)

- 선진국들은 내.외국인을 포괄하는 무차별적 수량제한, ECONOMIC NEED TEST, 독점등 무차별적 규제도 스케쥴에 기재되어야 하며, 제 6조 (국내규제)에 해당하는 내.외국인 공히 적용되는 인가기준도 무역 왜곡 효과가 있거나 필요이상으로 번잡한 규제, 객관적이지 못한 실질적 규제등에 회랙조치가 많으므로 제 6조의 조문작성에 세심한 주의를 기울여야 한다고 한 반면 개도국들은 내.외국인에 공히 적용되는 무차별적 규제는 스케쥴 등재 대상이 아니라고 반박함.

- 아국은 무차별적인 수량제한등은 OFFER 에 기재하지 않았으나 제 6조 및 스케쥴에 등재되어야할 무차별적 규제의 범위에 합의가 형성되면 이를 기재할 용의가 있다고 하였음(보험,여행알선업, 유통등 미국에 약속한 분야에 대한 추후 수량제한, ECONOMIC NEED TEST 등을 OFFER에 추가 기재하기 위한 포석의 일환)

다. 국내 규제에 대한 공개주의 적용

- 이씨, 스웨덴, 스위스, 뉴질랜드등은 제 6조에 해당하는 규제사항도 스케쥴에등재된 분야의 무역에 영향을 미치는 경우 (NON-VIOLATION CASE)에는 제 3조 (공개주의)의 규정을 확대적용하여 통지의무등을 부과할 필요가 있으며, 이와관련 제 3조의 수정 필요성까지도 언급하였으나 캐나다는 그럴경우 과도한 문서가 생산될것이라는 이유로 유보적 입장을 표명함.

라. 서비스 공급형태 (MODE OF SUPPLY) 의 구분

- 북구는 4개 공급 형태의 구분이 스케쥴 작성에 유용하지 못하다고 한 반면 다른 선진국들은 명확한 입장을 표명하지 않았음.

마. 수평적 규제(토지 취득 제한등)의 기재 방법

- 대부분의 나라가 분야별로 반복 기재하기 보다는 OFFER 앞부분에 일관 기재하는 방법을 선호하였으며, 각 분야별 자유화 약속과의 법률적관계를 명확히 하여야 한다는

점을 강조하였음.

첨부: 사무국 작성 서비스 분야 분류표 1부. 끝

(GVW(F)-0175)

(대사 박수길-국장)

배부처:법무부,상공부,건설부,보사부,공보처,교통부,체신부,문화부,공보처,과기처,
행 DN

원 본

외 무 부

종 별 :

번 호 : GVW-0991　　　　일 시 : 91 0529 1930

수 신 : 장 관(통기,경기원,재무부,법무부,상공부,교육부,건설부,보사부,노동부,(교통부,체신부,문화부,공보처,과기처,항만청)

발 신 : 주 제네바 대사

제 목 : UR/GNS 회의 (2)

5.28(화) 속간더 보고함.

1. 스케쥴 작성방법(공식회의 계속)

- EC 및 캐나다의 제안으로 사무국에서 스케쥴 작성방법에 관한 대안을 마련하여 다음주회의에서 논의키로 하였음.

2. 서비스 분야 분류표 (공식회의)

- 사무국에서 새로이 작성한 분류표 (기송부)에 대한 설명이 있었으며, 일부 국가로 부터 다음 사항을 재확인하는 논평이 있었음.

0 동 목록은 전적으로 사무국 책임하에 만들어지는 것임.

0 동 목록은 참고 목록 (ILLUSTRATIVE LIST) 으로 사용될 것이나 각국의 최대한 동 분류 체계에 따르려고 노력할 필요가 있음.

0 각국 고유의 국내 규제 체계에 따른 신축성이 허용되어야 함.

3. 사업 서비스 (전문직업, 교육, 보건, 개인 서비스포함) 분야 각국 OFFER 에 대한 명료화 (비공식회의)

- EC, 캐나다, 미국등이 자국 관심분야인 법률, 회계, 보건 서비스등과 관련 각국 OFFER 에 대하여 질의하고 인도, 헝가리가 인력이동 문제를 제기한 이외에 다른 나라는 상대국 OFFER 에 대한 질의를 하지 않았는바, 주요 내용은 다음과같음.

0 CROSS-BORDER SUPPLY 에 전문인력 (회계사,엔지니어등)의 일시적 이동에 의한 서비스 공급이 포함되는지 여부와 관련 홍콩은 통신수단등에 의한 서비스 자체의 국경간 공급으로 정의하는반면, 미국은 회사 설립등 상업적 주재 형태가 아닌 일시적 주재에 의한 서비스 공급도 포함된다는 입장을 견지함.

0 헝가리는 많은 나라의 OFFER 에 CROSS-BORDERSUPPLY 에는 제한 없음.

통상국 2차보 법무부 보사부 문화부 교통부 체신부 교육부 경기원
재무부 상공부 건설부 노동부 과기처 해항청 공보처

PAGE 1　　　　91.05.30 09:16 WG
외신 1과 통제관

0201

인력이동란은 UNBOUND로 표기하고 있는바 동 서비스 공급에는 전문인력의 일시적 주재가 필요한 점을 고려할때 동 COMMITMENT 가 실질적으로 무슨 의미가 있는지 문제를 제기함.

0 호주, 캐나다등과 같은 연방국가의 경우 주 정부차원의 규제가 명확하게 기재되어야 한다는 점이 지적됨.(EC, 스웨덴등)

0 EC 회원국중 한 국가에서 전문자격을 인정 받은 경우 동 자격이 다른 EC회원국에서도 인정되는지 (미국)에 대하여 EC는 EC 법규상의 자격의 상호 인정 (MUTUALRECOGNITION OF DIPLOMA) 은 EC 회원국민에 한정된다고 함.

0 미국은 인도네시아 OFFER 등의 보건 관련 서비스에 병원 경영 서비스가 포함되는지 여부에 대하여 관심을 표명함.

0 EC 는 오지리의 전문 직업 서비스 OFFER 와관련, CROSS-BORDER SUPPLY 에 '제한 없음' 으로 표기하는 한편 변호사등의 명칭 사용을 제한하고 있는바 자격의 상호 인정과정없이 어떻게 서비스 공급이 이루어질수 있는지, 상업적주재에 '제한 없음'으로 표기하면서도 국적요건을 부과하고 있는바 어떻게 시장접근이 이루어질수 있는지 의문을 표시함.

0 EC 는 아국 OFFER 중 회계 서비스와 관련 CROSS-BODER SUPPLY 에는 COMMITMENT 하는 반면 상업적 주재는 UNBOND 한 이유를 질의한바 아국은 국내 여건이 외국 회계법인의 설립을 허용할 단계에 있지 않으며 추후 국내산업이 어느정도 발전한 이후에 협상대상이 될수 있을것이라고 답변함.

0 EC 는 또한 일본 OFFER 중 법무서비스에 제한 없음 이라고 표시한데 대하여 의문을 표시한바 일본은 내.외국인간 차별이 없다고 답변함.

4. 표제회의는 5.30(목) 오후 속개하여 건설, 노동력이동 분야에 대한 합의를 계속할 예정임.끝

(대사 박수길-국장)

2 3항 조치

원 본

외 무 부

종 별 :

번 호 : GVW-1009 일 시 : 91 0531 1700

수 신 : 장 관(통기,경기원,재무부,법무부,교육부,상공부,건설부,보사부,노동부,

발 신 : 주 제네바 대사 교통부,체신부,공보처,과기처,항만청)

제 목 : UR/GNS 회의(3)

5.30(목) 오후 속개된 표제회의 내용을 하기 보고함.

1. 회의개요

- 건설분야 각국 OFFER 에 대한 질의 답변과 노동력 이동관련 헝가리 및 인도와선진국간 의견 개진 형태로 진행되었음.

2. 주요내용

가. 건설분야

- 인도 및 헝가리는 CROSS-BORDER SUPPLY 에 자유화 약속을 하더라도 노동력 이동이 UNBOUND 상태면 무의미한 OFFER 가 된다고 지적하였음.

0 특히 미국 OFFER 의 경우 상업적 주재와 연계된 인력 이동만 BINDING 되었으므로 CROSS-BORDER SUPPLY 에는 의미를 가지지 못한다고 지적한 바 미국은 과거의 경험에 비추어 볼때 CROSS-BORDER SUPPLY 라 하더라도 현장 사무소등 어느정도의 설립은 필요하므로 이와 관련한 인력이동은 가능할 것이라고 함.

- 폴란드는 TEAM WORK 에 의하여 이루어지는 건설공사의 특성을 고려할때 미국 OFFER 상의 SPECIALIST 를 어떻게 정의하는지 질의한바 미국은 자산적 가치를 갖는 지식을 보유한 사람에 한정되며 일반화 된 지식을 보유한자는 제외된다고 함.

0 EC 는 주정부 차원의 규제를 밝힐 것을 요청한 바 미국은 중앙 정부 뿐만 아니라 주정부차원에서도 아무런 규제가 없으며 (정부 조달은 제외)아무 제한없이 BINDING하는 것이라고 함.

- 미국은 EC 역내의 기술장벽 제거 혜택이 역외국에게도 제공될 것인지 문의한바 EC 는 그렇다고 답변함.

- 아국 OFFER 와 관련 내국민 대우란에 UNBOUND 한 이유 (스웨덴), 건설업 면허기준에 수량제한, 질적제한 기준, 또는 ECONOMIC NEED TEST등이 있는지 (EC),

통상국 2차보 법무부 보사부 교통부 체신부 교육부 경기원 재무부
상공부 건설부 노동부 과기처 해항청 공보처

PAGE 1 91.06.01 08:54 WG

외신 1과 통제관

0203

합작부자는 어떻게 처리되고 있는지 (캐나다)등의 질의가 있었는바

0 아국은 '90년부터 건설시장 개방을 시작하였기 때문에 내국민 대우에 관한 조건을 검토중에 있으며 건설업 면허는 자본금 규모, 기술인력보유등 객관적이고 무차별적인 기준에 의하여 합작부자는 '94년까지 외국인 지분 참여가 허용되나 그이후는 100 퍼센트 단독부자가 허용될 것이라고 답변함.

- 일본 OFFER 상에 모두 '제한없음'으로 기재된데 대하여 많은 나라로 부터 의문이 제기 되었는바

0 일본은 자국이 이해하고 있는바에 따라 내.외국인 차별조치가 없는 경우에'제한없음'으로 표기하였으며 무차별조치는 포함되지 않았다고 함. 또한 자국 OFFER 상의 건설분야에는 28개 종류의 산업활동이 포함된다고 함.

나. 노동력 이동

- 인도 및 헝가리는 개도국이 비교우위가 있는 분야는 오직 노동집약 서비스뿐이라는 관점에서 노동력 이동에 관한 각국의 COMMITMENT 의 시급성을 강조하였는바

0 EC, 호주, 스위스등은 자국 OFFER 의 개정시인력 이동에 관한 COMMITMENT 가 포함될 것이며 미국과 캐나다의 접근방식 (분야별 구분없이 KEYPERSONNEL 에 한하여 BINDING)을 고려하고 있다고 함

- 캐나다는 모두에게 똑같이 적용되는 일반부속서 방식 (GENERAL ANNEX APPROACH: 사전에 정의된 특정 범주의 인력에 대하여 분야별 구분없이 모든 나라가 COMMITMENT 하는 방식)이 인력이동에 관한 각국의 COMMITMENT 를 촉진시킬 수 있을 것이라고한 바

0 인도는 그러한 대원칙이 다수국에 의해 받아들여진다면 그다음 문제는 일반부속서상에 규정할 인력의 범주를 정하는 것인바 동 인력 범위가 협상에 의하여 확대될 수 있을 것이라고 주장함.

3. 기타

- 금일 칠레가 OFFER 를 제출함으로써 총 23개국의 OFFER 가 제출되었으며 알젠틴도 OFFER 제출 의사를 표명하였음

0 구체적 OFFER 를 제출한 국가 (20개국): 스위스, 미국, 일본, EC, 호주, 뉴질랜드, 홍콩, 캐나다, 스웨덴, 아국, 노르웨이, 핀랜드, 싱가폴, 인도네시아, 터키, 멕시코, 오지리, 콜롬비아, 아이슬랜드, 칠레

0 일부 분야에 대한 동결 약속만 제시한 국가 (3개국): 폴란드, 체코, 루마니아

- 다음주에 토의할 양허협상절차에 관한 사무국 문서가 배부되었는 바, 별첨 (FAX) 송부함

- 다음주 회의 참석을 위하여 경기원 김사무관의 출장일정을 6.6(목) 까지 연장건의함

첨부: 양허협상 절차에 관한 사무국 문서 1부.(GVW(F)-0181). 끝

(대사 박수길-국장)

GVW(W)-0181 10531 1900
" GV-1009 첨부"

Procedural Guidelines for Negotiations on Initial Commitments

1. Participants shall submit initial offers in which they specify commitments they are willing to assume in accordance with the provisions of Parts III and IV of the General Agreement on Trade in Services.

2. All initial offers shall be circulated to all participants in the Uruguay Round in order to provide transparency.

3. The initial offers will be the subject of multilateral consultations as well as a periodic review and assessment process open to all participants which have submitted offers and to those which have notified their intentions to do so in the context of the negotiations on initial commitments.

4. Negotiations on initial commitments shall proceed on the basis of the substantive guidelines attached to the text of the Agreement.

5. Participants may present requests for improvements on offers bilaterally. Such requests shall be made available, through the Secretariat, to other participants in these negotiations.

6. Negotiations shall take place among participants which have submitted initial offers and/or requests on the basis of the submitted offers, requests as well as any other proposals.

7. After negotiations on initial commitments are concluded each participant shall consolidate its schedule of specific commitments and communicate it to the Secretariat.

Participants may wish to establish appropriate deadlines for the presentation of initial offers and the conclusion of the negotiations on initial commitments. To this end, participants will also finalize the guidelines referred to in paragraph 4 above at the earliest possible date.

0206

1991-05-31 15:37 KOREAN MISSION GENEVA 2 022 791 0525 P.01

원 본

외 무 부

종 별 :

번 호 : GVW-1014 일 시 : 91 0531 1930

수 신 : 장 관(통기, 경기원, 재무부, 법무부, 교육부, 상공부, 건설부, 보사부, 노동부, 교통부, 체신부, 문화부, 공보처, 과기처, 항만청)

발 신 : 주 제네바 대사

제 목 : UR/GNS 회의(4)

5.31(금) 속개된표제회의 내용을 하기 보고함.

1. 회의 개요

- 유통 서비스 및 관광 관련 서비스 (AUDIO VISUAL포함)분야 각국 OFFER 에 대한 질의 답변이있었으며, 운송분야는 각국의 소극적 태도로 토의되지 않았음.

2. 주요 내용

가. 유통 서비스

- 인도는 스위스 OFFER 에 무역업 (COUNTERTRADING) 을 도매업으로 부터 구분한 이유 및 오지리 OFFER 상의 도매업중 국가 독점 무역업이 존재하는지 질의한바

0 스위스는 자국 분류체계에 따라 구분하였으며, 도매업과 무역업은 구분되어야 할 것이라고 함.한편 오지리는 무역업에 국가 독점은 없으며, 정상적 사업 활동의 하나라고 답변함.

- EC 는 스웨덴 OFFER 중 ' RULES ON COMMISSION, LICENSED AGENCIES' 상의 구체적 규제사항에 대하여 질의한바

0 스웨덴은 동 규제는 내.외국인간 무역차별적인 것이며, 내.외국인간 무차별적 수량제한 같은 규제도 없다고 함.

- 핀랜드는 아국 OFFER 와 관련 700 평방미터 이하의 점포 개설에 대한 허가 절차 유무에 대하여 질의한바

0 아국은 수산물, 의약품등 외에는 개별법상의허가 절차는 없으나 외자 도입법상의 인가 절차는 필요하다고 답변함.

- 한편 미국은 자국 OFFER 개성시 유통분야를 포함 시킬 것이라고 발언함.

나. 관광 관련 서비스

- 미국은 관광 분야에 있어서 소비자 (관광객)이동의 중요성을 강조하고 관광객출

통상국 2차보 법무부 보사부 문화부 교통부 체신부 교육부 경기원
재무부 상공부 건설부 노동부 과기처 해항정 공보처

91.06.01 09:25 WG

외신 1과 통제관

0207

국제한 (여권발급 제한), 해외 여행객수제한, 여행경비, 유학경비, 해외 의료비, CREDITCARD 등 해외 지불수단 제한등 모든 제한이 스케쥴에 기재되어야 한다고 함.

0 인도 및 헝가리는 해외 여행 경비제한은 재정정책 목적상의 제한이며, FRAMEWORK 제 11조 (지급 및 이전) 및 제 12조 (국제 수지)에서 다루어져야 한다고 반박함.

0 또한 캐나다는 의료 경비는 의료 서비스 분야에 유학 경비는 교육 서비스 분야에 기재되어야 할것이라고 함.

- 미국은 또한 관광객이 출발하는 국가에서의 제한 만이 협상 대상이며, 관광객이 입국하는 국가에서의 제한은 수출통제이므로 FRAMEWORK 으로부터 벗어나는 사항이며, 이와 같은 관점에서 소비자이동의 내국민 대우란은 NOT APPLICABLE 이 적절하다고한바

0 헝가리는 갓트에서는 수출통제도 취급하고있는바, 서비스 협정에서도 더 논의되어야 할사항이라고 하였으며, 멕시코는 자국의 경우 소비자의 출국과 입국 양쪽을 다 고려하였다고 함.

- EC, 캐나다, 중국등은 아국관광, 진흥법상의 호텔 등록 요건과 해외여행관련 여권 발급 및 여행 경비 제한현황에 대하여 질의하였는바

0 아국은 호텔 등록에는 자본금과 시설기준이있으며, 여권 발급에는 제한이 없다고 하는 한편 아국의 CREDIT CARD 해외 사용에 관한 제도를 상세히 설명하였음.

- 스위스 OFFER 와 관련 아국은 공무원의 자국항공기 이용 의무는 정부 조달 문제라고 지적, 스웨덴은 주정부의 자유재량에 의한 식당인가 OFFER 내용의 적절성 여부에 대하여 지적한바

0 스위스는 자국 항공기 이용 의무는 정부조달 문제라고 긍정하는 한편, 식당인가 제한은 국민보건상의 이유에 기초한 것이라고 함.

- 말련은 호텔업을 BINDING 하였을 경우 세탁, 물품소매, 식당등의 부수 서비스도 당연히 포함되는지 문제를 제기한바 홍콩은 호텔부숙객에게 제공되는 서비스라면 포함될 것이라고 답변함.

- 해외 여행객에 대한 차별적인 출국세 부과에관한 질문 (캐나다)에 대하여 EC 는 한 회원국이 목적지에 따라 출국세를 부과하는 사례가 있으며, 항공이나 관광분야에 기재하는 방안을 고려하겠다고 함.

- 아국은 외국 영화 필름에 대한 수입제한이 상품 무역에 해당하는지, 상품에 체화된 서비스무역인지 문제를 제기한바, 오지리 및 멕시코는 상품 무역이라고 답변한 반면 말련은 기본적으로 상품 무역이라는 점에는 동의하나 무역업이 취급품목에 대한

PAGE 2

0208

제한으로 영향을 받는 것과 같이 서비스 산업 활동에도 상당한 영향을 미치는 조치라고 언급함.

3. 각국 OFFER 평가에 관한 기준

- 호주는 각국 OFFER 에 대한 평가가 양자협상에 의하여 주관적으로 행해지는 점을 지적하고 다자적인 평가 기준을 만들것을 제의한바 칠레, 폴란드 등의 일부 반대가 있었으나 다수국의 지지에 따라 사무국에서 각국 OFFER 평가과정에서 고려하여야 할 요소를 취합한 ISSUE PAPER (OFFER 의 실질 가치를 계량적으로 평가하기 위한것은 아님) 를 작성하기로 합의하였음.

4. 표제 회의는 6.3(월) 속개하여 FRAMEWORK 중분쟁해결 절차등 조문에 대하여 토의할 예정임.끝

(대사 박수길-국장)

외교문서 비밀해제: 우루과이라운드2 19
우루과이라운드 서비스 협상 1

초판인쇄 2024년 03월 15일
초판발행 2024년 03월 15일

지은이 한국학술정보(주)
펴낸이 채종준
펴낸곳 한국학술정보(주)
주 소 경기도 파주시 회동길 230(문발동)
전 화 031-908-3181(대표)
팩 스 031-908-3189
홈페이지 http://ebook.kstudy.com
E-mail 출판사업부 publish@kstudy.com
등 록 제일산-115호(2000. 6. 19)

ISBN 979-11-7217-121-6 94340
979-11-7217-102-5 94340 (set)

책에 대한 더 나은 생각, 끊임없는 고민, 독자를 생각하는 마음으로 보다 좋은 책을 만들어갑니다.